GRAND CANYON

TIM HULL

Contents

Although every effort was made to make sure the information in this book was accurate when going to press, research was impacted by the COVID-19 pandemic and things may have changed since the time of writing. Be sure to confirm specific details, like opening hours, closures, and travel guidelines and restrictions, when making your travel plans. For more detailed information, see p. 285.

GRAND CANYON VICINITY

NEVADA

UTAH
ARIZONA

Dixie National Forest

Dixie National Forest

Zion National Park

Bryce Canyon National Park

Grand Staircase Escalante National Monument

Shivwitz Reservation

St. George

Washington

Hurricane

Kanab

Vermilion Cliffs National Monument

Lee Ferry

Marble Canyon

To Las Vegas

Mesquite

Hildale

Colorado City

Fredonia

Kaibab Reservation

Pipe Spring National Monument

Kaibab National Forest

Grand Canyon-Parashant National Monument

Lake Mead National Recreation Area

Colorado River

Supai

Havasupai Reservation

Grand Canyon National Park

Phantom Ranch

Grand Canyon Village

Lake Mead

Meadview

Grand Canyon West

Grand Canyon National Park

Hualapai Reservation

Tusayan

Kaibab National Forest

Valle

Peach Springs

Nelson

Audley

Kaibab National Forest

Kingman

Ash Fork

Pinaveta

Williams

Flagstaff

To Phoenix

Prescott National Forest

Prescott National Forest

Sedona

To Phoenix

Virgin River

Paria River

Colorado River

0   20 mi

0   20 km

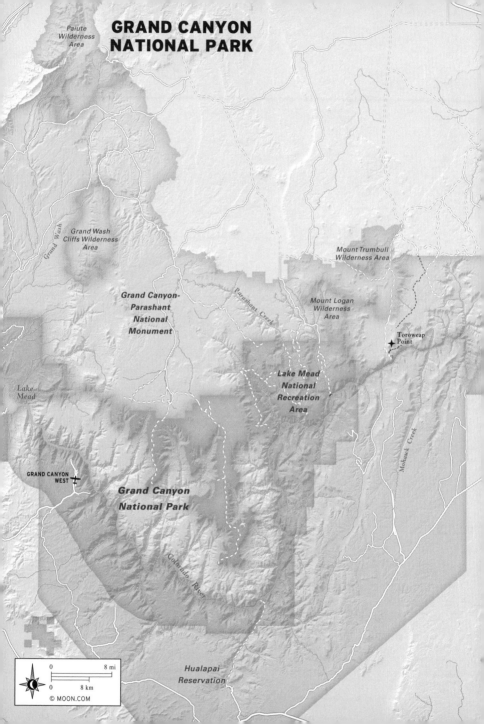

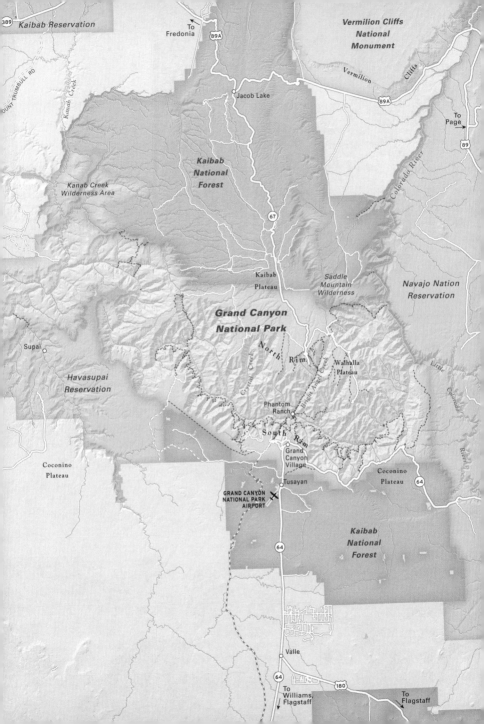

DISCOVER

Grand Canyon

There's a reason why Arizona's official nickname is "The Grand Canyon State." Any state with one of the true wonders of the world would be keen to advertise its good luck.

The canyon must simply be seen to be believed. If you stand for the first time on one of the South Rim's easily accessible lookouts and don't have to catch your breath, you might need to check your pulse. Staring into the canyon brings up all kinds of existential questions; its brash vastness can't be taken in without conjuring some big ideas and questions about life and humanity. The canyon is a water-wrought cathedral, and no matter what beliefs or preconceptions you approach the rim with, they are likely to be challenged, molded, cut away, and revealed—like the layers of primordial earth that compose this deep rock labyrinth and tell the history of the planet. Take your time here—you'll need it.

The more adventurous can make reservations, obtain a permit, and enter the desert depths of the canyon, taking a hike, or even a mule ride, to the Colorado River or spending a weekend trekking rim to rim with an overnight at the famous Phantom Ranch, deep in the canyon's inner gorge. The really brave can hire

Clockwise from top left: twisted pines lining the South Rim; picture window at the North Rim's Grand Canyon Lodge; Colorado River rushing through the inner gorge below Plateau Point; recording the sunset at Hopi Point; natural rock sculpture on the North Rim; canyon vista from Desert View.

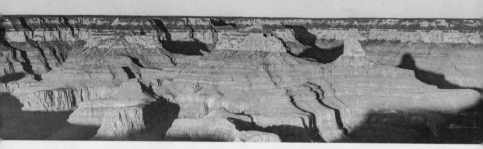

a guide and take a once-in-a-lifetime trip down the great river, riding the roiling rapids and camping on its serene beaches.

There are plenty of places to stay and eat, many of them charming and historic, on the canyon's South Rim. If you decide to go to the high, forested, and often snowy North Rim, you'll drive through a corner of the desolate Arizona Strip and onto the Kaibab Plateau, which have a beauty and a history all their own.

It is folly to try too hard to describe and boost the Grand Canyon. You just have to see it for yourself. Perhaps the most poetic words ever spoken about the Grand Canyon, profound for their obvious simplicity, came from President Theodore Roosevelt, speaking on the South Rim in 1903. "Leave it as it is," he said. "You cannot improve on it; not a bit."

Clockwise from top left: sunset and moonrise from Hopi Point on the South Rim; near Cape Royal on the North Rim; a biker's view from the South Rim; along the South Kaibab Trail.

10 TOP EXPERIENCES

1 Catch your breath looking at the Grand Canyon from **Mather Point** (page 55).

2 Watch the **sunrise or sunset** from the ideal vantage of popular **Hopi Point** (page 65).

3 **Hike** the **Rim Trail** for all the best views from the South Rim (page 71).

4 **Climb Desert View Watchtower** for an expansive view of canyon country (page 69).

5 Descend the **Bright Angel Trail** into Grand Canyon's inner depths (page 74).

6 **Raft or kayak** the legendary **Colorado River** (page 160).

>>>

7 Take in a different side of the Grand Canyon from the North Rim's **Bright Angel Point** (page 116).

>>>

8 Dip your toes in the Colorado River at **Lees Ferry**—without having to hike deep into the gorge (page 218).

>>>

9 Stay at **Phantom Ranch,** an enchanting oasis hidden in Grand Canyon's inner gorge (page 155).

<<<

10 Swim under **waterfalls** in **Havasupai** (page 184).

>>>

Planning Your Trip

Where to Go

The South Rim

For the vast majority of canyonland tourists, the **South Rim** *is* Grand Canyon National Park. The park's busiest section by far, the South Rim offers amazing views of Grand Canyon from timeless spots such as **Mather Point, Yavapai Geology Museum**, and **Desert View Watchtower**. Take an easy hike along the **Rim Trail** with the canyon spread out before you, or venture on a day hike deep into the canyon along the **Bright Angel Trail.** The South Rim's popular scenic drive or bike ride to **Hermit's Rest**, in the park's evergreen western reaches, should not be missed, nor should a bus tour or road trip along **Desert View Drive** to the rim's eastern, desert section.

The North Rim

Wrapped in a highland forest at the edge of the **Kaibab Plateau,** the remote and lesser-known **North Rim** section of Grand Canyon National Park boasts some of the best views in the park from the veranda in back of the enchanting and historic **Grand Canyon Lodge.** Here you can rent a **rimside cabin** and hike or **ride a mule** along the forest trails and down into the green-and-red canyon. Don't skip the scenic drive to **Point Imperial** and **Cape Royal,** stopping along the way at several wondrous viewpoints and trails known only to a small and passionate percentage of canyon visitors.

The Inner Canyon

While a day hike into Grand Canyon from the

gnarled evergreens clinging to the North Rim

If You're Looking for . . .

HIKING

- Descend a few miles into the Grand Canyon from the **South Rim** on the **Bright Angel Trail** or **South Kaibab Trail.**

- On the **North Rim,** enter the canyon via the **North Kaibab Trail** or hike through the forest along the rim on the **Widforss Trail.**

BIKING

- Bring your bike or rent one on the **South Rim** and ride around the park on paved **greenway trails,** including several miles along the rim, or dare the 14-mile (22.5-km) round-trip **Hermit Road** ride.

- On the **North Rim,** hit the **Arizona Trail** through the park on your mountain bike.

RAFTING

- Book a 3- to 18-day trip with a **National Park Service-approved river trip outfitter** for the adventure of a lifetime on the Colorado River.

- Contact the **Hualapai Tribe** at **Grand Canyon West** for one-day rafting trips.

CAMPING

- Reserve a spot at **Mather Campground** on the South Rim or the **North Rim Campground** through www.recreation.gov.

DRIVING TOURS

- Take the **Desert View Drive** on the **South Rim** east to **Desert View Watchtower.**

- Don't miss the scenic drive to **Cape Royal** and **Point Imperial** on the **North Rim.**

BUDGET-FRIENDLY

- Visit the park during **January** or **February** for the best prices on **South Rim** accommodations.

- On the **North Rim,** bring your own food and drinks in a cooler to save money.

KID-FRIENDLY

- Take a guided **bike tour** along the **South Rim.**

- Take an easy hike to **Bright Angel Point** on the **North Rim.**

- Go on a **walk with a ranger** to learn about all the canyon's critters.

South or North Rim is an excellent introduction to the hard beauty and magic of the **Inner Canyon,** for an experience like no other take a two- to three-day **backpacking trip** down the Bright Angel, South Kaibab, or North Kaibab Trails to the green and shady oasis of **Phantom Ranch,** or dare a multiday **white-water rafting** trip along the roiling **Colorado River** through the canyon's **inner gorge** of ancient rock.

Beyond the Boundaries: Canyon Country

Where Grand Canyon National Park ends, the canyonlands begin. Head toward the North Rim and **Glen Canyon National Recreation Area,** the **Arizona Strip,** and the **Kaibab Plateau**—and make sure to take along your hiking shoes and kayaks. Head east to gaze into the **Navajo Nation's Canyon de Chelly** and to tour the fascinating **Hopi villages** on three remote mesas. West of the park, hike to the canyon home of the **Havasupai,** swim beneath their world-famous blue-green waterfalls, and then take the historic remains of **Route 66** toward the **Hualapai Tribe's Skywalk** hovering over the western Grand Canyon.

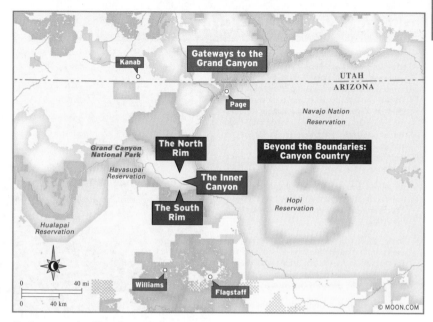

Gateways to the Grand Canyon

Phoenix's Sky Harbor is the closet major airport to Grand Canyon National Park's popular **South Rim** section, and many visitors drive north from the Valley of the Sun and enter the park from either **Williams** or **Flagstaff.** Williams, a small town about an hour from the park, is home to the **Grand Canyon Railway,** and Flagstaff has the most varied dining and accommodations near the park. For trips that include the **North Rim** and Glen Canyon National Recreation Area, the small town of **Page** makes a good base, while a visit to the North Rim, nearby Zion and Bryce Canyon National Parks, and the state parks in southern Utah is better launched from **Kanab, Utah.**

When to Go

No matter which season you choose for your visit to Grand Canyon National Park, the overwhelming beauty of the place will be on full display, sometimes drenched in summer rain, sometimes dusted with winter snow, but always a view for the ages. However, just about everything else—how much you spend, the size of the crowds, your choice of accommodations, the services offered in the park, how long you can comfortably stand on the rim, and how far you can safely hike into the canyon—depends on *when* you go.

High Season (Summer)

The **high season** on the park's **South and North Rims** comes in **summer,** from roughly **May through August.** Expect crowds at the most popular viewpoints and sights along the South Rim, lines at the main South Entrance and the shuttle bus stops, full lodges, campgrounds, and eateries, and busloads of tourists from around the globe. With average daytime rim temperatures in the 70s F (21-26°C) and 80s F (27-32°C), the crowds can hardly spoil a day spent walking

- Lose the crowds and get off on your own a bit while visiting the **South Rim** by spending some time at the less-visited **Desert View Drive** viewpoints and the park's eastern **Desert View** section. While still busy during the high season and on weekends and holidays in spring and fall, Desert View is more spread out and far less crowded than Grand Canyon Village and the area around the Grand Canyon Visitor Center.

- Another way to find solitude on the South Rim even during the high season is to hike the **Rim Trail** east from the visitor center and west from the village.

- To skip the long lines at the main South Rim entrance station during the high season, take the **free shuttle bus from Tusayan** (Tusayan Route/Purple Line) or ride your **bike** into the park along the **Tusayan Greenway.**

- While relatively busy during the height of summer, the cool highlands of the **North Rim** draw much smaller crowds than those that inundate the South Rim. There are many places on the beautiful forested North Rim where you may find yourself far away from everything except the grand wilderness.

- Take your own **food and drinks** in a cooler

early morning on the veranda at the North Rim's Grand Canyon Lodge

and have **scenic picnics** to avoid the packed restaurants and food courts at the South and North Rims.

along the Rim Trail and exploring Grand Canyon Village. Summer inside Grand Canyon is pleasant and safe only in the early morning and evening; high temperatures regularly exceed 110°F (43°C) during the hottest part of the day, when all creatures within the gorge seek their hidden recesses of shade. Late-afternoon thunderstorms, often with spectacular displays of lightning, are a common occurrence throughout the region from July to September.

Mid-Season (Spring and Fall)

Still busy but with a more welcoming **inner canyon,** the park's **mid-season** comes in

spring (roughly **mid-March through April**) and **fall** (roughly **September through October**). Inside the canyon, spring starts in **early March** and fall stretches into **November.** Mid-season offers something of the best of both worlds—pleasant (though often windy) days and cool nights on the rims and **near-ideal conditions for backpacking** and exploring inside the canyon. Backcountry permits and river-trip reservations are, as a result, more difficult to obtain during the mid-season months.

Low Season (Winter)

The remote **North Rim closes for the season**

sandstone walls looming above the inner canyon

winter hiking on the South Rim's Grandview Trail

by early November, with the Kaibab Plateau blanketed in snow. (The only road leading to the North Rim, AZ 67, is closed December to mid-May.) Around the holidays there is usually an early-winter rush at the **South Rim.** By **January** the South Rim has entered its relatively slow **low season,** which lasts through about **mid-March** when the first of the spring break crowds arrive. Though cold and periodically snowy, the days and nights of the low season are a great time to be at the South Rim. A light but warm coat, a wool hat, and a pair of gloves is all you need to enjoy a winter visit to the canyon. You may find significant discounts on accommodations throughout the region during this season, but also curtailed services. On a **winter backpacking** trip into the **inner canyon** from the South Rim, you'll encounter cool days, cold nights, and fewer people (permit required). Commercial river trips through the inner canyon do not run during winter (rafting season runs April-October).

Before You Go

Park Fees and Passes

The **entrance fee** for Grand Canyon National park is $35 for a private vehicle with up to 15 people. The pass is good on both the South and North Rims for seven consecutive days. Motorcyclists pay $30 to enter, and those walking, cycling, or riding the free Purple Route shuttle bus from Tusayan or the Grand Canyon Railway from Williams, or who are part of a tour group, pay $20.

You can purchase a digital entrance pass at www.recreation.gov and https://yourpassnow. com, or pick one up on your way to the park at the **Williams-Kaibab National Forest Visitor Center** (200 W. Railroad Ave., Williams, 928/635-1418 or 800/863-0546, 8am-6:30pm

Trying to figure out how many days you need for your Grand Canyon adventure? It depends on how many areas of the canyon you want to explore.

The ideal **South Rim** trip lasts **four days and three nights,** with one day in each of the park's three major sections (Grand Canyon Village, Hermit Road, and East Rim/Desert View Drive) plus a day spent hiking into the canyon. **Three days and two nights** (with the first and last days including the trip to and from the rim) allows you to see all the sights on the rim, to take in a sunset and sunrise over the canyon, and even to do a day hike or mule trip below the rim.

If you include a **North Rim** or **West Rim** excursion, add at least **one or two more days and nights.** It takes about 4.5 hours to reach the North Rim from the South Rim (perhaps longer if you take the daily shuttle instead of your own vehicle). The West Rim, home to the **Hualapai and Havasupai Reservations,** is some 225 miles (360 km) from the South Rim over slow roads—although it makes sense if you're coming from Las Vegas and on your way to the South Rim anyway. A visit to the Hualapai Reservation's **Skywalk** should not be substituted for the South Rim (and isn't recommended to those seeing the Grand Canyon for the first time; you have not truly seen the Grand Canyon unless you have seen the South or North Rim).

If you want to add a trip into the **inner canyon,** plan to spend at least **one full day and night** below the rim. Camping overnight below the rim requires a backcountry permit.

The most important thing to remember when considering a trip to the canyon is to **plan far ahead,** even if you're just, like the vast majority of visitors, going to spend time on the South Rim. At least **six months' advance planning** is the norm, longer if you are going to ride a mule down or stay overnight at Phantom Ranch in the inner canyon.

daily spring-summer, 8am-5pm daily fall-winter), the **Flagstaff Visitor Center** (1 E. Route 66, Flagstaff, 928/774-9541 or 800/379-0065, www.flagstaffarizona.org, 8am-5pm Mon.-Sat., 9am-4pm Sun.), the **Chevron Travel Stop** in **Valle** (through a machine that only takes credit cards), or the **Grand Canyon Visitor Center** (Rte. 64, Tusayan, 928/638-2468, www.explorethecanyon.com, 8am-10pm daily Mar.-Oct., 10am-8pm daily Nov.-Feb.).

If you plan to visit more than two national parks in one year (or one park more than twice), purchase an $80 **America the Beautiful Pass,** which allows unlimited visits to any federal park or forest for one year. The pass is free to active military personnel and their dependents, and to all U.S. citizens or permanent residents 62 years old or older.

Reservations

Start making reservations for **in-park hotels and activities** up to a year in advance.

- **South Rim and inner-canyon lodging and mule rides:** Contact **Xanterra Parks and Resorts** (888/297-2757, www.grandcayonlodges.com) for reservations at most of the South Rim lodgings—El Tovar, Bright Angel Lodge, Kachina Lodge, Thunderbird Lodge, and Maswik Lodge)—and Phantom Ranch. Also book South Rim mule rides and motorcoach tours through Xanterra. To reserve a room at Yavapai Lodge (which has the park's only pet-friendly rooms), contact **Delaware North** (877/404-4611, www.visitgrandcanyon.com). While in-park hotels seem to always be booked solid, it often pays to call the local numbers several times to check for cancellations and lucky breaks (928/638-2631 for the Xanterra lodgings, 928/638-4001 for Yavapai Lodge).

- **North Rim lodging and mule rides:** For Grand Canyon Lodge on the North Rim, contact **Forever Resorts** (877/386-4383, www.grandcanyonforever.com), and go through **Grand Canyon Trail Rides** (435/679-8665,

photographing the sunset from Hopi Point on the South Rim

www.canyonrides.com) to book mule rides there.

- **Campground reservations:** All reservations for the South Rim's Mather Campground and the North Rim Campground go through **Recreation.gov** (877/444-6777, www.recreation.gov). To make reservations for the South Rim's Trailer Village, contact **Delaware North** (877/404-4611, www.visitgrandcanyon.com).

Inner-canyon adventures such as **backpacking** and **river trips** require long-term planning as well. You must apply for a **backcountry permit** by the first day of the month that is four months before your planned backpacking trip; for more information about obtaining a permit, contact the **Backcountry Information Center** (928/638-7875, www.nps.gov/grca). River trips must be booked about a year in advance and through an approved park concessionaire; the best place to start is the website of the **Grand Canyon River Outfitters Association** (www.gcroa.org), a nonprofit group of licensed river outfitters.

Entrance Stations
SOUTH RIM
MAIN ENTRANCE (SOUTH)
The park's primary and busiest entrance station is the **South Entrance Station,** reached via AZ 64 from **Williams** or via U.S. 180 to AZ 64 from **Flagstaff.**

DESERT VIEW ENTRANCE (EAST)
The South Rim has a secondary and far less busy entrance: the **East Entrance Station,** in the park's **Desert View** section, about 25 miles (40 km) east of **Grand Canyon Village.** This entrance can be reached via AZ 64 from U.S. 89 near **Cameron.**

NORTH RIM
The lone **North Rim Entrance Station** is located on AZ 67, the only road leading into and out of the park. The North Rim closes for the season by early November, and AZ 67 is closed December-mid-May.

In the Park

Visitors Centers

The main visitors center on the South Rim is the **Grand Canyon Visitor Center** (7am-6pm daily May-Sept., 9am-4pm daily Oct.-Apr.) near Mather Point, just a short drive from the main South Entrance and surrounded by parking lots. The **North Rim Visitor Center** (8am-6pm daily May 15-Oct. 16, 9am-3pm daily Oct. 17-30) is located at the end of AZ 67.

Where to Stay

Staying at one of the **lodges** inside the park offers the most convenience, with a bit of charm, history, and style thrown in. The in-park lodges are operated by concessionaires **Xanterra** (www.grandcanyonlodges.com) and **Delaware North** (www.visitgrandcanyon.com).

Outside the **South Rim** section of the park, **Williams** (60 mi/97 km, 1 hour) and **Flagstaff** (80 mi/129 km, 1.5 hours) have the most varied options in the region, while **Tusayan,** about 1 mile (1.6 km) outside the main gates, has a small selection of mid- to high-end hotels.

The **North Rim** section has only **Grand Canyon Lodge** within the park, **Kaibab Lodge** about 18 miles (29 km) north of the rim, and **Jacob Lake Inn** some 45 miles (72 km) north of the rim.

The **best campgrounds** are **Mather Campground, Desert View Campground,** and **North Rim Campground** inside the park and those administered by the **Kaibab National Forest.** Make reservations through **Recreation.gov** (877/444-6677, www.recreation.gov).

Getting Around

The free *South Rim Pocket Map & Services Guide* is a handy resource for exploring the South Rim, available at entrance stations and most visitors centers in the park (or download at www.nps.gov/grca). It includes a map of shuttle bus routes and stops as well as a comprehensive list of greenway trails.

FREE SHUTTLE

Park your car and take the **free, natural gas-powered shuttle buses** around the **South Rim.** The buses run several different routes around the park, including the Village Route (Blue) and the Kaibab/Rim Route (Orange), which both operate year-round; the Hermit's Rest Route (Red), which operates March-November; and the Tusayan Route (Purple), which operates from early spring to fall, running from the nearby town of Tusayan into the park.

The shuttle buses run every 10-30 minutes, generally beginning about an hour before sunrise and stopping about an hour after sunset. You may have to wait in relatively long lines, especially on busy summer days, and watch several buses fill up and depart before making it on.

The 14-mile (22.5-km) round-trip **Hermit Road** is closed to private cars from March to November, and the shuttle bus is the only way to see the essential viewpoints on this route, other than walking the Rim Trail or riding a bike.

The buses only go east as far as Yaki Point and the South Kaibab Trailhead, so to reach the Desert View section you have to drive yourself or book a tour through Xanterra.

BIKING

An increasingly bike-friendly national park, Grand Canyon's **South Rim** has miles of **greenway trails** for pedestrians and cyclists, including a section along the western **Rim Trail** on which bikes are allowed. You can also ride your bike into the park via the **Tusayan Greenway** (6.5 mi/10.5 km one-way), a paved bike path through the forest. Closed to cars for most of the year, the 14-mile (22.5-km) round-trip **Hermit Road,** along which you'll find some of the park's best viewpoints, is

In-Park Lodging

	Location	Rates	Season	Lodging Type
Mather Campground	South Rim	$18	year-round	tent and RV sites
Trailer Village	South Rim	$52-62	year-round	RV sites
Bright Angel Lodge	South Rim	$95-210	year-round	"hikers" rooms, hotel rooms, cabins, restaurants
Maswik Lodge	South Rim	$215	year-round	motel rooms, restaurant
Yavapai Lodge	South Rim	$150-200	year-round	motel rooms, restaurant
Kachina Lodge	South Rim	$225-243	year-round	motel rooms
Thunderbird Lodge	South Rim	$225-243	year-round	motel rooms
El Tovar	South Rim	$217-263	year-round	hotel rooms, restaurant
Desert View Campground	East Rim	$12	May-mid-Oct.	tent sites
North Rim Campground	North Rim	$18-25	mid-May-mid-Oct.	tent and RV sites
Grand Canyon Lodge	North Rim	$148-301	mid-May-mid-Oct.	cabins, motel rooms, restaurant
Bright Angel Campground	inner canyon	permit required	year-round	hike-in tent sites
Cottonwood Campground	inner canyon	permit required	year-round	hike-in tent sites
Indian Garden Campground	inner canyon	permit required	year-round	hike-in tent sites
Phantom Ranch	inner canyon	$51-149	year-round	hike-in dorms, cabins, food

open to bicycles, as is the **Desert View Drive,** which is open to and busy with cars year-round. Most viewpoints and all the stores, restaurants, and lodges on the South Rim provide outdoor racks to lock up your bike. For rentals, gear, and tours, head over to **Bright Angel Bicycles** near the Grand Canyon Visitor Center.

WALKING

The paved **greenway trails** between the South Rim's lodges, campgrounds, visitors centers, historic buildings, and other sights make Grand Canyon National Park very pedestrian-friendly. For sightseeing, the best walks to take are along the easy and relatively

The Hermit Road Greenway Trail allows bicyclists to ride along the South Rim.

level **Rim Trail,** a 12.8-mile (20.6-km) one-way trail along the rim that runs from the South Kaibab Trailhead to Hermit's Rest. Hike the whole thing or a few stretches—either way the Rim Trail will lead you to the best the South Rim has to offer.

Sustainability Tips

It's not difficult to be an eco-conscious tourist at Grand Canyon National Park. Just by choosing Grand Canyon over other destinations you've already made a good start. For several years now sustainability has been a priority at the park, and everywhere you go you see signs of this new era—water stations for refilling water bottles and reducing waste, greenway trails for bikes and pedestrians, an emphasis on locally produced food and beverages, and much more.

Before You Go

Consider staying at one of the **in-park lodges** (make reservations far in advance). This strategy cuts down on the amount of driving you will have to do; as soon as you arrive in the park you can park your car and walk, bike, or ride the free, natural gas-fueled shuttle buses for the rest of your stay. Moreover, the park concessionaires that operate the in-park lodges and hotels—**Xanterra** and **Delaware North**—have serious and energetic sustainability programs.

In the Park
WATER REFILL STATIONS
Bring your **reusable water bottles** along and refill them at stations across the park. The pure, delicious spring water comes from Roaring Springs near the North Rim and travels through a pipeline across the canyon to the South Rim. No plastic throwaway bottle of water could even come close.

Bring your water bottle and refill it at water refill stations throughout the park.

ECO-FRIENDLY HIKING AND BACKPACKING

Following basic **Leave No Trace** principles (Center for Outdoor Ethics, www.lnt.org) is the conscious, thinking hiker's bedrock responsibility.

The famous **Seven Principles** seem to take on an added seriousness in Grand Canyon, where every living thing exists in a perilous niche ruled by aridity. Follow these ideas, memorize these rules, spread these principles: (1) Plan ahead and prepare; (2) Travel and camp on durable surfaces; (3) Dispose of waste properly; (4) Leave what you find; (5) Minimize campfire impacts; (6) Respect wildlife; (7) Be considerate of others.

ECO-FRIENDLY BIKING

There's eco-friendly biking and then there's biking to be eco-friendly. The former requires basic common sense and adherence to the Seven Principles above. The latter is one of the most eco-conscious choices an individual Grand Canyon National Park visitor can make. **Leave your car outside the park** in a safe parking lot in Tusayan, and ride the 6.5-mile (10.5-km) one-way **Tusayan Greenway** into the park. You, Grand Canyon, and perhaps even the world will be better off for it.

Explore Grand Canyon

Best of Grand Canyon Country

A busy five days in Grand Canyon country may seem like ten when it's all said and done, and you'll have at least a month's worth of photographs and memories. There's a lot to do but no need to rush; always choose a view or a hike over your time table.

Note that high-season **reservations** for in-park lodging and dinner at El Tovar are required far in advance.

Day 1

Start your visit on the **South Rim** at the **Grand Canyon Visitor Center,** where you can watch a short movie about the park and check out displays on the natural and human history of the region. Walk the short path to **Mather Point** and join the crowds seeing **Grand Canyon** for the first time. Walk west on the **Rim Trail** to **Yavapai Point** and **Yavapai Geology Museum and Observation Station** and check out all the fascinating displays on Grand Canyon geology. Continue on the Rim Trail west to **Grand Canyon Village** and explore the historic lodges, gift shops, lookouts, and galleries. Have lunch at one of the many park eateries. After lunch catch the free shuttle bus at **Hermit Road** and continue west all the way to **Hermit's Rest,** stopping at the viewpoints along the way. You can also walk to the viewpoints along the Rim Trail or **ride a bike** along the Hermit Road. The trip to Hermit's Rest and back will take the rest of the day. Have dinner at **El Tovar** (reservations required) and then watch the **sunset** from the rim nearby.

descending the Bright Angel Trail

Best Adventures

Classic adventures in the park include a night or two spent deep within Grand Canyon, a ride on the Colorado River's legendary white water, and a precarious relationship with a mule.

BACKPACK INTO GRAND CANYON

Hike into Grand Canyon along the **Bright Angel Trail** or **South Kaibab Trail** from the South Rim and spend a night or two near the Colorado River at **Bright Angel Campground,** or venture on a **rim-to-rim** trek with three or more nights below the rim. (Permit required.)

RIDE A MULE TO PHANTOM RANCH

Follow a taciturn cowboy deep into Grand Canyon along the steep **Bright Angel Trail** to **Phantom Ranch,** spend the night in a cabin near the Colorado River, and then ride back up the trail the next morning. (Reservations required.)

RAFT THE COLORADO RIVER

Choose a National Park Service-approved outfitter and head off downriver on a **multiday rafting trip** through Grand Canyon, stopping

the Colorado River flowing through the Grand Canyon below Phantom Ranch

along the banks at **side hikes, waterfalls,** and **swimming holes.** (Reservations required.)

Day 2

Rise early and watch the **sunrise** before having a big breakfast at **Harvey Burger,** just off the Bright Angel Lodge's lobby. Then set off hiking into Grand Canyon on the **Bright Angel Trail** as far as you feel comfortable going—try to go at least to **Mile-and-a-Half Resthouse** (3 mi/4.8 km round-trip). Seasoned hikers may want to go as far as **Indian Garden** (9.6 mi/15.4 km round-trip). After your hike, cool off and rest with a local beer or a few cocktails at the **Bright Angel Cocktail Lounge.** About an hour before sunset, catch the Hermit's Rest Route (Red) shuttle bus to **Hopi Point** and watch the **sunset** with tourists from all over the globe.

Day 3

Rise early and explore the eastern **Desert View** section of the park, driving to the viewpoints and stopping at the **Tusayan Ruin & Museum** and **Desert View Watchtower** before leaving the park through the Desert View gate. Continue heading east on AZ 64, passing the **Little Colorado River Gorge,** and turn north onto U.S. 89, stopping for lunch at **Historic Cameron Trading Post** on the Navajo Reservation, just north of the junction with AZ 64. Continue north on U.S. 89 and pick up U.S. 89A going west. Stop and watch the Colorado River rolling along beneath the **Navajo Bridge,** then cross the **Arizona Strip** to the forested **Kaibab Plateau** and the **North**

Desert View Watchtower on the South Rim

Rim. Altogether, the drive from the South Rim to the North Rim takes about 4.5 hours.

Day 4

Spend the morning checking out the **North Rim Visitor Center, Grand Canyon Lodge,** and nearby **Bright Angel Point** before heading out on the scenic drive to **Cape Royal** and **Point Imperial,** stopping at viewpoints, trails, and ruins along the way. After dinner at the lodge (reservations highly recommended), sink into one of the chairs on the lodge's veranda and watch the sunset.

Day 5

Take an early-morning walk on the **Bright Angel Point Trail** (0.5 mi/0.8 km round-trip) or along the rimside **Transept Trail** (3 mi/4.8 km round-trip) near the lodge, or head out on one last proper hike into the canyon along the **North Kaibab Trail** to **Coconino Overlook** (1.5 mi/2.4 km round-trip) or **Supai Tunnel** (4 mi/6.4 km round-trip). When you climb out, sadly, it will be time to pack up, check out, and start the long drive to the airport in Phoenix, or wherever else you're headed to next....

Best Views

There's no one spot on the rims that provides the best all-around view of Grand Canyon, but a few come close. Ask the friendly rangers you meet for more suggestions.

LOOKOUT STUDIO

A Mary Colter-designed stone building hanging off the rim in **Grand Canyon Village,** Lookout Studio's **multi-level porches and verandas** provide breathtaking views of Grand Canyon and a chance to see **California condors** soaring overhead.

HOPI POINT

Probably the **most-recommended** spot on the **South Rim** for viewing the **sunset,** Hopi Point has **wide and long views** of the canyon and a fun, convivial atmosphere most nights, as travelers from around the world gather together to watch and photograph the performance.

CAPE ROYAL

On the **North Rim,** Cape Royal, a jutting **rock platform** hovering over the gorge among looming **rock temples and monuments,** waits

view from Lookout Studio in Grand Canyon Village

to be discovered at the end of a long forest drive along the rim.

Best Hikes

There are no truly easy hikes in Grand Canyon National Park; at around 7,000 feet (2,134 m) above sea level, even hikes along the South Rim's mostly flat Rim Trail can be challenging to low-landers. Even short hikes into the canyon require **preplanning** and **proper supplies** of water and food.

Family-Friendly Hikes
(UNDER 5 MILES/8 KM)
RIM TRAIL: BRIGHT ANGEL
LODGE TO MATHER POINT
Heading east from **Bright Angel Lodge** along

the **South Rim's** paved and generally level **Rim Trail,** this **2.5-mile (4-km) one-way** hike passes the historic lodges and shops at **Grand Canyon Village,** the **Trail of Time,** and **Yavapai Geology Museum and Observation Station** on the way to **Mather Point**—with Grand Canyon spreading out on your left side the whole way. If you don't feel like walking back, hop on a shuttle bus nearby.

BRIGHT ANGEL TRAIL TO
MILE-AND-A-HALF RESTHOUSE
Introduce yourself to the **inner canyon** on this

A short hike along the Bright Angel Trail is a good introduction for families.

3-mile (4.8-km) round-trip hike from the **South Rim** down the steep and twisting **Bright Angel Trail,** passing through a rock tunnel and ending at a **resthouse** along the trail, where you'll turn around and start your (eventually) rewarding climb back out.

NORTH KAIBAB TRAIL TO SUPAI TUNNEL

Step aside for the mule trains on this **4-mile (6.4-km) round-trip** hike into Grand Canyon from the **North Rim,** turning around at a **tunnel** blasted into the rock walls along the trail.

Day Hikes
(5-10 MILES/8-16.1 KM)
HERMIT TRAIL TO DRIPPING SPRING

Discover the lesser-used **Hermit Trail** on this **6.2-mile (10-km) round-trip** hike into the canyon from the **South Rim,** turning around at an **enchanting overhang** covered in greenery and trickling with spring water.

BRIGHT ANGEL TRAIL TO INDIAN GARDEN

Descend the precipitous **Bright Angel Trail** from the **South Rim** to the desert floor of the Tonto Platform and spring-fed **Indian Garden,** where you'll rest in the shade of a cottonwood tree before heading back up for the second leg of this tough but wonderful **9.6-mile (15.4-km) round-trip** hike.

WIDFORSS TRAIL

Get to know the **forests** of the **North Rim** on this **10-mile (16.1-km) round-trip** hike among pines, firs, and aspens to **Widforss Point,** a spectacular viewpoint named for the beloved Grand Canyon artist Gunnar Widforss.

Butt-Kickers
(OVER 10 MILES/16.1 KM)
BRIGHT ANGEL TRAIL TO PHANTOM RANCH

A classic backpacking expedition (permit

Widforss Point on the North Rim

required), this **19-mile (31-km) round-trip** journey from the **South Rim** to the **inner gorge** crosses a suspension footbridge over the **Colorado River** and ends at a **peaceful oasis.**

HERMIT TRAIL TO HERMIT CAMP
This **16.4-mile (26.4-km) round-trip** hike from the **South Rim** down the **Hermit Trail** (permit required) to primitive campsites near Hermit Creek is a great introduction to the **wilder side** of Grand Canyon backpacking. Add about **3 miles (4.8 km) round-trip** for a side hike to the **Colorado River** and roaring **Hermit Rapid.**

RIM-TO-RIM ON THE SOUTH KAIBAB AND NORTH KAIBAB TRAILS
Spend some quality time with the **inner canyon** on this **21-mile (34-km) one-way** hike across Grand Canyon from the **South Rim to the North Rim.** Some do it in one day, while most spend at least one night, and ideally two or three, at campgrounds along the trail (permit required).

Best in One Day

You can sample much of what Grand Canyon National Park has to offer in one day on the **South Rim.**

Best for First-Time Visitors

- See the canyon from **Mather Point,** which is a short walk from Grand Canyon Visitor Center, and **Yavapai Point,** 0.7 mile (1.1 km) west of Mather Point on the Rim Trail.

- Walk around **Grand Canyon Village** exploring the historic lodges, gift shops, and viewpoints.

- Take the free shuttle bus (Mar.-Nov.) to **Hermit's Rest,** stopping at the viewpoints along the way.

Best for Families

- Walk along the **Rim Trail** between **Mather Point** and **Grand Canyon Village.**

- Join the **Junior Rangers** at **Grand Canyon Visitor Center**—it's a fun and educational way to get kids engaged with nature.

- Attend free **ranger programs** about canyon animals and geology.

Best for Hikers

- Walk the **Rim Trail** from **Grand Canyon Village** west to **Hermit's Rest.**

- Take the **Bright Angel Trail** into the canyon, turning around at **Mile-and-a-Half Resthouse, Three-Mile Resthouse,** or **Indian Garden.**

Best for Return Visitors

- Hike into the canyon on the **Bright Angel Trail.**

- Take the scenic **Desert View Drive** to **Desert View Watchtower.**

- Book a **mule ride** along the South Rim.

view of the Colorado River from Desert View

Family Fun

Mile-and-a-Half Resthouse along the Bright Angel Trail

Try one of these family-friendly adventures on the **South Rim.**

SOUTH RIM MULE RIDE

Take a **guided mule ride** along the South Rim on the back of a friendly, sure-footed Grand Canyon mule, with many stops and stories along the way. Kids must be at least nine years old and at least four feet, nine inches (145 cm) tall to ride. (Reservations required.)

HIKE TO MILE-AND-A-HALF RESTHOUSE

A family expedition deep into the heart of the great gorge! Take your time and stop for lots of rests along the **Bright Angel Trail;** get younger kids into the experience by letting them carry a small backpack with water and snacks.

GUIDED BIKE RIDE

Guided bike tours of the South Rim include a 3-hour ride along **Hermit Road** and a 3.5-hour ride along the rim to **Yaki Point.** Kids must be 13 or older to ride a bike; trailers are available for younger children.

FREE RANGER PROGRAMS

Go on a **guided hike** with a ranger to learn about the canyon's animals and geology; attend select **night programs** for spooky tours of the Pioneer Cemetery and star gazing.

The South Rim

They come from all over the globe to Grand Canyon National Park's South Rim, to a fairy-tale stone-and-timber village hanging off the edge of an alien world. Walk or bike or ride the free shuttle bus to the high, jutting promontories scattered along the rim, and you'll hear a Babel of languages, see strange fashions, and perhaps meet new friends. Face the chaos or design of nature at its most awe-inspiring, rethinking your fears, desires, and preconceptions among the wind-wrinkled pinyon and juniper and the tall, skinny ponderosa pines.

   Something like six million people visit the South Rim every year, a number that has grown more or less steadily since the park opened in 1919. But the area actually went on the map as a world-wide tourist

Highlights

Look for ★ to find recommended sights, activities, dining, and lodging.

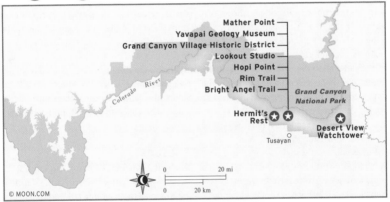

Mather Point
Yavapai Geology Museum
Grand Canyon Village Historic District
Lookout Studio
Hopi Point
Rim Trail
Bright Angel Trail

Grand Canyon National Park

Hermit's Rest ★ ★

Desert View Watchtower ★

Tusayan

Colorado River

0   20 mi
0   20 km

© MOON.COM

★ See Grand Canyon for the first time from the first and most popular viewpoint on the rim—**Mather Point,** a jutting rock platform that hovers over the canyon (page 55).

★ Learn about the incredible geologic story told in Grand Canyon's rock strata and see it all open before you from a scientifically chosen viewpoint at **Yavapai Geology Museum** (page 55).

★ Explore the **Grand Canyon Village Historic District** to learn the fascinating history of the canyon pioneers and the golden age of Southwest tourism (page 58).

★ Take your camera out to the patio of the **Lookout Studio** to photograph soaring California condors and an incredible view of the vast and labyrinthine canyon (page 64).

★ Watch the setting sun turn the canyon walls into fleeting works of art from popular **Hopi Point** (page 65).

★ Make your way west along the forested rim to the enchanting stone cottage called **Hermit's Rest** and watch the shiny black ravens gliding above (page 66).

★ Step inside one of architect Mary Jane Colter's finest accomplishments—**Desert View Watchtower,** standing tall on the edge of the canyon, an homage to Ancestral Puebloan-built towers that dot the great Southwest (page 69).

★ Walk along the easy, accessible **Rim Trail,** past historic buildings, famous lodges—and the most breathtaking views in the world (page 71).

★ Hike down **Bright Angel Trail,** the most popular trail on the South Rim, its construction based on old Native American routes twisting deep into the canyon (pages 74 and 81).

destination nearly two decades earlier, when the Santa Fe Railroad began easy passenger service to the South Rim in 1901. The railroad and the famous Fred Harvey Company worked for decades to make the South Rim a special place, to rival even the canyon itself, hiring Southwestern design masters like Charles Whittlesey and Mary Jane Colter to create enchanting and romantic structures along the rim—one-of-a-kind works of art made into shops, lookouts, and lodges that still stand and thrive today.

The most popular section of the park by far, the South Rim *is* the Grand Canyon for most visitors. To the west of the magical Grand Canyon Village, the center of all life and activity on the rim with its lodges, shops, restaurants, and lookouts, the park stretches west along the Hermit Road to a series of developed lookouts, each offering a different perspective on the canyon. To the east of the village, the Desert View area presents a wider view of the canyon and the meandering river, reached by driving the paved two-lane Desert View Drive through the evergreen forest, moving farther into natural solitude with every mile.

But as you stare at the canyon from places like Hopi Point, Powell Point, Hermit's Rest, and atop the sublime Desert View Watchtower, high above the inner gorge where the Colorado River continues its sculpting ways, you may find yourself challenged by the Grand Canyon's size. It sometimes takes mythology, magical thinking, and storytelling to see it for what it really is. When the first Europeans to see the Grand Canyon approached the South Rim in the Desert View area—a detachment of Spanish conquistadores sent by Coronado in 1540 after hearing rumors of the great gorge from the Hopi people—they were completely unprepared for the spectacle. The Spanish soldiers thought the spires and buttes rising from the bottom were about the size of a man; they were shocked, upon gaining a different perspective

below the rim, to learn that they were actually as high or higher than the greatest structures of Seville. Human comparisons do not work here. Preparation is not possible. You simply must come here, take that Grand Canyon trip, breath in the clean, high-country air, feel the warm wind rising out of the gorge, and witness the mystery for yourself.

PLANNING YOUR TIME

The ideal South Rim-only trip lasts four days and three nights, with one day in each of the park's three major sections (Grand Canyon Village, Hermit Road, and East Rim/Desert View Drive) plus a day spent hiking into the canyon. Three days and two nights (with the first and last days including the trip to and from the rim) allows you to see all the sights on the rim, to take in a sunset and sunrise over the canyon, and even to do a day hike or mule trip below the rim. If you just have a day, about five hours or so will allow you to see all the sights in Grand Canyon Village plus take a ride out to Hermit's Rest, stopping at viewpoints along the way.

Seasons

At about 7,000 feet (2,134 m), the South Rim has a temperate climate: warm in the summer months, cool in spring and fall, and cold in the winter. It rains and snows in winter, and thunderstorms, sometimes quite violent, appear in the late afternoons of July, August, and early September. Summer brings the park's busiest season, and it is *very* busy. About three million visitors from all over the world visit the South Rim each summer, offering rare opportunities for people-watching and hobnobbing with fellow tourists from the far corners of the globe. Summer (May-Sept.) temperatures often exceed 110°F (43°C) in the inner canyon, which has a desert climate, but are cooler by 20-30°F (11-16°C) up on the forested rims. There's no reason for anybody to hike deep into the canyon in summer. It's not fun,

---

Previous: shadowy Grand Canyon around sunset; Mather Point; Bright Angel Trail.

and it is potentially deadly. Instead, plan your epic trek in the spring or fall, perfect times to visit the park: It's light-jacket cool on the South Rim and warm but not hot in the inner canyon.

Wintertime at Grand Canyon's South Rim lasts from December to March, when the spring break traffic picks up. December is a festive and romantic time to be on the South Rim, and there's always a chance that you'll wake up to a white Christmas. January and February are generally the park's slowest months, with just over 200,000 visitors per month (compared to, say, 750,000 visitors in July). These are the coldest months on the rim, with high temperatures in the 30s F (-1°C to 4°C) and 40s F (4-9°C) in January and the 40s F (4-9°C) and 50s F (10-15°C) in February. There is often snow and ice on the rim and on the upper stretches of the trails, and hiking may require crampons, which most of the shops in the park sell ($25). The best thing about visiting the canyon in winter is the relative solitude. It's much easier to secure reservations, and you encounter far fewer people on the roads, at the viewpoints, in the restaurants, stores, and visitors centers, and especially on the trails. There are, however,

fewer services—there are no ranger programs at night during January and February, and the shuttle bus does not go to Hermit's Rest, though unlike during the summer months Hermit Road is open to private vehicles.

What to Take

Take along an easy-to-carry receptacle to refill at the water fountains situated throughout the park. A water bottle, CamelBak, or canteen is simply required gear for a visit; you are going to get thirsty in the high, dry air along the rim. You might even bring along a cooler with cold water and other drinks, which you can leave in your car and revisit as the need arises. Consider taking a hat, binoculars, and a camera along with your water bottle. The canyon's vastness can only be considered for so long before you start to notice the details hidden in plain sight; binoculars and cameras come in handy in such circumstances.

Bring along a light jacket even in summer, as the nights at 7,000 feet (2,134 m) can turn somewhat chilly. In the winter, when it is 70-something (21°C) in Phoenix, the South Rim is cold and often snowy. Several layers of cold-weather clothing will serve you well October-May.

Exploring the South Rim

The South Rim is by far the most developed portion of **Grand Canyon National Park** (928/638-7888, www.nps.gov/grca, 24 hours daily, $35 for seven-day pass for one private vehicle with up to 15 people; $30 for motorcycles; $20 for walk-ins, bikes, railway and shuttle bus; children 15 and under free; rates subject to change annually) and should be seen by every American, as Teddy Roosevelt once recommended. Here you'll stand side by side with people from all over the globe, each one breathless on their initial stare into the canyon and more often than not hit suddenly with an altered perception of time and human history. Don't let the rustic look of

the buildings fool you into thinking you're roughing it. The food here is above average for a national park. The restaurant at El Tovar offers some of the finest, most romantic dining in the state, and all with one of the great wonders of the world just 25 feet (7.6 m) away.

The best way to explore the South Rim is to park your vehicle in one of the large parking lots near the main visitors center or at Market Plaza, and then take the **free shuttle bus** to the viewpoints and sights. It's also possible to explore **on foot** via the Rim Trail and greenways, or **by bike** on the roads and greenways. You can rent a bike at Bright Angel Bicycles,

The South Rim

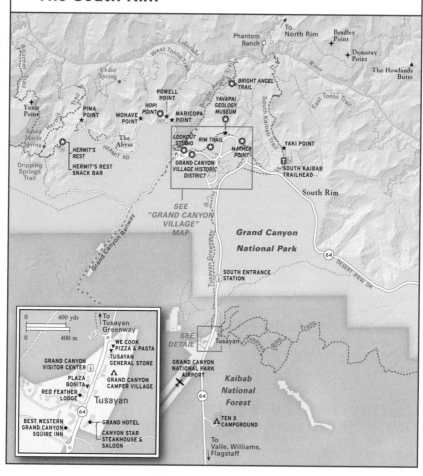

just across the plaza from the Grand Canyon Visitor Center.

VISITORS CENTERS
Inside the Park

While Historic Grand Canyon Village is the heart of the South Rim, Mather Point and **Grand Canyon Visitor Center** (7am-6pm daily May-Sept., 9am-4pm daily Oct.-Apr.), about 2.2 miles (3.5 km) east of the village along the rim, provide easy and in-depth introductions to the canyon and the park.

Entering from the main South Entrance on AZ 64 from Williams or Flagstaff, keep to the South Entrance Road for 5.1 miles (8.2 km) to reach four large parking lots around the visitors center complex. During the high season and on holidays, these parking lots can fill up by 9:30am, and most days they fill up by 10am regardless of the season. If you can't find parking here, proceed to Market Plaza and then Park Headquarters to find a spot; you can then backtrack to the visitors center via the Rim Trail or the free shuttle bus. Entering

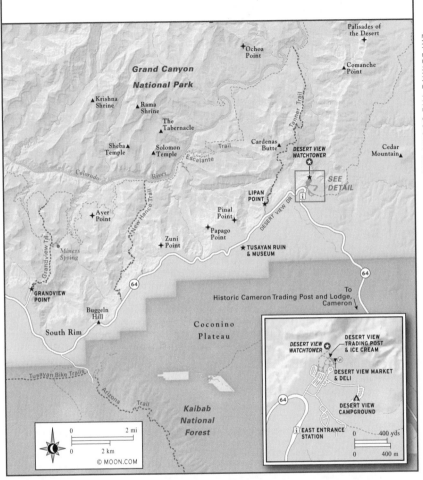

from the east through the Desert View area, turn right onto South Entrance Road at its junction with Desert View Drive, about 23 miles (37 km) from the East Entrance. From the junction it's only 1 mile (1.6 km) on the South Entrance Road to the main visitors center.

After finding a spot, head directly to Mather Point, which is just a short walk from the visitors center parking lots. After seeing the canyon from this famous first vantage, head back to the visitors center, where you

will find a water refill station, bathrooms, a bookstore with souvenirs and supplies, and a large, light-filled building with information about Grand Canyon and environs. Rangers staff the center all day to answer questions and help you plan your visit, and they offer ranger-led walks, hikes, and natural-history presentations around the park most days and evenings. A 20-minute film shown here on the hour and half hour, *Grand Canyon: A Journey of Wonder*, narrated by the great Peter Coyote, depicts the canyon's dawn-to-dusk cycle of

Four Days on the South Rim

The ideal South Rim trip lasts four days and three nights. The itinerary below assumes that you're driving to the South Rim from Phoenix's Sky Harbor Airport. High-season reservations for in-park hotels and dinner at El Tovar are required far in advance.

DAY 1

Arriving in the afternoon after the 3.5-hour journey across the desert and up to Arizona's highlands, enter Grand Canyon National Park through the **South Entrance** just past Tusayan, and park in one of four large parking lots near **Grand Canyon Visitor Center.** Walk the paved and signed pathways to **Mather Point** for your first look at Grand Canyon. After taking it in, take a short walk west (0.7 mi/1.1 km one-way) along the **Rim Trail** from Mather Point to the **Yavapai Point** and **Yavapai Geology Museum and Observation Station.** Spend some time in the small museum learning about the canyon's geology. Walk back to the visitors center and check it and the bookstore out, then drive to your in-park hotel to get checked in. Have a celebratory welcome dinner at **El Tovar** or **The Arizona Steakhouse** and then take in the sunset from the Rim Trail in the area of **Grand Canyon Village.** If you're not too tired, take in an **evening ranger program** at **McKee Amphitheater.**

DAY 2

The early risers in the group should hike the Rim Trail, take the shuttle bus, or book a tour to see the sunrise from one of the rim's viewpoints. Others can get a little extra rest before rising for a big breakfast at **Harvey Burger** or the **Maswik Food Court.** Today will be all about exploring the **Hermit Road** (western) portion of the park. During the high season, choose between biking, hiking, or riding the free shuttle bus. The route is about 7 miles (11.3 km) one-way, with several stops at viewpoints along the way and a final stop at the enchanting **Hermit's Rest** at the end of the road. Hikers can start out on foot and then pick up the shuttle bus at one of the viewpoints when tired. If you didn't bring your own bikes, rent some and even book a guided tour of the Hermit Road area at **Bright Angel Bicycles and Café,** near the main visitors center. This should take most of the day. Have dinner at one of the many park eateries, watch the sunset from one of the viewpoints, take in a ranger program, or have drinks and listen to some live music at **Yavapai Tavern.** But make it an early night, for tomorrow you descend deep into the Grand Canyon!

DAY 3

Rise early, have a hearty hiker's breakfast at **Harvey Burger,** and hit the world-famous **Bright Angel Trail.** To really experience the incredible world below the rim, hike to **Mile-and-a-Half Resthouse** (3 mi/4.8 km round-trip, 2-4 hours) or **Three-Mile Resthouse** (6 mi/9.7 km round-trip, 4-6 hours). If you don't feel like hiking, take a fun and memorable day trip to Williams and back aboard the historic **Grand Canyon Railway.** In the evening have a last dinner at your favorite in-park eatery and watch a final sunset from the rim.

DAY 4

Spend your final day on the South Rim exploring **Desert View Drive** (in the eastern portion of the park) in your vehicle, stopping at the viewpoints, the **Tusayan Museum,** and Mary Jane Colter's **Desert View Watchtower.** Leave the park through the **Desert View entrance** and drive to Cameron (about 30 mi/48 km), stopping at the **Little Colorado Gorge** and the historic bridge. Have lunch at **Historic Cameron Trading Post** and then drive back to Phoenix, about a three-hour drive via U.S. 89 to I-17.

Water Stations on the South Rim

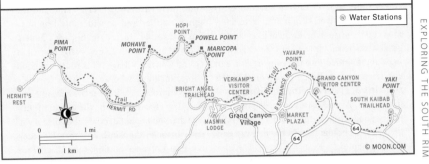

mystery and beauty, and there are several maps and other exhibitions that explain and illuminate the somewhat confusing grandeur just outside.

In Grand Canyon Village, along the rim about 2.2 miles (3.5 km) west of Grand Canyon Visitor Center, is the smaller **Verkamp's Visitor Center** (8am-7pm daily early Mar.-mid-May and early Sept.-Nov., 8am-8pm daily mid-May-mid-Aug., 9am-8pm daily mid-Aug.-early Sept., 8am-6pm daily Dec.-early Mar.), near Hopi House and El Tovar. It began in a white-canvas tent when Grand Canyon National Park opened and was a famous curio and souvenir shop right on the rim for 100 years. Since 2015 the historic building has housed a visitors center run by the Grand Canyon Conservancy, which includes books, souvenirs, and displays about the history of Grand Canyon Village.

Hikers going into the canyon during their trip to the South Rim should stop by the **Backcountry Information Center** (1 Backcountry Rd. Grand Canyon Village, 928/638-7875, www.nps.gov/grca/planyourvisit/backcountry.htm, 8am-noon and 1pm-5pm daily) for hiking tips and specific information about the latest on-the-ground trail conditions. If you have questions, concerns, or nagging trepidations before heading into the canyon, talk to one of the friendly, knowledgeable rangers here; it's likely you'll come away feeling confident and excited to hit the trail. The Backcountry

Information Center has a large parking lot that's only about 0.6 mile (1 km) from the Bright Angel Lodge in the heart of the village.

The farthest-flung of all the park's South Rim information and visitors centers is in the **Desert View Watchtower** (9am-5pm daily), about 25 miles (40 km) east of Grand Canyon Village. It is staffed with helpful rangers who have information about Desert View and the rest of the park.

Tusayan

About 1 mile (1.6 km) south of the park's South Entrance, the town of Tusayan is the home of the (non-NPS-affiliated) **Grand Canyon Visitor Center** (Rte. 64, 928/638-2468, www.explorethecanyon.com, 8am-10pm daily Mar.-Oct., 10am-8pm daily Nov.-Feb., IMAX tickets $13 over age 10, $10 children 6-10, children under 6 free), which has been a popular first stop for park visitors since the 1980s. You can purchase a park pass here, book tours, and check out some displays about the canyon, but the center wouldn't be worth the stop if not for its **IMAX Theater.** The colossal screen shows the 35-minute movie *Grand Canyon—The Hidden Secrets* every hour at half past. The most popular IMAX film ever (some 40 million people have reportedly seen it), the movie is quite thrilling, affording glimpses of the canyon's remote corners that feel like real time, if not reality. If you can afford the admission price, this is a fun way to learn about what you're about to see in the park. It's also a convenient place to book tours—everything from helicopter tours to river rafting adventures. If you're going budget, skip it and drive a few miles up the road, where you're likely to forget about both movies and money while staring dumbfounded into the canyon. You can also leave your car here and hop on the **free shuttle bus (Tusayan Route/Purple Line)** to the park. A small café here sells pizza and pretty good Chinese food to go. Don't miss the historic photographs in the hallway past the gift shop.

ENTRANCE STATIONS
Main Entrance (South)

The vast majority of visitors to Grand Canyon National Park enter through the **South Entrance Station** on AZ 64 from **Williams,** or via U.S. 180 to AZ 64 from **Flagstaff.** There are several lanes and generally the lines keep moving; however, on summer and holiday weekends you may experience a significant wait. As you enter a ranger will give you a *South Rim Pocket Map & Services Guide,* which is a helpful reference for exploring the park.

The most direct route to the South Rim is AZ 64 from Williams, 60 miles (97 km) of flat, dry, windswept plain, dotted with a few isolated trailers, manufactured homes, and gaudy for-sale signs offering cheap "ranchland." About 20 miles (32 km) longer but much more scenic is the route from Flagstaff via U.S. 180, which meets up with AZ 64 at Valle, about 30 miles (48 km) south of the South Entrance; it's a total of about 80 miles (129 km) from Flagstaff to the park gate. You can purchase your park pass ahead of time at www.recreation.gov or https://yourpassnow.com, the visitors centers in Flagstaff and Williams, the Chevron Travel Stop in Valle, or at the Grand Canyon Visitor Center in Tusayan, but doing so does not allow you to skip the lines unless you also ride the shuttle bus into the park rather than taking your car.

Desert View Entrance (East)

AZ 64 enters the park through the south but soon veers east toward Navajoland and the much smaller and considerably less busy **East Entrance Station,** in the park's **Desert View** section, about 25 miles (40 km) east of Grand Canyon Village. This route is a good choice for those who want a more leisurely and comprehensive look at the rim, as there are quite a few stops along the way to the village that you might not otherwise get to if you enter through the South Entrance. To reach the East Entrance Station, take U.S. 89 for 46 miles (74 km) north of **Flagstaff,** across a wide, big-sky landscape covered in volcanic rock, pine forests, and yellow wildflowers, to Cameron, on the Navajo Reservation. Then head west on AZ 64 for about 30 miles (48 km) to the entrance station. This is the best way to leave the park's South Rim section if you are heading to the Navajo or Hopi Reservations, or to the North Rim and Zion and Bryce Canyon in southern Utah.

SCENIC DRIVES
Desert View Driving Tour
25 MILES (40 KM)

The Desert View driving tour explores the eastern portion of the South Rim; its main draw, other than expansive views of the canyon, is Mary Jane Colter's Desert View Watchtower, the center of the area's action and appeal, about 25 miles (40 km) east of Grand Canyon Village. Without stopping at the many developed viewpoints, the drive to the watchtower, campground, and small eateries takes about 45 minutes to an hour; when you add in the many viewpoint stops, the drive could take several hours to most of the day. The viewpoints along this drive, which one ranger called the "quiet side of the South Rim," gradually change from forest to high-country desert, and are typically less crowded than those that can be reached by the shuttle.

The free shuttle goes only as far as **Yaki**

1: view from Desert View Watchtower 2: Desert View Drive leading through forest

Point, a great place to watch the sunrise and sunset, near the popular South Kaibab Trailhead. Yaki Point is at the end of a 1.5-mile (2.4-km) side road northeast of AZ 64. The area is closed to private vehicles, but all the other stops to the east can be reached only by private vehicle. If you want to make Yaki Point part of the Desert View driving tour, you can park your car at a small picnic area just east of the side road (about 2 mi/3.2 km from the village) and then cross the road and follow a path for about 0.5 mile (0.8 km) through the woods to the promontory and the South Kaibab Trailhead.

Along Desert View Drive, make sure not to miss the essential **Grandview Point,** where the original canyon lodge once stood long ago. From here the rough Grandview Trail leads below the rim. The viewpoint sits at 7,400 feet (2,256 m), about 12 miles (19.3 km) east of the village and then a mile (1.6 km) on a side road. It's considered one of the grandest views of them all, hence the name; the canyon spreads out willingly from here, and the sunrise in the east hits it strong and happy. To the east, look for the 7,844-foot (2,391-m) monument called the Sinking Ship, and to the north below look for Horseshoe Mesa.

Moran Point, east of Grandview, is just 8 miles (12.9 km) south of Cape Royal (as the condor flies) on the North Rim and offers some impressive views of the canyon and the river (18 mi/29 km from village).The point is named for the great painter of the canyon, Thomas Moran, whose brave attempts to capture the gorge on canvas helped create the buzz that led to the canyon's federal protection. Directly below the left side of the point you'll see Hance Rapid, one of the largest on the Colorado. It's 3 miles (4.8 km) away, but if you're quiet you might be able to hear the rushing and roaring.

Farther on Desert View Drive you'll come to **Tusayan Ruin & Museum** (22 mi/35 km from village). Stop here for a self-guided walking tour of the small Ancestral Puebloan ruin and a look around the small museum with exhibits about the rim's ancient inhabitants

and the descendants who still call the region home.

As the drive winds down and the trees turn from pine to pinyon to scrub, **Lipan Point** (23.3 mi/37 km from village) offers wide-open vistas and the best view of the river from the South Rim. It's one of the most popular viewpoints on the South Rim for watching the sunrise and sunset.

Finally, at Desert View, there's a large parking lot, bathrooms, gift shops, a deli, a gas station, and a campground. From the patio of the amazing, can't-miss **Desert View Watchtower** (25 mi/40 km from village), you'll be able to catch a faraway glimpse of sacred Navajo Mountain near the Utah-Arizona border, the most distant point visible from within the park.

Turn around and head back to the village on the same road, stopping again at the viewpoints or just cruising along through the forest.

Hermit Road Driving Tour
7 MILES (11.3 KM)

- **Hermit Road** is open to **private vehicles** in **winter only** (Dec.-Feb.).

- In **spring, summer,** and **fall** (Mar.-Nov.), this makes a great **walking tour** or **shuttle tour.**

March-November, the park's free shuttle goes all the way to architect and Southwestern-design queen Mary Jane Colter's **Hermit's Rest,** about 7 miles (11.3 km) from Grand Canyon Village along the park's western scenic drive called the **Hermit Road.** It takes approximately two hours to complete the loop, stopping at nine viewpoints along the way. On the return route, buses stop only at Mohave and Hopi Points. The Hermit Road viewpoints are some of the best in the park for viewing the sunsets. To make it in time for these dramatic solar performances, catch the bus at least an hour before sunset. There is often a long wait at the **Hermit's Rest Transfer Stop,** just west of the Bright Angel Lodge. The bus drivers generally know the times of sunrise and sunset. The route is open to cars beginning in December, when you can drive to most of the viewpoints and stare at your leisure.

Each of the Hermit Road lookouts provides a slightly different perspective on the canyon, whether it be a strange, unnoticed outcropping or a brief view of the white-tipped river rapids far, far below.

The first stop along the route is the **Trailview Overlook** (1.5 mi/2.4 km from village), from which you can see the Bright Angel Trail twisting down into the canyon and across the plateau to overlook the Colorado River.

The next major stop along the route is **Maricopa Point** (2.7 mi/4.3 km from village), which provides a vast, mostly unobstructed view of the canyon all the way to the river. The point is on a promontory that juts out into the canyon over 100 feet (30 m). This is the former site of the Orphan Mine, first opened in 1893 as a source of copper and silver—and, for a few busy years during the height of the Cold War, uranium.

Consider taking the 10- to 15-minute hike along the Rim Trail west through the piney rim world to the next viewing area, **Powell Point** (3.3 mi/5.3 km from village). Here stands a memorial to the one-armed explorer and writer John Wesley Powell, who led the first and second scientific river expeditions through the canyon in 1869 and 1871. The memorial is a flat-topped pyramid, which you can ascend to stand tall over the canyon.

About 0.3 mile (0.5 km) along Hermit Road from Powell Point is **Hopi Point** (2.9 mi/4.7 km from village), which offers sweeping, open views of the western canyon. As a result, it is the most popular west-end point for viewing the sun dropping red and orange in the west. North from here, across the canyon, look for the famous mesas named after Egyptian gods—Isis Temple, off to the northeast, and the Temple of Osiris to the northwest.

The next viewpoint heading west is **Mohave Point** (4.2 mi/6.8 km from village), from which you can see the Colorado River and a few white-tipped rapids. Also visible

from here are the 3,000-foot (914-m) red-and-green cliffs that surround the deep side canyon, appropriately named The Abyss. Right below the viewpoint you can see the red-rock mesa called the Alligator.

The last viewpoint before Hermit's Rest is **Pima Point** (7.5 mi/12.1 km from village), a wide-open view to the west and the east, from which you can see the winding Colorado River and the Hermit Trail twisting down into the depths of the canyon.

Finally you arrive at **Hermit's Rest,** a charming stone hovel built to look old and haphazard, about 7 miles (11.3 km) from the village. Inside there's a gift shop and a snack bar. There are also bathrooms here and access to the Hermit Trail.

Return to the village by the same route.

TOURS
Ranger-Led Tours
As part of a full schedule of activities and programs (go.nps.gov/gc_programs) on the busy South Rim, National Park Service rangers lead free daily hikes along the **Rim Trail** while discussing various fascinating aspects of the natural and human history of the South Rim and Grand Canyon. During the summer months rangers also take groups below the rim for a 3-mile (4.8-km) round-trip hike on the **Bright Angel Trail.** A hike with a ranger is a great way to learn about the canyon and the park, and the talks are generally entertaining and illuminating and geared toward families with children. Check the daily schedules at Grand Canyon Visitor Center or Verkamp's Visitor Center. Find out the time of your summer hike the day before, as the ranger is likely to get going very early to avoid the heat. It's a good idea to plan out all your ranger-led activities the first day you arrive.

Bike Tours
Bright Angel Bicycles and Café (10 S. Entrance Rd., 928/814-8704, www.bikegrandcanyon.com, 6am-8pm daily Apr.-Nov., 7am-7pm daily Dec.-Mar., adult rental $12.50 for 1 hour, $31.50 for 5 hours, $40 for

full day, child rental $9.50 for 1 hour, $20 for 5 hours, $31.50 for full day) rents comfortable, easy-to-ride bikes as well as safety equipment and trailers for the tots. It also offers guided bike tours of the South Rim departing from the bike shop, including a 5.5-mile (8.9-km), 3-hour ride along Hermit Road ($47-65) and a 6-mile (9.7-km), 3.5-hour ride along the rim to Yaki Point (kids must be 13 or older to ride a bike, $44 for youth bikes, $57.50 for adult bikes). Both rides are relatively easy, though the Hermit Road tour has significant ups and downs. Also remember that you are at 7,000 feet (2,134 m). The friendly staff members are quick to offer suggestions about the best places to ride. The little café serves excellent coffee and sells premade sandwiches and other snacks. Bright Angel Bicycles is located right next to the **Grand Canyon Visitor Center** near the South Entrance and Mather Point.

Air Tours

Though not ideal from the back-to-nature point of view, a helicopter or plane flight over the canyon is an exciting, rare experience and can be well worth the rather expensive price—a chance to take some unique photos from a condor's perspective. Flights are only allowed in a few sections of the canyon, and most spend time over the plateau forests and the eastern canyon. Five companies offer air tours out of **Grand Canyon Airport** (www. grandcanyonairport.org), along AZ 64 in Tusayan, and most of them offer many more flights originating in Las Vegas. They all prefer reservations. While some companies offer you the choice of paying a little more for a quieter EcoStar helicopter, others use only EcoStars. Most of the companies offer narration in at least nine different languages.

Maverick Helicopters (888/261-4414, www.maverickhelicopter.com) offers the Canyon Spirit Tour, which departs from Grand Canyon Airport in Tusayan and soars over the Kaibab National Forest, the

confluence of the Colorado River and Little Colorado River, and Marble Canyon (45 minutes, $299 pp).

Grand Canyon Helicopters (855/326-9617, www.grandcanyonhelicopter.com) is the South Rim's largest helicopter service with more than 450,000 passengers per year and has been around since 1965. The company offers 25-30-minute tours ($268 pp), flying over the North Rim and deep into the canyon over the Colorado. There's also a tour that starts in Las Vegas and lands in the western canyon outside the national park for a champagne toast (3.5-4 hours, $519).

Papillon (888/635-7272, www.papillon. com) offers one 25-30-minute tour ($219-259 pp) from Grand Canyon Airport and many more tours that originate in Las Vegas.

In business since 1927, **Grand Canyon Scenic Airlines** (928/638-2359, www. grandcanyonairlines.com) offers tours over the canyon in its small and "ultra-quiet" De Havilland Twin Otter Vistaliner and Cessna Caravan planes. The Grand Discovery Air Tour takes off from Grand Canyon Airport and flies over the North Rim's Imperial Point and Kaibab Plateau, the east canyon, the confluence of the Little Colorado, and Navajoland (40-45 minutes, $149 pp).

West Wind Air Service (480/941-5557, www.westwindairservice.com) has a rim-to-rim tour that soars over the eastern part of the canyon to the North Rim and the Kaibab Plateau (45 minutes, $152 pp), as well as a longer tour that flies over Monument Valley and Lake Powell (3-3.5 hours, $375 pp), with the option to take a 4x4 tour of Monument Valley with a Navajo guide (4-5 hours, $416 pp).

Bus Tours

Xanterra, the park's main concessionaire, offers in-park **motorcoach tours** (303/297-2757 or 888/297-2757, www. grandcanyonlodges.com, $70 pp adults, $30 pp kids 3-16). Options include sunrise and sunset tours, and longer drives to the eastern Desert View area and the western reaches of the park at Hermit's Rest. This is

---

1: bikes for rent at Bright Angel Bicycles and Café
2: Grand Canyon Railway

Grand Canyon's Human History (and Where to See It)

Never hospitable, Grand Canyon has nonetheless had a history of human occupation for around 5,000 years. For centuries Ancestral Puebloans farmed and hunted the rims and bottomlands of Grand Canyon, leaving behind little but stacked-rock ruins and animal fetishes twisted from cottonwood and willow. These were the mysterious ancestors of the Hopi, who believe that they emerged into this world from Grand Canyon and who have lived on three dry mesas not far from its depths for more than 1,000 years. Explore and discover more about Grand Canyon's Native American tribes along Desert View Drive at Tusayan Museum and Desert View Watchtower, and at Grand Canyon Village's Hopi House.

The first non-Native American explorers to see Grand Canyon were Spanish conquistadores attached to Coronado's blind search for the Seven Cities of Cibola in the 1540s. Hopi guides showed them the way to the rim but not how to enter the great gorge. Based on later descriptions, historians believe the Spanish attempted to descend into the canyon somewhere near Moran Point on Desert View Drive. They couldn't find a way in, and neither could they conceive that the vast impediment would be of any use to them. Many, many others thought the same way for centuries afterward, and thus the canyonlands would become one of the last regions of North America to be explored and mapped. That all began to change in 1869, when the one-armed explorer John Wesley Powell led the first scientific expedition on the Colorado River through Grand Canyon. For more on Powell's epic journeys, check out the Grand Canyon Visitor Center and the memorial to Powell at Powell Point along the Hermit Road.

John Hance, the first non-Native American to reside at the canyon, explored its depths in the 1880s and built trails based on ancient Native American routes. In the late 19th and early 20th centuries, a few other tough loners such as Buckey O'Neill and Ralph Cameron tried to develop mining operations in the canyon but soon found out that guiding avant-garde canyon tourists was the only sure financial bet in the canyonlands. In those early days a visit to the South Rim included a long, jarring, and expensive stagecoach ride from Flagstaff, and when you arrived Hance and Cameron and the other early tourism entrepreneurs didn't exactly put you up in luxury. It took another couple of decades and the coming of the railroad before the average American visitor could see Grand Canyon in something like style and comfort. To get a feel for what those early, pre-park days were like on the South Rim, check out the Pioneer Cemetery and Grandview Point, where one of the first rimside hotels once stood, and below which prospectors worked one of the first disappointing hard-rock mines in the canyon.

About 6 miles (9.7 km) from Grandview Point along Desert View Drive, outside the park boundary in a forest meadow surrounded by ponderosa pines and near a stock tank visited often by the area's wildlife, stands Hull Cabin, a rustic spread built in the 1880s as part of a sheep farm. The U.S. Forest Service took it over in the early 20th century and made it a ranger station, and these days you can rent the historic cabin (877/444-6777, www.recreation.gov, for more information call 928/638-2443) and experience something of what it was like to live near the rim back in the old pioneer days before the park.

By 1901 the Santa Fe Railroad had built a track from Williams to the South Rim and begun a new era that led to the creation of Grand Canyon National Park in 1919. In the decades to come, the Fred Harvey Company, architect Mary Jane Colter, National Park Service architect Daniel Hull, and others would create Grand Canyon Village, Desert View, and Hermit's Rest—more or less the park that we know and love today. To learn more about the Santa Fe Railroad, the Fred Harvey Company, and the formative years of Grand Canyon National Park, head to El Tovar, the Bright Angel Lodge History Room, and the Grand Canyon Railway Depot, from which you can still take a thrilling, retro train ride to Williams and back.

a comfortable, educational, and entertaining way to see the park, and odds are you will come away with a few new friends—possibly even a new email pal from abroad. Only pay for a tour if you like being around a lot of other people and listening to mildly entertaining banter from the tour guides for hours at a time. It's easy to see and learn about everything the park has to offer without spending extra money on a tour; as in most national parks, the highly informed and friendly rangers hanging around the South Rim's sites offer the same information that you'll get on an expensive tour, but for free. Also, if you like being on your own and getting out away from the crowds, a tour is not for you. To book a tour through Xanterra, you can either plan ahead and book online, or when you arrive check at the activities desk at Maswik and Bright Angel Lodges, from which the tours begin.

Train Tours

A fun, retro, and environmentally conscious way to reach the park or a memorable day trip from the South Rim, the **Grand Canyon Railway** (800/843-8724, www.thetrain.com, $67-226 pp round-trip depending on railway class) re-creates what it was like to visit the great gorge in the early 20th century. It takes about 2.5 hours to get to the South Rim depot in Grand Canyon Village from the station in Williams, where the Grand Canyon Railway Hotel just beyond the train station makes a good base, attempting as it does to match the atmosphere of the old Santa Fe Railroad's Harvey House that once stood on the same ground. The train has standard seats with great views, and also more-luxurious cars with observation domes and cocktails. Guides, called "Passenger Service Attendants," ride along in each car to answer questions and offer facts and anecdotes about northern Arizona and Grand Canyon.

During the trip you might wonder when the train is going to speed up, but it never really does, rocking at about 60 mph through pine forests and across a scrubby grassland

shared by cattle, elk, pronghorn, coyotes, and red-tailed hawks, all of which can be viewed from a comfortable seat in one of the old refurbished cars. Along the way look for ruins of the great railroad days, including ancient telegraph posts still lined up along the tracks.

A trip to and from the Grand Canyon on the old train is recommended for anyone who is interested in the heyday of train travel, the Old West, or the golden age of Southwestern tourism—or for anyone desiring a slower-paced journey across the northland. Besides, the fewer visitors who drive their vehicles to the rim, the better. Kids seem to especially enjoy the train trip, as comedian-fiddlers often stroll through the cars, and on some trips there's even a mock train robbery complete with bandits on horseback with blazing six-shooters.

Mule Trips

Mules do a good deal of the heavy lifting around Grand Canyon National Park, and when they are not working they relax at the historic and photo-ready Mule Barn across the train tracks from the main village area. This sturdy and dexterous hybrid has been carrying supplies and tourists into the canyon since before the national park took over. Though prohibitively expensive for many, mule riding is still a popular Grand Canyon exploit, made popular over the generations by riders from Teddy Roosevelt to the Brady Bunch.

Park concessionaire Xanterra offers a three-hour, 4-mile (6.4-km) mule ride along the rim east of the village, with many stops and stories along the way. The **Canyon Vistas Mule Ride** (303/297-2757 or 888/297-2757, www.grandcanyonlodges.com, 8am and noon Mar.-Oct., 10am Nov.-Feb., $152.85 pp) goes year-round and includes one hour of orientation and a two-hour ride. You must weigh less than 225 pounds (102 kg) fully dressed, be at least nine years old (under 18 must be accompanied by adult), at least four feet, nine inches (145 cm) tall, and in good health. Make sure to bring along a long-sleeve shirt, long pants, a hat, and closed-toe shoes. The tours start at the Mule Barn for orientation. To reach the barn, walk west 0.2 mile (0.3 km) from Bright Angel Lodge across the Village Loop Drive and the train tracks (follow the smell!). You can book online up to 15 months ahead. If you don't have a reservation, check to see if there's space available at the activities desk at Maswik or Bright Angel Lodges. Xanterra also offers overnight mule trips below the rim to Phantom Ranch in the inner canyon.

Horseback Trips

Outside the park, **Apache Stables** (928/638-2891, www.apachestables.com, $58.50 for 1-hour ride, $110.50 for 2-hour ride) offers one- and two-hour trail rides, an evening ride with a campfire, and an evening wagon ride with campfire (bring your own food). The stables are located in the beautiful Kaibab National Forest just outside the South Entrance. Drive 1 mile (1.6 km) north of Tusayan on AZ 64 and turn west on Forest Road 328 (Moqui Dr.); the stables are about a quarter mile (0.4 km) down on the left.

Guided Hikes

The **Grand Canyon Conservancy** (www. grandcanyon.org), Grand Canyon National Park's main nonprofit partner, offers a couple of easy guided hikes, perfect for families with older kids (children six or older preferred). The **Meet the Canyon Hike** (8am-11:30am and 1pm-4:30pm daily year-round, $55 pp) starts at Kolb Studio and then moves along the Rim Trail up to Trailview Overlook (1.3 mi/2.1 km one-way), from which you can see hikers ascending and descending the Bright Angel Trail. Along the way you'll learn about the geology, nature, and human history of the South Rim. Sign up for this popular guided hike on the GCC's website, where you can

also download an itinerary with a list of gear to bring along. The 3.75-mile (6-km) **Grand Canyon Adventure** (8am-noon Mon., Wed., and Fri. year-round, $55 pp) starts from Yavapai Lodge, east of the village, and travels the eastern section of the Rim Trail; book online or call the Yavapai Lodge front desk (928/638-4001, 8am-5pm daily).

The conservancy also leads backpacking trips below the South Rim to Indian Garden and the Bright Angel Campground, and also offers longer backpacking trips, river trips, and mule-assisted hikes ($700-5,500).

Self-Guided Tours

Two self-guided walking tours in Grand Canyon Village can be combined for an educational and illuminating few hours on the South Rim. The **Self-Guided Walking Tour of the Grand Canyon Village Historic District** (download pamphlet at www.grandcanyonlodges.com; click on Historic Village under Tours & Activities) is an easy stroll through the village that starts at the old Santa Fe Railroad station and ends at Kolb Studio, taking in all of the village's significant buildings (each one a National Historic Landmark) and telling their stories and those of their builders, owners, and famous residents. This is a great way to discover Grand Canyon Village, but for an even better tour take along the brochure for the **Self-Guided Civilian Conservation Corps Walking Tour** (download at www.nps.gov/grca/planyourvisit/brochures.htm) as well, and combine both tours into one in-depth look at the village. The CCC tour starts at the stairway near Kolb Studio and goes in a 1.5-mile (2.4-km) circle, passing walls, stairs, and buildings that the CCC helped build on the South Rim in the 1930s.

Sights

Divide the South Rim into several different sections to make it easier to explore. The first section is around the main visitors center, which you reach soon after entering the park at the main South Entrance, and is close to Mather Point, a wonderful option for your first look at Grand Canyon. Other areas include Market Plaza, Grand Canyon Village, Hermit Road, and East Rim/Desert View Drive.

GRAND CANYON VISITOR CENTER

★ Mather Point

As most South Rim visitors enter through the park's South Entrance, it's no surprise that the most visited viewpoint in the park is the first one along that route—**Mather Point,** named for the first National Park Service director, Stephen T. Mather. While crowded, Mather Point offers a typically astounding view of the canyon and is probably the mind's-eye view that most casual visitors take away. It can get busy, especially in the summer. Park at one of the four large lots near the visitors center complex and walk the short paved path from the **Grand Canyon Visitor Center.** At Mather Point you can walk out onto two railed-off jutting rocks to feel like you're hovering on the edge of an abyss, but you may have to stand in line to get right up to the edge.

Yavapai Point

A good way to see this part of the park is to leave your car at the visitors center and then walk a short way along the Rim Trail west to **Yavapai Point,** the best place to learn about the canyon's geology and get more than a passing understanding of what you're gazing at.

★ YAVAPAI GEOLOGY MUSEUM

Yavapai Geology Museum and Observation Station (928/638-7890, 8am-8pm daily summer, 8am-6pm daily winter, free) is the best place in the park to learn about the canyon's geology. This Kaibab limestone and ponderosa pine museum and bookstore is a must-visit for visitors interested in learning about what they're seeing.

Designed by architect Herbert Maier and first opened in 1928, the building itself is of interest. The stacked-stone structure, like Mary Jane Colter's buildings, merges with the rim itself to appear a foregone and inevitable part of the landscape. It's cool in here in the summer and warm in the winter. It's a place where time is easily lost, where you enter the gorge's timelessness, and you may even forget that you are in a museum while staring through the large windows that face the canyon. That's because you're not really in a museum, but rather an observation station. The site for the station, which was originally called the Trailside Museum, was handpicked by top geologists as the best for viewing the various strata and receiving a rimside lesson on the region's geologic history and present.

The museum features myriad displays about canyon geology. Particularly helpful is the huge topographic relief map of the canyon—a giant's-eye view that really helps you discern what you're seeing once you turn into an ant outside on the rim.

You can reach the museum by walking 0.8 mile (1.3 km) west from the visitors center or taking the shuttle bus on the Orange Route. There's also a small parking lot and bathrooms.

Trail of Time

After you've opened and flipped through Grand Canyon's wide-open geologic storybook at Yavapai Point, pick up the wheelchair-accessible **Trail of Time** just outside the little

stacked-rock museum building. A 2.83-mile (4.56-km) geologic timeline on the Rim Trail, the Trail of Time is a great way to put all that information into perspective while strolling along the rim. Each meter of the trail has a distinctive marker that equals one million years, and along the way there are rocks, viewing tubes, and exhibits explaining the incredible formation of Grand Canyon. If you walk from Yavapai to the village (1.3 mi/2.1 km, about 1 hour; the pamphlet *A Journey Through Time: Grand Canyon Geology* is available at both ends), you move backward in time toward the oldest rocks in Grand Canyon, Elves Chasm gneiss, which are about 1,840 million years old. Heading east from the village to Yavapai takes you forward in time toward the canyon's youngest rocks, Kaibab limestone, just 270 million years old.

MARKET PLAZA

About 4.4 miles (7.1 km) from the South Entrance and 1.3 miles (2.1 km) from Bright Angel Lodge, Market Plaza has a large parking lot and is home to the Canyon Village Market and Deli, Yavapai Lodge and Restaurant, a bank, and a post office. The Shrine of the Ages, McKee Amphitheater, and Park Headquarters sit just across the South Entrance Road. There's a free shuttle bus stop here, and it's close to the Mather Campground and Trailer Village. With the bike-friendly Grand Canyon Village Greenway passing right by Market Plaza, it's a good home base option for a park-and-ride visit.

Shrine of the Ages

Along the main road leading into Grand Canyon Village, the **Shrine of the Ages** (20 S. Entrance Rd., 928/638-7888) is a stylish multipurpose building for religious ceremonies, concerts, lectures, and presentations. Grand Canyon has always been considered a sacred space by the native inhabitants of the

region, and when new cultures moved in they inevitably attached religious significance to the inspiring grandeur all around. In 1952 an interfaith group started the push for a dedicated building for religious services along the rim, and architect Harold E. Wagner designed a building shaped like an Ancestral Puebloan kiva, complete with a wind-fed organ, hanging off the rim along the Hermit Road. The project never got off the ground, though, and instead the Shrine of the Ages opened in 1970 near the existing Pioneer Cemetery. The small, elegant building includes a large room for concerts and ranger programs in spring and fall, and several different churches hold Sunday services here throughout the year. Reach Shrine of the Ages by shuttle on the Village Route, by a spur off the Rim Trail that passes McKee Amphitheater, or by private vehicle year-round.

Pioneer Cemetery

When South Rim pioneer John Hance—a man who was sometimes *paid* to tell tourists tall tales—died in 1919, friends buried him along the rim not far east of Grand Canyon Village. A few years later, in 1922, Hance's resting place became the official graveyard of Grand Canyon. The **Pioneer Cemetery,** next to Shrine of the Ages, has over the decades become the final haunt of not just pioneers—those hardy folk who tried to make a living and a life here before the national park was established in 1919—but also of Harvey Girls, war veterans, National Park Service employees, and longtime residents of the area who had a special relationship with and impact on the canyon country. The peaceful and woodsy cemetery includes a memorial to the 128 people who died in the 1957 plane collision over the eastern part of Grand Canyon. Purchase a guide to the cemetery and its residents, *In a Better Place: At Rest in Grand Canyon Cemetery* ($3.99), at the Grand Canyon Conservancy bookstore next to the main visitors center. The cemetery is about 1.7 miles (2.7 km) west of the visitors center, and is reached via a spur off the Rim Trail, by

---

1: Yavapai Geology Museum and Observation Station at Yavapai Point 2: walking the deep history of Grand Canyon along the Trail of Time

The Canyon and the Railroad

It wasn't until the **Santa Fe Railroad** reached the South Rim of the Grand Canyon in 1901 that the great chasm's now-famous tourist trade really got going. Prior to that, travelers faced an all-day stagecoach ride from Flagstaff at a cost of $20, a high price to pay for sore bones and cramped quarters. Thanks to the railroad, even travelers of a less seasoned variety could see the wonders of the West, including the Grand Canyon, with relative ease.

The railroad's main concessionaire, the **Fred Harvey Company,** in those years operated "Harvey House" hotels, restaurants, and lunch counters all along the Santa Fe line. Widely celebrated for their high-quality fare and service, these eateries often became the nicest place in town in places that were still little more than frontier outposts. Each Harvey Company restaurant was staffed by the famous **"Harvey Girls,"** young women often recruited in cities, intensively trained as waitresses, and then sent out to work at far-flung spots along the railway. Hard-working and efficient, they were expected to adhere to strict company rules and were held to high standards of service. Being a Harvey Girl provided the opportunity for women to be adventurous pioneers, living and working independently and helping to settle the West. There are today several women who worked as Harvey Girls buried in Grand Canyon's Pioneer Cemetery.

Along with bringing its special brand of service to the South Rim, the Harvey Company in the 1920s and 1930s enlisted the considerable talents of Arts and Crafts designer and architect **Mary Jane Colter** to build lodges, lookouts, galleries, and stores on the South Rim. These treasured buildings still stand today, and are now considered to be some of the finest architectural accomplishments in the entire national parks system. The Harvey Company's dedication to simple elegance, and Colter's interest in and understanding of Pueblo Indian architecture and lifeways, created an artful human stamp on the rim that nearly lives up to the breathtaking canyon it serves.

For half a century or more, the Santa Fe line from Williams took millions of tourists to the edge of the canyon. But finally the American love affair with the automobile, the rising mythology of the go-west road trip, and the interstate highway system killed train travel to Grand Canyon National Park by the late 1960s. In the 1990s, however, entrepreneurs revived the railroad as an excursion and tourist line. Today, the **Grand Canyon Railway** carries more than 250,000 passengers to the South Rim every year, which has significantly reduced polluting automobile traffic in the cramped park.

shuttle on the Village Route, or by private vehicle year-round.

Grand Canyon Community Library

There are actually three libraries on Grand Canyon's South Rim—a school library; a research library for historians, students, and National Park Service employees with about 12,000 items at Park Headquarters; and the charming little **Grand Canyon Community Library** (11 Navajo St., 928/638-2718, www.grandcanyoncommunitylibrary.org, 10:30am-5pm Mon.-Sat.). Housed in a small National Park-rustic building near Market Plaza that used to be a one-room schoolhouse in the 1920s, the library has about 16,000 items and is open to the public, though only locals can borrow. Part of the Flagstaff-Coconino County Public Library system, there are a few computers with Internet access and free Wi-Fi in this cozy, old-fashioned space about 200 yards (183 m) from the rim, as well as books, magazines, and printing, faxing, scanning, and copying services.

★ GRAND CANYON VILLAGE HISTORIC DISTRICT

Largely the creation of the Santa Fe Railroad and National Park Service architects in the early 1900s, Grand Canyon Village today is a diverse and enchanting assemblage of historic

---

1: Pioneer Cemetery 2: Verkamp's visitors center and store

buildings still in use. The stylishly rustic village, which includes out-of-sight residential neighborhoods for park and concessionaire employees, has some 247 structures and is listed as a National Historic Landmark District. It's the center of the South Rim, and the busy area between El Tovar and Bright Angel Lodge is something of a town square.

El Tovar

El Tovar is the South Rim's first great hotel and the picture of haute-wilderness style. Designed in 1905 by Charles Whittlesey for the Santa Fe Railroad, El Tovar has the look of a Swiss chalet and a log-house interior, watched over by the wall-hung heads of elk and buffalo; it is at once rustic, cozy, and elegant. This Harvey Company jewel has hosted dozens of rich and famous canyon visitors over the years, including George Bernard Shaw and presidents Teddy Roosevelt and William Howard Taft. While it is a wonderfully romantic building up close, El Tovar looks even more picturesque from a few of the viewpoints along the Hermit Road, and you can really get a good idea of just how close the lodge is to the rim by seeing it from far away. Inside you'll find two gift shops and a cozy lounge where you can have a drink or two while looking at the canyon. El Tovar's restaurant is the best in the park, and it's quite pleasant to sink into one of the Arts and Crafts leather chairs in the rustic, dark-wood lobby and contemplate the former lives of the animals whose majestic heads grace the walls of this enchanting building.

Hopi House

A few steps from the front porch of El Tovar is Mary Jane Colter's **Hopi House,** designed and built in 1905 as if it sat not at the edge of the Grand Canyon but on the edge of Hopi's Third Mesa. Hopi workers used local materials to build this unique gift shop and gallery for Native American art. The Fred Harvey Company even hired the famous Hopi-Tewa potter Nampeyo to live here with her family while demonstrating her artistic talents and Hopi lifeways to tourists. This is one of the best places in the region for viewing and buying Hopi, Navajo, and Pueblo art (though most of the art is quite expensive), and there are even items made by Nampeyo's descendants on view and for sale here.

Verkamp's

Along the rim just east of El Tovar, **Verkamp's** was for a century a curio shop run by the Verkamp family, whose founding ancestor started out here selling Native American art and souvenirs to tourists out of a canvas tent. The business, the longest-running family concern in the national park system, closed down in 2008 due mostly to the reluctance of another generation to take it on. Verkamp's is now a Grand Canyon Conservancy bookstore and gift shop with a small museum about the history and growth of Grand Canyon Village. The building, a 1905 modified Mission-style house that is like nothing else on the rim, housed the Verkamp family upstairs until the 1970s and is now on the National Historic Register.

Bright Angel Lodge

The village's central hub of activity, rustic and charming **Bright Angel Lodge** was designed in 1935 by Mary Jane Colter to replace the old Bright Angel Hotel, which pioneer John Hance built in the 1890s, and the Bright Angel Camp tent-city near the trail of the same name. Originally meant to attract more middle-class tourists to the park, the lodge is still a romantic and comfortable place to stay, resembling a rough-hewn hunting lodge constructed of materials found nearby.

The **Bright Angel History Room,** just off the main lobby, has fascinating exhibits and artifacts telling the story of the Fred Harvey Company, architect Mary Jane Colter, the Santa Fe Railroad, and the early years of Southwestern tourism. Spend some time in here learning about the legendary Harvey Girls, who hosted a golden age of train travel from Chicago to Los Angeles. You'll also see Colter's "geologic fireplace," a 10-foot-high

(3-m) re-creation of the canyon's varied strata. Geologists collected the stones from the inner canyon and loaded them on the backs of mules for the journey out. The fireplace's strata appear exactly like those stacked throughout the canyon walls, equaling a couple of billion years of earth-building from bottom to rim.

For a break from the outdoors, step into the **Bright Angel Cocktail Lounge,** a dark and cozy bar off the lobby where you can relax over a pint of Arizona-brewed beer. Don't miss the charming murals on the walls depicting Native American imagery and greenhorn tourists riding mules into the canyon. The Bright Angel lobby also has one of the best gift shops in the park.

BUCKEY O'NEILL LOG CABIN AND RED HORSE STATION

Bright Angel Lodge includes several buildings with individual rooms as well as a collection of small cabins just to the west of the main lobby building. Two of these cabins were created out of historic buildings originally constructed and occupied by South Rim pioneers. The cabin closest to the rim, **Buckey O'Neill's Log Cabin,** was once the home of William "Buckey" O'Neill, an early canyon entrepreneur who died while fighting with Teddy Roosevelt's Rough Riders in Cuba. This cabin is the oldest continuously standing structure on the South Rim. O'Neill built it in the 1890s after coming to Arizona in 1879 at the age of 19. Still a popular figure in northern Arizona, O'Neill was a journalist, a judge, the mayor of nearby Prescott, a presidential candidate, and, like everyone in his day, a hard-luck miner. Though nobody made much money mining Grand Canyon in those days, O'Neill eventually sold his canyon mining claims and in doing so helped bring the Santa Fe Railroad to the rim, changing the region indelibly. There's a statue of him in Prescott, a charming small town about two hours south of the rim and the state's first territorial capital. The dramatic equestrian statue was sculpted by Solon Borglum, whose brother and nephew carved Mount Rushmore.

Also among the cabins here is **Red Horse Station,** built by Ralph Cameron, also an early canyon miner and entrepreneur (and eventually a U.S. senator who helped Arizona win statehood), after the railroad came to the rim. In 1902, Cameron constructed the two-room hotel from the remains of his obsolete stagecoach station, and the building later housed the South Rim's first post office. Cameron developed, with several partners, the Grandview and Bright Angel Trails. He later fought for decades to control the Bright Angel Trail and Indian Garden with a $1 per person toll and a string of questionable mining claims. Cameron eventually lost the fight and the National Park Service took over the trail in 1928.

Mary Jane Colter preserved the two structures in the 1930s and incorporated them into the new lodge. Though closed to the general public, both cabins are available as overnight accommodations. Over the years they have been updated for comfort, but they still retain much of their historic charm.

Grand Canyon Railway Depot

Grand Canyon changed forever when the Santa Fe Railroad came to the South Rim in 1901. Instead of being visited primarily by wealthy tourists willing to pay too much for a punishing stagecoach ride from Flagstaff only to stay in questionable accommodations on the rim, now wealthy and middle-class travelers could travel to the rim with relative ease. The tracks and the trains soon inspired a better class of cabin along the rim, and the Santa Fe Railroad in 1905 built the luxurious El Tovar Hotel. A few years later the railroad decided it needed a new depot to match the hotel's considerable rustic style. Designed by railroad architect Francis W. Wilson (who also built the Harvey House and train depot in Barstow, California), the log structure just down the hill from El Tovar opened in 1909. Today the **Grand Canyon Railway Depot** is the oldest standing wooden train depot in the national park system, a National Historic Landmark, and still in service as a train

Grand Canyon Village

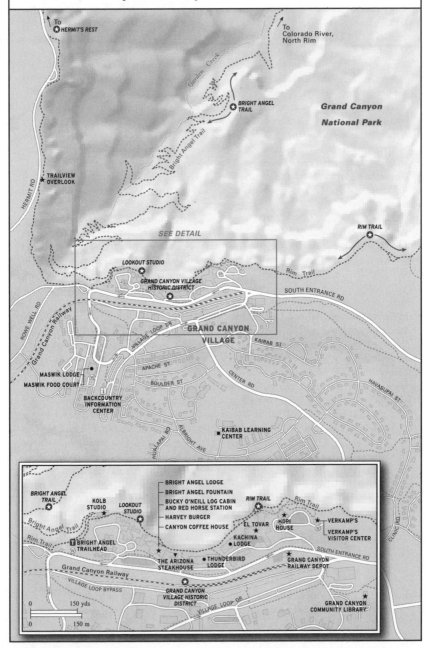

To HERMIT'S REST

To Colorado River, North Rim

Garden Creek

BRIGHT ANGEL TRAIL

Bright Angel Trail

Grand Canyon

National Park

TRAILVIEW OVERLOOK

HERMIT RD

RIM TRAIL

SEE DETAIL

LOOKOUT STUDIO

GRAND CANYON VILLAGE HISTORIC DISTRICT

Rim Trail

SOUTH ENTRANCE RD

ROME WELL RD

Grand Canyon Railway

VILLAGE LOOP DR

GRAND CANYON VILLAGE

KAIBAB ST

APACHE ST

BOULDER ST

CENTER RD

HAVASUPAI ST

MASWIK LODGE
MASWIK FOOD COURT

BACKCOUNTRY INFORMATION CENTER

HUALAPAI RD

ALBRIGHT AVE

KAIBAB LEARNING CENTER

KOLB STUDIO

LOOKOUT STUDIO

BRIGHT ANGEL TRAIL

Bright Angel Trail

BRIGHT ANGEL LODGE
BRIGHT ANGEL FOUNTAIN
BUCKY O'NEILL LOG CABIN AND RED HORSE STATION
HARVEY BURGER
CANYON COFFEE HOUSE

RIM TRAIL

Rim Trail

EL TOVAR

HOPI HOUSE

VERKAMP'S

VERKAMP'S VISITOR CENTER

KACHINA LODGE

CLINIC RD

Rim Trail

BRIGHT ANGEL TRAILHEAD

THE ARIZONA STEAKHOUSE

THUNDERBIRD LODGE

SOUTH ENTRANCE RD

GRAND CANYON RAILWAY DEPOT

Grand Canyon Railway

VILLAGE LOOP BYPASS

GRAND CANYON VILLAGE HISTORIC DISTRICT

VILLAGE LOOP DR

GRAND CANYON COMMUNITY LIBRARY

0   150 yds
0   150 m

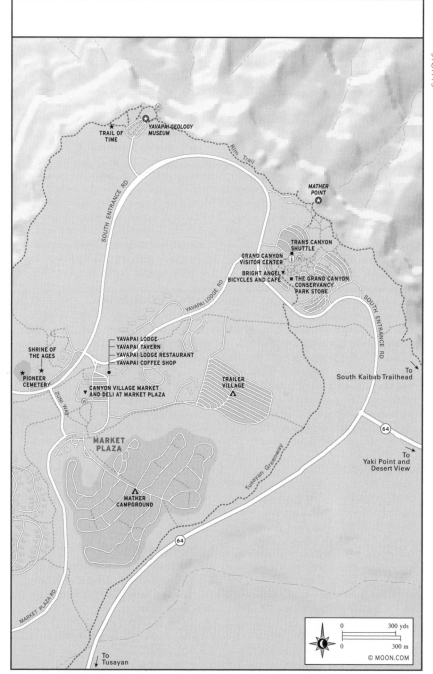

station, hosting hundreds of historic Grand Canyon Railway passengers every day.

★ Lookout Studio

Mary Jane Colter also designed the **Lookout Studio,** west of the Bright Angel Lodge, a little stacked-stone watch house that seems to be a mysterious extension of the rim itself. The stone patio juts out over the canyon and is a popular place for picture taking. The Lookout was built in 1914 exactly for that purpose—to provide a comfortable but "indigenous" building and deck from which visitors could gaze at and photograph the canyon. It was fitted with high-powered telescopes and soon became one of the most popular snapshot scenes on the rim. It still is today, and on many days you'll be standing elbow to elbow with camera-carrying tourists clicking away. As she did with her other buildings on the rim, Colter designed the Lookout to be a kind of amalgam of Native American ruins and backcountry pioneer utilitarianism. Her formula of using found and indigenous materials, stacked haphazardly, works wonderfully here. When it was first built, the little stone hovel was so "authentic" that it even had weeds growing out of the roof. Inside, where you'll find books and canyon souvenirs, the studio looks much as it did when it first opened. The jutting stone patio is still one of the best places from which to view the canyon.

Kolb Studio

Built in 1904 right on the canyon's rim, **Kolb Studio** is significant not so much for its design but for the human story that went on inside. It was the home and studio of the famous Kolb Brothers, pioneer canyon photographers, moviemakers, river rafters, and entrepreneurs. Inside there's a gift shop, a gallery, and a display about the brothers, who in 1912 rode the length of the Colorado in a boat with a movie camera rolling. The journey resulted in a classic book of exploration and river-running, Emery Kolb's 1914 *Through the Grand Canyon from Wyoming to Mexico.* The Kolb Brothers were some of the first entrepreneurs at the canyon. Around 1902 they set up a photography studio in a cave near the rim and later moved it to this house. After a falling-out between the brothers, the younger Emery Kolb stayed on at the canyon until his death in 1976, showing daily the film the brothers had made of their epic river trip to several generations of canyon visitors.

HERMIT ROAD

To the west of the village the rim juts out to various viewpoints that provide expansive and inspiring views of the canyon and Colorado River. December-February, the 7-mile (11.3-km) two-lane Hermit Road is open to private vehicles; March-November, it's accessible only on foot (via the Rim Trail), by bicycle, or on a free shuttle bus. Many of the viewpoints along this essential route, built in 1934-1935, are named for Arizona's Native American tribes.

Trailview Overlook

From Bright Angel Lodge it's a 0.5-mile (0.8-km) walk west along the Rim Trail to the **Trailview Overlook,** from which you can see hikers descending and ascending the mighty Bright Angel Trail. The walk includes an incline and some steps that lead to a couple of promontories facing east, a perfect vantage from which to view the impossibly twisty trail as well as Grand Canyon Village all tucked away behind a skirt of pine. Come here at night and watch flashlights and headlamps dancing on canyon walls as hikers trudge up the trail through the darkness. You can also ride the free shuttle bus on the Hermit Route to reach Trailview, and during winter you can drive there.

Maricopa Point

About 0.7 mile (1.1 km) west from Trailview Overlook along the Rim Trail, **Maricopa Point** offers gorgeous and inspiring canyon views from a jutting promontory at the end of a narrow, paved pathway. This area is best known as the site of the former Orphan Mine, one of the nation's richest uranium mines during the nuclear age of the 1950s and 1960s.

Finding the Best Canyon Viewpoints

The canyon's unrelenting vastness tends to blur the details. Viewing the gorge from many different points seems to cure this. There are 19 named viewpoints along the South Rim Road, from the easternmost Desert View to the westernmost Hermit's Rest. Is it necessary, or even a good idea, to see them all? No, not really. For many it's difficult to pick out the various named buttes, mesas, side canyons, drainages, and other features that rise and fall and undulate throughout the gorge, and one viewpoint ends up looking not that different from the next.

The best way to see the canyon viewpoints is to park your car and walk along the **Rim Trail.** Attempts to visit each viewpoint tend to speed up your visit and make you miss the subtleties of the different views. Consider really getting to know a few select viewpoints rather than trying to quickly and superficially hit each one. Any of the viewpoints along the **Hermit Road** and **Desert View Drive** are candidates for a long love affair. The views from just outside **El Tovar** or the **Bright Angel Lodge,** right in the middle of all the bustling village action, are as gorgeous as any others, and it can be fun and illuminating to watch people's reactions to what they're seeing.

There isn't a bad view of the canyon, but if you have limited time, ask the rangers at the main visitors center or Yavapai Geology Museum what their favorite viewpoint is and why. The shuttle bus drivers are also great sources of information and opinions. Try to see at least one sunset or sunrise at one of the developed viewpoints. The canyon's colors and details can seem monotonous after the initial thrill wears off (if it ever does), but the sun splashing and dancing at different strengths and angles against the multihued buttes and sheer, shadowy walls makes it all new again.

You used to be able to see the ruins of the mine's headframe from the point, but it has since been dismantled as the park works to clean and reform the land.

Powell Point

About 0.5 mile (0.8 km) west from Maricopa Point along the Rim Trail, **Powell Point** is named for John Wesley Powell, the one-armed Civil War veteran who organized and led the first two scientific expeditions down the Colorado River and through the Grand Canyon. Curiously, the altar-like half-pyramid that serves as the memorial to Powell and his 1869 and 1872 adventures is perched on a promontory from which you cannot see the river. Beyond the monument, benches await before a jutting flat-rock platform, without barriers and with stunning views to the north and east. It's inspiring and peaceful to sit out here and watch the day fade away.

Hopi Point is just a short walk (about 0.3 mi/0.5 km, or 10 minutes on the Rim Trail) from here, so consider strolling there instead of waiting for the shuttle bus.

★ Hopi Point

With an expansive and unbounded view, probably the best from the rim (certainly the best from the Hermit Road), **Hopi Point** gets very busy at sunrise and sunset, so much so that if you don't like crowds it should be avoided during these most popular viewing times. From here catch amazing views of the river and, to the north, the famous mesas named after Egyptian gods: Isis Temple, Horus Temple, and Osiris Temple. There's a small monument here to Colonel Claude Hale Birdseye, who headed the U.S. Geological Survey through the canyon in 1923, which marked the beginning of the drive to dam the Colorado and use its flow and power for profit. This has long been a favorite spot for photographers, so you are likely to see members of that curious tribe set up with their tripods. There are restrooms here, too. Don't miss seeing the decommissioned fire lookout along the Hermit Road between Hopi Point and Powell Point.

Mohave Point

About 0.8 mile (1.3 km) west from Hopi Point along the Rim Trail, **Mohave Point** provides near-equal vistas, including fantastic looks at the river, including Boucher and Granite Rapids. Mohave is a good alternative to Hopi Point at sunrise and sunset if you want to avoid the crowds. From here you can stare down into **The Abyss,** literally—a steep, vertical drop hemmed in by 3,000-foot (914-m) cliffs. You can also see from here the weird red sandstone formation called the **Alligator**— for very good reason.

Pima Point

Pima Point is the last developed viewpoint along the Hermit Road prior to Hermit's Rest. Two miles (3.2 km) west from Hopi Point along the Rim Trail, Pima Point has great views to the west, from **Bright Angel Canyon** all the way to **Powell Plateau** off in the hazy distance. The view to the east includes **Monument Creek** and the red-rock **Alligator,** and right across the canyon you can see **Ninetyfourmile Creek.** This is one of the best points to see the river, and on a quiet day you might be able to hear the rush and roar of the rapids.

★ Hermit's Rest

The final stop on the Hermit Road is the enchanting gift shop and resthouse called **Hermit's Rest,** a rest-stop designed by Mary Jane Colter in 1914. As you walk up a path past a stacked-boulder entranceway, from which hangs an old mission bell from New Mexico, the little stone cabin comes into view. It is meant to look as if some lonely hermit dug a hole in the side of a hill and then stacked rock on top of rock until something haphazard but cozy rose from the rim—a structure from the realm of fairy tales. Inside, the huge, yawning fireplace, tall and deep enough to be a room itself, dominates the warm, rustic front room, where there are a few chairs chopped out of stumps, a Navajo blanket or two splashing color against the gray stone, and elegant lantern lamps hanging from the rafters. Outside,

the views of the canyon and down the Hermit Trail are spectacular, but something about that little rock shelter makes it hard to leave. The large, often quite chubby Grand Canyon ravens seem to be big fans of Colter's rustic and romantic style; this is one of the best places on the South Rim to watch them glide and socialize.

EAST RIM AND DESERT VIEW DRIVE

Desert View Drive is a paved two-lane road through the forest east of Grand Canyon Village that eventually leaves the park and ends on the Navajo Reservation. The viewpoints along this 23-mile (37-km) journey toward the park's eastern boundaries are well worth the drive, ending at the amazing Desert View Watchtower. The free shuttle only goes as far as Yaki Point. Most visitors use their own vehicles, but park concessionaire Xanterra also offers bus tours of the area.

Yaki Point

The farthest east that the free shuttle will take you, **Yaki Point** is a fantastic viewpoint and provides access to the South Kaibab Trailhead, which is right next to the viewpoint. The point is about 2 miles (3.2 km) east toward Desert View on AZ 64 near Pipe Creek Vista. It's also the eastern terminus or trailhead for the Rim Trail. Yaki Point is at the end of a 1.5-mile (2.4-km) side road that's closed to private vehicles. You can walk there on the Rim Trail or take the free shuttle. If you want to make Yaki Point part of the Desert View Drive, you can park your car at a small picnic area just east of the side road, where there are bathrooms and parking, and then cross the road and follow an approximately 0.5-mile (0.8-km) path through the woods to the promontory and the South Kaibab Trailhead. From here you can see Zoroaster Temple, Wotans Throne, and the breathtakingly steep and twisty South Kaibab Trail along Cedar Ridge. The National

1: Hopi Point at sunset **2:** view from below Lookout Studio in Grand Canyon Village **3:** Tusayan Museum **4:** Desert View Watchtower

Park Service built the trail in 1925 to compete with the Bright Angel Trail, on which entrepreneurial prospector-turned-politician Ralph Cameron had a $1 per person stranglehold. A favorite trail of many canyon hikers, the South Kaibab is relatively short but very steep, and it's the quickest corridor route into the inner gorge.

Grandview Point

Back in the old pioneer days before the park, **Grandview Point,** a forested viewpoint along the Desert View Drive, was one of the main tourist areas along the South Rim, home to the Grandview Hotel, opened in 1897. Before that it was the main access point to Ralph Cameron and Pete Berry's Last Chance Mine, far below on Horseshoe Mesa. The two pioneers built what eventually became the Grandview Trail leading to the mesa in 1893. Today the trail remains open, but it is a wild and unkempt route into the gorge that is generally used only by experienced canyon hikers. There's a large interpretive sign here that tells the story of the mine and the hotel. While nothing remains of the old hotel, adventurous hikers will find remnants of the mining operation down on Horseshoe Mesa.

Tusayan Ruin & Museum

The **Tusayan Ruin & Museum** (928/638-7888, 9am-5pm daily, free) has a small but interesting group of exhibits on the canyon's early human settlers. The museum is located next to an 800-year-old Ancestral Puebloan ruin with a self-guided trail and regularly scheduled free ranger walks. Since the free shuttle bus doesn't come this far east, you have to drive to the museum and ruin; it's about 3 miles (4.8 km) west of Desert View and 22 miles (35 km) east of the village. It's worth the drive, though, especially if you're heading to the Desert View section anyway. The museum has displays on the history of human life in the region along with excellent artifacts of the Hopi, Navajo, Havasupai, and Paiute. Don't miss Roy Anderson's fascinating

1986 painting depicting a romantic vision of life at Tusayan some 800 years ago.

While the canyonlands haven't been exactly hospitable to humans over the eons, the oldest artifacts found in Grand Canyon date back about 12,000 years. They include little stick-built animal fetishes found in caves inside the canyon and throughout the Southwest. The ancient Kayenta people constructed and occupied a small village here around AD 1185. The unreconstructed ruin consists of several "rooms" surrounded by low and mostly fallen rock walls, scattered along a 0.1-mile (0.16-km) flat, paved, wheelchair-accessible trail through the pinyon-pine forest. The ruin was first excavated in 1930 by Harold S. Gladwin. Archaeologists believe the village included apartments around a large plaza facing south toward the sacred San Francisco Peaks, which was used as a general living area for about 16-20 people, along with several small storage rooms and a kiva—an underground structure used for religious ceremonies. Tusayan is thought to have been the westernmost outpost of the ancient Kayenta people and is linked to other nearby sites such as Keet Seel and White House ruin on the Navajo Reservation to the east. Follow the short entrance road off the Desert View Drive to the native-stone building and parking lot; you'll find bathrooms close by.

Lipan Point

From **Lipan Point,** a beautiful viewpoint near the Desert View Watchtower, you'll see the rocks from the Grand Canyon Supergroup, tilted formations at the canyon bottom that are some 740-1,200 million years old. From here you'll also see Hance Rapid 3.8 miles (6.1 km) below, the first major rapid below Lees Ferry. The expansive views from here include great looks at the North Rim, the Vermilion Cliffs, and the fertile Unkar Delta far below, where Ancestral Puebloan farmers lived for hundreds of years. Lipan Point is a popular vantage from which to view sunrise and sunset over Grand Canyon.

★ Desert View Watchtower

What is perhaps the most mysterious and thrilling of Mary Jane Colter's canyon creations, the **Desert View Watchtower** (built in 1932) is an artful homage to smaller Ancestral Puebloan-built towers found at Hovenweep National Monument and elsewhere in the Four Corners region, the exact purpose of which is still unknown.

You reach the tower's high, windy deck by climbing the twisting, steep steps winding around the open middle, past walls painted with visions of Hopi lore and religion by Hopi artist Fred Kabotie. From the deck of the watchtower, the South Rim's highest viewpoint, the whole arid expanse opens up, and you feel something like a lucky survivor at the very edge of existence, even among the crowds. Such is the evocative power, the rough-edged romanticism, of Colter's vision.

Recreation

DAY HIKES

Something about a well-built trail twisting deep into an unknown territory can spur even the most habitually sedentary canyon visitor to begin an epic trudge. This phenomenon is responsible for both the best and worst of the South Rim's busy recreation life. It is not uncommon to see hikers a mile or more below the rim picking along in high heels and sauntering blithely in flip-flops, not a drop of water between them. It's best to go to the canyon prepared to hike, with proper footwear and plenty of water and snacks. You'll probably want to hike a little, and since there's no such thing as an easy hike into the Grand Canyon, going in prepared, even if it's just for a few miles, will make your hike a pleasure rather than a chore. Also, remember that there aren't any loop hikes here: If you hike in (down) a mile, you also must hike out (up) a mile.

Planning Your Hike

To have a fun, illuminating, and happily memorable hike into Grand Canyon from the South Rim, it's essential that you **know**

Rim Trail running along the South Rim from the South Kaibab Trailhead to Hermit's Rest

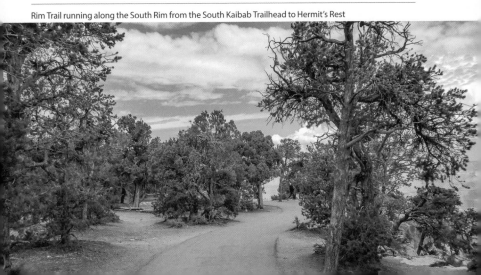

South Rim Hikes

Trail	Effort	Distance	Duration
Rim Trail	Easy	12.8 mi/20.6 km one-way	All day
Bright Angel Lodge to Powell Point	Easy	1.9 mi/3.1 km one-way	1-2 hours
Powell Point to Monument Creek Vista	Easy	3 mi/4.8 km one-way	1.5-2.5 hours
Monument Creek Vista to Hermit's Rest	Easy	2.8 mi/4.5 km one-way	1.5-2.5 hours
Bright Angel Lodge to Mather Point	Easy	2.5 mi/4 km one-way	1.5-2.5 hours
Mather Point to South Kaibab Trailhead	Easy	2.4 mi/3.9 km one-way	1.5-2 hours
Bright Angel Trail	Moderate to strenuous	9.5 mi/15.3 km one-way	2-3 days
Mile-and-a-Half Resthouse	Moderate	3 mi/4.8 km round-trip	2-4 hours
Three-Mile Resthouse	Moderate to strenuous	6 mi/9.7 km round-trip	4-6 hours
Indian Garden	Strenuous	9.6 mi/15.4 km round-trip	6-8 hours
South Kaibab Trail	Strenuous	7 mi/11.3 km one-way	2 days or more
Ooh Aah Point	Moderate	1.8 mi/2.9 km round-trip	1-2 hours

and admit your own limits. Social media is flooded these days with posts, pictures, and videos about neighborhood super-athletes and their one-day rim-to-rim-to-rim sprints, but that doesn't mean the trails have somehow been paved and flattened. Ignore those outliers, no matter how many of them there seem to be. The simple truth is that, even for experienced hikers, day hikes along the Bright Angel Trail and South Kaibab Trail are often challenging and exhausting. Don't underestimate even the shortest of hikes into the canyon. Follow the advice and heed the warnings posted around the park and at every trailhead: **Don't hike without proper supplies.** That means water, snacks, a hat, and seasonally appropriate footwear and clothing. All the gear you'll need is available for sale and rent at the Market Plaza general store.

Seasons

The best hiking days at the South Rim are in spring and fall—from around late March to early May, and late September to early November. During the winter months, the upper stretches of the trails (which are those most likely to be included in day hikes) are often wet, muddy, and icy. In the summer months the desert air below the rim heats up with every step down, and becomes unbearable—and deadly—for most of the day. Summer is nonetheless the busiest season on the South Rim.

Trail	Effort	Distance	Duration
Cedar Ridge	Moderate to strenuous	3 mi/4.8 km round-trip	2-4 hours
Skeleton Point	Strenuous	6 mi/9.7 km round-trip	4-6 hours
Hermit Trail	Very strenuous	9.7 mi/15.6 km one-way	2-3 days
Waldron Trail Junction	Strenuous	2.6 mi/4.2 km round-trip	2-4 hours
Dripping Spring	Strenuous	6.2 mi/10 km round-trip	5-7 hours
Santa Maria Spring	Strenuous	4.8 mi/7.7 km round-trip	4-6 hours
Vishnu Trail	Easy	1.1 mi/1.8 km round-trip	1 hour
Red Butte Trail	Moderate	2.5 mi/4 km round-trip	1-2 hours
Grandview Trail	Strenuous	3.2 mi/5.1 km one-way	1-2 days
South Bass Trail	Very strenuous	7.8 mi/12.6 km one-way	1-3 days
Boucher Trail	Very strenuous	10.5 mi/16.9 km one-way	3 days or more
New Hance Trail	Very strenuous	8 mi/12.9 km one-way	2-3 days
Tanner Trail	Very strenuous	10 mi/16.1 km one-way	3 days or more

TOP EXPERIENCE

★ Rim Trail

Distance: 12.8 miles (20.6 km) one-way
Duration: All day
Elevation gain: About 200 feet (61 m)
Effort: Easy
Trail conditions: Paved except for unpaved stretch between Powell Point and Monument Creek Vista (narrow, packed-dirt path); some steep parts heading west from Bright Angel Lodge to Hermit's Rest
Trailhead: Multiple access points, from South Kaibab Trailhead in the east to Hermit's Rest in the west

If you can manage a nearly 13-mile (20.9 km), relatively easy walk at an altitude of around 7,000 feet (2,134 m), the **Rim Trail** provides the single best way to see all of the South Rim.

The trail, paved for most of its length, runs from the South Kaibab Trailhead area on the east, through the village, and all the way west to Hermit's Rest, hitting every major point of interest and beauty along the way. The path gets a little tough as it rises a bit past the Bright Angel Trailhead just west of the village. Heading farther west, the trail becomes a thin, dirt single-track between Powell Point and Monument Creek Vista, but it never gets too difficult. (You can avoid these sections by walking on the road, which is paved.) It would be considered an easy, scenic walk by just about anybody, kids included. But perhaps the best thing about the Rim Trail is that you don't have to hike the whole 12.8 miles (20.6 km)—far from it. There are at least 16

Rim Trail

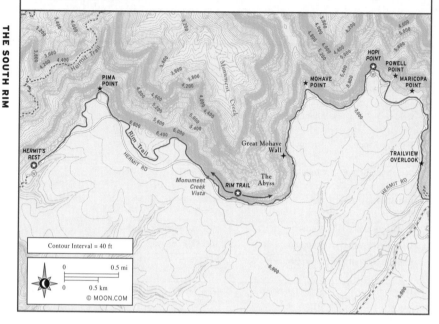

Contour Interval = 40 ft

0   0.5 mi

0   0.5 km

© MOON.COM

shuttle stops along the way, and you can hop on and off the trail at your pleasure. Dogs are allowed on the Rim Trail with a leash, but you can't take them on the shuttle buses.

Few will want to hike the entire way, of course. Such an epic walk would in fact require twice the miles (or at least one long ride on the shuttle bus), as the trail is not a loop but a ribbon stretched out flat along the rim from west to east. It's better to pick out a relatively short stretch and take your time.

BRIGHT ANGEL LODGE TO POWELL POINT

Distance: 1.9 miles (3.1 km) one-way
Duration: 1-2 hours
Effort: Easy
Trail conditions: Paved and wheelchair accessible, with a few steeper sections
Trailhead: Bright Angel Lodge
Shuttle Stop: Bright Angel Lodge, on Village Route (Blue) / Hermit's Rest Route (Red)

Heading west from Bright Angel Lodge and the village center, the Rim Trail climbs to a long plateau and then hugs the rim all the way to Hermit's Rest, about 7 miles (11.3 km) on. The long, wide, and unobstructed views at Hopi Point make it one of the most popular points from which to view sunset and sunrise.

About 0.5 mile (0.8 km) west from Bright Angel Lodge, you'll rise up to the **Trailview Overlook** and watch hikers descending and ascending the Bright Angel Trail. After traversing the plateau's east side, the trail winds around to face the north across the canyon at **Maricopa Point** (about 0.7 mi/1.1 km west from Trailview Overlook). Just a short walk on and you pass **Powell Point** (0.5 mi/0.8 km west from Maricopa Point), a stunning, unhemmed viewpoint and the site of the Powell Memorial, a monument dedicated to the first modern explorer of the Colorado River through Grand Canyon. The rim in these western regions is dominated by a pygmy forest of pinyon, juniper, and oak, and past

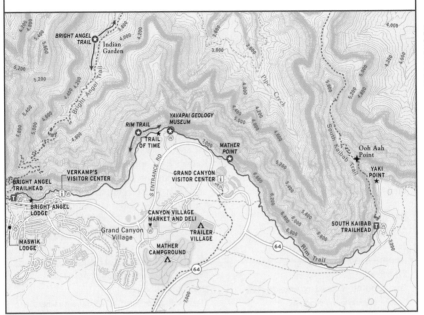

Powell Point begin some of the best views of the Colorado snaking far below.

POWELL POINT TO MONUMENT CREEK VISTA

Distance: 3 miles (4.8 km) one-way
Duration: 1.5-2.5 hours
Effort: Easy
Trail conditions: Narrow packed-dirt path, sometimes rocky
Trailhead: Hopi Point
Shuttle Stop: Hopi Point, on Hermit's Rest Route (Red)

From Powell Point to Monument Creek Vista, the Rim Trail is a narrow (3-ft/0.9-m-wide) dirt path. It gets a bit more difficult than the paved stretches because of the narrowness and the lack of pavement; it's not accessible to wheelchairs in this section.

It's just a 0.3-mile (0.5 km) walk along the Rim Trail from Powell Point to **Hopi Point,** which offers sweeping views of the western canyon. Moving west from Hopi Point, the trail turns slightly southward while still hugging the rim along the sheer drop called the **Hopi Wall,** and then leads out to a promontory called **Mohave Point,** just above the long red mesa called the **Alligator.** The trail then jogs south again, passing **The Abyss,** a 3,000-foot (914-m) drop straight down.

There are bathrooms at Hopi Point—the last ones before Hermit's Rest at the end of the trail.

MONUMENT CREEK VISTA TO HERMIT'S REST

Distance: 2.8 miles (4.5 km) one-way
Duration: 1.5-2.5 hours
Effort: Easy
Trail conditions: Wide paved road, open to bikes
Trailhead: Monument Creek Vista
Shuttle Stop: Monument Creek Vista, on Hermit's Rest Route (Red)

The Rim Trail widens out beginning at Monument Creek Vista and allows bikes for the next 2.8 miles (4.5 km); this section of the trail is called the Hermit Road Greenway. Below, Monument Creek descends to its marriage with the Colorado River. The Rim Trail reaches a promontory called **Pima Point** (1.8 mi/2.9 km from Monument Creek Vista) and then turns south following the rim, showing Hermit Creek and the Hermit Trail in the side canyon. At Hermit's Rest (1 mi/1.6 km from Pima Point), the enchanting gift shop and snack bar designed in the 1930s by Mary Jane Colter, you can catch the free shuttle bus back to the village (it will take at least 30 minutes to an hour to reach the village, as the shuttle buses stop at all the viewpoints on the way there and back). Or you can rest a bit here and then walk back to the village on the Rim Trail.

BRIGHT ANGEL LODGE TO MATHER POINT

Distance: 2.5 miles (4 km) one-way
Duration: 1.5-2.5 hours
Effort: Easy
Trail conditions: Paved and wheelchair accessible
Trailhead: Bright Angel Lodge
Shuttle Stop: Bright Angel Lodge, on Village Route (Blue)

Heading east on the Rim Trail from Bright Angel Lodge takes in all the essential sights within **Grand Canyon Village,** follows the **Trail of Time,** and then makes an important stop at **Yavapai Geology Museum and Observation Station** (1.8 mi/2.9 km from the lodge), the must-see geology museum and viewpoint that puts the amazing views you're seeing into some kind of approachable perspective. Continuing east along the forested stretch of the Rim Trail leads to Mather Point (0.7 mi/1.1 km east of Yavapai), the busiest viewpoint on the South Rim, from which it's a short and easy side stroll to the Grand Canyon Visitor Center and the shuttle bus station.

MATHER POINT TO SOUTH KAIBAB TRAILHEAD

Distance: 2.4 miles (3.9 km) one-way
Duration: 1.5-2 hours
Effort: Easy
Trail conditions: Paved and wheelchair accessible
Trailhead: Mather Point, near Grand Canyon Visitor Center
Shuttle Stop: Mather Point, on Rim Route (Orange)

The 2.4-mile (3.9-km) stretch of Rim Trail from Mather Point to the South Kaibab Trailhead passes along a wild section of rim with few developed viewpoints or stops. It's just you, the canyon, and the condors, which can often be seen gliding and diving around Pipe Creek Vista, about 1.5 miles (2.4 km) from Mather Point. The Rim Trail ends (and begins) at the parking lot for Yaki Point and the South Kaibab Trailhead. Here the South Kaibab Trail begins its precipitous drop to the river, and you can take a short walk out to Yaki Point for anther inspiring view. There are bathrooms here as well as a shuttle bus stop.

TOP EXPERIENCE

★ Bright Angel Trail

Distance: 3-9.6 miles (4.8-15.4 km) round-trip
Duration: 2-8 hours
Elevation gain: 3,040 feet (927 m) from trailhead to Indian Garden
Effort: Moderate to strenuous
Trail conditions: Narrow, rocky, steep, sandy
Trailhead: Just west of Bright Angel Lodge
Shuttle Stop: Bright Angel Lodge, on Village Route (Blue)

Hiking down the **Bright Angel Trail,** you quickly leave behind the piney rim and enter a sharp and arid landscape, twisting down and around switchbacks on a path that is sometimes all rock underfoot. Step aside for the many mule trains that use this route, and watch for the droppings, which are everywhere. It doesn't take long for the rim to look very far away, and you soon feel like you are deep within a chasm and those rim-top people are mere ants scurrying about.

The Bright Angel Trail is the most popular trail in the canyon owing in part to its starting just to the west of the Bright Angel Lodge in the village center. It's considered by park staff to be the safest trail because it has two resthouses with water. The Bright Angel was once the only easily accessible corridor trail

Bright Angel Trail

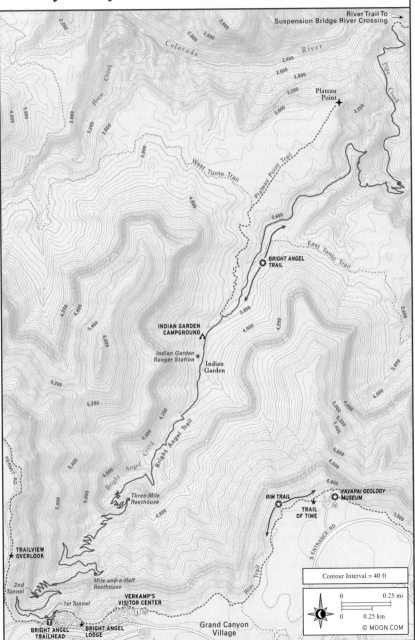

from the South Rim, and for years Grand Canyon pioneer Ralph Cameron charged $1 per person to use it. Many South Rim visitors choose to walk down the (now free) Bright Angel Trail a bit just to get a feeling of what it's like to be below the rim. If you want to do something a little more structured, the 3-mile (4.8-km) round-trip hike to the **Mile-and-a-Half Resthouse** is a good introduction to the steep, twisting trail. The going gets tougher on the way to **Three-Mile Resthouse,** a 6-mile (9.7 km) round-trip hike. Both rest-houses have water available from mid-May to mid-October, but don't rely on it; breaks in the trans-canyon waterline sometimes shuts them down. One of the best day hikes from the South Rim is the 9.6-mile (15.4-km) round-trip to beautiful **Indian Garden,** a cool and green oasis in the arid inner canyon. This is a rather punishing day hike, not recommended in the summer.

MILE-AND-A-HALF RESTHOUSE
Distance: 3 miles (4.8 km) round-trip
Duration: 2-4 hours
Elevation gain: 1,120 feet (341 m)
Effort: Moderate
Trail conditions: Narrow, rocky, steep, sandy
From its trailhead just west of Bright Angel Lodge, the Bright Angel Trail descends into Grand Canyon along the Bright Angel Fault, a lucky crack in the land along which humans have been entering the canyon for thousands of years. The trail starts out at about 6,850 feet (2,088 m) and drops somewhat gradually at first. At about 0.18 mile (0.29 km), you enter the first of two short tunnels through the rock layers. After passing through the tunnel, turn around and look up and to the left—though it's difficult to see, there's a panel of ancient **pictographs** here called **Mallery's Grotto.** If you're just in it to see the canyon from below the rim a bit, this is a good place to turn around.

At 0.45 mile (0.72 km), you come to the first of many, many switchbacks. This is a smart place to turn around if you have young kids in tow, as it gets noticeably steeper from here on

out. At 0.75 mile (1.2 km) you move through the second tunnel blasted out of the rock. After this the switchbacks turn a bit brutal.

Less than a mile (1.6 km) farther is Mile-and-a-Half Resthouse, which was built by the Civilian Conservation Corps in the mid-1930s along with most of the other infrastructure along the trail. The resthouse sits near north-facing cliffs that have allowed for the growth here of a small and improbable forest of Douglas fir.

Mile-and-a-Half Resthouse has potable water available from mid-May to mid-October, an emergency phone, and toilet facilities.

THREE-MILE RESTHOUSE
Distance: 6 miles (9.7 km) round-trip
Duration: 4-6 hours
Elevation gain: 2,120 feet (646 m)
Effort: Moderate to strenuous
Trail conditions: Narrow, rocky, steep, sandy
Continuing down from Mile-and-a-Half Resthouse you'll reach **Two-Mile Corner,** marked with a sign—this is a kind of line-in-the-red-sand after which the switchbacks become steeper and more difficult. From here to Three-Mile Resthouse the switchbacks require concentration, which is hard to muster with the incredibly expansive views all around. Once you reach Three-Mile Resthouse, take the short path behind it to a viewpoint looking down on Indian Garden and Plateau Point.

Three-Mile Resthouse has potable water available from mid-May to mid-October, an emergency phone, and toilet facilities.

INDIAN GARDEN
Distance: 9.6 miles (15.4 km) round-trip
Duration: 6-8 hours
Elevation gain: 3,040 feet (927 m)
Effort: Strenuous
Trail conditions: Narrow, rocky, steep, sandy
The notorious series of switchbacks through Redwall limestone known as **Jacob's Ladder** begins below Three-Mile Resthouse, as does the punishing and beautiful desert, asserting itself in a rocky lowland of dry washes,

mesquite, cliffrose, and bunched cacti. Indian Garden welcomes you like a spring-fed oasis should—all shade trees and trickling water. There's often a convivial atmosphere here with resting hikers and trailside picnics.

Indian Garden has a campground and ranger station. A permit and a reservation is required to stay the night at Indian Garden. There are a few picnic tables beneath the cottonwoods, and there's also potable water, pit toilets, and an emergency phone.

Grand Canyon rangers are adamant in advising hikers to go no farther than Indian Garden in one day in the summer. Nonetheless, the Bright Angel Trail continues along **Pipe and Garden Creeks** for another 3.1 miles (5 km) to the Colorado River. Then it's another 1.6 miles (2.6 km) via the **River Trail** and across the suspension bridge to **Bright Angel Campground** and **Phantom Ranch.**

From Indian Garden, there's also an easy (but sandy) 1.5-mile (2.4-km) one-way trail across the bushy Tonto Platform to **Plateau Point,** a cliff edge with amazing views of the Colorado River surging through the inner gorge. *Again, rangers advise against attempting this strenuous 12-mile (19.3-km) hike (round-trip from the rim) in one day in the summer.*

South Kaibab Trail

Distance: 1.8-6 miles (2.9-9.7 km) round-trip
Duration: 1-6 hours
Elevation gain: 2,040 feet (622 m) from trailhead to Skeleton Point
Effort: Moderate to strenuous
Trail conditions: Narrow, rocky, very steep, sandy in places; mule traffic, mule leavings
Trailhead: Near Yaki Point on the East Rim
Shuttle Stop: Yaki Point, on Rim Route (Orange)

Steep but relatively short, the 7-mile (11.3-km) **South Kaibab Trail** provides the quickest, most direct route from the South Rim to and from the river. It's popular with day hikers and those looking for the quickest way into the gorge, and many consider it superior to the often-crowded Bright Angel Trail. The trailhead is located a few miles east of the village

near Yaki Point, which is closed to private vehicles; take the shuttle bus on the Kaibab/Rim Route (Orange).

The 1.8-mile (2.9-km) round-trip hike to **Ooh Aah Point** has great views of the canyon from steep switchbacks. A common turnaround point for day hikers, **Cedar Ridge** is a 3-mile (4.8-km) round-trip hike. If you are interested in a longer haul, the 6-mile (9.7-km) round-trip hike to **Skeleton Point,** from which you can see the Colorado River, is probably as far along this trail as you'll want to go in one day, though in summer you might want to reconsider descending that far.

There's no water anywhere along the trail, and there's no shade to speak of. Bighorn sheep have been known to haunt this trail, and you might feel akin to those dexterous beasts while hiking the rocky ridgeline, which seems unbearably steep in a few places, especially on the way back up. Deer and California condors are also regular residents of the South Kaibab Trail. This is a trail the mules use, so make sure to step aside and wait while the mule trains pass.

OOH AAH POINT

Distance: 1.8 miles (2.9 km) round-trip
Duration: 1-2 hours
Elevation gain: 700 feet (213 m)
Effort: Moderate
Trail conditions: Narrow, rocky, very steep, sandy in places; mule traffic, mule leavings

The steep and scenic hike down the cliffside switchbacks called the Chimney begins the South Kaibab Trail, so for many the jaunt down to Ooh Aah Point is quite enough. There's no sign but it's obvious when you get there—you'll suddenly feel an urge to ooh and ahh right before the trail turns sharply left. The National Park Service designed and built the South Kaibab Trail in the mid-1920s, blasting most of it out of cliffsides and high ridges, making it probably the most scenic trail in the park.

CEDAR RIDGE

Distance: 3 miles (4.8 km) round-trip

Duration: 2-4 hours

Elevation gain: 1,120 feet (341 m)

Effort: Moderate to strenuous

Trail conditions: Narrow, rocky, very steep, sandy in places; mule traffic, mule leavings

The switchbacks continue to Cedar Ridge, about 1.5 miles (2.4 km) in. This is where most day hikers turn around for the 1,120-foot (341-m) climb back up to the rim. From here there are great views of O'Neill Butte, named for South Rim pioneer Buckey O'Neill, who by selling his mining claims helped bring the Santa Fe Railroad to the South Rim in 1901. O'Neill died while fighting with Teddy Roosevelt's Roughriders in Cuba. The mule trains stop here, so during the busy season there may be a wait to use the pit toilets, which are the only facilities along the trail.

SKELETON POINT

Distance: 6 miles (9.7 km) round-trip

Duration: 4-6 hours

Elevation gain: 2,040 feet (622 m)

Effort: Strenuous

Trail conditions: Narrow, rocky, very steep, sandy in places; mule traffic, mule leavings

While not recommended for casual hikers, another 1.5 miles (2.4 km) down the South Kaibab Trail into the bushy desert depths of the canyon takes you along the east side of Cedar Ridge and across a section called Mormon Flat, which was constructed by a crew of Latter-day Saints in 1924-1925. Some 2,040 feet (622 m) below the rim, Skeleton Point gets its name from the sun-whitened bones of fallen mules that once collected far below. There's a hitching rail here, and also wonderful views of the Colorado River and Phantom Ranch.

Hermit Trail

Distance: 2.6-6.2 miles (4.2-10 km) round-trip

Duration: 2-7 hours

Elevation gain: 1,600 feet (488 m) from trailhead to Dripping Spring

Effort: Moderate to strenuous

Trail conditions: Narrow, rocky, steep, sandy in places

Trailhead: Just west of Hermit's Rest

Shuttle Stop: Hermit's Rest, on Hermit's Rest Route (Red)

Built by the Santa Fe Railroad as a challenge to the fee-charging keeper of the Bright Angel Trail, the **Hermit Trail** just past Hermit's Rest leads to some less visited areas of the canyon. This trail isn't maintained with the same energy as the well-traveled corridor trails, and it has no potable water.

You could take the Hermit Trail 9 miles (14.5 km) deep into the canyon to the river, where Fred Harvey built the first below-rim camp for tourists, complete with a tramway from the rim, the ruins of which are still visible. But such a trudge should be left only to fully geared experts. Even a day hike on the Hermit Trail should be taken very seriously. A good idea for day hikers and backpackers is to try at least one of the maintained and patrolled corridor trails (Bright Angel or South Kaibab from the South Rim) before taking on the Hermit Trail.

The trailhead for the Hermit Trail is just west of Hermit's Rest, which is 7 miles (11.3 km) west of Grand Canyon Village via the Hermit Road. For most of the year Hermit Road is closed to private vehicles, so a day hike in this section of the park typically requires a 30-minute to one-hour one-way shuttle bus trip to Hermit's Rest and then a short walk to the trailhead. A permit for a backpacking trip down the Hermit Trail allows you to drive to the trailhead and leave your vehicle, no matter what the season.

Hikes to **Waldron Trail Junction, Dripping Spring,** and **Santa Maria Spring** make tough but rewarding day hikes along the Hermit Trail.

WALDRON TRAIL JUNCTION

Distance: 2.6 miles (4.2 km) round-trip

Duration: 2-4 hours

Elevation gain: 1,240 feet (378 m)

Effort: Strenuous

Trail conditions: Rock and dirt, sand in some places, narrow, steep, technical

A hike down to the **Waldron Trail Junction**

in Hermit Basin makes for a relatively short but quite difficult day hike. Cobblestone-lined switchbacks start the trail, and on these pinyon-juniper upper reaches it's easy to see why this trail was considered state-of-the-art when it was constructed in 1912. In this section you feel like you're in a relatively flat, pygmy forest valley on the very edge of the world, and it's a bit surprising to see a few cabins and corrals. A sign at the trail junction marks the turnaround spot.

DRIPPING SPRING

Distance: 6.2 miles (10 km) round-trip
Duration: 5-7 hours
Elevation gain: 1,600 feet (488 m)
Effort: Strenuous
Trail conditions: Rock and dirt, sand in some places, narrow, steep, technical

The 6.2-mile (10-km) round-trip hike to the secluded and green **Dripping Spring** is one of the best day hikes in the canyon for midlevel to expert hikers. Start out on the Hermit Trail's steep, rocky, almost stair-like switchbacks. You come to the Waldron Trail Junction after 1.3 miles (2.1 km). Look for the **Dripping Spring Trailhead** after about 0.2 mile (0.3 km) from the Waldron Trail Junction, once you reach a more level section dominated by pinyon pine and juniper. Veer left (west) on the trail, which begins to rise a bit and leads along a ridgeline across **Hermit Basin;** the views are so awe-inspiring that it's difficult to keep your eyes on the skinny trail. After about 1 mile (1.6 km), you'll come to the junction with the Boucher Trail. Continue heading west, hiking about 0.5 mile (0.8 km) up a side canyon to the cool and shady rock overhang known as Dripping Spring. And it really does drip: A shock of fernlike greenery creeps off the rock overhang, trickling cold spring water at a steady pace into a small collecting pool (don't drink without treating it). Get your head wet, have a picnic, and kick back in this out-of-the-way, hard-won oasis. But don't stay too long. The hike back up is nothing to take lightly: The switchbacks are punishing, and the end, as it always does when

one is hiking up a trail in the Grand Canyon, seems to get farther away as your legs begin to gain fatigue-weight. There's no water on the trail, so make sure to bring enough along and conserve it.

SANTA MARIA SPRING

Distance: 4.8 miles (7.7 km) round-trip
Duration: 4-6 hours
Elevation gain: 1,680 feet (512 m)
Effort: Strenuous
Trail conditions: Narrow, rocky, steep, sandy

To reach **Santa Maria Spring,** veer right at the junction with the **Dripping Spring Trailhead** to stay on the Hermit Trail and hike for another 0.9 mile (1.4 km). A welcome rest-stop for backpackers coming up out of the depths, the small stone shelter here was built in 1913. The water from the spring must be treated before drinking. If you're going to do a day hike on the Hermit Trail, consider going to Dripping Spring, not Santa Maria Spring. It's a longer hike to the former, but well worth it.

Kaibab National Forest

The 1.6-million-acre Kaibab National Forest surrounds Grand Canyon National Park, stretching across the Colorado Plateau southeast to Arizona's Mogollon Rim and from the North Rim almost to the Utah border. The forest of pinyon pine, juniper, ponderosa pine, spruce, fir, and aspen is divided into three separate ranger districts: the Williams Ranger District east of the canyon, the Tusayan Ranger District near the South Rim, and the North Kaibab Ranger District on the Kaibab Plateau and North Rim.

The 800-mile (1,290-km) **Arizona Trail** (www.aztrail.org) traverses the state from north to south and is divided into passages. **Passage 36,** also called the **Coconino Rim** section, runs through the Kaibab National Forest's Tusayan Ranger District, north and northwest of Grandview Lookout Tower and into Grand Canyon National Park. There are trailheads at various locations, including at Forest Road 605, about 0.4 mile (0.6 km) south of the Tusayan Ranger District (176 Lincoln Log Loop, 928/638-2443, www.fs.usda.gov) sign on the west side of AZ 64, and another near the historic Grandview Lookout Tower (take Forest Road 302 east from AZ 64 for 15 miles (24 km) to Forest Road 310, turn left, and look for the 80-foot-tall (24-m), 7-foot-square (2.1-m) metal tower built in the 1930s). The Arizona Trail is open to hikers, bikers, and horseback riders; however, part of the Arizona Trail's route includes the Bright Angel Trail through the canyon, on which only hikers are allowed.

VISHNU TRAIL

Distance: 1.1 miles (1.8 km) round-trip
Duration: 1 hour
Elevation gain: Negligible
Effort: Easy
Trail conditions: Dirt path
Trailhead: Grandview Lookout Tower trailhead

An easy loop, the **Vishnu Trail** makes for a pleasant forest stroll to a point on the Coconino Rim and excellent views of Grand Canyon and cone-shaped Vishnu Temple (7,829 ft/2,386 m high). The trail winds through the pine and scrub-oak forest from the fire tower to Vishnu Lookout, and then connects with the Arizona Trail to return to the tower.

RED BUTTE TRAIL

Distance: 2.5 miles (4 km) round-trip
Duration: 1-2 hours
Elevation gain: 866 feet (264 m)
Effort: Moderate
Trail conditions: Narrow, rocky, steep
Trailhead: Just east of AZ 64
Directions: Take AZ 64 to Forest Road 320, turn east and go 1.5 miles (2.4 km), then turn left on Forest Road 340, drive for 0.75 mile (1.2 km), and turn right onto a dirt road. Drive about 0.25 mile (0.4 km) to reach the trailhead, at the end of the road.

After you reach a certain elevation on the empty bunchgrass plain between Williams and Tusayan, a stout volcanic peak comes into view and does not go away until you pass it

by. This is Red Butte, on top of which there's a fire lookout built in the 1980s and staffed full-time during the region's often busy wildfire season. The Red Butte Trail, just off AZ 64, is short but exposed to the sun and fairly steep to the top, from which you can see for miles and miles.

BACKPACKING

On any given night there are only a few hundred visitors sleeping below the rim—at Phantom Ranch, a Mary Jane Colter-designed lodge near the mouth of Bright Angel Canyon; at three developed campgrounds along the corridor trails; or off somewhere in the canyon's wild primitive labyrinth. Until a few decades ago backpacking into the inner canyon was something of a free-for-all, but these days access to the interior is strictly controlled through a permit system.

Backcountry Permits

To camp overnight below the rim, you have to purchase a **permit** ($10, plus $8 pp per night), and they're not always easy to get—each year the park receives about 30,000 requests for backcountry permits and issues only about 13,000. The earlier you apply for a permit the better; the earliest you can apply is 10 days before the first of the month four months before your proposed trip date. The easiest way to get a permit is to go to the **park's website** (www.nps.gov/grca), print out a backcountry permit request form, fill it out, and then fax it first thing in the morning on the date in question—for example, if you want to hike in October, you would **fax** (928/638-2125) your request May 20-June 1. Have patience; on the first day of the month the fax number is usually busy throughout the day—keep trying. On the permit request form you'll indicate at which campgrounds you will stay. The permit is your reservation. For more information on obtaining a backcountry permit, call the **South Rim Backcountry Information Center** (928/638-7875, 8am-noon and 1pm-5pm daily).

Corridor Trails

Rangers divide Grand Canyon's rim-to-river and inner-canyon backpacking trails into **four zones—Corridor, Threshold, Primitive,** and **Wild**—based on several factors. The **corridor trails**—Bright Angel, South Kaibab, and North Kaibab (which starts on the North Rim)—are well maintained and signed, easy to follow, and patrolled, and backpackers have seasonal access to potable water, toilets, ranger stations, and emergency phones.

A **classic South Rim corridor trail backpacking trip** (4 days, 3 nights, 19.5 mi/31 km) starts on the **South Kaibab Trail,** on which you descend quickly to the inner gorge and stop for two nights at Bright Angel Campground, a shady creekside spot between the Colorado River and Phantom Ranch. On the third day, break camp early and hike up the **Bright Angel Trail** to Indian Garden. Camp here and hike 3 miles (4.8 km) round-trip to Plateau Point for an inspiring view of the gorge and the river. Set out early the next morning for the final leg up the Bright Angel Trail to the South Rim.

★ BRIGHT ANGEL TRAIL

Distance: 9.5 miles (15.3 km) one-way to Bright Angel Campground
Duration: 2-3 days
Elevation gain: 4,420 feet (1,347 m)
Effort: Moderate to strenuous
Trail conditions: Narrow, rocky, steep, sandy in places
Trailhead: Just west of Bright Angel Lodge
Shuttle Stop: Bright Angel Lodge, on Village Route (Blue)

The most popular and safest corridor trail, **Bright Angel Trail** provides one of the most scenic, memorable, and satisfying hikes in the world. All first-time Grand Canyon backpackers should take it into or out of the inner gorge. The trail, an ancient route for Native Americans, follows the Bright Angel Fault to the Colorado River, where the River Trail finishes the route to Bright Angel Campground, Phantom Ranch, and the North Kaibab Trail

to the North Rim. Rangers patrol the Bright Angel Trail regularly during the high season; for all of its accessibility and popular appeal, the trail is still difficult, steep, and deadly hot during the summer. Hikers who have overestimated their abilities are the ones most likely to get into trouble on this and the other corridor trails. In spring, summer, and early fall, drinking water is available at resthouses and campgrounds along the trail, and pit toilets are open year-round.

The Bright Angel is steepest in its upper reaches over the first (or last) 4 miles (6.4 km) of mind-bending switchbacks. The trail smooths out on the Tonto Platform's desert stretches and passes through the green and shady **Indian Garden,** once a seasonal home of the Havasupai Indians and later controlled via fraudulent mining claims by pioneer senator Ralph Cameron, who did the canyon a favor by planting the cottonwood trees here. A popular detour from Indian Garden is the 1.5-mile (2.4-km) one-way hike from the campground out to Plateau Point, from which you can see the Colorado River running through the inner gorge. Below Indian Garden there's a junction with the cross-canyon Tonto Trail, while Bright Angel Trail follows the trickling greenbelt of **Garden Creek** past the **Tapeats Narrows,** a series of natural pools and channels eroded into sandstone. The trail then plunges again and becomes a series of evil switchbacks known as the **Devil's Corkscrew,** whose dark Vishnu schist absorbs the sun and creates a stretch of intense heat during the infernal months. From the **River Resthouse** near the bottomlands there's a side trail to the river and **Pipe Creek Beach,** and then it's a sandy 1.5-mile (2.4-km) trudge through the dunes to the **Silver Bridge** across the mighty Colorado to reach the cool, green inner-canyon havens in Bright Angel Canyon.

SOUTH KAIBAB TRAIL

Distance: 7 miles (11.3 km) one-way to Bright Angel Campground
Duration: 2 days or more

Elevation gain: 4,780 feet (1,457 m)

Effort: Strenuous

Trail conditions: Narrow, rocky, steep, sandy in places

Trailhead: Near Yaki Point on the East Rim

Shuttle Stop: Yaki Point, on Rim Route (Orange)

The quickest route to the river and inner gorge, the **South Kaibab Trail** makes an outlandishly scenic descent into Grand Canyon, so beautiful that it becomes dangerous if you watch the scenery closer than you watch your step. This incredibly steep trail was blasted out of high ridges and sheer canyon walls, so it's narrow, technical, and often offers panoramic views. There is no water available, and there are often mule trains—and their festering leavings—along the trail, and they always have the right-of-way. In short, it's wonderful, difficult, and thankfully rather short. The trail starts at Yaki Point on the South Rim and runs precipitously down to the tip of the Tonto Platform, passing favorite dayhiking stops such as Ooh Aah Point, Cedar Ridge, and Skeleton Point. The final steep descent starts at a promontory called the Tip Off and the junction with the Tonto Trail, where you can see the Colorado River, and ends at a shallow tunnel blasted into the ancient rock. Coming out of the tunnel there's a bridge over the wide river, and on the far side Bright Angel Campground and Phantom Ranch await.

Threshold Trails

For experienced Grand Canyon backpackers only, trails in the **Threshold Zone** have no potable water and are not maintained with the same energy as the corridor trails. Trailheads are typically on dirt roads, and they are infrequently patrolled by rangers. Backpackers should hike at least one of the corridor trails before moving on to the threshold trails.

HERMIT TRAIL

Distance: 9.7 miles (15.6 km) one-way to Colorado River

Duration: 2-3 days

Elevation gain: 4,240 feet (1,292 m)

Effort: Very strenuous

Trail conditions: Narrow, rocky, steep, sandy in places

Trailhead: Just west of Hermit's Rest

Shuttle Stop: Hermit's Rest, on Hermit's Rest Route (Red)

From about 1911 to 1930, the Santa Fe Railroad and the Fred Harvey Company developed and operated the **Hermit Trail** and **Hermit Camp,** an early-20th-century glamp-ground complete with a tramway from the rim and chef on staff. Over the years the once state-of-the-art Hermit Trail fell into disrepair, but you can still see some of the old fitted slabs and cobblestone that used to line this steep and winding trail. Experienced canyon backpackers use this trail to access Hermit Camp and other areas of the inner canyon. The upper sections of the Hermit Trail are the steepest—though the lower sections are plenty steep—dropping about 2,000 feet (610 m) in just 2.5 miles (4 km) to Hermit Basin and the Waldron Trail Junction. In the basin there's a relatively level section through a pinyon-juniper forest and then the descent continues past the Santa Maria Spring to a series of nasty switchbacks called the Cathedral Stairs. When the trail intersects with the cross-canyon Tonto Trail, turn west toward Hermit Camp a mile (1.6 km) on. Hermit Camp is in a charming little desert riparian area about 1.5 miles (2.4 km) up-creek from the Colorado River and the raging and roaring Hermit Rapid. There's a series of primitive campsites above the creek with a pit toilet and a small amount of shade. Make sure to bring along a water filter. There is no potable water at Hermit Camp, but if treated the creek water is cold and delicious.

GRANDVIEW TRAIL

Distance: 3.2 miles (5.1 km) one-way to Horseshoe Mesa

Duration: 1-2 days

Elevation gain: 2,500 feet (762 m)

Effort: Strenuous

Trail conditions: Narrow, rocky, steep, sandy in places

Trailhead: Grandview Point, 12 miles (19.3 km) east of Grand Canyon Village

A steep, rocky, and largely unmaintained route built first to serve a copper mine at Horseshoe Mesa and then to entice tourists below the forested rim, the **Grandview Trail** should be left to hikers who are midlevel and above. The 6.4-mile (10.3-km) round-trip trek to Horseshoe Mesa and the mine's ruins makes a difficult but fun overnight backpacking trip. Hiking back up, you won't soon forget the steep slab-rock and cobblestone switchbacks, and hiking down will likely take longer than planned as the steepest parts of the route are quite technical and require heads-up attention. There are established primitive campsites at Horseshoe Mesa, including two group sites and pit toilets, but no potable water.

Primitive Trails

These trails are for highly experienced Grand Canyon backpackers only, as they are not maintained and often require routefinding over long stretches. There is no water to speak of available in these areas save for the Colorado River, which is silty and must be purified.

SOUTH BASS TRAIL

Distance: 7.8 miles (12.6 km) one-way to Colorado River

Duration: 1-3 days

Elevation gain: 4,400 feet (1,341 m)

Effort: Very strenuous

Trail conditions: Narrow, rocky, steep, sandy in places

Trailhead: 31 miles (50 km) west of Grand Canyon Village

Directions: Drive 31 miles (50 km) west of Grand Canyon Village via Rowe Well Road (off Hermit's Rest Road) and Forest Road 328, a rough, unpaved road that may be impassable during wet weather; a high-clearance vehicle is recommended and 4WD might be a necessity if the road is muddy. The drive crosses the Havasupai Reservation, and you may be asked to pay an entrance fee (typically $25). Plan to spend at least two hours getting to the trailhead. Check with rangers about current conditions before heading out.

The **South Bass Trail** is at the head of some 50 miles (81 km) of inner-canyon routes built by South Rim pioneer William Bass over more than 40 years of living on the rim, starting in the 1880s. It's strictly for expert Grand Canyon backpackers. Not even the trailhead is easy to reach—it's 31 miles (50 km) from the village via unpaved forest roads. The trail drops below the Esplanade sandstone and twists, rises, and falls down Bass Canyon through the Redwall. A rockfall blocks the mouth of the canyon but a cairn marks a way around to the beach and the river, where there's an old abandoned river boat chained to the rocks. The South Bass Trail is within the Bass Canyon Use Area and at-large camping is allowed. You'll find pre-used sites on the Esplanade, the Tonto Platform, and at the river.

BOUCHER TRAIL

Distance: 10.5 miles (16.9 km) one-way to Colorado River and Boucher Rapid

Duration: 3 days or more

Elevation gain: 2,950 feet (899 m)

Effort: Very strenuous

Trail conditions: Narrow, rocky, steep, sandy in places, technical

Trailhead: Take Hermit Trail to Dripping Spring Trail (3.1 mi/5 km) and follow west for about 1 mile (1.6 km) to signed Boucher Trail.

Pioneer Louis D. Boucher (Boo-SHAY), the "Hermit" of Hermit's Rest, Hermit Creek, and Hermit Road, lived in Hermit Basin for 20 years in the late 19th and early 20th centuries, making seasonal homes at Dripping Spring and Boucher Creek. The trail that bears his name begins in Hermit Basin, reached via the Hermit Trail, and falls to the Colorado River, where there are at-large camping sites. The Boucher Trailhead is just below the Hermit Trail's intersection with the Dripping Spring Trail. This is one of the most difficult and hard-to-follow trails from the South Rim and should be left to expert Grand Canyon backpackers.

NEW HANCE TRAIL

Distance: 8 miles (12.9 km) one-way to Colorado River
Duration: 2-3 days
Elevation gain: 4,400 feet (1,341 m)
Effort: Very strenuous
Trail conditions: Narrow, rocky, step, sandy
Trailhead: Off Desert View Drive near Moran Point
Directions: Park at Moran Point along the Desert View Drive and walk 1 mile (1.6 km) east along the road until you reach the No Parking signs; follow the path through the forest to the signed trailhead.

Grand Canyon pioneer John Hance, who around 1883 became the first non-Native American to live on the South Rim, constructed this old miner's route through Red Canyon, an aptly named gorge cut through the variegated rocks that ends in riverside dunelands and camping spots on the beach. This trail is for highly experienced canyon backpackers only.

The trailhead is 16 miles (26 km) east of the junction of Desert View Drive and the South Entrance Road, but there's no sign to announce it except for ones that say No Parking. Ask a friend to drop you off, or park at Moran Point and walk about 1 mile (1.6 km) east to the signs, then follow the path through the pinyon-juniper forest to the trailhead sign that stands like a warning before the descending trail.

TANNER TRAIL

Distance: 10 miles (16.1 km) one-way to Colorado River
Duration: 3 days or more
Elevation gain: 4,600 feet (1,402 m)
Effort: Very strenuous
Trail conditions: Narrow, rocky, steep, sandy in places
Trailhead: Lipan Point

An amazing but difficult trail through the Desert View Supergroup, the **Tanner Trail** is the main route into the eastern canyon. The ancient trail has been used by Native Americans for untold generations and was improved in 1890 by its namesake, prospector John Tanner. From the trailhead at Lipan Point along Desert View Drive, the trail starts with an easy rimtop walk but soon drops into a ravine and descends to the Colorado without mercy. There are at-large primitive campsites at Seventyfivemile Creek and the east side of Tanner Canyon, where there's also a composting toilet.

BIKING

There are about 13 miles (20.9 km) of roads and greenways through the park that allow bikes, including a route from the Grand Canyon Visitor Center to Grand Canyon Village, and routes from the village to Mather Campground and Market Plaza—basically anywhere you need to go inside the park.

While the main park roads are open to bikes, they don't have wide shoulders or bike lanes. The exception is **Hermit Road,** which is closed to cars March-November. Seven miles (11.3 km) one-way between the village and the western end of the park at Hermit's Rest, the Hermit Road is the best and most popular bikeway on the South Rim. The only traffic you'll have to deal with on this rolling ride of tough ups and fun downs is the occasional shuttle bus. Just pull over and let them pass.

Only experienced road-bikers should attempt the 23-mile (37-km) ride along **Desert View Drive** to the park's eastern boundaries. It's a beautiful and only moderately difficult ride, but there isn't much of a shoulder and the traffic here is typically heavy during the high seasons.

Bikes are not allowed on the Rim Trail except for a 2.8-mile (4.5-km) section called the **Hermit Road Greenway Trail.** The paved trail begins at Monument Creek Vista along the Hermit Road and ends close to Hermit's Rest. This is about as close as you can get to the rim on a bike, and it's a fun and beautiful stretch of trail highly recommended to bicyclists. To get to the very edge of the rim, you have to park your bike and walk a bit, but

---

1: Grandview Trail **2:** New Hance Trail

Biking into Grand Canyon National Park... the Easy Way

Tusayan Greenway

Drive past the Grand Canyon Visitor Center in Tusayan and take a left from the traffic circle up the road to the **Tusayan Greenway** trailhead. Park your rig, unload the bikes, and start riding. You are now on your way to the very rim of Grand Canyon, riding a smooth and worthy human-powered machine over the undulating forest terrain where others have struggled astride mule, horse, tour bus, or motorhome. You are the future of the national parks while they are long past.

Yes, it's a 6.5-mile (10.5-km) one-way ride, trending uphill but not to an outlandish degree. Look out for wildlife as you race through the forest on the paved trail with the pine-scented breeze tickling your smiling face. However, you can also leave your car at the visitors center in Tusayan and, with your bike in tow, catch the **free shuttle bus** a few steps away (Tusayan Route or Purple Route). Or if you decide to ride into the park, you can always leave on a shuttle bus with your bike, or vice versa.

Pick up a *South Rim Pocket Map & Services Guide* when you enter the park (or download and print one in advance) and note all the green dotted routes. These are the park's bike trails, aka greenways. Stick to these and the park roads and you'll easily get wherever you want to go. Don't forget to bring a bike lock.

For a **fun biking day trip** at the South Rim (about 32 mi/52 km of riding round-trip), leave your car at the Tusayan Greenway trailhead outside the park; ride the greenways into and across the park, making stops at the main visitors center, Market Plaza, and Grand Canyon Village along the way; and then ride the 7-mile (11.3-km) Hermit Road all the way to Hermit's Rest, including the 2.8-mile (4.5-km) Greenway Trail along the rim. To get back to your car, head out of the park the same way you came in.

never very far, and there are bike racks at each developed viewpoint.

You can also reach the rim by bike at Yaki Point and the South Kaibab Trailhead. Take the greenway near Grand Canyon Visitor Center to the Yaki Point Road, which is closed to private vehicles.

Bright Angel Bicycles and Café (10 S. Entrance Rd., 928/814-8704, www. bikegrandcanyon.com, 6am-8pm daily

Apr.-Nov., 7am-7pm daily Dec.-Mar., adult rental $12.50 for 1 hour, $31.50 for 5 hours, $40 for full day, child rental $9.50 for 1 hour, $20 for 5 hours, $31.50 for full day) rents comfortable, easy-to-ride bikes as well as safety equipment and trailers for the tots. It also offers bike tours of varying length and difficulty. Bright Angel Bicycles is located next to the Grand Canyon Visitor Center, near the South Entrance.

Mountain Biking

The **Tusayan Bike Trails** are a series of single-track trails and old mining and logging roads organized into several easy to moderate loop trails for mountain bikers near the park's South Entrance. The trails wind through a forest of pine, juniper, and pinyon. The longest loop is 16 miles (26 km), and the shortest is 3 miles (4.8 km) long. There's a map at the beginning of the trails that shows the various loops. Pick up the trails at Forest Road 605 on the west side of AZ 64 north of Tusayan. Coming south from the park, the trailhead is 0.4 mile (0.6 km) south of the Tusayan Ranger District (176 Lincoln Log Loop, 928/638-2443, www.fs.usda.gov) sign on the west side of AZ 64. Coming from Tusayan toward the park on

AZ 64, go 0.3 mile (0.5 km) past town and turn west on Forest Road 605.

Bikes are also allowed on the **Arizona Trail** (www.aztrail.org) outside of the national park. There are trailheads at Forest Road 605, about 0.4 mile (0.6 km) south of the Tusayan Ranger District sign on the west side of AZ 64, and at the historic Grandview Lookout Tower, reached by taking Forest Road 302 east from AZ 64 for 15 miles (24 km) to Forest Road 310 and turning left. The Arizona Trail, composed of several different trails, moves through the **Kaibab National Forest,** sometimes close to the rim of the Grand Canyon and sometimes deep within the pine forest. The trails are generally hardpacked dirt with some rocks and sand. Watch for hikers and horseback riders.

CLIMBING

Though much of the rock in and around Grand Canyon is not ideal for rock climbing, being mostly too soft and loose (chossy, in the parlance of the sport), there are a few established short climbs along the South Rim in Kaibab limestone, including rocks near the Bright Angel Trailhead and in the Desert View area. Talk to a ranger for more information.

Entertainment and Shopping

RANGER PROGRAMS
Day Programs

Every day the park offers many free ranger-guided hikes and nature walks, as well as lectures and discussions on the animals, human history, and geology of the canyon, at various spots around the park. The programs are most numerous and varied in the high seasons of spring, summer, and fall. In January and February rangers typically offer only two programs per day—one on canyon critters and another on the geology of Grand Canyon. To make up for this, the park offers several special "Cultural Demonstrator" programs (though not daily) in winter featuring

Native American artists at the Desert View Watchtower. During the high season the ranger programs can get crowded, so it's best to plan ahead by checking the schedule at the visitors center, the activity desks at Bright Angel and Maswik Lodges, or online (go.nps.gov/gc_programs).

Night Programs

Most nights during the summer there's a typically fascinating and free evening ranger program at the **McKee Amphitheater** if the weather's nice and the **Shrine of the Ages** if it isn't. Night programs are generally not offered during January and February, ending

after Christmas and beginning again during spring break in March. This varied program of lectures and night walks, on subjects ranging from astronomy to the Colorado River to "Surviving the Apocalypse at the Grand Canyon," is usually very popular, so it's best to plan ahead. For some of the most popular programs you must get a ticket to secure a spot, starting at 7:30pm at the Shrine of the Ages venue near Park Headquarters for an 8:30pm program at either venue. The amphitheater is behind and east of the Shrine of the Ages and can be reached via a spur from the Rim Trail, about 1.4 miles (2.3 km) east of the village.

Junior Rangers

If you've got kids ages 4-12, before you start sightseeing, take them to the **Grand Canyon Visitor Center** and get them in the **Junior Rangers** program. The ranger will give them age-appropriate booklets, and throughout the day they'll earn a Junior Ranger badge and patch by fulfilling the fun and educational requirements, which include attending one of the ranger-led programs offered throughout the day.

EVENTS

In late June join the Tucson Amateur Astronomy Association at the South Rim for the annual **Star Party** (www.tucsonastronomy.org, free)—eight days of viewing the dark night skies over the canyonlands, scanning for planets and galaxies, and mingling with starry-eyed astronomers from around the world. During the event, park rangers offer constellation walks every night at 9pm, 9:30pm, and 10pm.

Over several weekends in late August to mid-September, classical music-lovers come to the canyon rim for a series of popular concerts during the **Grand Canyon Music Festival** (https://grandcanyonmusicfest.org, Fri. and Sat. nights, requested donation of $15 adults and $10 kids), which often features

some of the top musicians in the country playing live at the beautiful Shrine of the Ages.

From mid-September to late January, the Grand Canyon Conservancy hosts the **Grand Canyon Celebration of Art** (www.grandcanyon.org), a plein-air competition and exhibition featuring about 25 artists. The paintings are later displayed and sold at the Kolb Gallery, with proceeds going to fund a new art space on the South Rim.

In early November the South Rim hosts the **Native American Heritage Celebration** with free exhibits, lectures, performances, and demonstrations by and about the many Native American tribes that have a deep spiritual and cultural connection to Grand Canyon. The events are held over two days at various spots around the South Rim.

SHOPPING
Essentials

If you check in to your in-park hotel and discover that you forget something essential, whatever it might be, don't panic. Head to the **Canyon Village Market and Deli at Market Plaza** (1 Market Plaza Rd., 928/638-2262, 8am-8pm daily) and look around—chances are it is stocked there. A full grocery store, liquor store, hiking store, and gift shop, the general store also has a deli inside and a bank and post office nearby.

Gift Shops

Business hours at the various South Rim gift shops vary somewhat by season; what the National Park Service calls their "core hours" are listed below. Plan for somewhat shorter hours December-March.

The **Grand Canyon Conservancy Park Store** (8am-6pm daily), near the main visitors center, is the park's largest gift shop. Four of the in-park hotels have serious gift shops: **El Tovar** (7am-10pm daily), **Bright Angel Lodge** (7am-10pm daily), **Maswik Lodge** (7am-10pm daily), and **Yavapai Lodge** (8am-8pm daily). There's also three stand-alone shops in the village that should not be missed on any canyon shopping spree—**Lookout**

1: Grand Canyon Conservancy Park Store **2:** Hopi House

Studio (9am-5pm daily), **Hopi House** (8am-5pm daily), and **Verkamp's** (9am-6pm daily). The same items more or less can be found in all of them—T-shirts, sweatshirts, jackets, hats, stickers, water bottles, books, stuffed animals (super-cute mountain lions and condors), and various Native American arts and crafts. The best of the arts and crafts are sold and displayed at Mary Jane Colter's Hopi House near El Tovar, and at El Tovar itself.

The gift shop at **Hermit's Rest** (9am-5pm daily), where large shiny-black ravens proliferate, has various charming gift items featuring these rowdy canyon residents.

To the east, there's a gift shop and bookstore at **Desert View Watchtower** (9am-5pm daily), and gifts, souvenirs, and supplies are sold at the **Desert View Trading Post** (9am-5pm daily) and **Desert View Market and Deli** (8am-5pm daily).

Bookstores

The **Grand Canyon Conservancy** (www.grandcanyon.org), the park's nonprofit partner, publishes many excellent books about the history of Grand Canyon and the region, most of them deeply researched, finely written, and sumptuously illustrated. If you're a booklover, don't miss browsing these and other books—including a substantial selection of children's readers and picture books—at the **Grand Canyon Conservancy Park Store** (8am-6pm daily), right across the plaza from the main visitors center. Here you'll find books about how to hike the canyon, including

detailed trail guides, nature guides, and maps, along with beautiful coffee table books, and volumes on the history of the human activity in the park from the rim's pioneer miners to the golden days of the 1930s. You'll find roughly the same few books in almost all the gift shops in the park, but the widest selection is at the GCC park store, **Verkamp's** (9am-6pm daily) in the village, and at **Yavapai Geology Museum** (8am-8pm daily summer, 8am-6pm daily winter) in between.

Supplies and Gear

Whether you forgot your water bottle, your crampons, your tent, or even your backpack itself, **Grand Canyon Outfitters** inside **Canyon Village Market and Deli** (1 Market Plaza Rd., 928/638-2262, 8am-8pm daily) likely has a last-minute top-shelf replacement. Here you'll find hiking boots, clothing, tents, hiking poles, sleeping bags, packs (to rent or buy), books, maps, and friendly and helpful staff members to recommend the best gear for your canyon hike. Nobody's getting any deals here, of course, but you honestly could outfit a multiday expedition at a moment's notice, if the mood should strike you. Most of the lobby gift shops around the park have a small section of hiking gear such as water bottles, crampons, bandannas, hiking poles, and hats. In the east, there are a few hiking supplies and gear for sale at the **Desert View Market** (8am-5pm daily), but the best place to go is the Canyon Village Market and Deli at Market Plaza.

The Greening of Grand Canyon National Park

There are signs of it all around the South Rim section of Grand Canyon National Park—the ethos of sustainability, the new normal. It's been seeping in over the last couple of decades but has now become a flood of programs and progress. Look around while visiting the South Rim and you'll see evidence of it everywhere: in the lodges encouraging you to forgo changing your linens and using extra towels; in the restaurants serving produce, meat, beer, wine, coffee, and much more grown and made close by; and in the growing numbers of visitors who are choosing to leave their vehicles parked and walk, bike, or ride the free natural gas-fueled shuttle buses around the park.

Concessionaire **Xanterra Parks and Resorts** (www.grandcanyonlodges.com) runs most of the hotels and eateries at Grand Canyon National Park, as well as the Grand Hotel in Tusayan and the Grand Canyon Railway Hotel in Williams, where it also operates the historic Grand Canyon Railway. Xanterra traces its roots back to the great Fred Harvey Company and operates at several other major national parks, including Zion, Glacier, and Yellowstone. At Grand Canyon, Xanterra serves about two million meals and rents about 260,000 rooms each year.

Since 2000, the company has used 48.6 percent less water, 17.4 percent less electricity, and 32.5 percent less waste overall, including 40 percent less construction waste per project. Currently about 40 percent of the food used in its South Rim restaurants comes from sustainable sources, and there are now electric vehicle charging stations in the park and in Tusayan.

Xanterra is particularly dedicated to water conservation, which is fitting out here in the high and dry wilderness of the Colorado Plateau. The company works with **Change the Course** (www.changethecourse.us), a nonprofit that helps corporations encourage water conservation, with a goal of returning 1,000 gallons of water to the Colorado River Basin with every pledge. (To make the pledge, take a picture of yourself filling up your water bottle at one of the park's water stations and post it to Twitter or Instagram with the hashtag #waterforparks, or text "Rivers" to 474747.)

A few years ago Xanterra took a big step toward its goal of a zero-waste near-future when it started its innovative "single-stream" trash and recycling programs in which all trash, save for that from restaurants, is put in one receptacle and sorted by a company in Flagstaff, making high-level, targeted recycling easier.

Other creative green solutions include running the Grand Canyon Railway's historic steam engines on biodiesel made from Xanterra's kitchen grease, and feeding leftover food scraps to the mules and then selling their manure as compost to local nurseries and farms. The greening of Grand Canyon even extends to Xanterra's gift shops, where you can purchase souvenir T-shirts and jackets made from recycled water and soda bottles.

The South Rim's other major concessionaire, **Delaware North** (www.visitgrandcanyon.com), is equally dedicated to sustainability and a zero-waste future. The company operates Yavapai Lodge and its restaurants, the stores and delis at Market Plaza and Desert View, and Trailer Village. Five of its restaurants and snack bars on the South Rim have been certified by the Green Restaurant Association; some 70 percent of its retail products are made in the USA; 30 percent of its food is local, sustainable, or organic; and 90 percent of its ingredients come from within 190 miles (305 km). And in 2020, Delaware North at the Grand Canyon was named a Bike-Friendly Workplace based on its free bike rentals for employees and encouraging them to ride to work.

Food

Most of the in-park eateries are certified green restaurants (certified by the Green Restaurant Association) and strive to serve dishes using local and organic produce and meats. Foodies, food-lovers, and world-class diners should not miss a stop at El Tovar.

INSIDE THE PARK
Near the Visitors Center

Bright Angel Bicycles and Café (10 S. Entrance Rd., 928/638-3055, www.bikegrandcanyon.com, 6am-8pm daily Apr.-Nov., 7am-7pm daily Dec.-Mar., $3-10) is a convenient spot to pick up a quick breakfast, lunch, or coffee. The small bike shop and café near the main visitors center serves premade sandwiches provided by a Flagstaff-based deli, along with soups, wraps, bagels, sweets, and excellent coffee drinks made with Firehouse Coffee Company beans from nearby Prescott. **Fred Harvey Taco Truck** (11am-4pm daily in good weather, $2.50-10.50) sells magnificent tacos, burritos, rice, and quesadillas from a colorful food truck parked near the main visitors center area. It's only open during the high season and only during good weather. This is a great choice for vegetarians.

Grand Canyon Village

★ **El Tovar Dining Room** (928/638-2631, ext. 6432, www.grandcanyonlodges.com, 6:30am-11am, 11:30am-2pm, and 5pm-10pm daily, $10-40, reservations highly recommended) truly carries on the Fred Harvey Company traditions on which it was founded in 1905. A serious, competent staff serves fresh, creative, locally inspired and sourced dishes in a cozy, mural-lined dining room that has not been significantly altered from the way it looked back when Teddy Roosevelt and Zane Grey ate here. The wine, entrées, and desserts are all top-notch and would be appreciated anywhere in the world—but they always seem to be that much tastier with the

sun going down over the canyon. Pay attention to the specials, which usually feature some in-season local edible; they are always the best thing to eat within several hundred miles in any direction.

The Arizona Steakhouse (928/638-2631, www.grandcanyonlodges.com, 11:30am-3pm and 4:30pm-10pm daily Mar.-Oct., 4:30pm-10pm daily Nov.-Dec., $14-36), next to the Bright Angel Lodge, serves locally sourced, Southwestern-inspired steak, prime rib, fish, and chicken dishes in a stylish but still casual atmosphere. There's a full bar, and the steaks are excellent—hand-cut and cooked just right with unexpected sauces and marinades. The Arizona Steakhouse is closed for dinner in January and February and closes to the lunch crowd November-February.

★ **Harvey Burger** (928/638-2631, www.grandcanyonlodges.com, 6:30am-10pm daily, $9-22), just off the Bright Angel Lodge's lobby, is a perfect place for a big, hearty breakfast before a day hike below the rim. It serves all the standard, rib-sticking dishes amid decorations and ephemera recalling the Fred Harvey heyday. At lunch there's stew, chili, salads, sandwiches, and burgers, and for dinner there's steak, pasta, and fish dishes called "Bright Angel Traditions," along with a few offerings from The Arizona Steakhouse's menu. Nearby is the **Bright Angel Fountain** (11am-5pm daily in season), which serves hot dogs, ice cream, and other quick treats. **The Canyon Coffee House** (928/638-2631, www.grandcanyonlodges.com, 6am-10am daily, $1.60-4), just outside the Bright Angel Lodge main lobby, is open early and serves cinnamon rolls, croissants, bagels, yogurt and fruit, juice and coffee, but no espresso drinks.

Maswik Food Court (928/638-2631, www.grandcanyonlodges.com, 6am-10pm daily, $5-15), located inside Maswik Lodge, is a good place for a quick, filling, and delicious meal. You can find just about everything—burgers, salads, country-style mashed potatoes, french fries, sandwiches, prime rib, chili, and soft-serve ice cream, to name just a few of the dozens of offerings. Just grab a tray and pick your favorite dish, and you'll be eating in a matter of a few minutes.

If you're getting worn out from hiking the Rim Trail, look for multiple **Sustain Your Hike Carts** (11am-4pm daily, $2-7.50) near Bright Angel Lodge and other spots in the village for some jerky, trail mix, fruit, electrolyte drinks, sweets, and premade sandwiches.

Hermit's Rest

The **Hermit's Rest Snack Bar** (8am-8pm daily spring-fall, 9am-5pm daily in winter, $1-5), just outside the little stone gift-shop cottage called Hermit's Rest, sells premade sandwiches, chips, trail mix, electrolyte drinks, hot chocolate, cookies, nuts, and ice cream.

Market Plaza

Yavapai Lodge Restaurant (11 Yavapai Lodge Rd., 928/638-4001, www.visitgrandcanyon.com, 6am-10pm daily, $8-19) is a cafeteria-style eatery off the Yavapai Lodge lobby. It's casual, and you order from computers and pick up at a counter, but the food is a cut above most cafeterias, serving tasty American grill food for breakfast, lunch, and dinner, including wonderful and healthy "Southwest bowls." Also off the lobby is the **Yavapai Tavern** (11 Yavapai Lodge Rd., 928/638-4001, www.visitgrandcanyon.com, noon-10pm daily, $5-15), a casual sports bar with large televisions, live music, a patio, Arizona-made beers on tap (also a full bar), and a pub-style menu with burgers, wings, and nachos. Nearby **Yavapai Coffee Shop** (11 Yavapai Lodge Rd., 928/638-4001, www.visitgrandcanyon.com, 6am-3pm daily, $3-6) is good for a quick coffee drink and to fuel up pre-hike with prepared sandwiches and salads, fruit, bagels, wraps, and sweets.

Across the parking lot from Yavapai Lodge, the **Canyon Village Market and Deli** (1 Market Plaza Rd., 928/638-2262, 8am-8pm daily) has Arizona brews and wines, fresh produce, meat, and cheese, while the deli has great breakfast sandwiches and oatmeal, coffee drinks, and premade sandwiches and salads to go.

Desert View

Near the watchtower, the **Desert View Market and Deli** (928/638-2393, www.visitgrandcanyon.com, 8am-8pm daily

Desert View Market and Deli

March 23-Sept. 3, 8am-6pm daily Sept. 4-Oct. 21, 9am-5pm daily Oct. 22-Mar. 22, $4-11) has groceries, sandwiches (both hot and made-to-order, and premade to go), breakfast sandwiches and burritos, Indian and Mexican tacos, soup, nachos, veggie subs, and even Nathan's hot dogs. Next door, the **Desert View Trading Post & Ice Cream** (928/638-3150, www.visitgrandcanyon.com, 8am-8pm daily Mar. 23-Sept. 3, 8am-6pm daily Sept. 4-Oct. 21, 9am-5pm daily Oct. 22-Mar. 22) has, of course, ice cream, but also coffee drinks, homemade fudge, and other sweets.

OUTSIDE THE PARK
Tusayan

Tusayan makes for a decent stop if you're hungry. However, the food is just as good if not better inside the park, only about a mile (1.6 km) away. A lot of tour buses stop here, so you might find yourself crowded into waiting for a table at some places, especially during the summer high season.

If you're craving pizza after a long day exploring the canyon, try **We Cook Pizza & Pasta** (605 N. AZ 64, 928/638-2278, www.wecookpizzaandpasta.com, 11am-10pm daily Mar.-Oct., 11am-8pm daily Nov.-Feb., $10-30) for an excellent, high-piled pizza pie. It calls to you just as you enter Tusayan heading south from the park. The pizza, served in slices or whole pies, is pretty good considering the locale, and there's a big salad bar with all the fixings, plus beer and wine. It's a casual place, with picnic tables and an often harried staff. It gets really busy in here during the high summer season.

In the center of town, **Plaza Bonita** (352 AZ 64, 928/638-8900, www.myplazabonita.com, 7am-10pm Sun.-Thurs., 7am-11pm Fri.-Sat., $10-20) serves good Mexican food and great margaritas in a pleasant, family-style setting.

Inside the beautiful three-diamond Grand Hotel, on the southern side of town, the **Canyon Star Steakhouse & Saloon** (149 AZ 64, 928/638-3333, www.grandcanyongrandhotel.com, 7am-10pm daily, $11-30), with its high timber ceilings and elegant Old West aesthetic, is something of a mess hall for fancy cowboys, serving steaks, barbecue, fish, pasta, burgers, and more, and featuring a saloon that has stools topped with old mule saddles, 24 draft beers, and live music.

Delaware North, the park concessionaire that operates Yavapai Lodge and Market View Plaza, owns and operates the excellent **Tusayan General Store** (577 AZ 64, 928/638-2854, visitgrandcanyon.com, 6am-9pm daily), on the north side of town toward the park entrance, where you can find fresh groceries, a Starbucks, Grand Canyon gifts, and even several Arizona-brewed draft beers in growlers to go.

Accommodations

The park's lodging rates are audited annually and compare favorably to those offered outside the park, but you can sometimes find excellent deals at one of several gateway towns around canyon country. Using one of these places as a base for a visit to the canyon makes sense if you're planning on touring the whole of the canyonlands and not just the park. There are six lodges within Grand Canyon National Park at the South Rim—five operated by **Xanterra** (www.grandcanyonlodges.com) and one, Yavapai Lodge, operated by **Delaware North** (www.visitgrandcanyon.com). The hotels within the park are a green and sustainable choice: Xanterra and Delaware North both have robust sustainability programs aimed at conserving water and energy, reducing pollution, and increasing recycling while decreasing use of landfills.

All the hotels within Grand Canyon National Park offer wheelchair-accessible rooms.

INSIDE THE PARK

A stay at ★ **El Tovar** (303/297-2757 or 888/297-2757, www.grandcanyonlodges.com, $217-263 standard room, $442-538 suite), one of the most distinctive and memorable hotels in the state, would be the secondary highlight—after the gorge itself—of any trip to the South Rim. Opened in 1905, the log-and-stone National Historic Landmark, standing about 20 feet (6.1 m) from the rim, has 78 rooms and suites. The hotel's restaurant serves some of the best food in Arizona for breakfast, lunch, and dinner, and there's a comfortable cocktail lounge off the lobby with a window on the canyon. A mezzanine sitting area overlooks the log-cabin lobby, and a gift shop sells Native American art and crafts as well as canyon souvenirs. If you're looking to splurge on something truly exceptional, there's a honeymoon suite overlooking the canyon.

When first built in the 1930s, the ★ **Bright Angel Lodge** (303/297-2757 or 888/297-2757, www.grandcanyonlodges.com, $95-210) was meant to serve the middle-class travelers then being lured by the Santa Fe Railroad, and it's still affordable and comfortable while retaining a rustic character that fits perfectly with the wild canyon just outside. Lodge rooms don't have TVs, and most have only one bed. The utilitarian "hikers" rooms have refrigerators and share several private showers, which have lockable doors and just enough room to dress. Bright Angel is the place to sleep before hiking into the canyon; you just roll out of bed onto the Bright Angel Trail. The lodge's cabins just west of the main building have private baths, TVs, and sitting rooms; these include two cabins created out of historic pioneer structures, Buckey O'Neill's Log Cabin and Red Horse Station. Drinking and dining options include a small bar and coffeehouse, a Harvey House diner, and a restaurant with big windows framing the canyon.

Standing along the rim between El Tovar and Bright Angel, the **Kachina Lodge** (303/297-2757 or 888/297-2757, www.grandcanyonlodges.com, $225-243) offers basic, comfortable rooms with TVs, safes, private baths, and refrigerators. There's not a lot of character, but its location and modern comforts make the Kachina an ideal place for families to stay. The **Thunderbird Lodge** (303/297-2757 or 888/297-2757, www.grandcanyonlodges.com, $225-243) is in the same area and has similar offerings. Both properties have some rooms facing the canyon.

Maswik Lodge (303/297-2757 or 888/297-2757, www.grandcanyonlodges.com, $215) is located on the west side of the village about 0.25 mile (0.4 km) from the rim. The hotel has a cafeteria-style restaurant that serves just about everything you'd want and a sports bar with a large-screen TV. The rooms are motel-style basic but clean and comfortable, with TVs, private baths, and refrigerators, located in a series of two-story buildings around a parking lot north of the main lobby building. There are no elevators.

About 5 miles (8 km) from the park entrance at Market Plaza, **Yavapai Lodge** (11 Yavapai Lodge Rd., 928/638-4001 or 877/404-4611, www.visitgrandcanyon.com, $150-200) offers clean and comfortable rooms in a central forested setting. The East Section is a two-story building featuring air-conditioned rooms with refrigerators and TVs, and the King Family Room is a great option for families, with a king bed and twin bunk beds. The West Section, a retro motel-style structure, lacks air-conditioning but has pet rooms for an extra $25. Run by concessionaire Delaware North, Yavapai Lodge has a good casual restaurant and a pleasant lobby with a fireplace, a gift shop, and a tavern.

OUTSIDE THE PARK
Tusayan

Lining AZ 64, accommodations in Tusayan are about 1 mile (1.6 km) south of the park's South Entrance.

Though more basic than some of the

other places in Tusayan, the **Red Feather Lodge** (300 Rte. 64, 928/638-2414, www.redfeatherlodge.com, $220-240) is a comfortable, affordable place to stay, with a welcoming lobby with Navajo rugs hanging on the walls, a pool, hot tub, and separate hotel and motel complexes.

Resembling a high-end hunting lodge, the **Grand Hotel** (149 Rte. 64, 928/638-3333, www.grandcanyongrandhotel.com, $200-400) is one of the more luxurious places to stay in the region, with prices to match. The sprawling sandstone-and-log hotel with a shining, green metal roof pops up just as you enter Tusayan, and its beautiful lobby sets the Craftsman, wood-and-leather tone of the whole place with a fireplace lounge and large gift shop. A cowboy wilderness chic and elegant Old West hunting lodge aesthetic pervades, with heads of beasts on the walls, including a mountain lion, a bobcat, and a buffalo. The hotel has very clean and comfortable rooms; a pool, hot tub, and fitness center; as well as a large saloon and steak house.

Across AZ 64 from the Grand Hotel, the **Best Western Grand Canyon Squire Inn** (74 Rte. 64, 928/638-2681, www.grandcanyonsquire.com, $197-239) has a fitness center, pool and spa, salon, game room, bowling alley, and myriad other amenities—so many that it may be difficult to get out of the hotel to enjoy the natural sights. The large complex features interior hallways and entrances, an outdoor fireplace, a huge pool, and, in the lobby, artist Kenton Pies's bronze fountain-sculpture *Desert Refreshment.* The hotel offers standard and deluxe rooms, as well as suites. The standard room has two comfy queen beds with crisp white sheets, a flat-screen TV, and a refrigerator and microwave. ADA-accessible and dog-friendly rooms are also available.

Cameron

On the Navajo Nation about 50 miles (81 km) north of Flagstaff along U.S. 89, near the junction with AZ 64 (the route to the park's east gate), sits the ★ **Historic Cameron Trading Post and Lodge** (800/338-7385, www.camerontradingpost.com, $79-199), established in 1916. It's about a one-hour drive from the Desert View area of the park and is a good place to start your tour. Starting from the East Entrance, you'll see the canyon gradually becoming grand. Before you reach the park, the Little Colorado drops some 2,000 feet (610 m) through the arid, scrubby land, cutting through gray rock on the way to its marriage with the big river and creating the **Little Colorado Gorge.** Stop here and get a barrier-free glimpse at this lesser chasm to prime yourself for what is to come. There are usually a few booths set up selling Navajo arts and crafts and a lot of touristy souvenirs at two developed pullouts along the road.

The Cameron Lodge is a charming and affordable place to stay, and it makes a perfect base for a visit to the Grand Canyon, Indian Country, Lake Powell, and the Arizona Strip. It has a good restaurant (6am-9:30pm daily summer, 7am-9pm daily winter, $7-16) serving American and Navajo food, including excellent beef stew, heaping Navajo tacos, chili, and burgers. There's also an art gallery, a visitors center, a huge trading post/gift shop, and an RV park ($35 full hookup, no bathroom or showers). A small grocery store has packaged sandwiches, chips, and sodas. The rooms are decorated in a Southwestern Native American style and are clean and comfortable, some with views of the Little Colorado River and the old 1911 suspension bridge that spans the stream just outside the lodge. There are single-bed rooms, rooms with two beds, and a few suites that are perfect for families. The stone-and-wood buildings and the garden patio, laid out with stacked sandstone bricks with picnic tables and red-stone walkways below the open-corridor rooms, create a cozy, history-soaked setting and make the lodge a memorable place to stay. The vast, empty red plains of the Navajo Reservation spread out all around and create a lonely,

1: El Tovar 2: Red Horse Station cabin at Bright Angel Lodge 3: Yavapai Lodge 4: Bright Angel Lodge

isolated atmosphere, especially at night, but the rooms have cable TV and free Wi-Fi so you can be connected and entertained even way out here. If you're visiting in the winter, the lodge drops its prices significantly during this less crowded touring season.

Camping

There are three in-park campgrounds on the South Rim. Mather Campground and Trailer Village are close to the village and all the action, while the Desert View Campground, about 25 miles (40 km) east of the village, is on the quieter side of the park. Reserve campsites as far ahead of time as possible. At 7,000 feet (2,134 m), the forested South Rim can get chilly at night even in the summer, so plan accordingly. Mather Campground has wheelchair-accessible sites, but Trailer Village and Desert View Campground do not.

INSIDE THE PARK

★ **Mather Campground** (877/444-6777, www.recreation.gov, $18 Mar.-Nov., $15 Dec.-Feb.) takes reservations up to six months ahead for the March-November 20 peak season and thereafter operates on a first-come, first-served basis. Located near the village and offering more than 300 basic campsites with grills and fire pits, the campground typically fills up by about noon during the summer busy season. It has restrooms with showers, and coin-operated laundry machines. The campground is open to tents and trailers but has no hookups and is closed to RVs longer than 30 feet (9.1 m). Even if you aren't an experienced camper, a stay at Mather is a fun and inexpensive alternative to sleeping indoors. Despite its large size and crowds, the campground gets pretty quiet at night. Even in summer, the night takes on a bit of a chill, making a campfire not exactly necessary but not out of the question. Bring your own wood or buy it at the store nearby. A large, clean restroom and shower facility is within walking distance from most sites, and they even have blow-dryers. Everything is coin operated, and there's an office on-site that gives change.

Consider bringing bikes along, especially for the kids. The village is about a 15-minute walk from the campground on forested, paved trails, or you can take the free shuttle from a stop nearby. Pets are allowed but must be kept on a leash, and they're not allowed on shuttle buses.

About 25 miles (40 km) east of the village, near the park's East Entrance, is **Desert View Campground** (877/444-6777, www. recreation.gov, first-come, first-served, May-mid-Oct. depending on weather, $12), with 50 sites for tents and small trailers only, with no hookups. There's a restroom with no showers and only two faucets with running water. Each site has a grill but little else. Pets are allowed but must be kept on a leash.

The South Rim concessionaire Delaware North operates **Trailer Village** (877/404-4611, www.visitgrandcanyon.com, $52-62), about half a mile (0.8 km) from the Mather Campground and right near Market Plaza. A clean, orderly, short tree-lined and paved area close to all the action and open year-round, Trailer Village has full hookups and pull-throughs for rolling mansions up to 50 feet (15.2 m) long. Only charcoal fires are allowed, and there's no Wi-Fi. Dogs are welcome but must be kept on a leash. Reservations are a must during the high seasons.

OUTSIDE THE PARK

In Tusayan about 1 mile (1.6 km) from the South Entrance, **Grand Canyon Camper Village** (549 Camper Village Ln., Tusayan, 928/638-2887, www.grandcanyoncampervillage.com, $33-66) is open year-round for trailers, motorhomes, and tents. Offering 30- and 50-amp spots, the campground has coin-op showers, laundry, and limited Wi-Fi. Take AZ 64 north (toward the park) through Tusayan to the Coyote Lane exit at the second traffic circle.

The beautiful **Ten X Campground** (877/444-6777, www.recreation.gov, mid-May-late Sept., $20), 2 miles (3.2 km) south of Tusayan off AZ 64, has 70 campsites for up to eight people, no hookups, pit toilets, and a 0.5-mile (0.8-km) nature trail through the ponderosa pines of the Kaibab National Forest. This is a great place for family camping only 4 miles (6.4 km) from the park entrance. You must reserve your spot in advance through Recreation.gov, which releases them on a six-month rolling basis.

You'll find one of the better deals in the whole canyon region in Valle, a tiny spot not far off AZ 64, about 30 miles (48 km) south of the South Entrance. The **Red Lake Campground and Hostel** (8850 N. Rte. 64, Valle, 928/635-4753, $20 pp per night), where you can rent a bed in a shared room, is a very basic but reasonably comfortable place sitting lonely on the grasslands next to a gas station; it has shared bathrooms with showers, free Wi-Fi, a common room with a kitchen and a TV, and an RV park ($25) with partial hookups. If you're going super-budget, you can't beat this place, though it is about 45 minutes from the park's south gate.

The **Kaibab National Forest** (www.fs.usda.gov/kaibab) rents out **Hull Cabin** (877/444-6777, www.recreation.gov, $140 per night May 1-Sept. 30), built in the 1880s as part of a sheep farm. The cabin is about 6 miles (9.7 km) from Grandview Point along Desert View Drive, outside the park boundary in a forest meadow. For more information, contact the Tusayan Ranger District office (928/638-2443).

Dispersed Camping

The **Kaibab National Forest,** which surrounds the canyon, allows **dispersed camping** outside the park (www.fs.usda.gov/kaibab, free) for up to 14 days per month. Forest officials want you to reuse already established dispersed camping spots and fire rings, and not to drive more than 30 feet (9.1 m) from the side of the road or camp within a mile (1.6 km) of a developed campground or 0.25 mile (0.4 km) of a livestock watering hole. Remember to tread lightly (www.treadlightly.org) and leave no trace (https://lnt.org), which means packing out everything that you pack in.

Transportation and Services

GETTING THERE
Driving

The majority of Grand Canyon visitors drive here, reaching the South Rim from either **Flagstaff** or **Williams** and entering the park through the south or east gates. The South Entrance is usually the busiest, and during the summer traffic is likely to be backed up somewhat.

To get to the **South Entrance** from Flagstaff, take U.S. 180 through the forest past the San Francisco Peaks. The road merges with AZ 64 at Valle, for a total distance of about 80 miles (129 km) from Flagstaff to the park gate, which takes about 1.5 hours. The drive from Williams to the South Entrance on AZ 64 is a more direct but less scenic route; it's about 60 miles (97 km) and takes about an hour. To reach the **East Entrance,** take U.S. 89 north from Flagstaff to Cameron, then take AZ 64 west to the entrance. The drive is about 80 miles (129 km) and takes about 1.5 hours. This route is recommended if you want to see portions of Navajo Country on your way to the canyon, and entering through the East Entrance will put you right at Desert View, the Desert View Watchtower, and Tusayan Ruin & Museum—sights that otherwise you'll have to travel 25 miles (40 km) or so east from Grand Canyon Village to see.

Where Can I Find...?

- **Accessible Lodging and Camping:** All hotels within the park offer wheelchair-accessible rooms. Mather Campground has wheelchair-accessible sites.

- **Accessible Trails:** A large portion of the Rim Trail is accessible to wheelchairs.

- **Laundry:** There are coin-operated washing machines and dryers at Mather Campground.

- **Lost and Found:** If you find a lost item, take it to the main visitors center. If you're looking for a lost item, call 928/638-7798, 928/638-2631, or 928/638-4001.

- **Pay Phone:** There's a pay phone outside Canyon Village Market and Deli at Market Plaza.

- **Post Office:** Next to the Canyon Village Market and Deli at Market Plaza.

- **Public Restrooms:** Grand Canyon Visitor Center, Market Plaza, Grand Canyon Village, lobbies of all the lodges, Hopi Point, Hermit's Rest, South Kaibab Trailhead, Mather Campground, Desert View restaurants.

- **Religious Services:** Shrine of the Ages; a list of services and times is posted at the main visitors center and Mather Campground, or ask at the activities desk at Bright Angel or Maswik Lodges.

- **Showers:** There are coin-operated showers at Mather Campground.

- **Water:** There are water stations at the Grand Canyon Visitor Center complex, Market Plaza, and Grand Canyon Village, as well as at all the lodges.

- **Wi-Fi:** Find free Wi-Fi in the Canyon Village Market and Deli (8am-8pm daily), at Park Headquarters (8am-5pm Mon.-Fri., computers in research library available 8am-4:30pm), and at the Grand Canyon Community Library (10:30am-5pm Mon.-Sat., computers also available). If you are a guest at one of the in-park lodges, you will be able to access free Wi-Fi in the lobby, though probably not in the rooms.

The Grand Canyon's South Rim is 225 miles (360 km) from **Phoenix,** which has in Sky Harbor International Airport the closest major airport to the park. The best way to reach the canyon from out of state is to fly into Phoenix, rent a car, and drive north on I-17. Once you reach the northland, you can either take the route through Williams along AZ 64 or the Flagstaff route along U.S. 180 and AZ 64; the latter route is the more scenic of the two. Expect the drive from Phoenix to take about four hours, barring heavy traffic on the interstate.

The roughly five-hour, 280-mile (450-km) drive from **Las Vegas** to the South Rim—a very popular trip—is a relatively short one by Southwestern standards. Even if you get a late-morning start and make a few stops along the way, you're still likely to arrive at the park by dinnertime. Take U.S. 93 from Las Vegas to Kingman, then take I-40 to reach Williams or Flagstaff and head north to the park. The speed limit on most sections of I-40 in Arizona is 75 mph, so all that highland forest scenery flashes by unless you stop a few times to take it in. Most summer weekends you'll find the route crowded but manageable. At all times of the year you'll be surrounded by 18-wheelers barreling across the land. If you feel like stopping overnight—and perhaps it is better to see the great canyon with fresh morning eyes—do so in Williams. It's just an hour or so from the park's South Entrance, has a bit of Route 66 charm, and offers several distinctive and memorable hotels and restaurants, all of which you'll miss if you breeze through town in a hurry.

Grand Canyon National Park's South Rim

is 494 miles (795 km) from **Los Angeles,** the capital of the American West. Most of the seven- or eight-hour drive is along I-40. It's an approximately two-hour drive north on I-15 from L.A. to Barstow, where I-40 begins (or ends, if you're coming from the east), but it's sure to take considerably longer on the weekends and during the morning and evening rush hours, which in Southern California tend to be interminable. Expect snarls and delays around Barstow as well.

Shuttle from and to Flagstaff

Groome Transporation aka Arizona Shuttle (928/350-8466, https://groometransportation.com/arizona) offers comfortable rides from Flagstaff to the Grand Canyon three times daily (Mar.-Oct., $60 round-trip for adults). The company also goes between Phoenix's Sky Harbor International Airport and Flagstaff ($48 pp one-way) several times a day as well as from Flagstaff to Sedona, the Verde Valley, and Williams ($35-43 one-way).

GETTING AROUND
Car
PARKING

The best way to explore Grand Canyon National Park's South Rim is to park your car near a shuttle stop and use a combination of walking and riding the free shuttle to get around. First try the four lots around the **main visitors center,** which include trailer and RV parking spots. In the high season these large parking lots generally fill up by 10am. Next move on to **Market Plaza,** where you can park cars, trailers, and RVs in a large lot, and then the mid-sized lot at **Park Headquarters** across from Market Plaza, where you can park an RV up to 22 feet (6.7 m) long. Both of these lots usually fill up by noon. There are a number of parking spots within the village outside Bright Angel Lodge and El Tovar, but you'll be lucky to get one of these prime spots, which are typically all taken by 2pm. The **Backcountry Information Center** (928/638-7875) also

has a large parking lot, the southern portion of which can accommodate RVs and trailers. This lot across the train tracks from the village typically fills by 2pm.

GAS AND REPAIRS

The closest gas station to Grand Canyon Village is Conoco in Tusayan (928/638-2608), about 7 miles (11.3 km) to the south. There's a gas station in the park's Desert View section, about 26 miles (42 km) east of the village.

For small repairs like a flat tire, drained battery, blown fuses, or split hoses, try the **Public Garage** (928/638-2621, 8am-noon and 1pm-5pm daily) behind the National Park Service General Office Building by the railroad depot. Anything more serious and you'll have to call a tow truck from Williams or Flagstaff. This will likely take a long time and it won't be cheap. One tow truck driver recently said that there's a shortage of his kind in the region, and that if you don't have AAA, which generally takes priority, it will take even longer than usual. He said he's out on AZ 64 nearly every day, especially in the high season, helping tourists, and typical calls include tourists losing the keys to their rentals and run-ins with elk.

Free Shuttle Buses

The park operates excellent **free shuttle services** along the South Rim, with comfortable buses fueled by compressed natural gas. It's strongly encouraged you park your car for the duration of your visit and use the shuttle. It's nearly impossible to find parking at the various sights, and traffic through the park is not always easy to navigate—there are a lot of one-way routes and oblivious pedestrians that can lead to needless frustration. Make sure you pick up a free *Pocket Map,* which has a map of the various shuttle routes and stops, available at the entrance gate and at most visitors centers throughout the park.

Pretty much anywhere you want to go in the park a shuttle will get you there, and you rarely have to wait more than 10 minutes at any stop. That being said, there is no shuttle that goes all the way to the Tusayan Ruin & Museum or the Desert View Watchtower near the East Entrance.

Shuttle drivers are a good source of information about the park. They are generally very friendly and knowledgeable, and a few of them are genuinely entertaining. The shuttle conveniently runs from around sunup until about 9pm, and drivers always know the expected sunrise and sundown times and seem to be intent on getting people to the best overlooks to view these two popular daily park events.

Park shuttles have racks that fit 2-3 bikes. All shuttle buses are wheelchair accessible (up to 30 in/76 cm wide and 48 in/122 cm long), with wheelchair ramps and low entrances and exits.

If you are in a hurry to get somewhere, the free shuttle bus is not what you need. Especially during the summer and on spring and early fall weekends, expect to stand in a line and watch several buses fill and depart before you get on.

FROM TUSAYAN TO THE PARK

From early spring to fall, the **Tusayan Route (Purple)** operates from the Grand Canyon Visitor Center and IMAX theater in Tusayan into the park, all day every day. You must have your park entrance pass before you board the shuttle. Entrance passes can be purchased at the IMAX theater as well as various other places around Tusayan, or online at www.recreation.gov. Just leave your car in the parking lot in Tusayan and take the free shuttles everywhere you want to go inside the park. Shuttles from the theater begin at 8am daily, and the last trip is at 9:45pm. The Tusayan shuttle drops you off at the Grand Canyon Visitor Center; the last shuttle out of the park leaves at 9:30pm. The shuttle runs every 20 minutes and takes about 20 minutes from Tusayan to the visitors center.

INSIDE THE PARK

The year-round **Kaibab/Rim Route (Orange)** will take you from Grand Canyon

Visitor Center west to Yavapai Geology Museum and back, and east to the South Kaibab Trailhead, Yaki Point, and Pipe Creek Vista and back. Ride the year-round **Village Route (Blue)** west from the visitors center to Market Plaza, Shrine of the Ages, the Grand Canyon Railway Depot, Bright Angel Lodge, and the Hermit's Rest Route transfer area. Eastbound the Village Route goes from the transfer area to Maswik Lodge, the Backcountry Information Center, Shrine of the Ages, Mather Campground, Trailer Village, Market Plaza, and then back to the visitors center.

The **Hermit's Rest Route (Red)** runs March-November (Dec.-Feb. Hermit Road is open to private vehicles) and is the way most visitors reach the must-see western viewpoints along the South Rim. The route starts at the Village Route transfer area at the head of Hermit Road and heads west, stopping at Trailview Overlook, Maricopa Point, Powell Point, Mohave Point, The Abyss, Monument Creek Vista, Pima Point, and Hermit's Rest. Headed back east it makes stops only at Pima Point, Mohave Point, and Powell Point before returning to the Village Route transfer.

Taxi

Xanterra's taxi service (928/638-2822 or 928/638-2631, ext. 6563) operates 24/7, offering rides around the park, including to Desert View ($48 for 1-3 people), and outside the park to Tusayan ($14 for 1-3 people) and the Grand Canyon Airport ($21 for 1-3 people). It is perhaps handiest as a ride to the trailheads—$16 to Hermit's Rest for Hermit Trail backpackers and $10 to the South Kaibab Trailhead. There are only a few cabs in service so trips may end up taking longer than planned.

Bike

Whether you're staying in the park or just visiting for the day, consider bringing your bike along. You can park your car at the **South Rim Backcountry Information Center parking lot** (across the train tracks from the village) and ride your bike all around the park from there using the paved **Tuyasan Greenway Trail**. Every hotel, restaurant, store, and sight has a bike rack; don't forget your bike lock. If you get tired, park shuttles have racks that fit 2-3 bikes. Remember, though, that the shuttles take a lot longer because they make many stops. There's a good map of all the in-park bike routes in the free *Pocket Map* guide, and staff members at **Bright Angel Bicycles and Café** (928/814-8704, www.bikegrandcanyon.com, 6am-8pm daily Apr.-Nov., 7am-7pm daily Dec.-Mar.), right next to the Grand Canyon Visitor Center near the South Entrance and Mather Point, can answer your questions and also offer bike rentals.

TO THE NORTH RIM

The 215-mile (345-km), 4.5-hour drive from the Grand Canyon National Park's South Rim section to the park's lesser-visited North Rim is a memorable journey through a true American outback: across the western edge of the Navajo Nation, over the Colorado River, through the lonely Arizona Strip, up onto the high Kaibab Plateau, and ending at the Grand Canyon Lodge hanging off the forest rim.

Leave the South Rim through the Desert View area along AZ 64, which meets U.S. 89 North at Cameron. Head north across Navajo land to Bitter Springs, about an hour north of Cameron. Pick up U.S. 89A going west, cross the Colorado River via the Navajo Bridge, and then head across the Arizona Strip to the Kaibab Plateau. U.S. 89A meets AZ 67 to the North Rim on top of the plateau at Jacob Lake. From there it's about 45 miles (72 km), a drive of about an hour, to Grand Canyon National Park.

The **Trans-Canyon Shuttle** (928/638-2820, www.trans-canyonshuttle.com, $90 one-way, reservations required) makes a daily round-trip excursion between the North and South Rims, departing the North Rim at 7am and arriving at the South Rim at 11:30am. The shuttle then leaves the South Rim at 1:30pm and arrives back at the North Rim at 6pm.

During the spring and summer, shuttles run twice daily from the South Rim to the North Rim (8am-12:30pm and 1:30pm-6pm), and twice daily from the North Rim to the South Rim (7am-11:30am and 2pm-6:30pm).

TO SKYWALK
From the South Rim

To get to the Hualapai Reservation's Skywalk from Grand Canyon Village, take AZ 64 south to Williams. Head west on I-40 to Ash Fork, where you can pick up Route 66 to Peach Springs. The drive from Peach Springs to Grand Canyon West is 85 miles via Route 66, Antares Road, Pearce Ferry Road, and Diamond Bar Road, and it takes about two hours. The total drive from the South Rim to Grand Canyon West is about 225 miles (360 km) and takes about 4.5 hours.

From Las Vegas

It's only 125 miles (201 km) from Las Vegas to the Skywalk (about a 2.5-hour drive), so it makes sense to include this remote side trip if you're headed to the South Rim from Vegas anyway. To reach Grand Canyon West from Las Vegas, take U.S. 93 out of the city, heading south for about 65 miles (105 km) to mile marker 42, where you'll see the Dolan Springs/Meadview City/Pearce Ferry exit. Turn north onto Pearce Ferry Road. About 30 miles (48 km) in, turn east on Diamond Bar Road. Then it's about 20 miles (32 km) to Grand Canyon West.

To continue on from Grand Canyon West to the South Rim, head to Peach Springs along Historic Route 66. You can stop here for the night, at the Hualapai Lodge; continue on for about an hour east on Route 66 to Seligman, which has several small hotels and a few good restaurants; or drive Route 66 to Ash Fork, where you can pick up I-40 east to Williams, the gateway to the South Rim. The journey from the Skywalk to Williams is about 170 miles (275 km) and takes a little over three hours.

SERVICES
Internet, ATMs, and Post Office

Most of the quotidian services on the South Rim are at **Market Plaza,** where there's a general store, **Chase Bank** and an ATM (foreign currency exchange for bank members only, 928/638-2437), a **post office** (928/638-2512), and **free Wi-Fi** in the **Canyon Village Market and Deli** (8am-8pm daily). There are also **ATMs** in the lobbies of the Bright Angel Lodge, El Tovar, and Maswik Lodge.

Free Wi-Fi can also be harnessed at **Park Headquarters** (8am-5pm Mon.-Fri., computers in research library available 8am-4:30pm) and the **Community Library** (10:30am-5pm Mon.-Sat., computers also available). If you are a guest at one of the in-park lodges, you will be able to access free Wi-Fi in the lobby, though probably not in the rooms.

Day Care

Plan far ahead if you're going to need day care during your trip and reserve a spot at **Kaibab Learning Center** (1 Mohave St., Grand Canyon Village, 928/638-6333, 7:30am-5pm Mon.-Fri.), a school and day care center on the South Rim. Bring along a copy of your child's immunizations, two changes of clothing, a water bottle, a hat, two healthy snacks, and a healthy lunch.

Pets

Leashed pets are allowed on the Rim Trail and the park greenways, but they are barred from the lodges, restaurants, shuttle buses, stores, and all other trails. Yavapai Lodge offers pet-friendly rooms.

Xanterra's **South Rim Kennel** (928/638-0534), next to Maswik Lodge, keeps dogs and cats for the day and overnight. You must make a reservation in advance, especially during the high season. Prices vary and food is included. Only animals with proof of vaccinations are allowed.

Religious Services

The **Shrine of the Ages** hosts Catholic, Latter-day Saint, Baptist, Jewish, and other religious services year-round. Check the schedules posted at the main visitors center, Shrine of the Ages, the post office, and Mather Campground.

Lost and Found

If you find something that you think someone lost, take it to the main visitors center. If you lost something that you want back, call 928/638-7798, 928/638-2631, or 928/638-4001.

Emergencies

North Country HealthCare operates an **urgent care clinic and pharmacy** on the South Rim (1 Clinic Rd., 928/638-2551, https://northcountryhealthcare.org, 9am-6pm daily Memorial Day-Labor Day, 8am-5pm daily Labor Day-Memorial Day). For after-hours emergencies dial 911 from your room.

The North Rim

Standing at Bright Angel Point on Grand

Canyon's North Rim, crowded together with several other gazers as if stranded on a jetty over a wide, hazy sea, someone whispers, "It looks pretty much the same as the other rim."

It's not true—far from it—but the comment brings up the main point about the North Rim: Should you go? Only about 10 percent of canyon visitors make the trip to the North Rim, which is significantly less developed than the South; there aren't many activities other than gazing, unless you are a hiker and a backcountry wilderness lover. The coniferous mountain forests of the Kaibab Plateau are themselves worth the trip—broken by grassy meadows and painted with summer wildflowers, and dappled with aspens that turn yellow and red in the fall and

Highlights

Look for ★ to find recommended sights, activities, dining, and lodging.

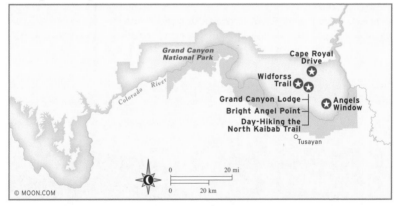

© MOON.COM

Grand Canyon National Park

Colorado River

Cape Royal Drive

Widforss Trail

Grand Canyon Lodge
Bright Angel Point
Day-Hiking the North Kaibab Trail

Angels Window

Tusayan

0   20 mi
0   20 km

★ Spend the day negotiating **Cape Royal Drive** as it winds through the forest, taking in several incredible viewpoints and hiking easy trails to the very edge of Grand Canyon (page 111).

★ Stare at the canyon from historic **Grand Canyon Lodge**'s famous veranda or through large picture windows in the wonderful sunroom (page 116).

★ Walk an easy, paved trail to **Bright Angel Point,** the North Rim's most popular viewpoint, an unbelievable spectacle of red rock covered with evergreens above a hazy blue labyrinth (page 116).

★ Catch a peek of the mighty Colorado River perfectly framed in the artfully eroded natural arch known as **Angels Window** (page 118).

★ Descend toward the desert depths of the great gorge as you day-hike on the steep **North Kaibab Trail,** frequented by mule trains (page 124).

★ Hike undulating **Widforss Trail** through the forest and along the rim to a view beloved of its namesake, North Rim artist Gunnar Widforss (page 128).

burst out of the otherwise uniform dark green like solitary flames. You may also catch sight of elk and mule deer. But it is a long trip, and you need to be prepared for a land of scant services—in return you'll find the simple, contemplative pleasures of nature in the raw.

PLANNING YOUR TIME

Summer and early fall are the best times to visit the Kaibab Plateau and the North Rim. In a good year, expect afternoon thunderstorms during July, August, and early September. High temperatures from May to September range from the mid-60s F (18°C) to the high 70s F (24-26°C), and when the monsoon storms don't come it's sunny and warm all day beneath a bright, cloudless turquoise sky, perfect weather for hiking, the North Rim's primary activity. Indeed, when packing to visit highland forest at around 8,000 feet (2,438 m) above sea level, think like a hiker: dress in layers and bring a light, waterproof jacket (or even a proper coat if you tend to get cold); early mornings and nights on the North Rim turn cool, and summer thunderstorms often bring chill winds. Don't forget a hat, and a bandana to protect your neck from the sun.

By early October the aspens flame orange and red among the evergreens and all of life starts to cool down. Grand Canyon Lodge and the restaurants, shops, and visitors centers close from October 31 to May 15. AZ 67, the only road into and out of the park on this side, closes from December 1 to May 15. Between October 31 and December 1, you can drive into the park and look around but you can't stay overnight. From December 1, when AZ 67 closes, until May 15, the North Rim Campground remains open as a primitive campground. To stay here, however, you need a backcountry permit and the energy to hike or ski 45 miles (72 km) from Jacob Lake.

A visit to the North Rim demands a gaze from at least **three essential viewpoints:** Bright Angel Point, Point Imperial, and Cape Royal. Luckily the trails to all three of these special places on the rim of the great canyon are accessible to pretty much everybody, though you need a vehicle to reach Cape Royal and Point Imperial.

Exploring the North Rim

You could spend all your time on the North Rim kicking back in an Adirondack chair on Grand Canyon Lodge's veranda and you would still have a full and memorable visit. Here it's about the remote quietude, the canyon seen from the sap-scented Arizona highlands, and the improbable stamp of elegance and style way out here at the edge of the world. However, you will get even more out of this truly special place if you drive the scenic Cape Royal Road and undertake at least one major hike, preferably below the rim on the North Kaibab Trail. During your explorations make sure to have your refillable water bottle with you, or buy one in the park gift shop. Water stations are located behind the North Rim Visitor Center, at the North Rim Backcountry Information Center, and at the North Kaibab Trailhead about 1.5 miles (2.4 km) north of the lodge.

VISITORS CENTERS
Inside the Park

The **North Rim Visitor Center** (8am-6pm daily May 15-Oct. 16, 9am-3pm daily Oct. 17-30) is next to Grand Canyon Lodge and is staffed with several rangers and volunteers who can direct you to the best sights and

---

Previous: view from a chair at Grand Canyon Lodge; Angels Window; Grand Canyon Lodge.

The North Rim

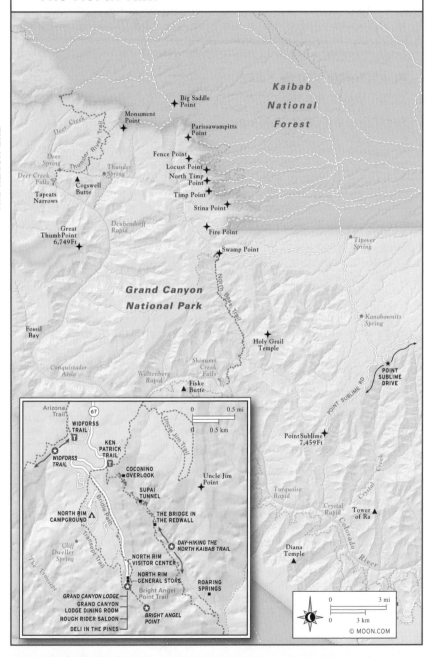

Kaibab National Forest

Big Saddle Point

Monument Point

Parissawampitts Point

Deer Creek

Fence Point

Locust Point

North Timp Point

Thunder River Trail

Deer Spring

Thunder Spring

Timp Point

Deer Creek Falls

Stina Point

Tapeats Narrows

Cogswell Butte

Deubendorff Rapid

Fire Point

Great Thumb Point 6,749 Ft

Swamp Point

Grand Canyon National Park

North Bass Trail

Tipover Spring

Fossil Bay

Kanabownits Spring

Conquistador Aisle

Waltenberg Rapid

Shinumo Creek Falls

Holy Grail Temple

Fiske Butte

POINT SUBLIME DRIVE

POINT SUBLIME RD

Arizona Trail

WIDFORSS TRAIL

67

0   0.5 mi

0   0.5 km

KEN PATRICK TRAIL

WIDFORSS TRAIL

Uncle Jim Trail

COCONINO OVERLOOK

Point Sublime 7,459 Ft

SUPAI TUNNEL

Uncle Jim Point

NORTH RIM CAMPGROUND

Bridle Path

THE BRIDGE IN THE REDWALL

Turquoise Rapid

DAY-HIKING THE NORTH KAIBAB TRAIL

Crystal Rapid

Tower of Ra

Cliff Dweller Spring

NORTH RIM VISITOR CENTER

Transept Trail

NORTH RIM GENERAL STORE

ROARING SPRINGS

Colorado River

The Transept

Bright Angel Point Trail

GRAND CANYON LODGE

Diana Temple

GRAND CANYON LODGE DINING ROOM

ROUGH RIDER SALOON

BRIGHT ANGEL POINT

DELI IN THE PINES

0   3 mi

0   3 km

© MOON.COM

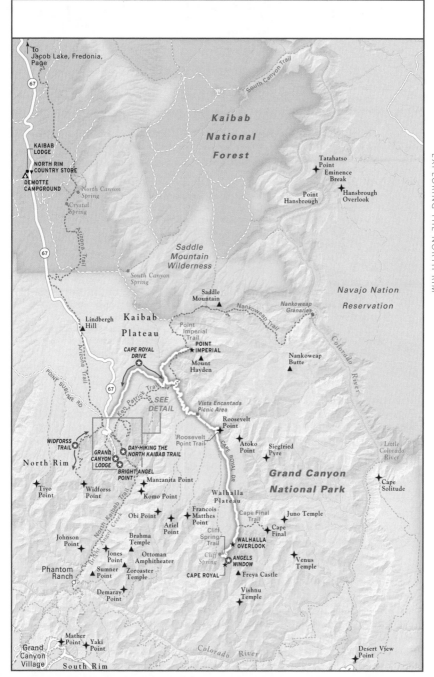

Three Days on the North Rim

An ideal visit to the North Rim lasts three full days.

DAY 1

Explore the area around **Grand Canyon Lodge** and the viewpoints reached by easy trails. Sit for a while in the lodge's sunroom and on the veranda, and walk to the edge of **Bright Angel Point** and on the rimside **Transept Trail** from the lodge to the campground and back. Then pile in the car and head north on AZ 67 to the Cape Royal Road. First veer left to **Point Imperial** and then backtrack and drive all the way to **Cape Royal** at the end of the road, stopping along the way to see the canyon from different points of view. Head back to the lodge for dinner and a nighttime ranger program.

DAY 2

Take a hike. Plan ahead the night before and pack up a picnic and other supplies while deciding which major trek to undertake. Before anything else, consider hiking a few miles down the **North Kaibab Trail** into the canyon and having a picnic and some relaxing wilderness meditation along the way. If you're up to the punishing switchbacks, try the **Widforss Trail** or the **Uncle Jim Trail** for forest-and-rim beauty and long views of the gorge.

DAY 3

Leave the park and explore one of the many fascinating areas within about a two-hour drive of the lodge, such as the **Kaibab National Forest,** which covers the Kaibab Plateau; the little-visited viewpoint at **Tuweep** (which requires a high-clearance or four-wheel-drive vehicle); or **Lees Ferry** (which can be reached easily via paved roads in a regular passenger car).

About 90 miles (145 km) northeast of the lodge below the plateau, Lees Ferry is where most canyon river trips begin, and it's one of the few places in the whole of the canyonlands where you can stick your toes in the Colorado River without having to hike deep into the gorge.

---

trails. Here you'll find fascinating exhibits on canyon science and lore, as well as a bathroom and water station. Within the visitors center the nonprofit Grand Canyon Conservancy operates an excellent bookstore with all the essential tomes and other media about Grand Canyon and the Great Southwest. This is where you go to find out the current ranger programs on offer and to bombard a hard-working ranger with all your questions about the canyon and the park.

Head to the **North Rim Backcountry Information Center** (North Rim Administration Bldg., 8am-noon and 1pm-5pm daily May 15-Oct. 15) for information and advice on hiking around the North Rim, and to apply for permits to spend the night below the rim or camping outside the North Rim Campground. There's also a bathroom and water station here.

Jacob Lake

At the junction of U.S. 89A and AZ 67, the small **Kaibab Plateau Visitor Center** (928/643-7298, www.fs.usda.gov, 8am-5pm daily mid-May-mid-Oct., free), about 44 miles (71 km) north of Grand Canyon Lodge and the North Rim, is usually staffed with a Forest Service ranger in season and offers information on the Kaibab Plateau and the Kaibab National Forest, including maps and assistance choosing and finding hiking trails. Stop here for an introduction to the canyon and the region before heading toward the rim. The visitors center is next to Jacob Lake, a small settlement without a lake of any kind, which was named for the great Mormon pathfinder Jacob Hamblin. While there is one gas station along AZ 67 between Jacob Lake and the park entrance, and there's also one inside the park, consider fueling up here to be on the safe side.

The Jacob Lake Inn is one of only three places on the entire plateau with a restaurant, and many visitors who cannot secure a hotel reservation inside the park choose to stay here.

ENTRANCE STATIONS

The lone North Rim Entrance Station to **Grand Canyon National Park** (928/638-7888, www.nps.gov/grca, 24 hours daily, $35 for seven-day pass for one private vehicle with up to 15 people; $30 for motorcycles; $20 for walk-ins, bikes, railway, and shuttle bus; children 15 and under free; rates subject to change annually) stands along AZ 67 about 30 miles (48 km) south of Jacob Lake and the U.S. 89A junction. After you pay your entrance fee, a ranger will give you a free copy of the *North Rim Pocket Map & Services Guide,* which is a valuable reference for exploring the park. If you plan to arrive outside of regular hours, you can buy a pass at www.recreation.gov and download the guide at www.nps.gov/grca, or there is a self-pay station at the visitors center where you can also pick up a free guide. From here it's another 14 miles (22.5 km) to the rim and the stately Grand Canyon Lodge and most of the park's services. AZ 67, a beautiful stretch of blacktop running through a forest mixed with evergreens, fire-blackened husks, white aspens, and green meadows, is the only road into and out of the park.

SCENIC DRIVES
★ Cape Royal Drive
23 MILES (37 KM) ONE-WAY, PLUS 3-MILE (4.8-KM) ONE-WAY SIDE TRIP

This outrageously scenic drive along the rim to Cape Royal is an essential part of the North Rim experience. The paved two-lane road twists and undulates through the green, white, and fire-blackened highland forest of tall and skinny quaking aspen, thick and shaggy conifers, and black stumps and husks of all sizes. There are several developed viewpoints along the rimside with parking, picnic tables, interpretive signs, and a few rustic benches on which you can sit back and contemplate the views. Plan to spend at least two hours one-way (it's 23 mi/37 km from Grand Canyon Lodge to Cape Royal), and at least another 30-40 minutes at nearby Point Imperial (a 3-mi/4.8-km one-way side trip; the route branches off from Cape Royal Road at mile 5.4/km 8.7). You reach several of the viewpoints via short and easy trails, so plan on doing some walking. Bring water, food, and warm clothing, and make sure that your vehicle is road-ready (no rigs over 30 ft/9.1 m long); there are no services of any kind on this road, though there are small bathrooms at Point Imperial and Cape Royal. Keep a look out for wildlife along this road, especially wild turkeys.

Get an early start and take AZ 67 north from **Grand Canyon Lodge** for 3 miles (4.8 km) to **Cape Royal Road** and turn right. At mile 5.4 (km 8.7) you need to decide whether to veer left to **Point Imperial,** a southeast-facing view of the white-rock peak **Mount Hayden** and across the red-and-green canyon to the Painted Desert on Navajoland, or continue on to the right and catch it on the way back. Either way, Point Imperial is a stop that should not be missed. Each viewpoint provides a different perspective on the canyon, so it's best to stop and spend some time at each one.

At mile 8 (km 12.9) is **Greenland Lake,** a beautiful lush meadow with a natural sink that traps rainwater and snowmelt, making this "lake" a highly variable prospect. There's also an old ranching cabin in this peaceful clearing about 200 yards (183 m) off the road, which you can reach by a short dirt trail.

At mile 10 (km 16.1) is **Vista Encantada** ("enchanting view"), which has a gorgeous view and is a great spot for a picnic. Stop here and contemplate another white-tipped, attention-grabbing peak—**Brady Peak,** just east of the picnic spot. The peak was named for Arizona pioneer Peter Brady (no relation to the Brady Bunch), who came to the territory in the impossibly early days of the 1850s and was a longtime elected official. Here you'll also see the often dry Nankoweap Creek

Cape Royal Drive

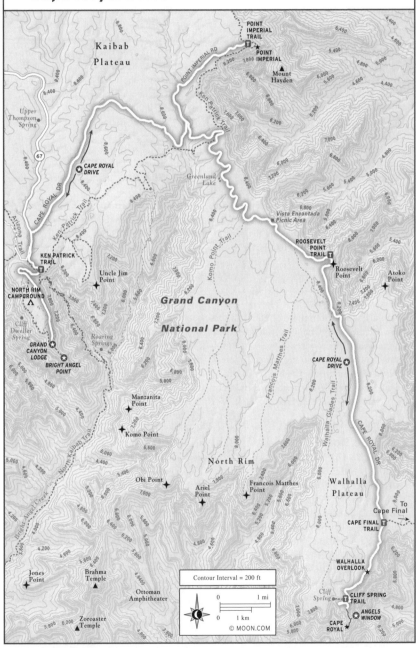

Kaibab Plateau

POINT IMPERIAL TRAIL

POINT IMPERIAL RD

POINT IMPERIAL

Mount Hayden

Ken Patrick Trail

Upper Thompson Spring

67

CAPE ROYAL DRIVE

CAPE ROYAL DR

Greenland Lake

Vista Encantada Picnic Area

Arizona Trail

Ken Patrick Trail

ROOSEVELT POINT TRAIL

Roosevelt Point

Atoko Point

KEN PATRICK TRAIL

Uncle Jim Point

Komo Point Trail

NORTH RIM CAMPGROUND

Grand Canyon

National Park

Cliff Dweller Spring

Roaring Springs

GRAND CANYON LODGE

BRIGHT ANGEL POINT

CAPE ROYAL DRIVE

CAPE ROYAL DR

Francois Matthes Trail

Manzanita Point

Walhalla Glades Trail

Komo Point

North Rim

Walhalla Plateau

North Kaibab Trail

Obi Point

Ariel Point

Francois Matthes Point

To Cape Final

CAPE FINAL TRAIL

Bright Angel Creek

WALHALLA OVERLOOK

Contour Interval = 200 ft

0   1 mi

0   1 km

© MOON.COM

Cliff Spring

CLIFF SPRING TRAIL

Jones Point

Brahma Temple

Ottoman Amphitheater

ANGELS WINDOW

Zoroaster Temple

CAPE ROYAL

etched beige against the red-and-green canyon landscape, and beyond that, if it's a clear day, you may see all the way to Navajoland and the Painted Desert.

Just up the road a bit at mile 11.7 (km 18.8) is **Roosevelt Point,** named for Teddy Roosevelt, the former U.S. president who loved Grand Canyon and spent time hunting game on the North Rim. A short loop trail (0.2 mi/0.3 km round-trip) provides the best views; take some time here strolling the trail and relaxing on the well-placed benches. Roosevelt Point, like Point Imperial and Vista Encantada, has awesome views of the eastern canyon off the **Walhalla Plateau,** a sliver plateau that sits alongside the Kaibab Plateau on its southeast side. **Tritle Peak,** topped white Kaibab limestone same as Brady and Hayden, rises 8,300 feet (2,530 m) to the east along a ridge that juts out into the canyon. It was named for F. A. Tritle, a territorial governor in 1881-1885 and early owner of the famous Jerome Copper Mine.

At mile 17.2 (km 27.7) you'll come to the **Cape Final Trailhead;** the trail is 4.2 miles (6.8 km) round-trip to a spectacular viewpoint with awesome looks at **Unkar Creek,** the **Painted Desert,** and **Freya Castle.**

Just ahead at mile 18 (km 29) are **Walhalla Overlook** and the ruin of **Walhalla Glades Pueblo,** which was occupied for about 100 years (about AD 1050-1150) by seasonal farmers from the **Unkar Delta** inside the canyon. A great red deposit at the confluence of Unkar Creek and the Colorado River, the Unkar Delta was populated and farmed from about AD 850 to AD 1200 and is visible from Walhalla Overlook. In the visitors center there's a pamphlet describing a self-guided tour of the ruin across the road.

To see where the farmers of Walhalla Glades likely obtained some of their water, stop at mile 19.1 (km 31) and take the approximately 1-mile (1.6-km) round-trip trail into the forest to **Cliff Spring.**

Finally, at mile 19.7 (km 32) you come to **Cape Royal,** a wonderful terminus with breathtaking views of the Colorado River and across the canyon to the South Rim, reached by an easy, paved trail (about 1 mi/1.6 km round-trip) lined with cliffrose, wind-sculpted pinyons and junipers, and random multicolored boulders. Along the trail you'll pass the rock arch **Angels Window,** which offers a perfectly framed view of the river.

Drive back to the lodge via the same road, and don't forget to stop at Point Imperial if you didn't already.

Point Sublime Drive
17.7 MILES (28.5 KM) ONE-WAY

Point Sublime is a hard-won viewpoint—some say the best on either rim—with 200-degree views of the canyon from a jutting rock promontory at the end of about 18 miles (29 km) of rough, rocky, narrow dirt road. It is not to be trifled with in a regular passenger car—especially not a rental! The **Point Sublime Road** is for high-clearance SUVs, Jeeps, Subarus, and trucks only (plus mountain bikes, of course).

For most of its length the road is one lane and hemmed in hard by overgrowth on either side. There are a few places where you run the risk of getting an "Arizona paint job," with the brush scratching the sides of your rig as you pass. The road winds west across the plateau through a stretch of wonderful old-growth forest—ponderosa pine, quaking aspen, spruce-fir evergreens, fallen trees, and burned areas covered in wildflowers.

Expect the drive to take at least an hour one-way, with a few stops along the way. Figure on spending half the day on this trip, better the first half; sunset out here is amazing, but driving back in the dark could be dangerous. You can camp at primitive sites out here with a permit from the **North Rim Backcountry Information Center** (North Rim Administration Bldg., 8am-noon and 1pm-5pm daily May 15-Oct. 15).

The Grand Canyon comes into view about two-thirds of the way in, and there's a small pullout and short path to an overlook. As you come up to the main attraction, **Point Sublime,** the vegetation changes quite

suddenly to wind-sculpted pinyon-juniper and desert scrub. Follow the short path out to the promontory. There are picnic tables near the parking lot at the end of the road.

To reach the Point Sublime Road, take AZ 67 north from the lodge 2.7 miles (4.3 km) and turn left (west).

Before you head out, check the most current road conditions with a ranger at the North Rim Visitor Center or the North Rim Backcountry Information Center. Also, take plenty of water and food and warm clothing, as well as tools and other backcountry-driving supplies.

TOURS
Ranger-Guided Tours

Hanging out with a park ranger, whether on a short natural-history stroll along the rim or a casual hike-and-talk through the piney forest, is an easy, free, and illuminating activity, and one that is really at the heart of the whole wonderful national park experience. For generations rangers have been our primary public-lands tour guides and educators, and it's fun and even a little nostalgic to take part in such a uniquely American tradition. Weather permitting during the high season, rangers offer a few daily walks and hikes focusing on some aspect of the natural setting and the history of human habitation in and around Grand Canyon. None of these walks is strenuous, and the rangers are typically witty and knowledgeable, having honed their presentations to a sharp edge. Check the visitors center for a daily list of the ranger-guided tours on offer. You can also check online (go. nps.gov/gc_programs).

Mule Rides

Sure-footed and indomitable mules work hard all season on the North Rim just as they do on the South, carrying tourists up and down the North Kaibab Trail and through the rimtop forest in one of the foundational experiences of Grand Canyon National Park. Look at the old photos and you'll see that everybody used to do it—presidents, celebrities, aristocrats, and the Brady kids. Of course, that was long ago in those leisurely days before rushing rim-to-rim in one day became the fashion. Mules are fascinating creatures, and if you don't mind being in a large group, a ride can be a memorable and anecdote-inspiring activity. **Grand Canyon Trail Rides** (desk inside Grand Canyon Lodge, 435/679-8665, www. canyonrides.com, 8:30am-1:30pm daily May 15-Oct. 15, $45-90), the same company that works the mules at nearby Zion and Bryce Canyon National Parks, offers three daily options during the high season: a one-hour trail ride through the forest and along the rim (must be at least 7 years old and 222 lbs/101 kg or less, $45); a three-hour trail ride along the rim to Uncle Jim's Point (at least 10 years old, 200 lbs/91 kg or less, $90); and a three-hour trail ride 2 miles (3.2 km) down the North Kaibab Trail (2,300 ft/701 m) to Supai Tunnel (at least 10 years old, 200 lbs/91 kg or less, $90), where there are pit toilets and drinking water. If you are trying to choose between the two three-hour tours, take the ride into the canyon to Supai Tunnel. It's a whole different world below the rim and you have a chance to see some of it on this ride, so take it. A shuttle bus picks you up at the lodge a half hour before your ride and takes you to the trailhead.

Backcountry and Educational Tours

Other than the North Kaibab Trail, the backpacking routes from the North Rim are all remote and difficult, requiring expert knowledge and a lot of planning and preparation. They also provide some of the purest wilderness solitude and mystical grandeur in the park. A great way to mount an expedition to one of these more out-of-the-way spots above and below the rim is to follow a guide from the **Grand Canyon Conservancy Field Institute** (928/638-2485 or 866/471-4435, www.grandcanyon. org, gccfi@grandcanyon.org, $200-1,000).

1: Point Imperial, the highest spot on the North Rim
2: Unkar Delta region along the Cape Royal Drive

Recent North Rim guided backpacking offerings from the nonprofit canyon advocacy group have included "Natural and Cultural History" trips to Nankoweap Canyon, along the Kanab Creek Trail, and rim-to-rim. The field institute also offers shorter, less strenuous North Rim retreats for artists, painters, and photographers. Check the website for a list of scheduled trips and workshops, which change every year.

Sights

Other than the unmissable Grand Canyon Lodge, the sights here are primarily views of Grand Canyon from different points on the rim. All but two of these viewpoints are reached by Cape Royal Road, a 23-mile (37-km) winding paved road over the forested Walhalla Plateau. Bright Angel Point is reached via a short walk along a paved trail behind Grand Canyon Lodge; Toroweap Overlook in the remote Tuweep area is quite a bit wilder, requiring at least a full day and a long, rough drive.

★ GRAND CANYON LODGE

You don't need to have a reservation to enjoy the best parts of **Grand Canyon Lodge**, the very center of the North Rim universe and one of the most dramatic and enchanting railroad-built lodges in the West. Here's a plan for your first sight of Grand Canyon from this high forested rim: Park at the lodge, enter through the front doors, and proceed down a short flight of stairs to the sunroom. Through the large, south-facing picture windows you will catch your first glimpse of the awful, impossible labyrinth, accompanied by clear, streaming sunlight and the soft, sinking comfort of a couch facing the edge of world. After a while, if you can bring yourself to rise, head out to the lodge's amazing veranda, sit back down in one of the Adirondack chairs hanging over the canyon, and explore the forest-and-desert dichotomy with the added benefit of a cool, sap-scented breeze. Once you've taken in the view from both of these comfortable and contemplative vantages, descend the veranda stairs and walk the easy trail down to Bright Angel Point.

Working for the Union Pacific Railroad and North Rim concessionaire Utah Parks Co. in 1927, Gilbert Stanley Underwood, a master of the National Park Service Rustic style who also designed Bryce Canyon Lodge and Zion Lodge, created the original lodge building out of local plateau rock and wood. After a fire in 1932 destroyed all but the limestone foundation, a scaled-back lodge was built on the ruin using similar local materials; it reopened in 1937. This treasured National Historic Landmark is still a dreamed-of destination nearly a century on.

Don't miss the adorable sunroom statue of **Brighty,** a legendary North Rim mule and the subject of the 1953 children's book *Brighty of the Grand Canyon* by Marguerite Henry, for sale in the gift shop. The lodge is closed mid-October-mid-May.

TOP EXPERIENCE

★ BRIGHT ANGEL POINT

A kind of natural stone jetty hovering above an empty red-and-green sea, **Bright Angel Point** (8,161 ft/2,487 m) is the primary North Rim lookout, reached via a paved but somewhat steep 0.25-mile (0.4-km) one-way trail behind Grand Canyon Lodge.

Not only does this often-crowded area provide several jutting views of the canyon (including of Roaring Springs Canyon, the side canyon called the Transept, and on a clear day

1: mule train descending the North Kaibab Trail
2: Grand Canyon Lodge

the South Rim), it also offers the perfect vantage from which to view the lodge as it looms above like a natural extension of the rim itself. You will not likely be alone in this area. To spend some quality time here without crowds, get up early and watch the new morning sun hit the red rocks covered with dewy evergreens, welcoming the day on the precipice of a hazy labyrinth whose intricacies defy belief.

POINT IMPERIAL

A view to the southeast toward Navajoland and the Painted Desert, **Point Imperial** is absolutely worth the scenic 11-mile (17.7-km) drive from the visitors center. At 8,803 feet (2,683 m) it's the highest point on the North Rim, providing glimpses for the sharp-eyed of the mouth of the **Little Colorado River,** the imposing canyon cliffs known as **Palisades of the Desert,** and even **Humphreys Peak,** Arizona's highest at 12,633 feet (3,851 m), some 67 miles (108 km) away in the blue distance. Much closer to the rim, you can see the celebrated **Mount Hayden,** an 8,372-foot (2,552-m) white sandstone peak at the end of a long ridge of red dirt. Named for Arizona pioneer businessman Charles T. Hayden (as are many buildings in Tempe and at Arizona State University, both of which he helped establish), the elegantly eroded peak is a frequent subject for North Rim photographers.

Take AZ 67 north from the visitors center and after 3 miles (4.8 km) turn right onto Cape Royal Road. At mile 5.4 (km 8.7) veer left to Point Imperial. The developed viewpoint has parking, bathrooms, picnic tables, and benches for sitting down when the view buckles your knees.

WALHALLA OVERLOOK AND WALHALLA GLADES PUEBLO

Stop at **Walhalla Overlook,** along Cape Royal Drive about 18 miles (29 km) from the turnoff, for a view into the history of human life in Grand Canyon and on the North Rim. From here you can see the red deposits at the confluence of Unkar Creek and the Colorado River known as the Unkar Delta. A relatively large group of Ancestral Puebloan farmers lived inside the great canyon and worked the delta from about AD 850 to AD 1200. During the latter part of this period the people of the Unkar Delta most likely built the **Walhalla Glades Pueblo** on the rim just across the road from the overlook, occupying it in summer from about AD 1050 to AD 1150. This part of the high country is called the Walhalla Plateau, a "peninsula" surrounded on three sides by the canyon that's slightly lower than the rest of the Kaibab and therefore subject to warmer air and earlier snowmelts, which is likely why the farmers chose this area to build their small summer-farming homes and storage rooms. There's a pamphlet describing a self-guided tour of the six-room ruin at the visitors center. All that remains of this once bustling little outpost is a series of low rock walls that outline what used to be the rooms of the Pueblo, but with a little imagination it's possible to speculate about what life would have been like for these hardy North Rim pioneers.

CAPE ROYAL

Offering the most expansive view of the canyon on either rim, **Cape Royal** provides long and wide vistas extending from the Palisades of the Desert, to the Colorado River deep within, to the bustling South Rim off in the hazy distance. About 23 miles (37 km) from the visitors center at the very edge of the plateau, the final stop on the rim, Cape Royal begins with a large gravel parking lot and a couple of rustic bathrooms. Walk the easy and paved 0.6-mile (1 km) round-trip trail lined with interpretive signs and high-country flora like pinyon pine and cliffrose. At the end of the path you'll be at Cape Royal, from which you can see such lonely and silent, isolated eroded-rock islands as Vishnu Temple, Horseshoe Mesa, and Wotan's Throne.

★ Angels Window

Along the trail to the viewpoint, you'll pass the amazing natural arch called **Angels**

Window, a squiggly upside-down triangle of sandstone somehow knocked out of an imposing white-rock outcropping. The window is also a perfect frame for a small section of the Colorado River, and you can walk over the rock out to the very edge of the outcropping (on top of the window), which is protected by a railing, for one of the most thrilling views on the North Rim.

TUWEEP

A far-flung unit of Grand Canyon National Park, **Tuweep** (www.nps.gov/grca/planyourvisit/tuweep.htm) includes a high desert rimside viewpoint, **Toroweap Overlook** (4,552 ft/1,387 m elevation), and a primitive campground. Few visitors make it out to this dry, scrubby country, but those who do report solitude and adventure. A trip here requires a lot of preplanning and the right weather (dry). Still, if you have the wherewithal and the time to do it safely, a trip to this backcountry spot will not soon be forgotten.

A former haunt of the Paiute, Tuweep (pronounced tu-VEEP) sits 3,000 precipitous feet (914 m) above the Colorado River on a volcanic landform called the Esplanade, between the piney highlands of the plateau and the canyon's scorched desert bottomlands. Toroweap Overlook here is less than a mile (1.6 km) across the gorge from the South Rim; this is one of the narrowest and deepest parts of the canyon. Just west of the overlook, look for a 5,102-foot (1,555-m) cinder cone called Vulcans Throne. From the lookout you'll get almost close-up views of the Colorado River below, and if you're lucky you might see a few rafters going by.

Toroweap is a Paiute term meaning, roughly, "dry and barren valley." The word is used to describe the arid flatlands that stretch west along the rim below the plateau and are significantly lower in elevation than the North and South Rims. Tuweep (meaning "earth"

in Paiute) was the name of the old ranching and mining settlement in the area, and now refers to this remote area of Grand Canyon National Park.

To cross this brushy volcanic landscape of juniper and pinyon, devoid of water and succor, lonely and now the domain of desert rats, canyon hoppers, and backcountry explorers, you must have a high-clearance vehicle, or better yet a four-wheel drive. Bring along extra water, food, and warm clothing as well as a tire pump, patches, and maybe even a few extra tires, as the route is known to be particularly hard on them. If you get stuck out here, you really can't be sure of getting any help, and don't expect to have cell coverage; you must be prepared for anything.

Camping

The campground at Tuweep has nine small sites for up to six people each with a picnic table. You must obtain a backcountry permit (www.nps.gov/grca/planyourvisit/backcountry-permit.htm, $10 plus $8 pp per night) and a reservation. Fires and charcoal grills are prohibited. There is no water here, but there are compost toilets; you must pack out everything else.

Getting There

The 126-mile (203-km) drive from the Grand Canyon Lodge on the North Rim to Tuweep will take you at least 3.5 hours in perfect conditions. Do not attempt to go during the summer rainy season—or if you do, go before afternoon when the storms typically start. When the road gets wet you are bound to get hopelessly stuck in the mud. Take AZ 67 to Jacob Lake (44 mi/71 km), and then descend the plateau via U.S. 89A to Fredonia (30 mi/48 km). In Fredonia go west on AZ 389 (Pratt St.) to Country Road 109 (8 mi/12.9 km west of Fredonia). Turn left onto Country Road 109 and drive 61 miles (98 km) of rough road to the rim.

Winter on the North Rim

Ranging in elevation from about 6,000 feet (1,829 m) to 9,200 feet (2,804 m), the forested Kaibab Plateau towers over the surrounding desert grasslands of the Arizona Strip, an island of pine, spruce-fir, aspen, and green meadows whose southern edge falls away into the vast maze-like canyon that spreads out beyond comprehension. The Colorado River moves through the deep gorge below, inaccessible and useless to rim life, while snowmelt seeps into the Kaibab limestone that forms the top layer of the plateau and creates the life-giving springs that make life and vacations possible here.

Already one of the most remote and isolated regions in the continental United States, the Kaibab Plateau and the North Rim of Grand Canyon become even more so during the long highland winter. While U.S. 89A across the plateau's northern tip generally remains open (if snowbound and sparsely traveled) and the Jacob Lake Inn provides a tiny spark of warm civilization during the cold months, the North Rim section of Grand Canyon National Park is closed from late fall until May 15—more than half the year! Grand Canyon Lodge closes in mid-October, taking most of the park's services with it. The campground is open for a bit longer, and remains a primitive campground without perks of any kind and requiring a backcountry permit to access throughout the winter.

The plateau averages about 142 inches (361 cm) of snow every year, with the most snow and the coldest temperatures coming in January and February. The record annual snowfall happened in 1978, when the Kaibab received about 273 inches (693 cm). From November to March temperatures generally range from highs in the 30s F (-1°C to 4°C) and 40s F (4-9°C) to lows in the teens (-12°C to -7°C) and 20s F (-7°C to -2°C). The days at least start to warm up a bit in April and May, but there are often patches of snow remaining when the park opens for the summer. Back in February 1985 the low plummeted to -22°F (-30°C), a record that remains unbroken.

But it's the getting there after the first snowfall (typically around early December) closes AZ 67, the 45-mile (72-km) road to the rim from Jacob Lake, that really limits the North Rim's use as a winter playground. After the first major storm, AZ 67 stays closed until May 15—whether there's snow on it or not. Snowmobiles, the fastest and easiest way to move across great swaths of snow, are not allowed on AZ 67. Only snowshoe backpackers and cross-country skiers make the journey to the rim or across the plateau during winter, enjoying a sense of solitude and faraway feelings unavailable anywhere else.

Recreation

The North Rim is a hiker's destination, a land where narrow trails snake through open pine forests woven through with white-and-yellow quaking aspens, past cool green meadows and swaths of tilting black burnout sprouting new life—and all along there's this unbelievably vast, sculpted maze of variegated stone on your right or your left or directly in front of you.

Though it's covered with green forests, remember that the Kaibab Plateau is essentially an 8,000-foot-high (2,438-m) desert. There's no water to speak of anywhere, and the high altitude might make lowlanders sick. Just as it is on the South Rim, the rangers on the North Rim warn hikers strenuously and repeatedly not to take the trails here lightly, especially those that lead below the rim. Most of the day hikes listed here are easy to moderate. For serious day-hikers, there are a few hikes around 10 miles (16.1 km) long. The trail to watch out for is also the best—the steep, switchback-haunted North Kaibab, the only corridor trail from the North Rim. Never let it out of your mind that for every step you take down it, you'll have to muster a heavier step back up. Most visitors should end their North Kaibab day hikes at Supai Tunnel. For most backpackers, the North Kaibab Trail is the best way to enter the canyon from the North Rim. It's one of the three major corridor trails inside the Grand Canyon that are patrolled and recommended for first-timers by rangers. The other backpacking routes from the North Rim to the Colorado River should be left to experienced Grand Canyon explorers.

DAY HIKES
Bright Angel Point Trail
Distance: 0.5 mile (0.8 km) round-trip
Duration: 30 minutes
Elevation gain: 200 feet (61 m)
Effort: Easy
Trail conditions: Paved
Trailheads: Log shelter in the parking lot near the visitors center, or in the back of the lodge off the veranda

This paved rim-edge pathway lined with warped boulders and gnarled pines leads down a relatively steep incline to one of the most popular spots on the North Rim, a jutting lookout called **Bright Angel Point,** which provides a sweeping, jaw-dropping view of **Bright Angel Canyon, Roaring Springs,** and across the great maze to **Grand Canyon Village** on the South Rim about 10 miles (16.1 km) away. From Bright Angel and two other jutting viewpoints behind the lodge, you'll see the side canyon called the **Transept,** the **San Francisco Peaks** far away near Flagstaff, as well as popular god-titled landmarks such as **Brahma Temple, Deva Temple,** and **Zoroaster Temple.** The trail can be negotiated by just about everyone, but should not be underestimated due to its stairs and steepness. There are benches here and there for rest and contemplation. During the summer high season this area behind Grand Canyon Lodge can become crowded. For a more solitary experience, walk this trail early in the morning. There are pamphlets available at the trailheads that explain the geology of the area, including pointing out the many ancient fossils in the rocks along the trail.

Transept Trail
Distance: 3 miles (4.8 km) round-trip
Duration: 1.5 hours
Elevation gain: 200 feet (61 m)
Effort: Easy
Trail conditions: Mostly flat and hard-packed dirt, some sand and dust
Trailheads: Grand Canyon Lodge or North Rim Campground

The **Transept Trail** leads north from behind Grand Canyon Lodge along the forested rim of the **Transept,** a deep side canyon southwest of the lodge, and ends in the woods just beyond the North Rim Campground. It's a useful trail if you're staying at the campground and don't want to use your car every time you go to the lodge area. This is also a good trail to take if you are going to the general store from the lodge area. Even if you're not staying at the campground or going to the store, this trail is worth walking to see the canyon from different points along the rim and to spend some time in the oak-and-pine forest.

There are benches along the trail for resting and staring, and it's a good spot, especially early in the morning, for seeing small groups of grazing deer, busy squirrels running up and down the pines trees, and maybe even a prissy and hurried wild turkey with a line of chicks following close behind. Don't miss the small **Ancestral Puebloan ruin** along this trail about midway to the campground, once a two-room home for seasonal farmers. This trail can be made into a 3.6-mile (5.8-km) loop by taking the **Bridle Path** back to the lodge area.

Bridle Path
Distance: 3 miles (4.8 km) round-trip
Duration: 1 hour
Elevation gain: Negligible
Effort: Easy
Trail conditions: Flat and hard-packed dirt
Trailheads: Grand Canyon Lodge or North Kaibab Trail parking lot

The **Bridle Path** is another very useful trail for exploring the park or just getting from one place to another. The trail of hard-packed

North Rim Hikes

Trail	Effort	Distance	Duration
Bright Angel Point Trail	Easy	0.5 mi/0.8 km round-trip	30 minutes
Transept Trail	Easy	3 mi/4.8 km round-trip	1.5 hours
Bridle Path	Easy	3 mi/4.8 km round-trip	1 hour
North Kaibab Trail	Strenuous to very strenuous	28 mi/45 km round-trip to Phantom Ranch and river	2-3 days or more
Coconino Overlook	Moderate	1.5 mi/2.4 km round-trip	· 1-2 hours
Supai Tunnel	Strenuous	4 mi/6.4 km round-trip	3-4 hours
The Bridge in the Redwall	Strenuous	5.2 mi/8.4 km round-trip	4-6 hours
Roaring Springs	Very strenuous	9.4 mi/15.1 km round-trip	7-8 hours
Point Imperial Trail	Easy	4.4 mi/7.1 km round-trip	2 hours
Roosevelt Point Trail	Easy	0.2 mi/0.3 km round-trip	20 minutes
Cape Final Trail	Easy	4.2 mi/6.8 km round-trip	2 hours
Cliff Spring Trail	Easy	1 mi/1.6 km round-trip	1 hour
Cape Royal Trail	Easy	0.6 mi/1 km round-trip	30 minutes
Widforss Trail	Easy to moderate	10 mi/16.1 km round-trip	4-6 hours
Self-guided tour	Easy	5 mi/8 km round-trip	2-3 hours
Uncle Jim Trail	Easy to moderate	5 mi/8 km round-trip	2-3 hours
Ken Patrick Trail	Moderate	10 mi/16.1 km one-way	5-6 hours
Arizona Trail	Moderate	12 mi/19.3 km one-way	5-6 hours
Thunder River Trail and Deer Creek	Very strenuous	15 mi/24 km one-way to river	2-3 days or more
North Bass Trail	Very strenuous	13.5 mi/21.7 km one-way to river	3-4 days or more
Nankoweap Trail	Very strenuous	14 mi/22.5 km one-way to river	3-4 days or more

1: Transept Trail **2:** North Kaibab Trail

dirt is open to walkers, bicycles, and dogs on leashes—the only trail in the North Rim section of the park that allows pets and bikes. It runs for about 1.5 miles through tall pines, passing all the main park buildings and paralleling AZ 67 all the way to the **North Kaibab Trailhead.** This trail can get busy, and with the bikes and dogs added into the mix it requires heads-up hiking at all times. One of the best ways to use this trail if you are staying at the campground is to bring your bikes along and ride it back and forth from the lodge complex to your campsite.

★ North Kaibab Trail

Distance: 1.5-9.4 miles (2.4-15.1 km) round-trip
Duration: 2-8 hours
Elevation gain: 3,050 feet (930 m) from trailhead to Roaring Springs
Effort: Moderate to very strenuous
Trail conditions: Rocky, sandy in places, mule leavings on upper sections, dusty and technical in parts
Trailhead: 1.5 miles (2.4 km) north of Grand Canyon Lodge on east side of AZ 67

The **North Kaibab Trail** starts out among the coniferous heights of the North Rim. The forest surrounding the trail soon dries out and becomes a red-rock desert, the trail cut into the rock face of the cliffs and twisting down improbable routes hard against the cliffs, with nothing but your sanity keeping you away from the gorge. This is the only patrolled North Rim route down into the inner canyon and to the Colorado River. Sooner than you realize, the walls close in, and you are deep in the canyon, the trees on the rim just green blurs now.

A good introduction to this corridor trail and ancient native route is the short, 1.5-mile (2.4-km) round-trip jog down to the **Coconino Overlook,** from which, on a clear day, you can see the San Francisco Peaks and the South Rim. A 4-mile (6.4-km) round-trip hike down will get you to **Supai Tunnel,** opened up out of the red rock in the 1930s by the Civilian Conservation Corps. A little more than a mile (1.6 km) onward you'll reach **The**

Bridge in the Redwall (5.2 miles round-trip), built in 1966 after a flood ruined this portion of the trail.

For a tough, all-day hike that will likely have you sore but smiling the next morning, take the North Kaibab roughly 5 miles (8 km) down to **Roaring Springs,** the source of life-giving Bright Angel Creek. The springs fall headlong out of the cliffside and spray mist and rainbows into the hot air. Just remember, you also have to go 5 miles (8 km) back up.

Start hiking as early as you can no matter what the season. In the summer it's not even debatable. You may be on the North Rim, but it's still dangerously hot inside the canyon. Try to be out and done by 10am during the hot months. Though not as important from a safety perspective in spring and early fall, an early start will then put you ahead of the crowds and more likely to see wildlife along the trail.

The trailhead has a decent-sized parking lot, though it fills up during the high season, so the earlier you get here the better. You can also arrange for a shuttle from Grand Canyon Lodge, or walk 1.5 miles (2.4 km) from the lodge to the trailhead via the Bridle Path.

COCONINO OVERLOOK

Distance: 1.5 miles (2.4 km) round-trip
Duration: 1-2 hours
Elevation gain: 800 feet (244 m)
Effort: Moderate
Trail conditions: Rocky, sandy in parks, dusty, steep; mule leavings

A casual hiker's first curious and tentative step below the rim, **Coconino Overlook** provides a natural turnaround spot just under a mile (1.6 km) down from the North Kaibab Trailhead. This early stretch is still home to dark and shady highland pine and oak and juniper, and you feel enclosed in the forest as you stop and rest and gawk at the large table of sandstone at Coconino Overlook. But off in the distance the desert world of the inner canyon comes into view in **Bright Angel and Roaring Springs Canyons** below. Keep an eye out for mule trains, and watch your feet

Day-Hiking the North Kaibab Trail

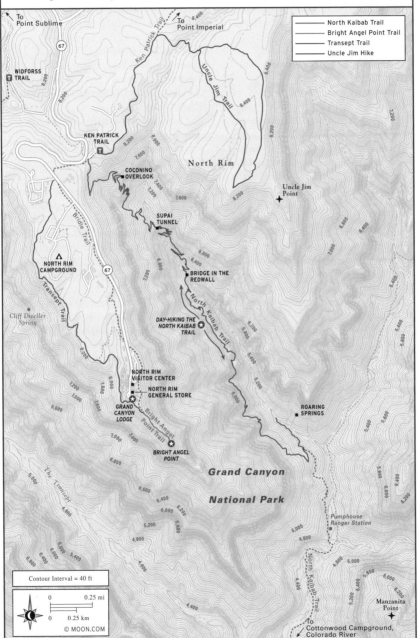

Legend:
- North Kaibab Trail
- Bright Angel Point Trail
- Transept Trail
- Uncle Jim Hike

To Point Sublime

To Point Imperial

67

WIDFORSS TRAIL

Ken Patrick Trail

Uncle Jim Trail

KEN PATRICK TRAIL

North Rim

COCONINO OVERLOOK

Uncle Jim Point

Bridle Trail

SUPAI TUNNEL

NORTH RIM CAMPGROUND

67

BRIDGE IN THE REDWALL

Transept Trail

Cliff Dweller Spring

North Kaibab Trail

DAY-HIKING THE NORTH KAIBAB TRAIL

NORTH RIM VISITOR CENTER

NORTH RIM GENERAL STORE

GRAND CANYON LODGE

ROARING SPRINGS

Bright Angel Point Trail

BRIGHT ANGEL POINT

Grand Canyon

National Park

The Transept

Pumphouse Ranger Station

North Kaibab Trail

Manzanita Point

Contour Interval = 40 ft

0   0.25 mi

0   0.25 km

© MOON.COM

To Cottonwood Campground, Colorado River

THE NORTH RIM

RECREATION

for the puddles and piles of the mule leavings. This is a short hike, but the North Kaibab Trail isn't easy at any point, so make sure you take plenty of water and snacks with you.

SUPAI TUNNEL

Distance: 4 miles (6.4 km) round-trip
Duration: 3-4 hours
Elevation gain: 1,450 feet (442 m)
Effort: Strenuous
Trail conditions: Rocky, sandy in parks, dusty, steep; mule leavings

Active hikers who want to get a true idea of the world below the rim should go at least as far as **Supai Tunnel,** a steep and strenuous hike but one that is rewarded with awesome views and a new, hard-won perspective on the canyon. However, unless you are a highly prepared, experienced, and healthy day-hiker, don't go beyond this point. Among the spring-fed greenery around Supai Tunnel, which makes for a great picture, there is a potable water spigot and a vault toilet. Here you are surrounded by the 300-million-year-old Supai Group, which Civilian Conservation Corps crews blew up back in the 1930s to create the short tunnel. At this elevation a brushy and gnarled pinyon-juniper woodland prevails, which will soon give way to the desert scrub and riparian vegetation along the canyon floor.

THE BRIDGE IN THE REDWALL

Distance: 5.2 miles (8.4 km) round-trip
Duration: 4-6 hours
Elevation gain: 2,150 feet (655 m)
Effort: Strenuous
Trail conditions: Rocky, steep, sandy in parts, dusty, technical, narrow

Only the toughest, most experienced and prepared day-hikers should attempt to hike to **The Bridge in the Redwall,** a bridge across Roaring Springs Canyon far below the forested rim. After Supai Tunnel the trail drops steeply into **Roaring Springs Canyon** and becomes a series of brutal switchbacks with heat washing off the rock walls. Stop in the middle of the bridge and look both ways up and down the side canyon, with its strange mixture of evergreens and desert scrub. If you're quiet you can almost hear the water rushing from Roaring Springs up ahead.

ROARING SPRINGS

Distance: 9.4 miles (15.1 km) round-trip
Duration: 7-8 hours
Elevation gain: 3,050 feet (930 m)
Effort: Very strenuous
Trail conditions: Rocky, steep, sandy in parts, dusty, technical, narrow

A lush and beautiful desert mini-oasis, **Roaring Springs** provides water for both the North and South Rims, as the Muav limestone in this section forms an impervious layer of rock and traps the snowmelt seeping through the plateau's higher stone levels, creating a pool that drains out of the cliffs where it can.

Between the bridge and Roaring Springs, the trail runs along a Redwall limestone ridge to a thrilling cliff-face section from which you can see the old pump house at Roaring Springs and a line of greenery along the creek. The narrow rock trail has been chiseled and blasted out of the 340-million-year-old limestone here and passes a tall spire called **"The Needle."** At 4 miles (6.4 km) there's a short spur off the North Kaibab to the left. After about a quarter mile (0.4 km) the trail ends near the creek, where there's a few picnic tables and you can cool your feet in the cold rushing water. Don't drink the water without treating it.

A day hike to Roaring Springs is a major undertaking and should not be attempted by any but the most prepared and experienced day-hikers.

Point Imperial Trail

Distance: 4.4 miles (7.1 km) round-trip
Duration: 2 hours
Elevation gain: Negligible
Effort: Easy
Trail conditions: Dirt, some rocks and overgrowth
Trailhead: Point Imperial parking lot, at mile 5.4 (km 8.7) up Cape Royal Road

A primarily flat and easy trail, this route

leads through a large wildfire-altered landscape that's exploding with new life, sprouting young aspens and pines here at the highest point on the North Rim. This out-and-back trail provides an interesting perspective on the long cycle of destruction and creation that rules the Southwest's highland forests. This is the **Saddle Mountain** area, the eastern edge of the plateau, with excellent views of **Marble Canyon** and **Navajo Mountain**. The turnaround point is a gate that marks the park's northern edge about 2.2 miles (3.5 km) in.

Roosevelt Point Trail

Distance: 0.2 mile (0.3 km) round-trip
Duration: 20 minutes
Elevation gain: Negligible
Effort: Easy
Trail conditions: Flat and overgrown
Trailhead: Roosevelt Point, at mile 11.7 (km 18.8) on Cape Royal Road

This very short, very easy loop trail around **Roosevelt Point** goes through a burned area that is choked and overgrowing with new groundcover but missing the more mature ponderosa pines. The short hike past a few inviting benches and through the brushy rimland offers great views of the eastern canyon. This is a good choice for those who want to take a short walk and feel a bit of the solitude that the North Rim can provide without having to undertake a major expedition.

Cape Final Trail

Distance: 4.2 miles (6.8 km) round-trip
Duration: 2 hours
Elevation gain: 150 feet (46 m)
Effort: Easy
Trail conditions: Old dirt road with a few rocks
Trailhead: Dirt parking lot at mile 17.2 (km 27.7) on Cape Royal Road, about 3 miles (4.8 km) from Cape Royal

Geologist Clarence Dutton, whose love of grandeur and ancient world religions can be discerned in nearly every Grand Canyon landmark he named, gave **Cape Final** its rather peremptory title in 1882 after riding his horse out to the promontory and declaring it "doubtless the most interesting spot on the Kaibab." You can judge for yourself by hiking this easy trail through the pine trees, green brush, and burned spots to a promontory on the Walhalla Plateau with views of **Unkar Creek, Painted Desert,** and **Freya Castle.**

Cliff Spring Trail

Distance: 1 mile (1.6 km) round-trip
Duration: 1 hour
Elevation gain: 150 feet (46 m)
Effort: Easy
Trail conditions: Rocky, steep, narrow
Trailhead: Across the road from a small pullout at mile 19.1 (km 31) on Cape Royal Road, 0.3 mile (0.5 km) from Cape Royal

Take this short trail downhill into the forest of pine, oak, and aspen, away from the rim, to one of the many North Rim springs seeping and trickling out a shady overhang of Kaibab limestone. Like Dripping Spring down the South Rim's Hermit Trail, just a trickle of water creates a relatively lush microclimate here, surely one of the reasons why Ancestral Puebloan farmers lived nearby and built a **granary** along the trail, the ruins of which can be seen about 100 yards (91 m) from the trailhead. Don't drink the water without treating it first.

Cape Royal Trail

Distance: 0.6 mile (1 km) round-trip
Duration: 30 minutes
Elevation gain: Negligible
Effort: Easy
Trail conditions: Paved
Trailhead: Cape Royal parking lot, at mile 19.7 (km 32) on Cape Royal Road

The **Cape Royal Trail** is a paved pathway lined with strange multicolored boulders and cliffrose, pinyon, and juniper, ending at a fenced-in, rock-slab promontory from which you get one of the park's most expansive and thrilling views of Grand Canyon. Along the way to the **Cape Royal viewpoint,** you'll pass the improbable **Angels Window,** which frames the bending Colorado River far below. Take a detour and walk out on the rock promontory on top of Angels Window before moving on to the end. There are primitive bathrooms in the trailhead's large parking lot.

★ Widforss Trail

Distance: 10 miles (16.1 km) round-trip
Duration: 4-6 hours
Elevation gain: 1,000 feet (305 m)
Effort: Easy to moderate
Trail conditions: Packed dirt, sometimes rocky, dusty, undulating
Trailhead: From Grand Canyon Lodge, drive north on AZ 67 for 2.7 miles (4.3 km), turn left (west) onto a dirt road (Point Sublime Rd.), and follow signs to trailhead.

Named for the 1920s-1930s canyon painter Gunnar Widforss, the undulating, wildflower-lined **Widforss Trail** leads along the rim of Transept Canyon and through ponderosa pine, fir, and spruce forest, with a few stands of aspen and burned areas mixed in, for 5 miles (8 km) to **Widforss Point,** where you can stare across the great chasm and rest before heading back.

The trail starts out on the edge of **Harvey Meadow,** home to an early North Rim tourist camp. Across the meadow there's a cave with a doorway, which famed lion-killer Uncle Jim Owens used from time to time. Intermediate

to expert hikers will have no problem hiking the entire 10-mile (16.1-km) round-trip route in less than four hours.

For a **shorter hike,** pick up the **free guide** to the Widforss Trail at the trailhead or the visitors center. It proposes a **5-mile (8-km) round-trip hike** on the first half of the trail (about 2-3 hours) and includes a map and information on the natural and human history of the North Rim.

There is no water available along this trail, so come prepared.

Uncle Jim Trail

Distance: 5 miles (8 km) round-trip
Duration: 2-3 hours
Elevation gain: 200 feet (61 m)
Effort: Easy to moderate
Trail conditions: Packed dirt, rocky in parts
Trailhead: North Kaibab Trail parking lot

Take this easy, flat trail through the forest to watch backpackers winding their way down the North Kaibab Trail's twisting switchbacks and maybe be passed by a mule train or two along the way. The **Uncle Jim Trail,** named for an old game warden who bragged of killing more than 500 Kaibab Plateau mountain lions, winds through old stands of spruce and fir, sprinkled with quaking aspen, to **Uncle**

Widforss Trail

Widforss Trail

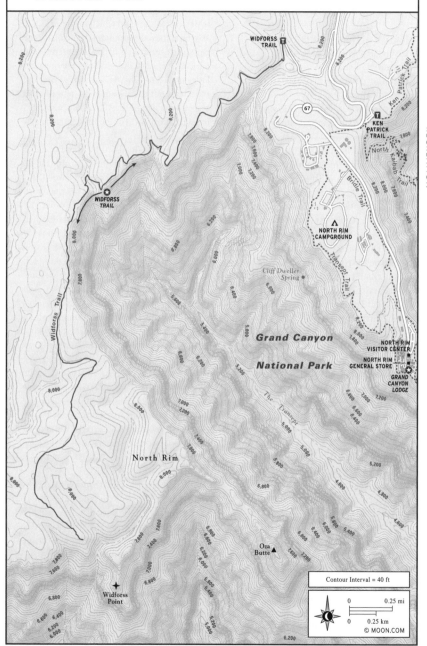

WIDFORSS
TRAIL

67

KEN
PATRICK
TRAIL

Ken Patrick Trail

WIDFORSS
TRAIL

Widforss Trail

North Kaibab Trail

Bridle Trail

NORTH RIM
CAMPGROUND

Transept Trail

Cliff Dweller
Spring

Grand Canyon

National Park

NORTH RIM
VISITOR CENTER
NORTH RIM
GENERAL STORE

GRAND
CANYON
LODGE

The Transept

North Rim

Oza
Butte

Widforss
Point

Contour Interval = 40 ft

| 0 | 0.25 mi |
| 0 | 0.25 km |

© MOON.COM

Jim Point, where you can let out your best roar into the tributary known as Roaring Springs Canyon.

Ken Patrick Trail

Distance: 10 miles (16.1 km) one-way
Duration: 5-6 hours
Elevation gain: 1,000 feet (305 m)
Effort: Moderate
Trail conditions: Packed dirt, rocky in parts
Trailheads: Point Imperial or North Kaibab Trail parking lot

The beautiful and tranquil Ken Patrick Trail winds through thick, sun-dappled forest of pine, spruce-fir, and aspen, much of it burned out and blackened by wildfire, for 10 miles (16.1 km) between the North Kaibab Trail parking lot and Point Imperial (the highest point on the North Rim) off the Cape Royal Road. This and the Widforss Trail are the best routes on the North Rim for getting to know the highland forest. If you want to do the whole trail as a day hike, have a friend drop you off at Point Imperial and then pick you up at North Kaibab, or the other way around. You could also leave a car at Point Imperial and then drive another car to the other end.

A lot of hikers will cut the hike down to **6 miles (9.7 km) round-trip** (2.5-3 hours) by starting at Point Imperial and turning around when the trail reaches the Cape Royal Road after a set of sandstone steps.

There's no water on the trail.

Arizona Trail

Distance: 12 miles (19.3 km) one-way
Duration: 5-6 hours
Elevation gain: Negligible
Effort: Moderate
Trail conditions: Dirt, rocky, sand in places
Trailhead: Near North Kaibab Trail parking lot

A 12-mile (19.3-km) section of the monumental **Arizona Trail,** which traverses the state from south to north, starts at the North Kaibab Trail parking lot, winds and undulates through the thick plateau forest, and then ends at the boundary line of the Kaibab National Forest. To do the whole 12-mile (19.3-km) North Rim section of the AZT, have someone drop you off at one end and pick you up at the other. The question then becomes which end to start and which end to end. If you're staying at the lodge or campground inside the park, start from the North Kaibab Trailhead parking lot, 1.5 miles (2.4 km) north of the lodge on AZ 67. The AZT trailhead is at the south end of the parking lot. The trail ends at a pullout along Forest Road 610, about 5.5 miles (8.9 km) north of the park entrance station. If you're coming from Jacob Lake, start from the Forest Road 610 trailhead and end at the North Kaibab Trailhead parking lot. To reach the southern trailhead from Jacob Lake, take AZ 67 south for 26 miles (42 km), turn left on Forest Road 611, drive 1.1 miles (1.8 km) and turn right on Forest Road 610, then drive 5.1 miles (8.2 km) to a pullout. Look for the AZT trail sign.

From the North Kaibab Trail parking lot, the AZT crosses AZ 67, skirts Harvey Meadow and the Widforss Trailhead, runs north through the forest and winds back around to the North Rim Entrance Station and along the highway, and ends at the forest boundary. Leashed dogs and even bicycles are allowed on the trail (though make certain that you know for sure when the Arizona Trail ends and the North Kaibab begins—otherwise you'll have to contend with a ranger if you have a dog or a bike on the wrong one). Look for the brown posts with a Kaibab Plateau Trail decal to be sure you are on the Arizona Trail.

BACKPACKING

Backpacking into and through the canyon from the North Rim is not as popular as starting out from the South Rim. It takes so much longer to get to the Kaibab Plateau from Phoenix, home to the state's only major airport, so most expeditions start on the South Rim on one of the two corridor trails, the Bright Angel Trail or the South Kaibab Trail. The South Kaibab Trail becomes the North Kaibab Trail at Phantom Ranch inside the canyon, and from there it's 14 miles (22.5 km) to the North Rim. The North Rim

Gunnar Widforss, North Rim Artist

It's an unfamiliar name, Widforss, but one that echoes across Grand Canyon from the South Rim to the North Rim and back, a name that has become a symbol for the heroic plein air struggle to capture the gorge on canvas. Born in Stockholm, Sweden, in 1879, Gunnar Mauritz Widforss had 12 brothers and sisters. Perhaps such over-crowding at home had something to do with his peripatetic artist's life spent wandering across Europe with paintbrushes and watercolors. He eventually ran out of space on the continent and landed on American shores, visiting the nation's greatest natural wonder for the first time in 1923. In a way, he never really left after that.

Widforss famously traded his watercolors and oil paintings for room and board in the Fred Harvey Company employee dorms on the South Rim. His highly re-alistic and technically exact paintings were often sold in the El Tovar gift shop. During his years exploring the canyon country, Widforss developed an affinity for the forested heights of the North Rim, where he would paint among the trees and was particularly adept at depicting the plateau's aspen groves. A gorgeous point at the end of the North Rim trail that bears his name was one of his favorite spots.

Widforss Trail leads through the forest and along the rim to Widforss Point, named for Gunnar Widforss.

In the early 1930s Widforss worked as an artist for the Works Progress Administration, for which he completed several large watercolors depicting Grand Canyon and Arizona's desert Salt River Valley, then at least 30 years away from becoming the vast Phoenix metropolitan area as we know it today. Widforss's death came too soon, in 1934, under tragic circumstances. He had just been diagnosed with a deadly heart condition that required him to immediately move to an elevation much lower than the South Rim's 7,000 feet (2,134 m). Resigned to his fate, Widforss returned to the park one last time to say goodbye to friends and gather his things. He was headed to a farewell luncheon with friends when he had a heart attack and died at the young age of 55. He is buried in the Grand Canyon Pioneer Cemetery on the South Rim.

is often the final destination for a rim-to-rim hike, or a brief stopover on the increasingly popular rim-to-rim-to-rim hike—South Rim to North Rim and then back to the South Rim! If you want to stay at the North Rim lodge after hiking across the canyon from the south, October is the last month that's pos-sible. However, you can hike from the South Rim throughout the winter, spend the night at Cottonwood Campground (permit required) on the North Kaibab, and then do a day hike from the campground to the North Rim, re-turning to the canyon for the night. With a backcountry permit you can also camp at the North Rim Campground November 1-May 15,

though the conditions are primitive and there may be snow on the ground.

For all but the most highly experienced and prepared Grand Canyon backpackers, the North Kaibab is the only viable route into the canyon from the North Rim. Though there are several rim-to-river trails mentioned below, these are some of the most difficult and remote trails in the canyon and should not be undertaken by first-timers or casual backpackers.

Permits and Hiker Shuttle

All overnight trips below the rim require a backcountry permit from Grand Canyon

National Park's **Backcountry Information Center** (928/638-7875, fax 928/638-2125, www.nps.gov/grca, grca_bic@nps.gov, $10 plus $8 pp per night). The earlier you apply for a permit the better; the earliest you can apply is 10 days before the first of the month four months before your proposed trip date. The Grand Canyon Lodge offers a **hiker shuttle** (daily May 15-Oct. 15, first person $7, each additional person $4) to the North Kaibab Trailhead, which leaves every morning from the lodge at 5:30am and 6am. Tickets must be purchased 24 hours in advance at the lodge.

North Kaibab Trail

Distance: 28 miles (45 km) round-trip to Phantom Ranch and Colorado River
Duration: 2-3 days or more
Elevation gain: 5,770 feet (1,759 m) to river
Effort: Strenuous to very strenuous
Trail conditions: Rocky, sandy, dusty, narrow, technical
Trailhead: 1.5 miles (2.4 km) north of Grand Canyon Lodge on east side of AZ 67

Hiking the 14-mile (22.5-km) length of the **North Kaibab Trail** to the Colorado River is like walking southward from Canada to Mexico, beginning high up on the North Rim among the spruce, fir, and pine and ending at a cottonwood-shaded riparian oasis in a desert surrounded by high rock walls. It's an amazing and unforgettable journey, part of it on high and narrow cliffside paths blasted and carved into the Redwall, much of it within sight of life-giving **Bright Angel Creek** (which the trail crosses six times) as it falls across the hard land from Roaring Springs to its communion with the great river. You pass the wet greenery of **Roaring Springs** about 5 miles (8 km) from the rim, and just beyond is the old **Pumphouse Residence,** now a ranger station, and the **Manzanita Resthouse** near the creek, where there's seasonal drinking water and shade. At around the halfway point, 6.8 miles (10.9 km) from the rim, you reach the enchanting **Cottonwood Campground,** a creekside campground and a great place to spend the night or even a couple of days exploring this less-visited end of the canyon. Another 2 miles (3.2 km) or so down the trail is **Ribbon Falls,** a wonderful spot with falling water and moss and other shocking greenery on the dry red land. The final section of the trail before **Phantom Ranch, Bright Angel Campground,** and the **Colorado River** is a narrow stretch through the **inner gorge,** easy and flat but low and hot, boxed in by Vishnu schist about 1.7 billion years old. In the summer it's generally too hot to hike through the inner gorge after 10am.

There's drinking water available along the trail, but don't rely on it. May 15-October 14, you can refill your water bottle at the North Kaibab Trailhead, Supai Tunnel, Roaring Springs, Manzanita Rest Area, and Cottonwood Campground. All the water stations along the trail are turned off October 15-May 15. Always carry a water filter for use in Bright Angel Creek, which is close by for much of the hike.

Thunder River Trail and Deer Creek

Distance: 15 miles (24 km) one-way to Colorado River
Duration: 2-3 days or more
Elevation gain: 4,400 feet (1,341 m) to river
Effort: Very strenuous
Trail conditions: Steep, rocky, sandy, dusty, technical
Trailhead: Indian Hollow or Monument Point in Kaibab National Forest

This steep and difficult, wild and unmaintained trail of punishing switchbacks leads from the North Rim to a rare and enchanting oasis of riparian greenery and amazing waterfalls deep within the canyon. This wondrous place is a popular stop on river trips (it's at Mile 136 on the river), so there are bound to be crowds of day-hikers in this area that otherwise feels so far away and deeply hidden.

In this area, at-large camping is allowed in the Esplanade and Surprise Valley Use Areas, and there are designated campsites in the Deer Creek and Tapeats Creek Use Areas. The Deer

Creek and Upper Tapeats areas have vault toilets and group sites.

From Grand Canyon Lodge drive north for 18.4 miles (30 km) on AZ 67 to Forest Road 22, just before the Kaibab Lodge. Turn left (west) on Forest Road 22 to Forest Road 425. Starting at **Monument Point** via the Bill Hale Trail takes 2.5 miles (4 km) off the hike in exchange for increased difficulty and short spurts of scrambling. For this trail take Forest Road 425 to Forest Road 292 to 292A. The longer but easier Thunder River Trail begins at **Indian Hollow,** reached by taking Forest Road 425 to Forest Road 232.

The roads to these remote trailheads are not to be traveled lightly, especially during bad weather. It will take at least half the day to reach the trailheads, going slow over dusty washboard roads. Talk to a ranger at the **North Rim Backcountry Information Center** (North Rim Administration Bldg., 8am-noon and 1pm-5pm daily May 15-Oct. 15) for advice, road conditions, and more specific directions to the trailheads.

North Bass Trail

Distance: 13.5 miles (21.7 km) one-way to Colorado River
Duration: 3-4 days or more
Elevation gain: 3,300 feet (1,006 m) to river
Effort: Very strenuous
Trail conditions: Steep, rocky, sandy, dusty, technical
Trailhead: Swamp Point

This extremely difficult trail from the North Rim to the Colorado River runs along **White and Shinumo Creeks,** past waterfalls and the remains of the old **Bass tourist camp,** ending at a large beach and terrace above the mighty river. The trail is named for canyonland pioneer Bill Bass, and is considered one of the most technically demanding routes in the canyon.

The trail is in the North Bass Use Area, and there are excellent campsites along Shinumo Creek and on a beach at the river, though you may be sharing it with river-runners.

Just getting to the remote trailhead is difficult, requiring a high-profile vehicle or four-wheel drive. Talk to a ranger at the **North Rim Backcountry Information Center** (North Rim Administration Bldg., 8am-noon and 1pm-5pm daily May 15-Oct. 15) about the best way to access the trailhead; the roads to it often don't open until late May or June.

Nankoweap Trail

Distance: 14 miles (22.5 km) one-way to Colorado River
Duration: 3-4 days or more
Elevation gain: 5,640 feet (1,719 m)
Effort: Very strenuous
Trail conditions: Steep, rocky, sandy, dusty, technical
Trailhead: Saddle Mountain; take Forest Road 610 for 4.6 miles (7.4 km) north of North Rim Entrance Station

Wait to tackle the **Nankoweap Trail** until you've done all the other rim-to-river trails in the canyon. Of all the named trails in this vast canyonland, the Nankoweap is the most difficult. Officially. Its rim-to-river descent of 5,640 feet (1,719 m) is the largest total drop of any trail. The National Park Service warns that "hikers must be experienced in canyon route finding" to survive this trail, which is narrow, brushy, rocky, slow, and has stretches that are less than a foot wide beside a 100-foot (30-m) drop-off. Rangers warn away casual hikers, those with a fear of heights, and solo hikers whatever their skill level. Those who do take on this trail will be rewarded with the ultimate canyon adventure, amazing views, and a rare form of wilderness solitude.

There are campsites at the trailhead in the Kaibab National Forest, as well as along the trail between Marion Point and Tilted Mesa, at Nankoweap Creek, and at the river.

BIKING

Bring your **mountain bikes** with you to the North Rim and try out the Kaibab Plateau's exciting, rugged, and technical mountain bike trails (there are no bike rentals available on the North Rim). One of the most popular is the 22.5-mile (36-km) one-way **Rainbow Rim Trail,** an amazing single-track through forests and meadows and along the rim outside the national park. The trail has five overlooks with awesome views of the canyon right from the saddle of your bike. Plan on the ride taking 5-6 hours or more, depending on how fast you go and how many times you stop along the way. To start at Parissawampitts Viewpoint, take AZ 67 south from its junction with U.S. 89A for 26.5 miles (43 km). Turn right on Forest Road 22 and drive 10.5 miles (16.9 km). Turn left onto Forest Road 206 and drive 3.5 miles (5.6 km). Turn right on Forest Road 214 and drive 8 miles (12.9 km) to Parissawampitts Viewpoint. The drive to the trailheads from the Kaibab Plateau Visitor Center may take up to 1.5-2 hours one-way. The total round-trip drive to Parissawampitts is 100 miles (161 km), and it is 97 miles (156 km) round-trip to the other trailheads. To start from Timp Viewpoint at the other end, take Forest Road 206 for 1.5 miles (2.4 km) to Forest Road 271, turn right, and then drive 8 miles (12.9 km) to the trailhead.

The **Bridle Path** (3 mi/4.8 km round-trip), which runs between Grand Canyon Lodge and the North Rim Campground, is the only hiking trail inside the North Rim section of the park that allows bikes. The 12-mile (19.3-km) portion of the **Arizona Trail** that starts at the North Kaibab Trail parking lot also allows bikes (but make certain that you know for sure when the Arizona Trail ends and the North Kaibab begins—otherwise you'll have to contend with a ranger if you have a bike on the wrong one). Look for the brown posts with a Kaibab Plateau Trail decal to be sure you are on the Arizona Trail. The rugged **Point Sublime Road** (17.7 mi/28.5 km one-way) inside the park is also a popular mountain bike ride.

AZ 67 through the forest from Jacob Lake (44 mi/71 km) makes an excellent **road-bike ride,** though the road does not have much of a shoulder.

TRAIL RIDING

All primitive roads open to vehicles and most of the trails within the national park are open to private stock. If you can get it here, you can ride your own trusty mule or horse on the Arizona Trail, the Bridle Path, the Ken Patrick Trail, the Uncle Jim Trail, and even the North Kaibab Trail. You have to check in first thing with the rangers at the **North Rim Backcountry Information Center** (North Rim Administration Bldg., 8am-noon and 1pm-5pm daily May 15-Oct. 15) when you bring your own stock to the North Rim.

Grand Canyon Trail Rides (desk inside Grand Canyon Lodge, 435/679-8665, www. canyonrides.com, 8:30am-1:30pm daily May 15-Oct. 15, $45-90) offers three daily mule rides: a one-hour trail ride through the forest and along the rim (must be at least 7 years old and 222 lbs/101 kg or less, $45); a three-hour trail ride along the rim to Uncle Jim's Point (at least 10 years old, 200 lbs/91 kg or less, $90); and a three-hour trail ride 2 miles (3.2 km) down the North Kaibab Trail (2,300 ft/701 m) to Supai Tunnel (at least 10 years old, 200 lbs/91 kg or less, $90).

The **North Rim Horse Camp** within the park has one group site for up to six people, six equines, two cars, and a trailer up to 30 feet (9.1 m) long. The camp, 0.25 mile (0.4 km) north of the North Kaibab Trailhead and about 2 miles (3.2 km) north of the lodge complex, has water, a small corral, a pit toilet, and picnic tables. A permit is required for overnight use ($10 plus $8 pp per night and $8 per equine per night).

WINTER RECREATION

Once snowfall closes AZ 67 to the rim, the snowshoe backpackers and cross-country skiers head for the plateau for some deep, muffled solitude. The forested plateau all covered in snow is a breathtakingly beautiful sight, but the icy cold air will cut at your throat once you start breathing again. The 45-mile (72 km) journey from Jacob Lake to the North Rim Campground inside the otherwise dormant national park is an epic undertaking on foot

Where Does the Water Come From?

It's probably not a question you would ask unless the water suddenly stopped flowing—a not unimaginable possibility considering Grand Canyon National Park's recent water woes.

The answer is more complex than you might think: Rain and snowmelt on the Kaibab Plateau seeps and percolates into sandstone layers, where it collects and then flows underground until it emerges as a spring. There are springs all over the plateau, but the most important one is called **Roaring Springs,** a shower of pure water falling out of the rock walls some 3,800 feet (1,158 m) below the rim. Not only is Roaring Springs the fountainhead of Bright Angel Creek—which gives the North Kaibab Trail, Cottonwood Campground, Phantom Ranch, and Bright Angel Campground their rare riparian beauty—it's also the source of all the drinking water on both rims of Grand Canyon National Park.

Roaring Springs has been providing fresh water to the North Rim since 1928, when the Union Pacific Railroad dammed Bright Angel Creek below the springs and installed generators and a pumphouse to light up the lodge and bring water to the tourists. In the 1960s the park service began constructing a trans-canyon pipeline to take Roaring Springs water through the gorge and up to the South Rim, and since the 1970s Roaring Springs has been the sole source of fresh water for one of the nation's most popular national parks.

Over the last few years, the old pipeline has sprung several leaks, which have caused disruptions in service on both the North and South Rims. The pipeline is, according to the National Park Service, "beyond its useful life, experiences frequent failures, and requires continual maintenance to repair frequent leaks." While both sections of the park have water stored on the rim, when leaks occur the park institutes water conservation policies such as turning off some water stations inside the canyon, cutting back on landscape watering, and offering drinking water in restaurants only by request.

To hopefully avoid more serious and long-lasting water issues, the park in 2019 began constructing a new "Transcanyon Water Distribution Pipeline" that is expected to last at least 50 years. One of the biggest changes that the new pipeline will bring is that it will relocate the intake for the pipeline from Roaring Springs to an area along Bright Angel Creek near Phantom Ranch in an effort to make it more reliable and easier to access.

or ski, and you need a back-country permit ($10 plus $8 pp per night) to stay at the North Rim Campground after November 1, when it becomes a primitive campground without water. The park service in 2017 closed the yurt that was once available in winter.

Entertainment and Shopping

RANGER PROGRAMS

The North Rim's rangers offer a full schedule of free programs throughout the day, and after dark the huge and clear sky above this sparsely populated plateau is ideal for stargazing. You can follow a ranger on a guided and narrated walk along the rim or on a hike to an essential promontory, or listen to a talk about the history, both natural and human, of the North Rim and maybe even see some of the resident wildlife—or at least learn a bit about it. These programs are always rewarding, and you are bound to hear some things about these isolated forestlands that only someone who lives here could know. The North Rim Visitor Center next to the lodge posts the daily schedule. When you decide which programs to attend, find out from one of the rangers if they usually fill up and whether you need to sign up ahead of time.

EVENTS

In mid-June the annual **Grand Canyon Star Party** (www.saguaroastro.org/grand-canyon-star-party, free) goes all night and all week, with a host of astronomers offering free gazes at the vast and starry North Rim sky.

In early August the annual **North Rim Native American Heritage Week** (www.nps.gov/grca/planyourvisit) brings to the high country members of the 11 different tribes that have a cultural connection to Grand Canyon. These include the Paiute of the nearby Arizona Strip and southern Utah, and the Hopi, who believe their ancestors emerged into this reality from the great chasm. During the week the usual ranger programs are replaced with ones led by tribal members and focused on the deep human history of the region; all programs are free.

In mid-August, the sublime views from the patio of Grand Canyon Lodge pair perfectly with the ethereal music of the Kanab, Utah-based **Symphony of the Canyons** (https://symphonyofthecanyons.org, free) during a popular yearly concert.

SHOPPING
Gift Shops and Bookstores

The North Rim's **main gift shop** (next to Roughrider Saloon, 7am-9pm daily mid-May-mid-Oct.) is stocked with all the souvenir T-shirts, hats, water bottles, sweatshirts, postcards, and stuffed animals you could want, as well as Grand Canyon-stamped coats for the cool North Rim nights. The shop also has one-of-a kind Native American jewelry, pottery, baskets, and more. If you've just arrived from the South Rim via the North Kaibab Trail, head here to buy your Rim-to-Rim T-shirt (or even a Rim-to-Rim-to-Rim T-shirt if you are slightly mad).

General Store

Next to the North Rim Campground, northeast of Grand Canyon Lodge, the **North Rim General Store** (928/638-2611, 7am-8pm daily mid-May-mid-Oct.) sells a staggering variety of foodstuffs, supplies, gifts, and souvenirs at only moderately inflated prices. Packaged loaves of bread and plastic jars of peanut butter give way to enough backpacking gear to outfit an inner-canyon expedition, should the mood strike you. Poor planners and free spirits will find in these aisles most of the groceries and camping gear they left behind, including firewood. And with fresh coffee, a few coffeehouse chairs and tables, and spotty Wi-Fi, this is the place to attempt to reconnect, if you must, with the real world. From the lodge complex, drive 1.4 miles (2.3 km) northeast on AZ 67 and turn left, or walk the Transept Trail between the lodge and the campground.

Food

The dining options on the North Rim are few and far apart, with only three full-service restaurants on the Kaibab Plateau to choose from. If you are on a tight budget, have a lot of dietary restrictions or food allergies, or just like to make your own dinner, consider filling a cooler with foodstuffs before you ascend the plateau. Most of the cabins and rooms at the Grand Canyon Lodge come with small refrigerators, and some of the cabins at Kaibab Lodge have refrigerators and microwave ovens. You can also find groceries, though not a lot of fresh fruits and vegetables, at the general store inside the park or at the North Rim Country Store, about 18 miles (29 km) north of the lodge on AZ 67. If you are only going to eat at one restaurant, make it the Grand Canyon Lodge Dining Room. The atmosphere, the views, and the history—not to mention the excellent, regionally sourced food—make for an enchanting dining experience.

INSIDE THE PARK

With its native stone walls and picture windows framing the impossible vastness of the canyon, the ★ **Grand Canyon Lodge Dining Room** must be seen even if you don't eat here. Its high ceilings, wrought-iron chandeliers, Native American symbols, and exposed wood rafters give this large, bright, and open space an unforgettable atmosphere and represent the height of the National Park Service Rustic style. Reservations for dinner are highly recommended (928/638-8560 or gnrfbmgr@gcnr.com, 9am-4pm Mon.-Fri.). All the dining options at Grand Canyon Lodge are closed from mid-October to mid-May. To make reservations for spring, summer, or fall while the lodge and restaurants are closed, call Forever Resorts (877/386-4383).

The restaurant is a member of the Green Restaurant Association and serves dishes with a touch of regional and national park history made from fresh, organic, and sustainable produce, meat, chicken, and fish. Breakfast (6:30am-10am daily, $6.70-17.50; buffet $17.50 adults, $9.25 children) features all the hearty and healthy (yogurt, oatmeal, etc.) classics plus Arizona favorites like tamales and eggs and huevos rancheros. Vegetarians will like the grilled vegetable wrap and the braised portobello on offer at lunch (11:30am-2:30pm daily, $6.20-19.50), and everybody will love the fantastic soup, salad, and sandwich buffet ($17.50 adults, $9.25 children). For dinner (4:30pm-9:30pm daily, $11.35-33.95) choose between the Bright Angel Buffet with prime rib (4:30pm-6:30pm daily, $32.95 adults, $18.95 children) and a menu featuring fresh fish, grilled veggie kabobs, pasta, steaks, and bison burgers.

To the left as you exit the Grand Canyon Lodge through the main doors, **Deli in the Pines** (10:30am-9pm daily) is an ultracasual eatery serving premade sandwiches, salads, pizza, chips, cookies, and more, primarily for takeout back to your cabin or to put in your backpack for a lunchtime picnic on the rim. This is really the only place within the park

that you can get a quick and relatively inexpensive bite to eat (most items are under $10). There's often a line for dinner. Grab some plastic forks and paper plates before you leave, or sit down and relax at one of the few tables inside.

Next to the lodge, a **coffee shop** (5:30am-11am daily) serves espresso and lattes, baked goods, and breakfast burritos before 11am. After 11am and for the rest of the day into the night (11am-11pm) it becomes the **Roughrider Saloon,** named for Teddy Roosevelt's personal fighting crew in the Spanish-American War, several volunteers for which he found in Arizona's northland. The cozy wood interiors here are the perfect complement to a cold regional brew, of which there is an excellent selection on tap ($6.50). They also serve canyon-themed cocktails ($9-10), a range of bottled beer ($5), and various bar snacks.

OUTSIDE THE PARK

The restaurant at the **Kaibab Lodge** (5 mi/8 km north of park entrance at AZ 67, mile marker 605, 928/638-2389) is a charming knotty-pine space with picture windows, checkered tablecloths, and an old woodstove for atmosphere. The food is generally homemade, hearty, and delicious. About 18 miles (29 km) north of the rim along AZ 67, the lodge serves breakfast ($6-12) and dinner ($11-30)—burgers, pasta, ribs, steaks, etc.—daily during the high season (mid-May-mid-Oct.) and is closed in the winter (mid-Oct.-mid-May). It offers gluten-free options, and for vegetarians there's a garden burger and few pasta dishes.

Though a full 45 miles (72 km) from the rim, the diner-style **counter** (6:30am-close daily) at **Jacob Lake Inn** (U.S. 89A and AZ 67, 928/643-7232, www.jacoblake.com, open year-round) is a popular eatery, and on any given summer evening you are likely to find a long line of travelers waiting for their spot. The menu features delicious steak burgers called "bull" sandwiches, a selection of fantastic grilled cheese sandwiches, and a homemade veggie burger that aficionados simply must try. The counter serves breakfast 6:30am-11am ($3-10) and lunch 11am-close ($5-15). The inn's small **dining room** (5:30pm-9pm daily, $10-25), lined with Navajo blankets, serves meat loaf, fresh fish, steak, chicken, and other high-country dinner staples.

The only convenience store within 100 miles (161 km) of lonely blacktop, the **North Rim Country Store** (AZ 67, mile marker 605, 18 mi/29 km north of the rim, 928/638-2383, www.northrimcountrystore.com, 7am-7pm daily mid-May-late Oct.), across AZ 67 from Kaibab Lodge, has a small selection of premade packaged sandwiches, along with cheese, fruit, a few vegetables, sodas, and a pretty good range of beer and wine—certainly there's enough here for a hiker's picnic or to stock up on road food before you descend the plateau. It also sells gas, vehicle supplies, and souvenirs.

Accommodations

There are three hotels on the Kaibab Plateau, but only one inside the park, Grand Canyon Lodge. Reservations are hard to come by, so start planning at least a year ahead of time. Of the three hotels, the Jacob Lake Inn, 45 miles (72 km) north of the rim, is the most likely to have a room available, especially last-minute. Kaibab Lodge, about 18 miles (29 km) north of the rim, is often booked up early for the summer.

INSIDE THE PARK

The historic ★ **Grand Canyon Lodge** (877/386-4383, www.grandcanyonforever. com, mid-May-mid-Oct.) rises from the North Rim at the end of AZ 67, a rustic masterpiece of local sandstone and pine gloriously isolated at 8,000 feet (2,438 m) on what feels like the very edge of the known world. The main lodge building hangs rimside above Bright Angel Point, the bottom of a U-shaped complex connected by porticos, and it houses the reception desk, the bright and high-ceilinged dining room, and the enchanting sunroom with its huge picture windows overlooking the canyon. Even if you aren't staying here, spend some time in the sunroom and on the lodge's terrace, both of which are essential North Rim experiences.

Cabins of various sizes dot the forest north, east, and west of the lodge, along with two large outbuildings with motel-style rooms. The motel rooms ($148 per night) are charming and comfortable, and some have connecting doors useful for families, but the cabins—including some with incredible views of the canyon—are the lodge's main draw. The stone-and-pine cabins all have private bathrooms and romantic stone fireplaces that have been converted to gas. Staying in one can make you feel like a wilderness wanderer bedded down in rare comfort. They come in three sizes: the small and basic Frontier Cabin ($163); the two-room Pioneer Cabin, which sleeps up to six ($188-191); and the larger Western Cabin ($262-301) with two queen beds and a front porch with rough-hewn rocking chairs. There are mini-fridges and coffeemakers in most of the rooms and cabins, and kids under 15 stay free (though it's an extra $15 per night if you want a rollaway bed, which are not allowed in the Frontier Cabins).

If you want to stay here, and you should, start hunting for a reservation at least 13 months ahead of your trip. Because the lodge closes during the winter (mid-Oct.-mid-May), there's a relatively small window for a visit, so planning far ahead is the only strategy that works consistently. It is possible, however, to stumble onto a last-minute reservation if the dates of your trip are flexible, you inquire over

1: cabins at Grand Canyon Lodge **2:** Jacob Lake Inn

the phone several times, and you get lucky with a cancellation. But this is not the norm.

Four of the Western Cabins are ADA accessible, as are two of the Pioneer Cabins and two of the Frontier Cabins. Additionally, the lodge's main lobby, sunroom, veranda, and dining room are all accessible via three lifts. Outside the main building, the gift shop, the deli, and the coffee shop/saloon are accessible via wide, wheelchair-friendly walkways.

OUTSIDE THE PARK

The **Jacob Lake Inn** (U.S. 89A and AZ 67, 928/643-7232, www.jacoblake.com, open year-round, $128-165 rooms, $96-144 cabins) is the third-best hotel on a plateau that has only three. The biggest drawback of this historic waystation, owned by the same family since 1923, is that it's 41 miles (66 km) from the North Kaibab Trailhead and 45 miles (72 km), about an hour's drive, from the park and the rim. Jacob Lake, which also has a gas station and a campground but not a lake, is the center of the action on the Kaibab Plateau, and at the inn you'll find all the non-campers that couldn't get a reservation inside the park or at Kaibab Lodge. The forested complex includes a main lobby building with a lunch counter, dining room, bakery, and gift shop; a scattering of very rustic cabins that have seen a lot of hard wear and history; and a host of motel- and hotel-style rooms in various states of decline (all rooms and cabins have private bathrooms). The cabins and some of the motel rooms do not have TVs, phones, or Wi-Fi. That being said, Jacob Lake is a fine place to stay, clean and comfortable and bustling with fellow travelers and activity during the summer. The nicest rooms are in the newer hotel building behind the main lodge, and have up-to-date decor, air-conditioning, cable TV, and Wi-Fi. Jacob Lake Inn offers ADA-accessible rooms.

Tucked along the tree line on the edge of an expansive green meadow, 18 miles (29 km) from the rim and 16 miles (26 km) from the North Kaibab Trailhead, the **Kaibab Lodge** (5 mi/8 km north of park entrance at AZ 67, mile marker 605, 928/638-2389, mid-May-mid-Oct., $100-185) is a rustic wilderness haven that's been welcoming North Rim wanderers since the late 1920s. The charming main lodge building has a warm, inviting atmosphere with a fire crackling in the corner and hearty smells wafting from the restaurant. Guests and their pets stay in a variety of cabins and motel-style rooms hiding among the pines and aspens. While all the rooms and cabins are generally rustic but comfortable (and all have private bathrooms), some are more rustic than others, and there's a reason why the older cabins and rooms are less expensive. There are no TVs here, no Wi-Fi, and cell phones don't work. The Hiker's Special is one of the best deals on the plateau: $100 per night for a small, basic room with a double bed and a bathroom. Kaibab Lodge offers ADA-accessible rooms.

Camping

The campgrounds on the North Rim are open with full services from mid-May to mid-October, and you must reserve a spot in advance. For the park and national forest campgrounds, individual sites are "released" for reservations six months ahead of time on www.recreation.gov (so if your preferred date is, say, July 15, you must reserve a site, if you can, on January 15 starting at 8am MST). Even summer nights on the plateau can be chilly, so pack accordingly.

INSIDE THE PARK

The North Rim's warm summer days and cool, star-filled nights are often ideal for camping out; the park's 90-site **North Rim Campground** (www.recreation.gov, mid-May-mid-Oct., $6 for walk-to sites,

$18-25 standard nonelectric) typically fills up quickly during the summer and early fall. Keep in mind that, during a good year, you can expect regular late-afternoon rainstorms, often quite dramatic with thunder and lightning, from July to September. All sites are nonelectric with picnic tables, fire rings, and grills. The campground offers tent-only sites, ADA-accessible sites, and pull-through sites for rigs up to 27 feet (8.2 m) long. There's a dump station here but no hookups. A central complex has coin-op showers, laundry, and a drinking-water station, and there's a nearby general store with spotty Wi-Fi and a good selection of groceries and supplies. The campground spreads through an open, parklike forest of pine and aspen about 1.5 miles (2.4 km) north of the lodge, and some of the more expensive spots have rimside views. The easy Transept Trail runs along the rim from the campground to the lodge area, as does the Bridle Path (along AZ 67 rather than the rim), the only trail in the North Rim section of the park that allows bikes and dogs.

From December 1 to May 15, AZ 67 is closed to vehicles, but the North Rim Campground remains open as a primitive campground. Requiring a backcountry permit, which is also your reservation ($10 plus $8 pp per night), the campground offers no services and is primarily used by wintertime rim-to-rim hikers.

OUTSIDE THE PARK

About 18 miles (29 km) north of the rim along AZ 67, the **DeMotte Campground** (Forest Road 616, 877/444-6777, www. recreation.gov, mid-May-mid-Oct., $22) has 38 nonelectric campsites for tents, trailers, and small motorhomes. There are no hookups. Operated by the Kaibab National Forest, the sites have tables and fire grills, and there are drinking-water stations and vault toilets within the campground, which is woodsy and peaceful like the rest of the plateau. You may be able to get spotty cell coverage here, especially if you have T-Mobile.

Located across the road from the Jacob Lake Inn, about 44 miles (71 km) from the rim, **Jacob Lake Campground** (Jacob Lake, U.S. 89A and AZ 67, 928/643-7770, www.recreation.gov, mid-May-mid-Oct., $18) and Recreation Area is a relatively long drive from the park and North Kaibab Trail, but it's a great alternative if you can't get reservations somewhere closer. The Kaibab National Forest-administered campground has 51 nonelectric campsites, ADA-accessible vault toilets, and drinking water, and is close to hiking, biking, and equestrian trails. There are no hookups here, mostly tent and car camping, with gravel tent pads, picnic tables, fire rings, and grills. Cell coverage is fairly good here.

Also in Jacob Lake, about 45 miles (72 km) north of the rim, **Kaibab Camper Village** (928/643-7804, www.kaibabcampervillage. com, mid-May-mid-Oct., $20-45) has the only sites on the plateau with full hookups. The village has pull-through and back-in spots for rigs up to 40 feet (12.2 m), as well as tent sites with tables and fire pits. The complex has chemical toilets, coin-op laundry and showers, and a store. Head south on AZ 67 from the U.S. 89A junction for 0.25 mile (0.4 km) and turn right on Forest Road 461, then drive 1 mile (1.6 km). This campground is owned and operated by the folks from the nearby Kaibab Lodge.

For campers who prefer to be off on their own a few extra steps to the side of human civilization, the **Kaibab National Forest** (www.fs.usda.gov/kaibab, free) allows free dispersed camping across the green plateau for up to 14 days per month. Try to reuse already established dispersed camping spots and fire rings (you will know them when you see them), and never drive more than 30 feet (9.1 m) from the side of the road, or camp within a mile (1.6 km) of a developed campground or one-quarter mile (0.4 km) of a livestock watering hole. When camping out in the wilds like this, remember to tread lightly (www.treadlightly.org) and leave no trace (800/322-4100, https://lnt.org).

Transportation and Services

DRIVING

A road trip to Grand Canyon's North Rim is not to be taken lightly. The Kaibab Plateau is an isolated highland country crisscrossed by rough forest roads that is sparsely populated and dormant for half the year. A road-ready vehicle is essential. Take along extra water, food, and supplies even if you're staying in one of the three hotels on the plateau; being overprepared is better than the alternative.

There is only one way into Grand Canyon National Park's North Rim section—U.S. 89A to AZ 67, a paved (only since 1941) two-lane through the forest that ends at the rim and is one of the most scenic and thrilling roads in Arizona. While driving on the plateau, keep an eye out for motorcycles, which proliferate during the summer, and for cyclists riding on the nonexistent shoulder. Also keep a watch out for wildlife, including elk, deer, turkeys, and all sorts of other scurrying furry creatures that pay little heed to the highway.

The many Forest Service roads around the Kaibab Plateau are mostly dirt or gravel and should be taken on a case-by-case basis; some should be avoided unless you have a high-profile vehicle. In July, August, and September, expect daily late-afternoon thunderstorms that can quickly wash out a road or inspire a flash flood. To reach some of the backpacking trails here, you will need a high-profile vehicle or even a four-wheel drive. If you don't have one of these, and especially if you are driving a rental car, consider trying a trail that's easier to access.

Gas and Repairs

There are only three gas stations on the plateau: Jacob Lake, about 45 miles (72 km) from the rim; the North Rim Country Store, on AZ 67 about 18 miles (29 km) north of the rim; and inside the park. The latter, a small Chevron station with unleaded and diesel at the entrance to the campground, is not equipped for repairs. The North Rim Country Store (928/638-2383) fixes tires and sells a small selection of car supplies. For repairs involving batteries, belts, hoses, and other auto emergencies, you'll have to make it 45 miles (72 km) north of the rim to the service station at Jacob Lake (928/643-7232).

Parking

Inside the park there's parking at the lodge and the campground. On any given summer day, especially on a weekend, parking can be a challenge. However, patience and a willingness to walk a good distance are generally rewarded. There's a decent-sized parking lot at the North Kaibab Trailhead north of the lodge, but it generally fills up during the high season, so the earlier you start your hike into the gorge the more likely you are to find a parking spot.

To the South Rim

The drive from the North Rim to the South Rim, 215 miles (345 km) by car, takes about 4.5 hours. The first leg of the journey starts at Grand Canyon Lodge. Head north on AZ 67 about 45 miles (72 km) to Jacob Lake, at the junction with U.S. 89A. Take 89A down the Kaibab Plateau and through the Arizona Strip at the base of the Vermilion Cliffs, crossing the Colorado River at Navajo Bridge. U.S. 89A joins U.S. 89 South at Bitter Springs, about 50 miles (81 km) from Jacob Lake. Head south on U.S. 89 for about an hour to Cameron Trading Post on the Navajo Reservation. Just south of Cameron is the junction with AZ 64, which leads west along the Little Colorado Gorge to the Desert View entrance of Grand Canyon National Park's South Rim. From there it's about an hour's drive to Grand Canyon Village and the heart of the South Rim.

Where Can I Find...?

- **Accessible Lodging and Camping:** Grand Canyon Lodge offers ADA-accessible cabins. The North Rim Campground has ADA-accessible sites.

- **Accessible Trails:** The Cape Royal Trail is paved and wheelchair accessible.

- **Laundry:** There are coin-operated washing machines and dryers at the North Rim Campground.

- **Lost and Found:** Check at the North Rim Visitor Center and the Grand Canyon Lodge front desk.

- **Pay Phone:** There's a pay phone outside the North Rim General Store.

- **Post Office:** There is a small post office in the east wing of Grand Canyon Lodge.

- **Public Restrooms:** Find public restrooms behind the North Rim Visitor Center, at the North Rim Backcountry Information Center, and at the North Rim Campground.

- **Religious Services:** Ask at the Grand Canyon Lodge front desk.

- **Showers:** There are coin-operated showers at the North Rim Campground.

- **Water:** There are water stations behind the North Rim Visitor Center, at the North Rim Backcountry Information Center, at the North Rim Campground, and at the North Kaibab Trailhead.

- **Wi-Fi:** Spotty Wi-Fi is available at the North Rim General Store.

SHUTTLES

While you really need your own vehicle to do the North Rim right, for hikers the **Trans-Canyon Shuttle** (928/638-2820, www.trans-canyonshuttle.com, $90 one-way, reservations required) is also a good option. Rim-to-rim hikers starting on the North Kaibab Trail can take the shuttle to the North Rim after leaving a car on the South Rim for when they finally ascend from the depths. Or, they can start from the South Rim via the Bright Angel or South Kaibab Trail and then ride the shuttle back to the South Rim and their car. Of course the plan also would work if they left a car on the North Rim and then took the shuttle back from the South Rim. For most visitors, though, it's better to end a rim-to-rim hike on the South Rim, as it is much closer to Sky Harbor Airport in Phoenix. During the high season (spring and summer), shuttles run twice daily from the South Rim to the North Rim (8am-12:30pm

and 1:30pm-6pm) and twice daily from the North Rim to the South Rim (7am-11:30am and 2pm-6:30pm). The 215-mile (345-km) drive—through the Navajo Reservation, across the Colorado River at Marble Canyon, onto the lonely bunchgrass plains of the Arizona Strip, and then twisting up to the high forested Kaibab Plateau—takes about 4.5 hours.

SERVICES
Pets

The Bridle Path is the only trail in the North Rim section of the park that allows pets. Dogs are not allowed in the lodge, cabins, or hotel rooms, and there is no kennel.

Emergencies

The Kaibab Plateau and Grand Canyon National Park's North Rim have no emergency medical resources save for rangers. The closest hospital is 81 miles (130 km) away in Kanab, Utah, about a 1.5-hour drive. The closest emergency room is in Page, Arizona, 124 miles (200 km) away, a drive of about 2.5 hours.

To reach the ranger on duty during an emergency, call 911 from a pay phone (at the general store), or 9911 from a lodge room or cabin, or talk to someone at the visitors center or the lodge's front desk.

The Inner Canyon

Inside the canyon is a strange desert, red and green, pink and rocky. It's those sheer rock walls, tight and claustrophobic in the interior's narrowest slots, that make this place a different world altogether. A large part of a canyon-crossing hike along the corridor trails takes place in Bright Angel Canyon along Bright Angel Creek. As you hike along the trail beside the creek, greenery and the cool rushing water clash with the silent heat washing off the cliffs.

On any given night there are only a few hundred visitors sleeping below the rim—at Phantom Ranch, a Mary Jane Colter-designed lodge near the mouth of Bright Angel Canyon; at three campgrounds along the corridor trails; or off in the canyon's wild backcountry. Until a few decades ago visiting the inner canyon was something of a free-for-all,

Highlights

Look for ★ to find recommended sights, activities, dining, and lodging.

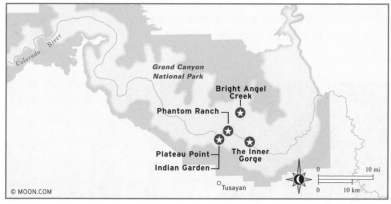

Grand Canyon
National Park

Bright Angel
Creek

Phantom Ranch

Plateau Point
Indian Garden

The Inner
Gorge

Colorado River

Tusayan

0   10 mi

0   10 km

© MOON.COM

★ Stop at **Indian Garden,** a spring-fed oasis on the Bright Angel Trail, where you can rest below the tall cottonwoods and watch wildlife flit through the greenery (page 152).

★ Look down on the roiling Colorado River from amazing **Plateau Point** (page 153).

★ Stay at peaceful **Phantom Ranch,** the wonderful green heart of the inner canyon (page 155).

★ Raft through the **inner gorge,** where you can marvel at some of the oldest rocks on the planet, along with two amazing, improbable bridges hanging over the river (page 166).

★ Listen to the musical flow of **Bright Angel Creek,** a shining, trickling lifeline along the North Kaibab Trail that spills into the Colorado near Phantom Ranch (page 168).

but these days access to the interior is strictly controlled; you have to purchase a permit, and they're not always easy to get—each year the park receives about 30,000 requests for backcountry permits and issues only 13,000.

No matter which trail you use, there's no avoiding an arduous, leg- and spirit-punishing hike there and back if you really want to see the inner canyon. It's not easy, no matter who you are, but it is worth it; it's a true accomplishment, a hard walk you'll never forget.

PLANNING YOUR TIME

There are many, many routes into and around Grand Canyon, a lot of them remote, rough, and better left to highly experienced and prepared canyon experts. Rangers at Grand Canyon's **Backcountry Information Center** on both the South and North Rims can assist you in choosing the best routes and itineraries. If you're new to Grand Canyon backpacking, even if you are an expert backpacker in other regions, you should consider starting out on one of the **corridor trails** from the South or North Rim—**Bright Angel Trail, South Kaibab,** and **North Kaibab.**

While there are many athletes these days who like to rush through the canyon from rim-to-rim in one day, the truly magical part of a canyon backpacking trip is not so much the getting there but the being there. Spend as much time inside the canyon as you can; it takes a lot to get here, and it's a wonderous, unique place that should not be hurried through.

The **standard backpacking trip** from the **South Rim** lasts **three days.** One day hiking in, one day inside the canyon, and one day hiking out. The trip starts on either the South Kaibab or the Bright Angel Trail and ends at **Bright Angel Campground** or **Phantom Ranch** in the inner gorge near the Colorado River. During the high season (March 1 to November 14), you're allowed to spend up to two consecutive nights at Bright Angel or the other corridor campgrounds—Indian Garden Campground on the Bright Angel Trail and Cottonwood Campground on the North Kaibab Trail below the North Rim. (From November 15 to February 28, the limit is four consecutive nights.) Going in, it's best to take the **South Kaibab Trail**—it's very steep but dramatically beautiful and shorter than the Bright Angel. You'll be inside the canyon kicking back under the cottonwoods along Bright Angel Creek in no time. Going out, take the **Bright Angel Trail,** an arduous, punishing, and amazing hike out of the gorge, stopping for a rest at beautiful **Indian Garden.** For those who want to spend even more time inside the canyon, make a reservation to camp the third night at Indian Garden, and then hike out the rest of the way the next day. The **best times** to take this classic backpacking trip into the inner gorge are **March-April** and **October-early November.** Avoid this area in the summer.

Rim-to-rim hikes are also popular, though after October the **North Rim** is closed down and you may find yourself camping in snow at the North Rim Campground (and possibly even inside the canyon as well). If you're set on a rim-to-rim hike with multiple days of camping below the rim, the **best times** to do it are in the early spring or the fall, **April or October**—but these are also some of the most difficult times to get permits. These months are the best all-around times to backpack in the canyon. Summer, **May-September,** is **not a good time;** the canyon and the rims will be busy, and it will be 100-120°F (38-49°C) inside the canyon during the day and stay in the 80s (27-32°C) and 90s (32-37°C) once the sun goes down. Summer hiking in the canyon should be done before 10am. During October high temperatures inside the canyon range 80-90°F (27-32°C), and then drop to the high 60s (19-21°C) and 70s (21-26°C) come November,

THE INNER CANYON

The Inner Canyon

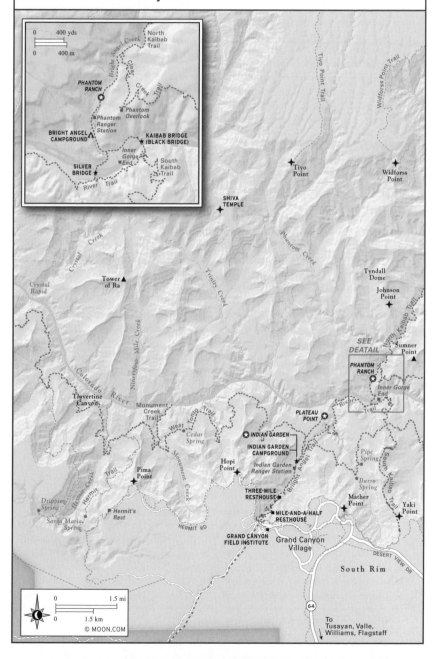

0   400 yds
0   400 m

Bright Angel Creek

North Kaibab Trail

Creek

Creek Trail

PHANTOM RANCH

Phantom Overlook

Phantom Ranger Station

BRIGHT ANGEL CAMPGROUND

KAIBAB BRIDGE (BLACK BRIDGE)

Inner Gorge End

South Kaibab Trail

SILVER BRIDGE

River   Trail

Tiyo Point Trail

Widforss Point Trail

Tiyo Point

Widforss Point

SHIVA TEMPLE

Phantom Creek

Crystal Creek

Crystal Creek

Tyndall Dome

Johnson Point

Crystal Rapid

Tower of Ra

Trinity Creek

North Kaibab Trail

SEE DEATAIL

Sumner Point

PHANTOM RANCH

Inner Gorge End

Colorado River

Ninetyfour Mile Creek

Travertine Canyon

Monument Creek Trail

West Tonto Trail

Cedar Spring

PLATEAU POINT

River   Trail

Pipe Spring

INDIAN GARDEN

INDIAN GARDEN CAMPGROUND

Indian Garden Ranger Station

Burro Spring

South Kaibab Trail

Hermit Creek

Hermit Trail

Pima Point

Monument Creek

Hopi Point

THREE-MILE RESTHOUSE

Bright Angel Trail

Mather Point

Yaki Point

Dripping Spring

Santa Maria Spring

Hermit's Rest

HERMIT RD

MILE-AND-A-HALF RESTHOUSE

GRAND CANYON FIELD INSTITUTE

Grand Canyon Village

DESERT VIEW DR

South Rim

0   1.5 mi
0   1.5 km

© MOON.COM

64

To Tusayan, Valle, Williams, Flagstaff

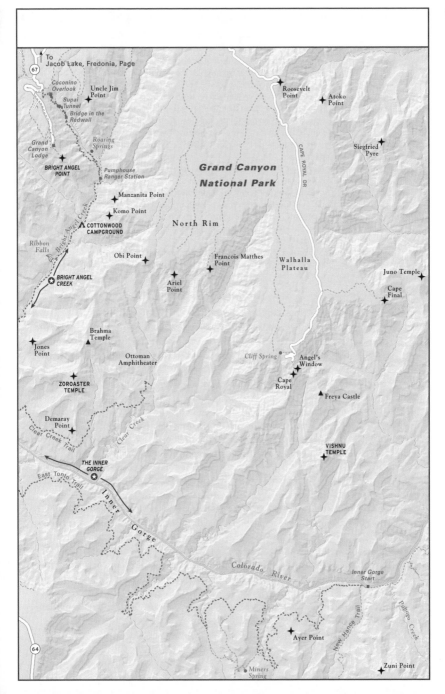

Hiking Rim to Rim . . . the Easy Way

One of the first things you notice while journeying through the inner canyon is the advanced age of many of your fellow hikers. It is not uncommon to see men and women in their 70s and 80s hiking along at a good clip, packs on their backs and big smiles on their faces.

At the same time, all over the South Rim you'll see warning signs about overexertion, each featuring a buff young man in incredible shape suffering from heatstroke or exhaustion, with the warning that most of the people who die in the canyon—and people die every year—are people like him. You need not be a wilderness expert or marathon runner to enjoy even a long, 27-mile (43-km), rim-to-rim hike through the inner canyon. Don't let your fears hold you back from what is often a life-changing trip.

There are several strategies that can make a canyon hike much easier than a forced march with a 30-pound (13.6-kg) pack of gear on your back. First of all, don't go in the summer; wait until October or even November, when it's cooler, though still quite warm, in the inner canyon. Second, try your best to book a cabin or a dorm room at Phantom Ranch rather than camping. That way, you'll need less equipment, you'll have all or most of your food taken care of, and there will be a shower and a beer waiting for you upon your arrival. Also, for $76 each way, you can hire a mule to carry up to 30 pounds (13.6 kg) of gear for you, so all you have to bring is a daypack with water and snacks. This way, instead of suffering while you descend and ascend the trail, you'll be able to better enjoy the magnificence of this wonder of the world.

making hiking much more pleasant than it is during the infernal summer months. High temperatures mostly stay around the 50s (10-15°C) and 60s (16-21°C) December-February, though nighttime temps in the canyon drop precipitously. In March expect inner-canyon highs in the low 70s (21-23°C) and lows in the high 40s (8-9°C); in April typical highs warm up to the low 80s (27-29°C), with lows in the high 50s (13-15°C); and in early May expect highs in the low 90s (32-34°C) and lows in the low 60s (16-18°C).

The Colorado River **rafting season** through the inner canyon runs **April-October,** and just as it is with backpacking trips, rafting in the summer is dangerous and uncomfortable in the extreme heat. The **best times** for a river trip through the canyon are **April-early May** and **October,** though of course these are the most difficult reservations to secure. The length of river trips varies greatly; a shorter, motorized trip may be a better choice in the deep summer.

Backcountry Permits

To camp overnight below the rim, you have to purchase a **permit** ($10 plus $8 pp per night). The earliest you can apply for an inner-canyon permit is 10 days before the first of the month that is four months before your proposed trip date. The easiest way to get a permit is to go to the **park's website** (www.nps.gov/grca), print out a backcountry permit request form, fill it out, and then fax it first thing in the morning on the date in question—for example, if you want to hike in October, you would **fax** (928/638-2125) your request May 20-June 1. On June 1 rangers will begin randomly processing all the requests for October, and they'll let you know in about three weeks. On the permit request form you'll indicate at which campgrounds you plan to stay. The permit is your reservation. For more information on obtaining a backcountry permit, call the **Backcountry Information Center** (928/638-7875, 8am-noon and 1pm-5pm daily year-round).

Exploring the Inner Canyon

If you want to be one of the small minority of canyon visitors to spend some quality time below the rim, stay at least one full day and night in the inner canyon. Even hikers in excellent shape find that they are sore after trekking down to the river, Phantom Ranch, and beyond. A rim-to-rim hike, either from the south or from the north, pretty much requires at least a day of rest below the rim. The ideal inner-canyon trip lasts three days and two nights: one day hiking in, one day of rest, and one day to hike out.

River trips range from three days up to three weeks and often include a hike down one of the corridor trails to the river. Depending on how long you want to spend on the river, plan far, far in advance, and consider making the river trip your only major activity on that particular canyon visit. Combining too much strenuous, mind-blowing, and life-changing activity into one trip tends to water down the entire experience.

TOURS
Mule Trips

For generations the famous Grand Canyon mules have been dexterously picking along the skinny trails, loaded with packs and people. Even the Brady Bunch rode them, so they come highly recommended. A descent into the canyon on the back of a friendly mule—with an often-taciturn cowboy-type leading the train—can be an unforgettable experience, but don't assume because you're riding and not walking that you won't be sore in the morning.

Park concessionaire **Xanterra** offers two mule trips to Phantom Ranch, a one-night excursion and a two-night expedition. The **one-night trip** is offered **year-round** and includes accommodations at Phantom Ranch (by booking a mule trip, you automatically reserve a spot at Phantom Ranch without having to enter the lottery), dinner and breakfast in the Phantom Ranch Canteen, and a sack lunch. The cost for the one-night trip is $692.59 per person, $1,204.51 for two people, and $533.31 for each additional person. The **two-night trip** is offered **November-March** and includes accommodations at Phantom Ranch, meals in the canteen, and sack lunches. The cost for the two-night trip is $1,009.42 per person, $1,657.50 for two people, and $690.86 for each additional person. For reservations call 888/297-2757 or visit www.grandcanyonlodges.com. You can make a reservation up to 13 months in advance, and you really should do it as soon as you know your plans. There's a 225-pound (102-kg) weight restriction.

The mule trips begin in the stone corral next to the Bright Angel Lodge and descend into the canyon via the Bright Angel Trail, stopping for a box lunch at Indian Garden. The trips ascend from the inner gorge via the South Kaibab Trail. Expect to be in the saddle for about 5.5 hours each way. You are provided with a small plastic bag about the size of a 10-pound (4.5-kg) bag of ice to carry your toiletries and other items. If you need more luggage than this, you can send a duffel bag ahead for $76 each way (30 lbs/13.6 kg maximum, 36 by 20 by 13 in/91 by 51 by 33 cm, www.grandcanyonlodges.com/lodging/phantom-ranch).

Guided Backpacking Trips

You certainly don't need a guide to take a classic backpacking trip into the Grand Canyon along one of the corridor trails. The National Park Service makes it a relatively simple process to plan and complete such a memorable expedition, and, while hikers die below the rim pretty much every year, the more popular regions of the inner canyon are as safe as can be expected in a vast wilderness. Then again, having some friendly, knowledgeable, and undoubtedly badass canyonlander plan and implement every detail of your trip sure couldn't hurt. Indeed, it would probably make the whole expedition infinitely more enjoyable. As long as you're willing to pay for it—and it is never cheap—hiring a guide is an especially good idea if you want to go places where few tourists and casual hikers dwell.

There are more than 20 companies authorized, through a **guide permit** issued by the National Park Service, to take trips below the rim. If your guide does not have such a permit, do not follow him or her into the Grand Canyon. For an up-to-date list, go to www.nps.gov/grca.

The **Grand Canyon Conservancy Field Institute** (928/638-2481, www.grandcanyon.org, $690-815), which is operated by the nonprofit Grand Canyon Conservancy, offers several three- to five-day guided backpacking trips to various points inside the canyon, including trips designed specifically for women, beginners, and those interested in the canyon's natural history. Operating out of Flagstaff, **Four Season Guides** (1051 S. Milton Rd., 928/779-6224, www.fsguides.com, $799-1,450) offers more than a dozen different backpacking trips below the rim, from a three-day frolic to Indian Garden to a nearly weeklong, 36-mile (58-km) expedition

on some of the canyon's lesser-known trails. The experienced and friendly guides tend to inspire a level of strength and ambition that you might not reach otherwise. These are the guys to call if you want to experience the lonely, out-of-the-way depths of the canyon but don't want to needlessly risk your life doing it alone.

SIGHTS
★ Indian Garden

A beautiful oasis about 3,000 feet (914 m) and 4.8 miles (7.7 km) below the South Rim, spring-fed **Indian Garden** entices hikers and backpackers down the twisting Bright Angel Trail, appearing as a thick line of green within an otherwise sharp and arid landscape from the bustling Grand Canyon Village high above. If you can handle a hard, steep, and mind-blowing 9.6 miles (15.4 km) round-trip (in spring and fall is best), a day hike to Indian Garden and back from the South Rim is one of the best things you can do in the national park.

In the desert Southwest, a little water makes all the difference, and the color green is all the more beautiful and inspiring because of its scarcity. So when you come across spring-fed oases like Indian Garden or riparian

Mule trips into the canyon are offered year-round.

paradises such as Bright Angel Canyon, you stay awhile and celebrate. Indian Garden has been a place of human activity in the harsh inner canyon for at least 13,000 years. More recently, archaeological sites around the area date from the Ancestral Puebloans and Cohoninas, from about AD 300 to AD 1300, including the remains of seasonal structures, granaries, and farming infrastructure. The Havasupai began farming this and the other spring-fed and riparian areas of the canyon in at least the 12th century, and were still doing so when Europeans and Americans arrived in the 19th century.

In the late 1800s, canyon pioneer Ralph Cameron prospected in the area with little success, and in 1903 opened a tourist camp with tent cabins, gardens, orchards, cottonwood trees, a laundry, a kitchen, and even a telephone line to the South Rim. The National Park Service took control of the area in the early 1920s after the formation of Grand Canyon National Park in 1919. Today Indian Garden is a cool and green resting stop and campground along the Bright Angel Trail, a haven for tired up-hikers still facing the Bright Angel's steepest sections.

★ Plateau Point

From Indian Garden, hike 1.5 miles (2.4 km) across the flat desert of the Tonto Platform to **Plateau Point,** an amazing cliff-edge viewpoint looking down on the roiling Colorado River snaking through the narrow inner gorge. The National Park Service discourages day hikes from the South Rim to Plateau Point in the summer (May–Sept.), but in spring or fall the strenuous 12-mile (19.3-km) round-trip hike is a wonderful day hike for experienced and fit hikers. The view and the atmosphere out here are best in the early to late evening, so if you want to take your time, obtain a permit and spend the night at Indian Garden's lush campground.

Colorado River Bridges

There are very few ways to cross the Colorado River through Grand Canyon. Navajo Bridge, near Lees Ferry (River Mile 0), crosses over the river at Marble Canyon, about 90 miles (145 km) upriver from its confluence with Bright Angel Creek inside the inner gorge, where the second and third bridges span the roiling green flow.

The first one you come to, heading downriver and arriving at a crossroads of the main corridor trails near Phantom Ranch, is **Kaibab Bridge,** also known as **Black Bridge,** which is open to both hikers and mule trains. Can you imagine what it took to build this bridge, the main route across the river for all the mule trains that supply Phantom Ranch, in such a remote, inaccessible location? It was 1928, and maybe people were a bit tougher back then. It's the only way to explain it. Actually, it was a crew of mostly Havasupai men who did a lot of the heavy lifting, carrying the 550-foot-long (168-m) suspension cables down the trail in single file. However, as it always seems to be at Grand Canyon, it was the mules that did most of the work, carrying some 122 tons of materials from the rim.

The construction of Black Bridge really changed the way people visited the inner canyon. Before the early 1920s (when a temporary wooden suspension bridge went up prior to Black Bridge's completion), intrepid canyon explorers and suppliers had to slide across a cable over the Colorado in a metal cage about the size of one mule. This contraption had, since about 1907, been the only way to cross the river safely at Bright Angel Canyon; it was set up by early canyon pioneer and tourism entrepreneur David Rust, when what is now Phantom Ranch was a remote tent camp called Rust's Camp.

Just downstream and connecting the Bright Angel Trail with Phantom Ranch and the North Kaibab Trail, the **Silver Bridge** opened in 1960. The bridge holds up the trans-canyon water pipeline as it crosses the river on its way from Roaring Springs, below the North Rim, to all the faucets on the South Rim. It's open only to foot traffic.

★ Phantom Ranch

A small scattering of wood-and-stone cabins, dormitories, and a canteen beneath the high red walls near the mouth of Bright Angel Canyon, **Phantom Ranch** is the closest thing there is to a town inside Grand Canyon National Park's section of the canyon. There's even a post office from which you can mail a postcard and have it carried out by a mule. But it's not a town, nor even a village; it is, however, the only truly busy spot of civilization in an otherwise hard and unforgiving stone labyrinth.

Sitting in the shade of towering cottonwood trees about 0.3 mile (0.5 km) from the mouth of the Bright Angel Canyon, near where Bright Angel Creek marries the Colorado River, Phantom Ranch has long been a site of human activity. The confluence of the spring-fed creek and the mighty river here has built a rich and lush delta where about 30 or 40 Ancestral Puebloan families lived, farmed, and hunted from around AD 1050 to AD 1140. There's a small **ruin** on the north side of the river with shallow, haphazard stone walls and shadowy pits, surrounded by brittlebush, prickly pear cactus, and other desert scrub. It's just above Boat Beach, a popular stop for river trips.

Phantom Ranch's canteen, which has air-conditioning and is crowded with family-style dining tables, acts as a lobby, restaurant, bar, and central meeting place. The complex also includes 11 cabins and four hiker dormitories (enough room for 92 overnight guests), scattered between high canyon walls in a green and shady setting with cottonwoods, the ubiquitous and invasive salt cedar, and even a few peach, pomegranate, fig, and olive trees left over from an old orchard.

The complex was designed in 1922 by Mary Jane Colter, the same architect who designed many of the charming and rustic structures on the South Rim for the Fred Harvey Company and Santa Fe Railroad. Before that

1: Indian Garden **2:** Plateau Point

it was a much less comfortable and inviting tourist tent camp run by pioneer David Rust, called Rust's Camp.

Between the river and the ranch, there are several structures from the 1920s and 1930s built from native materials, which you'll walk past as you make your way from the bridge over the river to Phantom. These are National Park Service buildings not open to the public, but they are rustic, romantic, and photo-worthy nonetheless, including the enchanting staff cabin called the Rock House, an old ranger station, an operator's cabin, and a mule corral. You will also pass Bright Angel Campground, which is about 0.4 mile (0.6 km) below Phantom Ranch. This popular corridor campground sits along the banks of Bright Angel Creek and was established by the Civilian Conservation Corps in the 1930s.

HIKING AND BACKPACKING

Although there are many lesser-known routes into and through the canyon, most hikers stick to the **corridor trails—Bright Angel, South Kaibab,** and **North Kaibab.**

A classic Grand Canyon backpacking journey begins at either the Bright Angel Trailhead or the South Kaibab Trailhead on the **South Rim.** Consider going up the one you don't use going down, mostly for variety's sake. Via the South Kaibab Trail, it's a 7-mile (11.3-km) hike to the **Bright Angel Campground,** which is just a short walk from the Colorado River and also from **Phantom Ranch.** Ideally, spend at least two days (the hike-in day and one full day after that) and two nights in the Phantom Ranch area, hiking up the North Kaibab a short way to see the narrow and close walls, talking to the rangers, sitting on the beach watching the river-trippers float by, and losing yourself to the calm, quiet soul of the wilderness.

When it's time to leave the oasis that is Bright Angel Campground and Phantom Ranch, a question arises: Should you rise headlong to the rim (7 mi/11.3 km up on the South Kaibab or 9.5 mi/15.3 km up on

Inner Canyon Hikes

Trail	Effort	Distance	Duration
River Trail	Easy	1.5 mi/2.4 km round-trip	1-2 hours
Clear Creek Loop	Easy to moderate	About 1.5 mi/2.4 km round-trip	1-2 hours
Clear Creek Trail	Strenuous	18 mi/29 km round-trip	2 days or more
Phantom Ranch to Ribbon Falls	Easy to moderate	11 mi/17.7 km round-trip	5-6 hours to all day
Tonto Trail	Moderate	93 mi/150 km from Garnet Canyon to Red Canyon	Many days

the Bright Angel) or move on leisurely to the next oasis? Those inclined to choose the latter should stay an **extra night** below the rim at the campground at **Indian Garden,** a green and lush spot 4.7 miles (7.6 km) up the Bright Angel Trail from the Bright Angel Campground. The small campground is primitive but charming, and the area around it is populated by deer and other creatures. After setting up camp and resting a bit, head out on the flat, 3-mile (4.8 km) round-trip hike to Plateau Point and a spectacular view of the canyon and river, especially at sunset. When you wake up beneath the shady trees at Indian Garden, you face a mere 4.8-mile (7.7-km) hike to the rim.

From the **North Rim,** the North Kaibab is the only major corridor trail to the river and Phantom Ranch.

Some people prefer to spend their time in the canyon recovering from the hard walk or mule ride that brought them here, and a day spent cooling your feet in Bright Angel Creek or drinking beer in the cantina is not a day wasted. However, if you want to do some exploring around Phantom Ranch, there are a few popular day hikes from which to choose. When you arrive, the friendly rangers will

usually tell you, unsolicited, all about these hikes and provide detailed directions. If you want to get deeper out in the bush and far from other hikers, ask one of the rangers to recommend a lesser-known route.

River Trail

Distance: 1.5 miles (2.4 km) round-trip
Duration: 1-2 hours
Elevation gain: Negligible
Effort: Easy
Trail conditions: Dirt, rocky, narrow, dusty
Trailhead: Start at Phantom Ranch on north side of river or at end of Bright Angel Trail on south side.

This short hike is along the precipitous **River Trail,** high above the Colorado just south of Phantom Ranch. The Civilian Conservation Corps (CCC) blasted this skinny cliffside trail out of the rock walls in the 1930s to provide a link between the Bright Angel and the South Kaibab Trails. Heading out from Phantom, it's about a 1.5-mile (2.4-km) loop that takes you across both **suspension bridges** and high above the river. It's an easy walk with fantastic views and is a good way to get your sore legs stretched and moving again. And you are likely to see a bighorn sheep's cute little face poking out from the rocks and shadows on the steep cliffs.

1: Kaibab Bridge 2: cabins at Phantom Ranch

Clear Creek Loop

Distance: About 1.5 miles (2.4 km) round-trip
Duration: 1-2 hours
Elevation gain: 826 feet (252 m)
Effort: Easy to moderate
Trail conditions: Dirt, rocky, narrow, dusty, steep, some sand
Trailhead: About 0.3 mile (0.5 km) north of Phantom Ranch on North Kaibab Trail

Another popular CCC-built trail near Phantom, the 1.5-mile (2.4-km) **Clear Creek Loop** takes you high above the river to **Phantom Overlook,** where there's an old stone bench and excellent views of the canyon and Phantom Ranch below. The rangers seem to recommend this hike the most, but, while it's not tough, it can be a little steep and rugged, especially if you're exhausted and sore. The views are, ultimately, well worth the pain.

Clear Creek Trail

Distance: 18 miles (29 km) round-trip
Duration: 2 days or more
Elevation gain: 1,500 feet (457 m)
Effort: Strenuous
Trail conditions: Dirt, rocky, narrow, dusty, some sand
Trailhead: 0.3 mile (0.5 km) north of Phantom Ranch on North Kaibab Trail

Just north of Phantom Ranch off the North Kaibab Trail, the **Clear Creek Trail** climbs steep switchbacks to **Phantom Overlook** above Phantom Ranch, and then the trail climbs to the Tapeats sandstone, an erosion-resistant layer of rock just above the one billion years of missing evidence called the Great Unconformity. From there the trail climbs up to the **Tonto Platform**'s desert expanse—the only trail across the Tonto Platform on the north side of the river. On the Tonto the trail runs relatively flat, heading east toward Zoroaster Temple, undulating through rocky and sandy washes, and then drops into **Clear Creek Canyon** (8.7 mi/14 km one-way) along a very narrow rock slope. Once you reach the floor of the canyon, the Clear Creek camping area is 0.25 mile (0.4

km) farther along the creek, with primitive campsites in a beautiful riparian area. From here, head about 4 miles (6.4 km) one-way up the creek to see the seasonal 800-foot (244-m) **Cheyava Falls,** which is best in spring when full of snowmelt; other times it slows to an underwhelming trickle, and in dry years there may be no falls at all. There's also a wet but amazing day hike downstream to the Colorado River from the camping area (6 mi/9.7 km round-trip).

The hike to the Clear Creek camping area is a popular backpacking trip in March and April; it requires a lot of planning, permits (of course), and for most a stay at Phantom Ranch or Bright Angel Campground one night on the way there from the South Rim and one night on the way back. The trail is wide open to the south and the hard sun all day, and should not be attempted in summer except at night and in the early morning.

Phantom Ranch to Ribbon Falls

Distance: 11 miles (17.7 km) round-trip
Duration: 5-6 hours to all day
Elevation gain: 1,174 feet (358 m)
Effort: Easy to moderate
Trail conditions: Dirt, rocky, some sand, narrow, high canyon walls
Trailhead: North Kaibab Trail, on north side of Phantom Ranch

If you hiked in from the South Rim and you have a long, approximately 11-mile (17.7-km) round-trip day hike in you, head north on the **North Kaibab Trail** from Phantom Ranch to beautiful **Ribbon Falls,** a mossy, cool-water oasis just off the hot, dusty trail. The falls are indeed a ribbon of cold water falling hard off the rock cliffs, and you can scramble up the slickrock and through the green creekside jungle and stand beneath the shower. Look for the sign for Ribbon Falls on the left side of the trail 5.5 miles (8.9 km) from Phantom. A section of this hike will also give you a chance to see the eerie, claustrophobic **"Box,"** one of the strangest and most exhilarating stretches of the North Kaibab (the last 4 miles/6.4 km of the trail going from north to south). This narrow stretch through the **inner gorge** is easy and flat but low and hot, boxed in by black Vishnu schist about 1.7 billion years old. Don't hike in the inner canyon after 10am in the summer.

Tonto Trail

Distance: 93 miles (150 km) from Garnet Canyon (western end) to Red Canyon (eastern end)
Duration: Many days
Elevation gain: 1,200 feet (366 m)
Effort: Moderate
Trail conditions: Dirt, rocky, sand, relatively flat, up and down through washes
Trailhead: Various access points on other canyon trails, including Bright Angel and South Kaibab Trails

This long, exposed trail crosses Grand Canyon's monotonous brushy desert known as the **Tonto Platform.** The trail connects the **Bright Angel and South Kaibab Trails** via a 4-mile (6.4-km) stretch, and a 12-mile (19.3-km) section connects the **Bright Angel Trail** with the **Hermit Trail** on the western edge of the park. The undulating Tonto Platform is composed of a large east-west deposit of Tapeats sandstone above the river and the inner gorge. There is no water along the

Tonto Trail, and it is not recommended for use in summer.

RUNNING

Grand Canyon runners (and really fast walkers) go light and lonely. It's best just to get out of their way; they are not really of this world, living instead in some runner's plane. They go rim-to-rim-to-rim without sleep, with few stops, with only a pocket water filter to drink out of Bright Angel Creek. This is a curious and awe-inspiring Grand Canyon species whose ranks are increasing daily. The best and easiest trails for running are the **corridor trails**—the Bright Angel, South Kaibab, and North Kaibab. You don't need a permit to run through the canyon as long as you do not stop for the night below the rim.

CLIMBING

Rock climbers can't help but be enticed by all that, well, rock inside Grand Canyon. Climbers have dared to scale more than 100 of the canyon's rock peaks. Some of the most popular peaks are **Zoroaster, Vishnu, and Shiva Temples.** The canyon's peaks, spires, and sheer cliffs are not for beginning climbers; it is, rather, a setting for the most

backpackers on the Tonto Trail

experienced climbers only. Unless you plan on hiking down into the canyon, climbing rocks, and then hiking out the same day (which is not a fun way to do anything), you'll need to obtain a permit and plan out your sleeping arrangements as well as your climb. For more information on rock climbing in Grand Canyon, talk to a ranger at the **Backcountry Information Center** (928/638-7875, 8am-noon and 1pm-5pm daily year-round).

FISHING

You'll need a valid Arizona fishing license from the **Arizona Game & Fish Department** (602/942-3000, www.azgfd.com, $55 nonresidents, $37 residents) to fish year-round in the Colorado River, Bright Angel Creek, or elsewhere inside Grand Canyon, where you'll find trout, striped and largemouth bass, catfish, and other species.

Exploring the Colorado River

TOP EXPERIENCE

People who have been inside the Grand Canyon often have one of two reactions—either they can't wait to return, or they swear never to return. This is even the case for those intrepid souls who ride the great river, braving white-water roller coasters while looking forward to a star-filled evening—dry, and full of gourmet camp food—camping on a white beach deep in the gorge. To boat the Colorado is one of the most exciting and potentially life-changing trips the American West has to offer.

COMMERCIAL RIVER TRIPS

Rafting season in the canyon runs **April-October,** and there are myriad trips to choose from—from a 3-day long-weekend ride to an 18-day full-canyon epic. An **upper-canyon trip** will take you from River Mile 0 at Lees Ferry through the canyon to Phantom Ranch, while a **lower-canyon trip** begins at Phantom, requiring a hike down the Bright Angel with your gear on your back. Furthermore, you can choose between a motorized pontoon boat (as some three-quarters of rafters do), a paddleboat, a kayak, or some other combination. It all depends on what you want and what you can afford.

Choosing a Trip

Expect to pay about $1,400 per person for a 3-day motor trip, $2,600 per person for a 6-day motor trip, $2,000 per person for a 6-day oar trip, and up to $5,000 per person for a 13-day oar trip. Many of the outfitters offer trips tailored to certain interests, such as trips with a naturalist or trips that make a lot of stops for hiking.

Choosing an Outfitter

If you are considering taking a river trip, the best place to start is the website of the **Grand Canyon River Outfitters Association** (www.gcroa.org), a nonprofit group of 13 licensed river outfitters, all of them monitored and approved by the National Park Service, each with a good safety record and relatively similar rates. Your guide takes care of all the permits you need to spend nights below the rim. After you decide what kind of trip you want, the website links to the individual outfitters for booking. Most of the companies offer trips lasting 3-18 days and have a variety of boat styles. It's a good idea to choose two or three companies, call them up, and talk to someone live. You'll be putting your life in their hands, so you want to make sure that you like the spirit of the company. Also consider the size of the group. These river trips are very social; you'll be spending a lot of time with your fellow boaters. Talk to a company representative about previous trips so you can get a gauge of what kind of people, and how many, you'll be floating with.

If you are one of the majority of river

Colorado River Outfitters

Below is a list of the National Park Service-approved river trip outfitters. No other companies are allowed to guide trips through the canyon, so you must pick from among these highly respected and well-established companies.

- **Aramark-Wilderness River Adventures** (P.O. Box 171, Page, AZ 86040, 928/645-3296 or 800/992-8022, www.riveradventures.com)

- **Arizona Raft Adventures** (4050 E. Huntington Dr., Flagstaff, AZ, 928/526-8246 or 800/786-7238, https://azraft.com)

- **Canyon Explorations/Expeditions** (675 W. Clay Ave., Flagstaff, AZ, 928/774-4559 or 800/654-0723, www.canyonexplorations.com)

- **Canyoneers** (7195 N. U.S. Hwy. 89, Flagstaff, AZ, 928/526-0924 or 800/525-0924, https://canyoneers.com)

- **Colorado River & Trail Expeditions** (P.O. Box 57575, Salt Lake City, UT 84157, 801/261-1789 or 800/253-7328, www.crateinc.com)

- **Grand Canyon Dories** (P.O. Box 216, Altaville, CA 95221, 209/736-0805 or 800/877-3679, www.oars.com)

- **Grand Canyon Expeditions** (P.O. Box 0, Kanab, UT 84741, 435/644-2691 or 800/544-2691, www.gcex.com)

- **Grand Canyon Whitewater** (100 N. Humphreys St., Ste. 202, Flagstaff, AZ, 928/779-2979 or 800/343-3121, www.grandcanyonwhitewater.com)

- **Hatch River Expeditions** (5348 E. Burris Ln., Flagstaff, AZ, 928/526-4700 or 800/856-8966, www.hatchriverexpeditions.com)

- **O.A.R.S.** (P.O. Box 67, Angels Camp, CA 95222, 209/736-2924 or 800/364-6277, www.oars.com)

- **Outdoors Unlimited** (6900 Townsend Winona Rd., Flagstaff, AZ, 800/637-7238, www.outdoorsunlimited.com)

- **Tour West** (P.O. Box 333, Orem, UT 84059, 801/225-0755 or 800/453-9107, www.twriver.com)

- **Western River Expeditions** (7258 Racquet Club Dr., Salt Lake City, UT, 801/942-6669 or 800/453-7450, www.westernriver.com)

explorers who can't wait to get back on the water once you've landed at the final port, remember that the National Park Service enforces a strict limit of one trip per year, per person.

Before You Go

There are a few things you can do long before your trip that will serve you well on the river. The most important of these is to get in shape. Colorado River trips are incredibly active affairs. Not only will you probably have to hike into or out of the canyon via the punishing Bright Angel Trail, every day on the river

there will be amazing, once-in-a-lifetime side trips on land—slick rocks over which to scramble, and steep trails (in the very loose sense of the word) to climb. Start training at least six months out with a steep trail or road and increase the difficulty over the months.

After you book your river trip, your guide company will send you a large packet of materials to look over. This generally includes information on what to expect from the trip, and offers suggestions about what to bring along and how to train for all the hiking. Make sure you read your packet over carefully and follow your guide's directions exactly.

Finally, it's a good idea to add travel insurance to the already steep price of your river trip. There's so much that could happen in the year or more between booking your trip and actually putting in at Lees Ferry or Phantom Ranch.

NONCOMMERCIAL RIVER TRIPS

Just imagine you and your best friends riding the great river together, piloting your own boat, choosing your own campsites, going at your own pace, free and easy and guideless in the vast red-rock wilderness. It's not easy, but it can be done with a noncommercial river trip through the Grand Canyon.

According to National Park Service (NPS) rules, the trip leader of a noncommercial rafting trip must be 18 or older and "must have a working knowledge of whitewater safety, general first aid, river equipment repair, and the techniques of whitewater navigation." Additionally, the leader must have whitewater experience in the Grand Canyon or other comparable western rivers such as the Green, the Rogue, the Yampa, and others (for a complete list of comparable rivers, go to https://grcariverpermits.nps.gov).

If you know somebody like that, a rare breed indeed, you are well on your way to heading out. The most important aspect of a noncommercial river trip is that it must be nonprofit, and all members must share equally in the cost. So if you don't know somebody who can run the river, you cannot hire a guide to do it for you.

Noncommercial trips are limited to 16 people for a standard trip and 8 people for a small group. You can apply to mount an **18- to 25-day river expedition** from **Lees Ferry to Diamond Creek** using inflatable rafts, fiberglass or plastic canoes and kayaks, or motorized boats with 55 horsepower or less (Apr. 1-Sept. 15 only). You can only take one trip per year.

A weighted **lottery** for a launch date is run by the **NPS Grand Canyon Permits Office** (1824 S. Thompson St., Ste. 201,

Flagstaff, AZ 86001, 928/638-7834 or 800/959-9164, grca_riv@nps.gov, www.nps. gov/grca, $25 lottery application fee, $200-400 trip deposit depending on size of group, $20 park entrance fee pp, $90 permit fee pp). You must fill out an online application at the website listed above, which are accepted during the first three weeks of February for dates the next year. You'll know if you got your launch date by the end of February. After the initial lottery, follow-ups are held throughout the year to assign leftover or cancelled launch dates (www.nps.gov/grca/ planyourvisit/cancelled-dates.htm).

You can also mount a shorter, **2- to 5-day noncommercial river trip** from **Diamond Creek to Pearce Ferry,** through the lower gorge and the Hualapai lands, ending at Lake Mead. There is no charge for an NPS permit (www.nps.gov/grca/planyourvisit/overview-diamond-ck.htm), which are awarded first-come, first-served up to a year ahead of time, but you will have to pay the tribe's access fees and camping fees ($100 pp per night).

If all this seems rather daunting, check out these **Flagstaff river equipment outfitters: Canyon R.E.O.** (1619 N. East St., Flagstaff, 928/774-3377 or 800/637-4604, www. canyonreo.com); **Moenkopi Riverworks** (5355 N. Dodge Ave., Flagstaff, 928/856-0012 or 928/526-6622, www.moenkopiriverworks. com); and **Professional River Outfitters, Inc.** (2800 W. Historic Rt. 66, Flagstaff, 928/779-1512 or 800/648-3236, www.proriver. com). They can provide you with boats and other gear rentals, food packs and kitchens, shuttle services, and even full packages with everything you need for a trip, including consulting (these packages usually run about $1,000-1,200 per person, which is still cheaper than a comparable commercial trip).

LEES FERRY TO PHANTOM RANCH

All river trips through the heart of Grand Canyon begin at Lees Ferry within the Glen Canyon National Recreation Area, which is River Mile 0 of the lower Colorado River. A popular trip is the 87 river miles (140 km) between Lees Ferry and Phantom Ranch in the inner gorge, often called the "upper-canyon trip." Such trips can last anywhere between three and seven days, depending on if you're in a motorboat or running on oars, and can cost upward of $1,500 to more than $3,000 per person. River rafters encounter 19 major rapids on this trip, and it usually requires a hike out the Bright Angel Trail (about 4,500 ft/1,372 m up) to the South Rim. Your trip will begin the night before at a chain hotel in Flagstaff with a must-attend orientation meeting. Early the next morning you'll pile into a van with your new friends and head to Lees Ferry, about a two-hour drive. When you arrive at Lees Ferry, the bustling begins, packing everything onto the boat and getting everyone settled on board, and soon enough you'll be off on the green, cold-water river with the sandstone walls closing in.

The hike up the Bright Angel Trail to the South Rim from Phantom Ranch is 9.9 miles (15.9 km), and it's an arduous, long, and sometimes dispiriting trudge, but it doesn't have to be. You'll hike out with your guide, and there are plenty of places to rest. You can send your bag ahead of you on a mule by booking duffel service ahead of time (30 lbs/13.6 kg maximum, $76 one-way).

Navajo Bridge
MILE 4

You're just getting settled and used to being off dry land when, about 4 miles (6.4 km) on from Lees Ferry, you pass beneath **Navajo Bridge,** which crosses the river some 500 feet (152 m) above you. This is the last place for 342 miles (545 km) that you can drive across the Colorado River, the next spot being Hoover Dam near Las Vegas, Nevada. Give a wave to all those sad tourists up there looking down on you, wishing they were going downriver too. Keep an eye out for California condors as you pass through this well-known haunt.

Marble Canyon
MILE 5

About another mile and you are officially in Grand Canyon. You'll know it when you see the ubiquitous top three layers appear here: the Kaibab Formation on top, the Toroweap Formation between, and the Coconino sandstone below that. There's actually no marble in **Marble Canyon;** the name came from canyon explorer John Wesley Powell, who thought the polished walls resembled marble. Marble Canyon stretches all the way to the Colorado River's confluence with the Little Colorado River. While geologically Marble Canyon is part of Grand Canyon, it is still known by its historical name. It was added to Grand Canyon National Park in 1975.

Soap Creek Rapid
MILE 11.2

It's not too long before you start to encounter the first rapids on the river, and you may already consider yourself a river-rat by the time you get through the **Badger Creek Rapid** at River Mile 7.8 and **Soap Creek Rapid** at Mile 11.2. There are nice sandy-beach campsites in this area, and it's where many first days on the river end. At Mile 12, there's a **carved inscription** on a rock commemorating the 1889 drowning death near here of Frank Brown, president of the Denver, Colorado, Canyon & Pacific Railroad Company, who along with engineer Robert B. Stanton journeyed into the canyon that year to complete a survey for a railroad project that, of course, never happened.

House Rock Rapid
MILE 17

At the mouth of the **Rider Canyon** tributary (down which rocks and other debris rush atop periodic flash floods, filling the river with rapid-creating materials), you encounter one of the more difficult stretches of Marble Canyon—**House Rock Rapid,** where boats have been known to flip from time to time. A short scramble up Rider Canyon is a good

way to stretch your legs and get off the boat for a while.

The Roaring Twenties
MILES 20-30

Almost universally described as akin to riding a roller coaster, the "Roaring Twenties" comprise **nine rapids** (including **Georgie, Hansbrough-Richards, Cave Springs,** and **Tiger Wash Rapids**), some spaced less than 1 mile (1.6 km) apart, making for a fast and super fun ride. You're soaked one minute, dry the next, then soaked again, and everybody's whooping and hollering all around you like kids at a waterpark. It's just pure fun, the river-running experience at its most enjoyable.

South Canyon
MILE 31

South Canyon is a popular spot to pull over and explore, especially in the beautiful area known as **Vasey's Paradise,** with cliffs covered in shaggy greenery and trickling white runnels falling close to the rocks. This area is also accessible from the North Rim and the House Rock Valley, so you may see hikers here as well as other river-runners. Nearby but not open to the public is **Stanton's Cave,** where archaeologists over the years have found the bones of extinct sloths and those mysterious bent-twig animal figures that were left by the canyon's ancient inhabitants. After the death of poor Frank Brown, Robert Stanton ended the 1889 railroad survey here, only to return the next year to continue the work down to the Gulf of California.

Redwall Cavern
MILES 33-50

Even if you can't afford to get there via the river, you've probably seen pictures of **Redwall Cavern,** which is one of the most popular and photographed places in the inner canyon. It's a huge chamber or amphitheater scooped out of the sandstone by eons of erosional forces. It's a must-stop along the river and truly amazing when seen up close. Cool and dark, Redwall Cavern is a wonderful place to hang out for a while during the infernal heat of a summertime river trip. There is no camping or fires allowed here. Moving on, the river bends around **Point Hansbrough,** a high, crumbling red-rock tower named for a member of the Brown-Stanton expedition, and through **President Harding Rapid** at Mile 43, a Class 4 rapid named for the 29th president.

Nankoweap Ruin Route
MILE 53

One of the highlights of an upper-canyon trip, this must-stop spot includes a steep but short (about 0.5 mi/0.8 km from the beach) hike to the **Nankoweap Granaries,** a small cliff ruin in which, around AD 1100, Ancestral Puebloans stored grain, seeds, and corn in dry, rodent-proof storehouses. The view of the river atop which you've just traveled 53 miles (85 km) is amazing. There are several campsites in this area, and you may see some very tired hikers fresh off the 14-mile (22.5-km) **Nankoweap Trail** from the North Rim, one of Grand Canyon National Park's most difficult.

Little Colorado River Confluence
MILE 61

And so you have come to the confluence, where the **Little Colorado River**'s warmish, milky-blue water from limestone springs joins the cold, green waters of the Colorado. This spot, which marks the official end of Marble Canyon and start of **Granite Gorge** (also known as the **inner gorge**), is a sacred landscape for the Hopi, who believe the Sipapu, or navel, through which they entered this world is located here. The Hopi also gathered salt from large deposits nearby via the salt trail, a route used for centuries. Also, under a sandstone cliff here is **Beamer's cabin,**

1: Lees Ferry, where most canyon river trips begin
2: river-trippers passing below Navajo Bridge at Marble Canyon

Colorado River Facts

- The Colorado River is 1,450 miles (2,335 km) long, the sixth-largest river in North America.

- It flows through seven states, two countries, and 11 U.S. national parks.

- Through Grand Canyon it ranges in width from just 76 feet (23 m) across at the Granite Narrows, River Mile 136, to about 750 feet at River Mile 193. It's about 200-300 feet (61-91 m) across on average.

- The Colorado River Basin comprises 260,000 square miles (673,400 sq km), about 8 percent of the continental United States, and has a population of about 36 million people.

- The river's headwaters are at La Poudre Pass Lake (elevation 10,174 ft/3,101 m) in Rocky Mountain National Park. The lake drains south at the Continental Divide, creating a mountain stream that eventually becomes the mighty Colorado River.

- The Colorado River enters Grand Canyon at Marble Canyon, just below Lees Ferry and Glen Canyon National Recreation Area, and exits the gorge some 296 miles (475 km) downriver at the Grand Wash Cliffs near Lake Mead.

- Glen Canyon Dam, just upriver from Lees Ferry, closed its gates in 1963, changing the river from a warm and muddy flow to one that is cold and green.

- The Colorado River through Grand Canyon is now between 48°F (9°C) and 55°F (13°C) year-round.

a small stone structure built by pioneer and miner Ben Beamer in 1890 out of a Pueblo ruin. There is no camping or fishing allowed in this area. The warmer waters of the Little Colorado make it a favorite spot for the humpback chub and other endangered native fish.

Confluence to Inner Gorge
MILES 62-76

For the next 10 miles (16.1 km) or so you'll pass the Crash Canyon, near where a United DC-7 crashed in 1956, along with Temple Butte, Carbon Creek, Lava Canyon, Espejo Creek, Tanner Rapid, and Tanner Canyon. The river then widens at the **Unkar Rapid** and the **Unkar Delta** (taking their name from the Paiute word for "red stone"). The Unkar Delta, a big bend in the river around River Mile 72.5, was a home of farming Ancestral Puebloans between about AD 850 and AD 1200. Leaving the Unkar Delta, you'll pass Escalante Creek, Escalante Rapid, and Nevills Rapid, named for Norman D. Nevills, the first man to offer commercial river trips through the canyon (1938).

★ The Inner Gorge
MILE 76

The walls become narrow and close in a bit claustrophobically as you enter **Granite Gorge,** also known as the **inner gorge.** Suddenly you're surrounded by the oldest rocks on earth, the so-called basement rocks—dark-gray-and-black Vishnu schist and the red-and-pink intrusive igneous of the Zoroaster granite. The first really serious, major challenge comes at **Hance Rapid,** at River Mile 76.5, named for the famous canyon pioneer, guide, and raconteur John Hance. The rapid was created by flash floods from **Red Canyon,** through which the **New Hance Trail** leads toward the South Rim. As you approach the beach at the Bright Angel Creek confluence, near Phantom Ranch, you'll see the **Black and Silver Bridges** over the Colorado River, the only permanent foot crossings since Navajo Bridge far upriver.

1: the inner gorge **2:** Bright Angel Creek

★ **Bright Angel Creek**

MILE 88

Bright Angel Creek flows from Roaring Springs just below the North Rim, careening down **Bright Angel Canyon** along much of the **North Kaibab Trail**, spilling into the Colorado River just below Phantom Ranch and Bright Angel Campground, through which the creek flows below tall, shady cottonwood trees, singing sweetly to campers all day and night. Coined by who else but explorer John Wesley Powell, the name "Bright Angel" is repeated ad nauseum throughout the national park, and is said to have come about as a commentary on the creek's clarity in contrast to the then very muddy Colorado River and many of its flood-stage tributaries. Ancestral Puebloans once lived in this lush riparian area, and there's a small **ruin** reached by a trail above the river on the same bank as **Boat Beach,** which is bound to have a few relaxing hikers on it as you float in looking all tough and grizzled from your time upriver.

Phantom Ranch

One of the most peaceful and beautiful places on earth despite its hot desert setting, **Phantom Ranch** is a green paradise near the banks of Bright Angel Creek, shaded by tall cottonwoods and kept close by high, reddish canyon walls all around. This is considered the halfway point on the river, and it's the end of the upper portion and the start of the lower portion. If you're just doing the upper-canyon trip, this is where you'll hop off the water and start your grueling journey on land out to the South Rim. But before you head off, take a short walk up to the Phantom Ranch Canteen for a lemonade or a cold beer.

PHANTOM RANCH TO LAKE MEAD

Commercial trips through the lower canyon begin at Boat Beach near Phantom Ranch and require a strenuous hike down the Bright Angel Trail from the South Rim, with all your gear on your back. (You can send your bag ahead of you on a mule by booking duffel

service ahead of time for $76 one-way.) This is the trip for those who want to experience the Colorado's rapids at their biggest and wildest. Lower-canyon trips take up to 10 days and cost at least $5,000 per person. You'll float through the western canyon to Lake Mead, a huge desert lake created by Hoover Dam on the lower Colorado near Las Vegas. Along the way you'll negotiate 28 major rapids and spend hours in the sunshine exploring red-and-green canyons beneath cool veils of falling water.

Crystal Rapid and the Gems

MILE 98

Leaving Phantom Ranch and heading downriver, fairly soon you'll encounter some challenging white water, including **Pipe Springs Rapid** below Plateau Point, where hikers look down from high above, and **Horn Rapid** at Horn Creek on the south bank, **Salt Creek Rapid** at Salt Creek on the south, **Granite Rapid** near Monument Creek on the south, and the roaring **Hermit Rapid** near Hermit Creek on the south. A moderate to difficult trail up Hermit Creek leads to **Hermit Camp,** the **Hermit Trail,** and eventually the South Rim. At River Mile 97 you'll pass **Boucher Rapid,** and then 1 mile (1.6 km) later you'll come to one of the most notorious and destructive spots along the river, **Crystal Rapid.** This is one of the top two most difficult rapids on the river (the other being the upcoming Lava Falls at Mile 179), formed by two side canyons (Crystal Creek from the north and Slate Creek from the south) meeting at the river. If you make it through Crystal, next comes the fun series of "gems"—**Agate, Sapphire, Turquoise, Jasper, Jade, Ruby,** and **Serpentine Rapids.**

Bass Canyon

MILE 107

A regular stop along the river and for rafters and inner-canyon explorers, **Bass Canyon** is the site of old **Bass Camp,** pioneer William Bass's tourist camp, established around 1899. It included a cable crossing over the river to connect his two trails, the **South Bass Trail** and the **North Bass Trail,** allowing for rim-to-rim travel before the bridges near Phantom Ranch were built.

Elves Chasm
MILE 116

After Bass Canyon you'll encounter the **Shinumo Rapid** near Shinumo Creek, **110-Mile Rapid, Hakatai Rapid** at Hakatai Canyon, and **Walthenberg Rapid,** and then pass **Garnet Canyon** before reaching beautiful **Elves Chasm** (a 0.25-mi/0.4 km hike from the river), an enchanting paradise with a shallow cave and pool below thin and misty waterfalls and red-and-white rock walls covered in moss and ferns.

Granite Narrows and Deer Creek Falls
MILE 136

The narrowest point between canyon walls at just 76 feet (23 m) wide, the short passage called the **Granite Narrows** provides an eerie thrill around River Mile 136, and soon after you're at the 110-foot (34-m) **Deer Creek Falls,** a beautiful green spot that is popular for stopping and exploring.

At Mile 148 you'll come to **Matkatamiba Canyon,** another gorgeous side canyon with a cool, green riparian habitat that's worth a stop.

Havasu Canyon
MILE 157

Perhaps the most famous tributary along the river through Grand Canyon, **Havasu Creek** is a perennial stream that spills into the Colorado River from the south after falling through **Havasu Canyon** and creating several waterfalls that are otherworldly in their beauty. **Beaver Falls** is about 3 miles (4.8 km) from the river; 6 miles (9.7 km) up-creek from the river will get you to **Mooney Falls.** The village of **Supai**—on the way to which is the most beautiful of the waterfalls, **Havasu Falls**—is 9 miles (14.5 km) from the river. Most river trips stop here at the mouth of Havasu Canyon for swimming and exploring.

Lava Falls
MILE 179

Often called the "climax" of the rough-and-tumble lower-canyon river trip, the Class 10 rapid called **Lava Falls** roils and crashes, waiting just for you with gnashing white teeth, at River Mile 179. Some of the most difficult white water in North America, Lava Falls is created by debris flooding out of **Prospect Canyon,** which has the second-largest debris fan of any tributary on the river. Neither Powell nor Stanton would try it during their pioneering trips down the Colorado. Both chose to portage around. But your guide won't. Prepare for the ride of your life.

Diamond Creek
MILE 226

Many lower-canyon river trips end at **Diamond Creek** on the Hualapai Reservation. The Diamond Creek Road, a 20-mile (32-km) dirt route from the banks of the river to Peach Springs (the reservation's capital), is one of the few ways to actually drive into Grand Canyon. The Hualapai Tribe offers fun, **one-day river trips** from the beach near Diamond Creek (928/769-2636, www. grandcanyonwest.com, May-Oct., $450 pp), which are a good substitute for the often prohibitively expensive and time-consuming trips starting at Lees Ferry or Phantom Ranch.

Separation Rapid
MILE 239

The last real white water of the trip, **Separation Rapid** at River Mile 239 was named by John Wesley Powell to commemorate the dissolution of his crew. The party camped near this rapid in August 1869, running short of food and spirit. Three of the men refused to run the rapid and chose instead to hike out. The next day Powell and the remaining men made easy work of it, and after that the river settled down considerably. Later Powell found out that the men had been

Hikes from the Colorado River

Trail	Effort	Distance	Duration	River Mile
South Canyon	Easy	0.5 mi/0.8 km round-trip	30-40 minutes	Mile 31 (right)
Nankoweap Granaries	Strenuous	1.5 mi/2.4 km round-trip	1.5-2 hours	Mile 53 (left)
Monument Creek	Easy	2 mi/3.2 km round-trip	1-1.5 hours	Mile 93 (left)
Shinumo Creek Falls	Easy	0.2 mi/0.3 km round-trip	30 minutes	Mile 108 (right)
Elves Chasm	Easy	0.5 mi/0.8 km round-trip	1 hour	Mile 116 (left)
Deer Creek Trail	Strenuous	10 mi/16.1 km round-trip	4-6 hours	Mile 136 (right)
Matkatamiba Canyon	Easy	0.5 mi/0.8 km round-trip	1 hour	Mile 148 (left)
Havasu Creek	Strenuous	Up to 19 mi/31 km	Varies	Mile 156 (left)
Fern Glen	Moderate	1 mi/1.6 km round-trip	1 hour	Mile 168 (right)
Travertine Canyon	Strenuous	Up to 4 mi/6.4 km round-trip	2-3 hours	Mile 229 (left)

murdered in the wilderness. The lesson here is stick with your river guide, no matter what.

Grand Wash Cliffs
MILE 276

The **Grand Wash Cliffs** at River Mile 276 are the official end of Grand Canyon and Grand Canyon National Park, and they mark as well the bittersweet end of your lower-canyon river trip. Here begins the Lake Mead National Recreation Area. Not far away are the towering Hoover Dam, the sprawling Lake Mead, and the flashing neon lights of Las Vegas.

Lake Mead

The 290-square-mile (751-sq-km) **Lake Mead National Recreation Area** comprises two desert reservoirs filled from the damming of the Colorado River. The largest is **Lake Mead,** 112 miles (180 km) long and the continent's largest man-made body of water.

On many commercial river trips a jet boat will meet you on the lake and take you and your gear the rest of the way to shore, where you'll load up in the awaiting van and head back across the desert to Flagstaff, a 3.5-hour drive.

HIKING AND BACKPACKING

Most river trips through Grand Canyon involve a lot of day hikes and land-scrambles from the shore to see all the amazing and otherwise inaccessible secrets that Grand Canyon has to offer. Many of the standard upper- and lower-canyon hikes aren't necessarily on trails, but rather tradition-established routes up dry, rocky creek beds and through spooky narrows to swimming holes and weeping red-and-green walls. Some of the hikes begin at the well-established camps along the river, while others can only be accessed by boat.

South Canyon

Distance: 0.5 mile (0.8 km) round-trip
Duration: 30-40 minutes
Elevation gain: 800 feet (244 m)
Effort: Easy
Trail conditions: Rock trails, slippery when wet, steep, narrow
Trailhead: River right, Mile 31

A must-stop on any river trip, **South Canyon** is home to the beautiful spring-fed oasis called **Vasey's Paradise.** This is one of the most beautiful and enchanting side hikes in the upper canyon. Near here is also **Stanton's Cave,** off limits to the public, where evidence of ancient canyon hunter-gatherers has been found. There's an Ancestral Puebloan **ruin** here, testifying to the area's long human habitation. South Canyon is also accessible from the North Rim and the House Rock Valley via a steep and difficult trail.

Nankoweap Granaries

Distance: 1.5 miles (2.4 km) round-trip
Duration: 1.5-2 hours
Elevation gain: 1,500 feet (457 m)
Effort: Strenuous
Trail conditions: Sandy, rocky, steep
Trailhead: River left, Mile 53

All the river trips stop at the **Nankoweap Granaries.** Hop off the boat near **Nankoweap Creek** and make the short but very steep climb up to the fascinating Ancestral Puebloan site—stone storehouses where farmers from the deltas kept their crops dry and rodent-free. It's a tough few minutes getting up there, but it's certainly worth it for a dramatic narrow view of the river and the high rock walls that contain it. The Nankoweap area is also accessible via a steep and difficult trail from the North Rim.

Monument Creek

Distance: 2 miles (3.2 km) round-trip
Duration: 1-1.5 hours
Elevation gain: 500 feet (152 m)
Effort: Easy
Trail conditions: Rocky, dirt, some sand
Trailhead: River left, Mile 93

Most river trips stop at **Monument Canyon,** from which flash-flood debris has spilled out over the eons to help create **Granite Rapid.** The canyon is named for its "monument"— a tall, thick spire of 545-million-year-old Tapeats sandstone; there are some cool and smooth narrows about 0.75 mile (1.2 km) up the drainage.

Shinumo Creek Falls

Distance: 0.2 mile (0.3 km) round-trip
Duration: 30 minutes
Elevation gain: 300 feet (91 m)
Effort: Easy
Trail conditions: Wet, rocky, sandy
Trailhead: River right, Mile 108

Head into shore and take an easy stroll up the wash (which will be more like wading if the water is high) to **Shinumo Creek Falls,** one of several magical waterfalls and swimming holes along the Colorado River through Grand Canyon. The swimming hole below the falls shrinks in summer and is at its best in the spring, but during flood times it may be dangerous.

Elves Chasm

Distance: 0.5 mile (0.8 km) round-trip
Duration: 1 hour
Elevation gain: 200 feet (61 m)
Effort: Easy
Trail conditions: Slick, wet, rocky, some sand
Trailhead: River left, Mile 116

There's little chance of your river trip failing to stop at this enchanting oasis at Mile 116, a shallow cave with a waterfall, swimming hole, and cool greenery all around. **Elves Chasm,** where it's easy to imagine some mythical group of gentle beings living out its days, is a short 0.25-mile (0.4-km) jaunt from the river.

Deer Creek Trail

Distance: 10 miles (16.1 km) round-trip
Duration: 4-6 hours
Elevation gain: 1,700 feet (518 m)
Effort: Strenuous
Trail conditions: Slick, wet, rocky, some sand
Trailhead: River right, Mile 136

Most commercial river trips stop at **Deer Creek Falls**, the cool narrows, and the **Deer Creek Trail** at Mile 136 along the river. The trail climbs up a ways and becomes a series of wondrous Tapeats sandstone narrows, and eventually leads to a smaller waterfall and joins the Thunder River Trail, which leads out of the canyon to the North Rim.

Matkatamiba Canyon

Distance: 0.5 mile (0.8 km) round-trip
Duration: 1 hour
Elevation gain: 400 feet (122 m)
Effort: Easy
Trail conditions: Rocky, wet, slick, some sand
Trailhead: River left, Mile 148

Stop the boat once again and take this short, wet hike (with some possible wading) up **Matkatamiba Canyon** about 0.25 mile (0.4 km) one-way to the "patio," a beautiful, green, and peaceful spot with ledges and narrows and waterfalls.

Havasu Creek

Distance: Up to 19 miles (31 km)
Duration: Varies
Elevation gain: 4,400 feet (1,341 m)
Effort: Strenuous
Trail conditions: Rocky, wet, slick, some sand
Trailhead: River left, Mile 157

Another popular stop along the river through Grand Canyon, **Havasu Creek** spills into the Colorado all blue green and beautiful around Mile 157. Most river-trippers stick to the mouth of the creek, relaxing and swimming in the pools here. You could conceivably leave the river here and hike to **Supai,** a small village inside Grand Canyon known for its wonderful nearby waterfalls—**Beaver Falls** (3 mi/4.8 km from river), gorgeous falls that tumble into deep, clear pools; **Mooney**

Falls (6 mi/9.7 km from river), a jaw-dropping 196-foot (60-m) ribbon of white water falling into a blue pool; and **Havasu Falls** (less than 9 mi/14.5 km from river), perhaps the most famous waterfall in the canyon, an amazing 200-foot (61 m) fall just below Supai Village. However, the wet creekside trail up the canyon to the falls is tough and long, and you won't be able to stay in the campground near the village without a prior reservation.

Fern Glen

Distance: 1 mile (1.6 km) round-trip
Duration: 1 hour
Elevation gain: 300 feet (91 m)
Effort: Moderate
Trail conditions: Rocky, wet, slick, some sand
Trailhead: River right, Mile 168

This side trip off the river leads to yet another beautiful and enchanting grotto covered in greenery and falling veils of spring water. Most river trips stop here for some splashing around and photography. The "trail" is a series of **sandstone stairs** that leads up **Fern Glen Canyon** to the grotto.

Travertine Canyon

Distance: Up to 4 miles (6.4 km) round-trip
Duration: 2-3 hours
Elevation gain: 900 feet (274 m)
Effort: Strenuous
Trail conditions: Rocky, wet, slick, some sand, some climbing
Trailhead: River left, Mile 229

Head up the wash (likely wet) for about an hour round-trip to see 35-foot (11-m) **Travertine Falls,** or scramble farther on, following **cairns** up the creek bed past several smaller waterfalls to a beautiful, green **spring-fed oasis,** the source of the canyon's water.

Food and Accommodations

PHANTOM RANCH

Designed by Mary Jane Colter for the Fred Harvey Company in 1922, ★ **Phantom Ranch** (888/297-2757, www.grandcanyonlodges.com, dormitory $51 pp, 2-person cabin $149, $13 each additional person), the only noncamping accommodations inside the canyon, is a shady, peaceful place that you're likely to miss and yearn for once you've visited and left it behind. Perhaps Phantom's strong draw is less about its intrinsic pleasures and more about it being the only sign of civilization in a deep wilderness that can feel like the end of the world, especially after the 14-mile (22.5-km) hike in from the North Rim.

Phantom Ranch has 11 rustic, air-conditioned **cabins** and four hiker-only **dormitories.** The cabins vary in size, sleeping 2-10 people. Each cabin has a sink with cold water, a toilet, bedding, and towels. Hot-water sinks and showers are available in a separate "showerhouse" building, where towels, soap, and shampoo are also provided. There are two dormitories for men and two for women (families with children five or under must stay in a cabin). Each dormitory has five bunk beds, a toilet, and a shower. Bedding, towels, soap, and shampoo are provided. The dorms and the cabins are all heated in the winter and air-conditioned in the summer.

The lodge's center point is the **Phantom Ranch Canteen,** a welcoming, air-conditioned, beer- and lemonade-selling sight for anyone who has just descended one of the trails. There is no central lodge building at Phantom Ranch, but the canteen is the closest thing to it, with its family-style tables often filling up during the heat of the day with beer-drinkers and tale-tellers. The canteen offers two meals per day—**breakfast,** made up of eggs, pancakes, and thick slices of bacon ($23.65), and **dinner,** with a choice of steak ($47.91), stew ($29.43), or vegetarian ($29.43). The cantina also offers a **box lunch** ($20.85) with a bagel, fruit, and salty snacks. Reservations for meals are also difficult to come by. You must make reservations at least a year ahead.

Most nights and afternoons, a ranger based at Phantom Ranch will give a talk on some aspect of canyon lore, history, or science. These events are always interesting and well attended, even in the 110°F (43°C) heat of summer.

Phantom is located near the mouth of Bright Angel Canyon, within a few yards of clear, babbling Bright Angel Creek, and shaded by large cottonwoods, some of them planted in the 1930s by the Civilian Conservation Corps. There are several day hikes within easy reach, and the Colorado River and the two awesome suspension bridges that link one bank to the other are only about 0.4 mile (0.6 km) from the lodge.

A **lottery system** governs Phantom Ranch **reservations.** You have to enter the lottery between the 1st and 25th of the month 15 months prior to your proposed trip. You'll be notified at least 14 months before your trip if you won a stay. Go to www.grandcanyonlodges.com/lodging/phantom-ranch/lottery for more details.

CAMPING

To stay overnight below the rim, you must obtain a **permit** from the **Backcountry Information Center** (928/638-7875, $10 plus $8 pp per night).

From March 1 to November 14, you're allowed to spend up to two consecutive nights at a corridor campground (Bright Angel, Indian Garden, or Cottonwood). From November 15 to February 28, the limit is four consecutive nights.

Developed Campgrounds

There are three developed campgrounds in the

inner canyon: **Cottonwood Campground,** along the North Kaibab Trail; **Bright Angel Campground,** near Phantom Ranch; and **Indian Garden Campground,** along the Bright Angel Trail. Your backcountry permit is your reservation. All three campgrounds offer toilets, a freshwater spigot (year-round at Bright Angel and Indian Garden only), picnic tables, food storage bins to keep the critters out, poles on which to hang your packs, and emergency phones. There are no showers or other amenities. It's a good idea to throw a roll of toilet paper into your pack just in case the campgrounds are out.

The best campground in the inner canyon is **Bright Angel Campground,** a shady, cottonwood-lined setting along cool Bright Angel Creek with 33 tent spots, each with pack poles, a picnic table, and ammo boxes to keep the raccoons out of your food. Because of its easy proximity to Phantom Ranch (about 0.4 mi/0.6 km), campers can make use of the Phantom Ranch Canteen, even eating meals there if they can get a reservation, and can attend the ranger talks offered at the lodge. There's nothing quite like sitting on the grassy banks beside your campsite and cooling your worn feet in the creek. Accessible from the Bright Angel Trail (9.5 mi/15.3 km one-way),

South Kaibab Trail (7 mi/11.3 km one-way) and North Kaibab Trail (14 mi/22.5 km one-way), Bright Angel Campground has an emergency phone, a year-round potable water spigot, and bathrooms with sinks and toilets. There's also a ranger on-site who will greet you once you get settled in your spot.

Cottonwood Campground is 6.8 miles (10.9 km) below the North Rim along the North Kaibab Trail, a small, bare-minimum stopover with 11 individual tent and two group sites near Bright Angel Creek, at about the halfway point between the North Rim and the Colorado River. Small and less visited than the other corridor campgrounds, Cottonwood is a mixture of desert scrub among the jagged and crumbling red buttes, towering above you against the star-smeared night skies, and a bit of riparian splendor among the titular cottonwood trees and salt cedar. Most of the sites lack shade of any kind and are exposed to the sun. Each site has a picnic table, an ammo box for food storage, and a pole on which to hang your pack. Near the historic ranger station, which is no longer in use, there is a faucet with potable water from mid-May to mid-October, but you should not count on it as the pipeline is subject to breaks. Take a filter along and get your water from the creek nearby. There's

Bright Angel Campground

also an emergency phone here and three compost toilets.

Indian Garden Campground is about 4.8 miles (7.7 km) from the South Rim along the Bright Angel Trail, a spring-fed oasis about halfway between the South Rim and Colorado River. A green and shady campground among the cottonwoods, each of the 15 individual tent sites has a shade structure, picnic table, pack pole, and ammo can to store your food. There's a ranger station on-site and potable water year-round, compost toilets, and an emergency phone. A great day hike from this area is the 3-mile (4.8-km) round-trip hike out to Plateau Point on the edge of the Tonto Platform, looking down at the river far below. One of the few drawbacks of Indian Garden is that the sites are relatively close together, so if you're next to a group of loud talkers you'll be joining in whether you want to or not. Look for deer and other common canyon critters among the overgrown greenery here.

Backcountry Camping

Off the popular corridor trails, the inner canyon's backcountry is divided into "use areas" with limited overnight access. Many of these areas, haunted by experienced canyon explorers year-round, allow **at-large camping** that follows standard Leave No Trace principles (https://lnt.org). Other areas have **primitive campsites** with pit toilets. The biggest obstacle to exploring these lesser-known spots is that there is no potable water provided anywhere off the corridor trails. When you're out camping and hiking in these areas, you must be able to filter and treat your water.

For backpackers who have already done the corridor trail thing, the next step would be to check out the **Threshold Zone,** such as Hermit Camp and Hermit Creek or Horseshoe Mesa. Threshold use areas typically have designated but primitive campsites. The **Primitive and Wild Zones** beyond allow at-large camping with a strict pack-out policy. These areas are typically explored by only the most experienced canyon hikers and often require route-finding and have trailheads that are difficult to access.

Transportation and Services

SHUTTLES

On the **South Rim,** you have to take the **free shuttle** to the **South Kaibab Trailhead** or else have somebody drop you off. There are no cars allowed near the trailhead and no overnight parking allowed. Take the **Kaibab/Rim Route (Orange)** to access the trailhead.

On the **North Rim,** to get from the **Grand Canyon Lodge**—the park's only accommodations on the North Rim—to the **North Kaibab Trailhead,** take the **hiker shuttle** (daily May 15-Oct. 15, $7 for first person, $4 for each additional person), which leaves the lodge twice daily first thing in the morning. Tickets must be purchased the day before at the lodge.

The **Trans-Canyon Shuttle** (928/638-2820, www.trans-canyonshuttle.com, $90 one-way, reservations required) makes a daily round-trip excursion between the North and South Rims, departing the North Rim at 7am and arriving at the South Rim at 11:30am. The shuttle then leaves the South Rim at 1:30pm and arrives back at the North Rim at 6pm. During the spring and summer, shuttles run twice daily from the South Rim to the North Rim (8am-12:30pm and 1:30pm-6pm), and twice daily from the North Rim to the South Rim (7am-11:30am and 2pm-6:30pm).

RESTHOUSES

There are several stone-and-wood resthouses along the corridor trails in which backpackers and day hikers can get out of the sun, have a rest, and, at some of them, even refill their water bottles.

On the **Bright Angel Trail,** look for **Mile-and-a-Half Resthouse** and **Three-Mile Resthouse,** 1.5 miles (2.4 km) and 3 miles (4.8 km), respectively, from the trailhead. Both resthouses have potable water available from mid-May to mid-October, emergency phones, and toilet facilities.

About 3 miles (4.8 km) down from Indian Garden, not long before you reach the river, the **River Resthouse** has an emergency phone and shade.

On the **South Kaibab Trail,** about 1.5 miles (2.4 km) from the trailhead, there are pit toilets at **Cedar Ridge,** but no resthouse or water.

DUFFEL SERVICE

Xanterra, the park concessionaire that operates Phantom Ranch, offers a convenient and freeing mule-back **duffel service** between the South Rim and Phantom Ranch (888/297-2757, www.grandcanyonlodges.com, 30 lbs/13.6-kg maximum, $76 one-way). The tough mule's burden becomes your salvation, as you breeze along the Bright Angel or the South Kaibab Trail with a light daypack on your back, free to look around and really take in the amazing landscape. It's easy to fit all you need for a few days in the canyon into a 30-pound (13.6-kg), 36 by 20 by 13-inch (91 by 51 by 33-cm) duffel bag. You provide the duffel bag and fill it yourself, then take it to the Xanterra Livery Barn (in Grand Canyon Village on the South Rim) to be weighed and accepted. You will need a reservation—make your duffel-service reservation at the same time you make all your other trip plans, up to a year out.

Inbound duffels headed to Phantom Ranch or nearby Boat Beach (this is a popular service with river-runners moving gear into and out of the canyon) must be at the Livery Barn by 3:30pm the day prior to the day they go down. Outbound duffels have to be at the Phantom Ranch loading area near the canteen no later than 6:30am on the day they are going out. You can pick up your duffels between 3pm and 4pm at the Livery Barn on the day that they come out, or between 6:30am and 4pm the next day.

EMERGENCIES

There are a lot of things that can go wrong on a backpacking trip into Grand Canyon. Most of these are completely avoidable if you plan ahead, have respect for the difficulty of what you are doing, follow the rules, and pay attention.

Three-Mile Resthouse on the Bright Angel Trail

If you or one of your party is injured or becomes sick while hiking on the corridor trails, head to one of the **emergency phones** at the resthouses, developed campgrounds, and ranger stations (Indian Garden and Phantom Ranch), and at the junction of the South Kaibab and Tonto Trails. Ask passersby to help get the message to rangers on the rim. Don't leave the injured or sick person alone. Soon enough, there will probably be a helicopter hovering over, ready to evacuate the patient to the rim and safety. While you may be able to get cell service in a few places inside the canyon if you're lucky, it should in no way be relied on for getting help.

There are regular ranger patrols below the rim on the Bright Angel, South Kaibab, and North Kaibab Trails, and at the ranger stations at Indian Garden on the Bright Angel Trail and Phantom Ranch in the inner gorge. River guides are generally trained for emergencies and first aid, and they will typically be a way to quickly contact civilization from the river.

Beyond the Boundaries: Canyon Country

Much of the hard, remote, and bewitching land around Grand Canyon National Park belongs to Native American tribes to whom the great gorge is an eternal and sacred place. The Hopi and Navajo live on their ancestral lands east of the canyon, the Havasupai and Hualapai to the west, and the Kaibab Paiute to the north. This is a world of vast high-desert plains and evergreen plateaus, of wind-sculpted buttes and narrow slickrock canyons, of lonely bunchgrass sweeps and red dirt.

Exploring these distant corners of North America is relatively easy save for the long distances between sights. There are several excursions into the far canyonlands that can be folded into a visit to the Park's South and North Rims.

Highlights

Look for ★ to find recommended sights, activities, dining, and lodging.

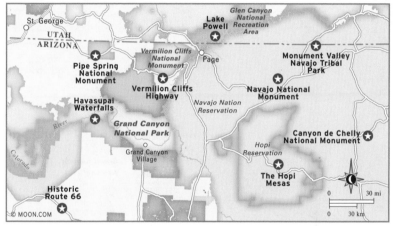

★ Trek into western Grand Canyon to the home of the **Havasupai,** where blue-green **waterfalls** create an enchanting desert oasis (page 184).

★ Drive back in time along the rough and remote remains of the old Mother Road, **Historic Route 66** (page 190).

★ Visit the **Hopi** and tour their 1,000-year-old villages, built on three high **mesas** in northeastern Arizona (page 197).

★ Stand on the edge of sacred Tsegi Canyon in **Navajo National Monument** and gaze at an ancient city rising out of the rock (page 203).

★ Drive through an otherworldly high-desert valley among fantastically eroded stone buttes and spires in **Monument Valley Navajo Tribal Park** (page 203).

★ Hike to the timeless White House Ruin along a precipitous rock-hewn trail in **Canyon de Chelly National Monument,** circled endlessly by ravens and silence (pages 205 and 209).

★ Kayak through a drowned labyrinth of strangely sculpted canyons at **Lake Powell,** a starkly beautiful man-made lake on the Colorado River (pages 216 and 221).

★ Traverse the Arizona Strip on the **Vermilion Cliffs Highway,** road-tripping on a mostly empty blacktop through a lonely red-rock landscape with towering cliffs and wide sweeping plains (page 224).

★ Tour a 19th-century ranch and fort at **Pipe Spring National Monument** and learn about the history of Native American and Latter-day Saint settlement on the isolated Arizona Strip (page 226).

Beyond the Boundaries: Canyon Country

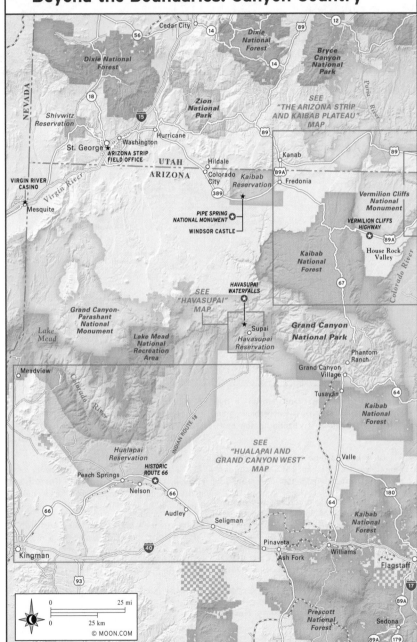

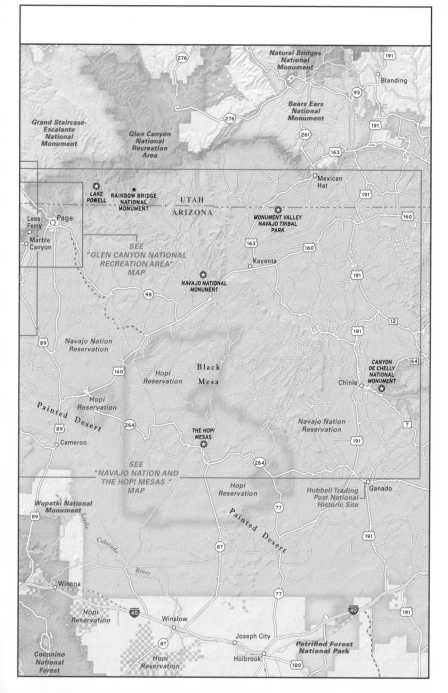

The region around Grand Canyon has stirred the souls of hikers, road-trippers, anglers, kayakers, artists, and photographers for generations, perhaps just as much as the great canyon itself. After all, it's a lot easier to reach the banks of the Colorado River from Lake Powell and Lees Ferry than from the South Rim—the latter requires a grueling hike, the former a scenic drive!

Alternative rims and alternative routes into Grand Canyon await tourists and explorers to the west of the South Rim, where the Hualapai Tribe watches over the Grand Canyon Skywalk, a glass horseshoe hovering over the gorge. Deep within the western canyon, members of the Havasupai Tribe live in a small village above a series of beautiful blue-green waterfalls. Closest to the South Rim, the Navajo and Hopi Reservations are just east of the park's Desert View section and offer otherworldly landscapes, fascinating history, and a chance to learn about unique cultural traditions tied inextricably to the great canyon itself.

PLANNING YOUR TIME

Side trips to spots on the **Navajo and Hopi Reservations** just a few hours east of Grand Canyon National Park are the easiest to add to your **South Rim** visit. The **Hopi Mesas** need a long day trip from the park, as does **Navajo National Monument.** Anything farther east needs two days at least. A side trip to **Glen Canyon National Recreation Area** (GCNRA) from the South Rim requires at least two days.

If you plan carefully and get lucky, you could include a two- or three-day visit to **Havasupai** with your excursion to the South Rim, but it's not easy to get reservations. It's more practical to plan a separate trip in April-June or September-October, the best months for a visit.

Most people visit the Hualapai Reservation's **Grand Canyon West** and **The Skywalk** from **Las Vegas.** It's a long drive from the South Rim (you'd need at least two extra days) and not worth it.

Any trip to the **North Rim** will necessarily include a visit to the **Kaibab Plateau** and **Arizona Strip,** and a side trip to **Lake Powell, Lees Ferry,** and other GCNRA spots from the North Rim requires at least two days.

Weather and Seasons

Spring, summer, and early fall are the best seasons to visit the Navajo and Hopi Reservations, the Skywalk, Glen Canyon National Recreation Area, and the Kaibab Plateau. If you're visiting Lake Powell or Havasupai, stick to spring and early fall—a summer trip is not recommended, as highs will be in the 100s F (38-43°C) and the sun unrelenting. Navajoland and Hopi also receive considerable heat in summer, though the relatively high elevations temper it somewhat. Nonetheless, summer is the busiest season throughout the canyonlands, so expect crowds, including droves of international tourists, everywhere you go. From July through September expect violent and sometimes damaging afternoon thunderstorms throughout the region.

From December to March you may find services curtailed in some areas, and in those areas that stay open all year, January and February will likely be the slowest months, and the least expensive. The Kaibab Plateau is often blanketed in snow December through March, closing the North Rim section of Grand Canyon National Park from the end of October until May.

Previous: Vermilion Cliffs Highway; White House Ruin in Canyon de Chelly; last remains of Historic Route 66.

Havasupai

Heavy with lime, the waters of Havasu Creek flow an almost tropical blue green. The creek passes below the weathered red walls of the western Grand Canyon and cuts Havasu Canyon, home these many centuries to the Havasupai (Havasu 'Baaja), the "people of the blue-green water."

Thousands of tourists from all over the world flock to **Havasupai** (928/448-2121, http://theofficialhavasupaitribe.com, entry fee $50 plus $10 environmental fee) every year just to see the canyon's blue-green waterfalls, to swim in their pools, and to visit one of the most remote hometowns in North America.

The Havasupai (Pai means "people" in the Yuman language) have been living in Grand Canyon since at least the 12th century, tending small irrigated fields of corn, melons, beans, and squash, and small orchards of peach, apple, and apricot trees. For centuries the Havasupai farmed in Havasu Canyon and in other spring-fed areas of Grand Canyon—Indian Garden along the Bright Angel Trail and Santa Maria Spring along the Hermit Trail—in the summer and then hunted and gathered on the rim during the winter, ancient patterns that were disrupted by the settling of northern Arizona in the late 19th century.

Today the Havasupai rely primarily on tourism to their little hidden oasis in Grand Canyon, and their beautiful land is known the world over for its striking waterfalls. The ease with which the Internet allows images to spread inevitably brought what once was a kind of poorly hidden secret to the attention of the globe. Now it's harder than ever to obtain a reservation in the tribe's small lodge and campground, which can only be reached via a **hike into the canyon** (8 mi/12.9 km to lodge, 10 mi/16.1 km to campground) or a 10-minute **helicopter ride.**

Reservations

The tribe requires that you **stay overnight** and have a **reservation** to visit Supai and the falls; **no day trips** are allowed. To make a reservation to camp in Havasu Canyon, you have to reserve a space online at www. havasupaireservations.com beginning at 8am on February 1 of the year you want to go. Camping permits sell out fast! To make reservations at the Havasupai Lodge (which you should do far in advance), call 928/448-2111 or visit www.havasupaireservations.com.

Planning Tips

A visit to Havasupai takes some planning. It's unbearably hot in the deep summer, when you can't hike except in the very early morning; the **best months** to visit are **September-October** and **April-June.** If you aren't into **backpacking,** you can hire a **pack mule** ($400 round-trip) or take the **helicopter** ($85 one-way). A popular way to visit is to hike in and take the helicopter out. It's a 10-minute thrill ride through the canyon to the rim, and the helipad is only about 50 yards (46 m) from the trailhead parking lot.

Most visitors stay the night at one of the motels along **Historic Route 66** before hiking in. Get an early start, especially during the summer. It's a **60-mile (97-km) drive** to the **trailhead at Hualapai Hill** from the junction of Route 66 and Indian Route 18, which leads to the trailhead. The closest hotels are the **Caverns Inn** and the **Hualapai Lodge** in **Peach Springs,** about 7 miles (11.3 km) west of the junction. You'll find cheaper accommodations in **Seligman,** about 30 miles (48 km) east of the junction.

SIGHTS
Supai Village

Havasu Creek falls through the canyon on its way to join the Colorado River, passing briefly by the ramshackle, inner-canyon village of **Supai,** where it is not unusual to see horses running free in the dusty streets, where

Visiting Native American Reservations

While the Native American communities in the canyonlands vary greatly in their cultures, histories, and ambitions for tourism, there are a few general rules to keep in mind when visiting their lands.

First and foremost, never forget that reservations are not national parks. Treat Native American reservations as you would private property. That means asking permission before entering them, and abiding by any permit rules each nation may have. Don't take pictures without asking first, and don't drive off road for any reason—that's somebody's land and livelihood. If you are lucky enough to be invited to watch a dance or other ceremony, treat it as you would any religious observance—with quiet reverence.

Again, remember that not all Native American nations are the same; research the requirements and the rules of each individual reservation before visiting.

reggae plays all day through some community speaker, and where the supply helicopter alights and then hops out again every 10 minutes or so in a field across from the post office. The village has a small café, a general store, and a small lodge.

TOP EXPERIENCE

★ Waterfalls

What used to be Navajo Falls, just down the trail from the village, was destroyed in a 2008 flash flood. Now there's a wider set of falls and a big pool that sits below a flood-eroded hill.

Perhaps the most famous of the canyon's blue-green falls, **Havasu Falls** comes on you all of a sudden as you get closer to the campground, which is about 2 miles (3.2 km) from the village. Few hikers refuse to toss their packs aside and strip to their swimsuits when they see Havasu Falls for the first time.

The other major waterfall, **Mooney Falls,** is another mile (1.6 km) down the trail, through the campground. It's not easy to reach the pool below; it requires a careful walk down a narrow, rock-hewn trail with chain handles, but most reasonably dexterous people can handle it.

Beaver Falls, somewhat underwhelming by comparison, is another 2 miles (3.2 km) toward the river, which is 7 miles (11.3 km) from the campground.

HIKING
Havasu Canyon Trail

Distance: 8 miles (12.9 km) one-way to Supai Village; 10 miles (16.1 km) one-way to campground
Duration: 3-5 hours one-way
Elevation gain: 2,000 feet (610 m)
Effort: Moderate
Trail conditions: Dirt, rocky, sandy in washes, open to mules
Trailhead: Hualapai Hilltop

The 8-mile (12.9-km) one-way hike to the **village of Supai** from the trailhead at Hualapai Hilltop is one of the easier treks into the Grand Canyon. For the first 2 miles (3.2 km) or so, rocky, moderately technical switchbacks lead to the canyon floor, a sandy bottomland where you're surrounded by eroded humps of seemingly melted, pockmarked sandstone. This is not Grand Canyon National Park: You'll know that for sure when you see the trash along the trail. It doesn't ruin the hike, but it nearly breaks the spell.

When you reach the village, you'll see the twin rock spires, called **Wii'Gliva,** which tower over the little farms and homes of Supai. The trail continues 2 miles (3.2 km) to the campground, passing **Havasu Falls,** and then moves on to the Colorado River 7 miles (11.3 km) downcreek, passing **Mooney and Beaver Falls** and through a gorgeous green riparian stretch. The Havasupai Reservation ends at Beaver Falls and Grand Canyon National Park begins.

Havasupai

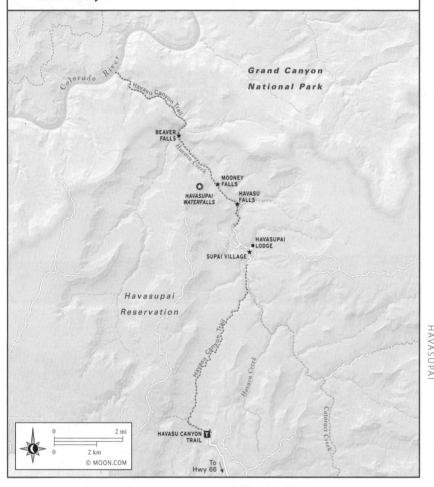

Grand Canyon
National Park

Colorado River

Havasu Canyon Trail

BEAVER
FALLS

Havasu Creek

MOONEY
FALLS

HAVASUPAI
WATERFALLS

HAVASU
FALLS

HAVASUPAI
LODGE

SUPAI VILLAGE

Havasupai
Reservation

Havasu Canyon Trail

Havasu Creek

Cataract Creek

0   2 mi

0   2 km

© MOON.COM

HAVASU CANYON
TRAIL

To
Hwy 66

It's difficult to the hike from the village or the campground to the Colorado River in one day—it's a long, wet route with many creek crossings and not always easy to follow; plus, there's no camping allowed at the river, so you must make it back by bedtime. Only experienced, strong hikers should attempt the trek to the Colorado River and back.

There are no water stations or toilets along the trail.

ACCOMMODATIONS AND FOOD

The **Havasupai Lodge** (928/448-2111, $145 up to 4 people) is a small two-story wood building in a quiet corner of the village. The rooms are basic though relatively large, with two queen beds, air-conditioning, and private baths. The village also has a small **café** that serves decent breakfast, lunch, and dinner, and a **general store.**

CAMPING

Most visitors pack in and stay at the primitive **campground** (first-come, first-served, water and toilets available, $25) about 2 miles (3.2 km) from the village between Havasu and Mooney Falls—an area the tribe once used to cremate the dead. The campground holds about 300 people in sites along the creek beneath shady cottonwoods.

TRANSPORTATION AND SERVICES
Getting to the Havasupai Trailhead and Supai Village

To reach **Havasu Canyon** from the South Rim, take I-40 to the Ash Fork exit and then drive west on Route 66, passing through Seligman. About 30 miles (48 km) past Seligman, turn north on Indian Route 18 and drive 60 miles (97 km) north to a parking area at **Hualapai Hilltop,** where the **trailhead** is located. The drive from the South Rim to Hualapai Hilltop is 195 miles (315 km) total and takes about four hours.

From there it's a moderate 8-mile (12.9 km) **hike** in to **Supai Village** and the lodge, and another 2 miles (3.2 km) to the campground. If you don't want to hike in, you can arrange to **rent a mule** (928/448-2121, 928/448-2174, or 928/448-2180, www.officialhavasupaitribe.

com, $400 round-trip to campground) or even hire a **helicopter.**

HELICOPTER

Airwest operates a helicopter service from Hualapai Hilltop to Supai (623/516-2790, 10am-1pm Sun.-Mon. and Thurs.-Fri. Mar. 15-Oct. 15, 10am-1pm Sun. and Fri. Oct. 16-Mar. 14, $85 one-way, cash or Mastercard/Visa/Discover). The helicopter takes off and lands every 10 minutes or so in a lot between the tourism office and the café in Supai. An ideal way to visit is to hike in and take the helicopter out. It's an approximately 10-minute ride through the canyon to the rim, and the helipad is only about 50 yards (46 m) from the trailhead parking lot.

Services

There is a small **tourism office** in the village where hikers stop for a permit check on their way to the campground, but there are very few other services offered at Supai. Indeed, if you are injured or get sick, there are no emergency health services in the village. In the event of such an emergency, you'll have to take a helicopter out, at your own expense, and family members cannot go with you. They will have to find their own way out of the canyon.

Hualapai and Grand Canyon West

Since the Hualapai (WALL-uh-pie) Tribe's Skywalk opened in 2007, the remote **Grand Canyon West** has become a fairly busy tourist attraction up on the **West Rim.** The Skywalk is about a two-hour drive from the Hualapai Reservation's capital, **Peach Springs,** which is located along Route 66 west of Seligman.

Although there's not much in Peach Springs other than a lodge and a few scattered houses, it makes an obvious base for a visit to

Grand Canyon West, which has several lookout points and a kitschy Old West-style tourist attraction called Hualapai Ranch, in addition to the famous Skywalk. The tribe's **Hualapai River Runners** (928/769-2636 or 888/868-9378) offer a one-day rafting trip on the river.

If you want to experience Grand Canyon West during your trip to the Grand Canyon National Park, remember that it is about 225 miles (360 km) from the South Rim and will take at least an extra two days.

1: hiking at Havasu Falls **2:** Mooney Falls

Hualapai and Grand Canyon West

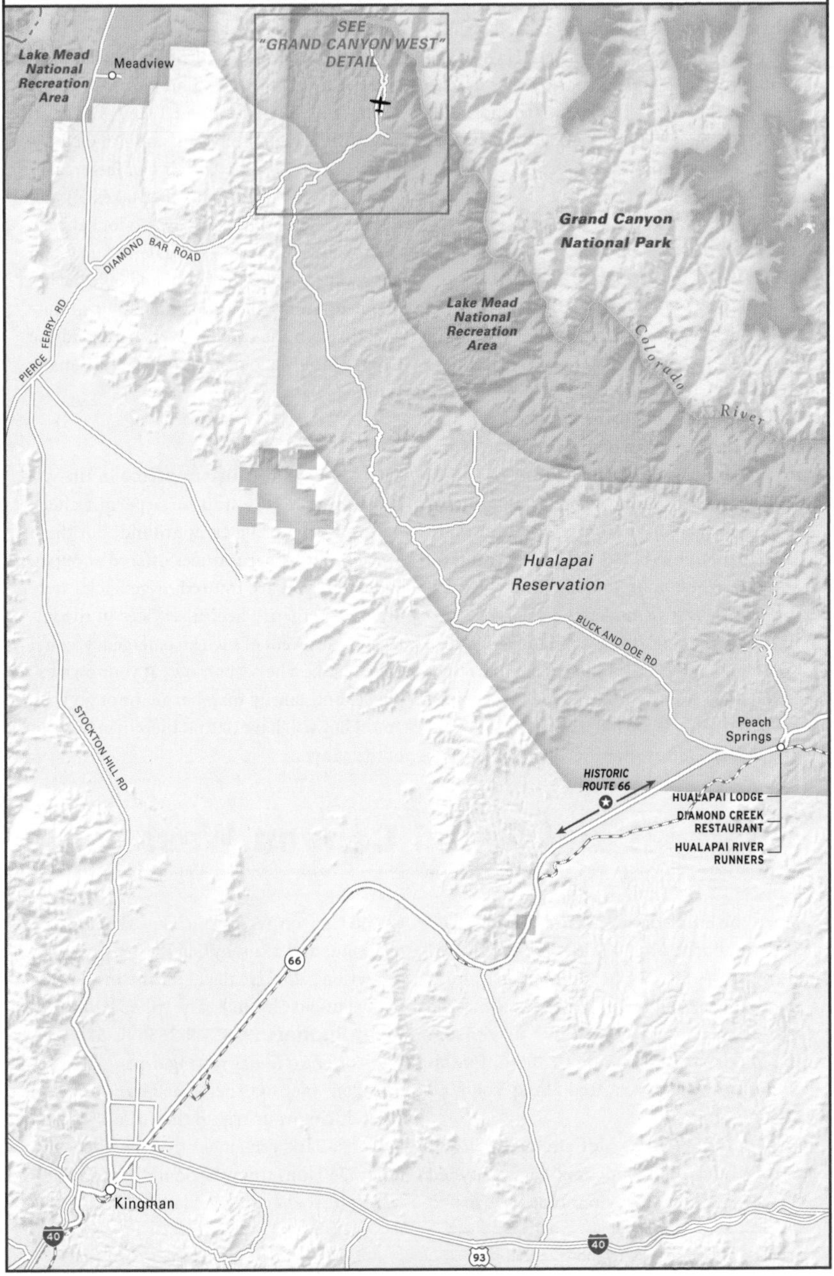

SEE
"GRAND CANYON WEST"
DETAIL

Lake Mead
National
Recreation
Area

Meadview

Grand Canyon
National Park

DIAMOND BAR ROAD

PIERCE FERRY RD

Lake Mead
National
Recreation
Area

Colorado River

Hualapai
Reservation

BUCK AND DOE RD

STOCKTON HILL RD

Peach
Springs

HISTORIC
ROUTE 66

HUALAPAI LODGE

DIAMOND CREEK
RESTAURANT

HUALAPAI RIVER
RUNNERS

66

93

40

40

Kingman

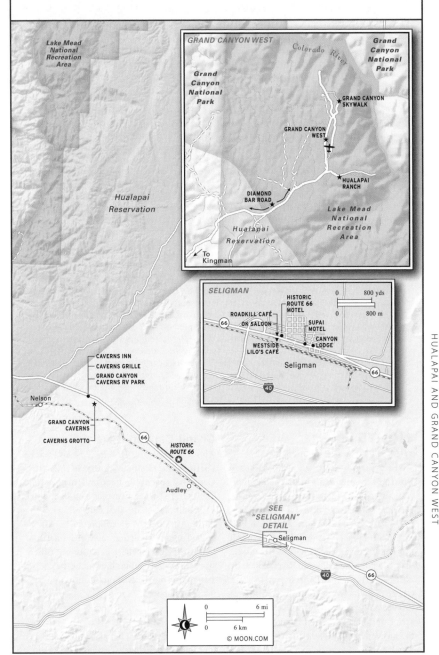

GRAND CANYON WEST

Lake Mead National Recreation Area

Colorado River

Grand Canyon National Park

Grand Canyon National Park

★ GRAND CANYON SKYWALK

GRAND CANYON WEST ★

Hualapai Reservation

★ HUALAPAI RANCH

DIAMOND BAR ROAD ★

Hualapai Reservation

Lake Mead National Recreation Area

↙ To Kingman

SELIGMAN

0   800 yds
0   800 m

HISTORIC ROUTE 66 MOTEL

ROADKILL CAFÉ
OK SALOON

SUPAI MOTEL

WESTSIDE LILO'S CAFÉ

CANYON LODGE

66

Seligman

66

40

CAVERNS INN
CAVERNS GRILLE
GRAND CANYON CAVERNS RV PARK

Nelson

★

GRAND CANYON CAVERNS

CAVERNS GROTTO

66

HISTORIC ROUTE 66

Audley

SEE "SELIGMAN" DETAIL

Seligman

40   66

0   6 mi
0   6 km

© MOON.COM

☆ Driving Historic Route 66

The longest remaining stretch of **Historic Route 66** (about 165 miles/265 km) runs from **Ash Fork,** on I-40, through the dry grasslands, cholla forests, and jagged hills of northwestern Arizona west to **Topock,** a tiny town on the Colorado River. There's not much out here but windswept landscapes and rocky hills, but there are a few quirky and memorable sights that old-school road-trippers will love.

The tiny roadside settlement of **Seligman,** 87 miles (140 km) east of Kingman, holds on tight to its Route 66 heritage. Fewer than 500 full-time residents live in this old ranching hub, railroad center, and Route 66 stop, but there is often, especially on summer weekends, twice that number in tourists driving through and stopping for a bite to eat and a look around the gift shops. Tour buses and large gangs of motorcycling Europeans even stop here and crowd up the one-strip town on occasion, as Seligman has become in recent years one of the top stops for a burgeoning sub-culture of classic car nuts, 50-something *Easy Rider* role-players, and lovers of mid-20th-century commercial architecture and road culture, all of whom prefer to eschew the interstate and take to the back roads. John Lasseter, codirector of the 2006 Disney-Pixar film *Cars,* has said that he based the movie's fictional town of **Radiator Springs** partly on Seligman, which, like Radiator Springs, nearly died out when it was bypassed by I-40 in the late 1970s.

A majority of the Route 66 argonauts who slide through Seligman stop at ★ **Delgadillo's Snow Cap Drive-In** (301 E. Chino Ave., Seligman, 928/422-3291, 10am-6pm daily, $5-10), a famous food shack whose family of owners have been dedicated to feeding, entertaining, and teasing Route 66 travelers for generations. They serve a mean chili burger, a famous "cheeseburger with cheese," hot dogs, malts, soft ice cream, and much more, but the food's not really the point. Originally built in 1953 out of found lumber, the Snow Cap has become one of the stars of the back-to-Route-66 movement. There's a lot to look at outside: a 1936 Chevy and other old cars (all of them with big eyes on their windshields, à la the film *Cars*), railroad junk, and several very silly signs; and inside, the close walls are covered with the business cards of customers from all over the world. Don't go here if you're grumpy: There will likely be a stand-up wait, especially on summer weekends, and you *will* be teased, especially if you have a question that requires a serious answer.

After Seligman, try *not* to stop at the picture-ready **Hackberry General Store** and junkyard museum. It can't be done. Maybe it's the cherry-red, 1957 Corvette parked conspicuously out front. Maybe it's because it's the only sign of life for miles in either direction along this forgotten

SIGHTS
Historic Route 66

Ash Fork, the tiny town where **Historic Route 66** begins, is off I-40 about 80 miles (129 km) and 1.5 hours from Grand Canyon National Park's South Rim. Take AZ 64 south to I-40 and then head west to the Ash Fork exit. The longest remaining stretch of the old Mother Road runs from here to **Topock,** a little town on the Colorado River, about 165 miles (265 km). It's the best way to reach Grand Canyon West from the South Rim, though many visitors to the West Rim area arrive on tour buses from Las Vegas. Along the way you'll find a few retro road-trip sights worth a stop.

Grand Canyon Caverns

About 13 miles (20.9 km) east of Peach Springs on Historic Route 66, **Grand Canyon Caverns** (Route 66, mile marker 115, 928/422-3223, www.gccaverns.com, 8am-6pm daily summer, 10am-4pm daily winter, $21-29 adults, $10.95-17.95 children 6-12) offers guided underground tours of North America's largest dry cave, where crystals and other strange rock formations hide in the darkness. The main tour lasts about 45 minutes and takes you about 0.75 mile (1.2 km) through the limestone cavern, but not before you descend 21 stories (210 feet/64 m) beneath the earth in an elevator. They also offer a shorter tour that is wheelchair accessible. There's a lot

Route 66 nostalgia is alive and well in Seligman.

stretch of the old Mother Road. Maybe it's the root beer. Cluttered with Route 66 and Americana road-culture memorabilia, including several rusting old cars that once made their way along the route, the general store (11255 E. Hwy. 66, Hackberry, 928/769-2605, www.hackberrygeneralstore. com, 9am-6pm daily) looks like it belongs to another era. Inside you'll find cold sodas, snacks, souvenirs, and a lot to look at, including some really cool road-map murals on the walls by artist Bob Waldmire. The owners, who bought the place on a whim years ago while driving Route 66, encourage visitors to walk around the property, examine the memorabilia, and take pictures.

You could spend a full day or more out in this quirky backcountry; those interested in Route 66 nostalgia will find a lot to look at, even if it's just the empty grasslands rolling by. For others, a stop in Seligman for lunch and a 30-minute stroll is a perfect way to visit this area.

of history here, too: During the Cold War the cavern served as a bomb-shelter-in-waiting, packed with enough food and water to sustain hundreds of blast-weary survivors if the unthinkable occurred. The friendly folks here at this old-school Route 66 tourist trap (in the best sense of the phrase) also offer an off-trail tour ($99) that goes much deeper into the caverns. And they'll be happy to take you out into the nearby ranchlands on horseback or in a Jeep.

Grand Canyon West

Grand Canyon West (5001 Diamond Bar Rd., 928/769-2636 or 888/868-9378, www. grandcanyonwest.com, 9am-sundown daily, $39 general admission, $20 add-on for

Skywalk, $19 add-on for meal) is the Hualapai Reservation's tourist area, comprising several viewpoints on the western rim of Grand Canyon and the Skywalk.

A general admission ticket gets you on the free hop-on/hop-off shuttle to **Eagle Point,** where the Skywalk juts out and there's a restaurant and a café, and on to **Guano Point,** with a wonderful view of the western canyon and a café on the edge of the rim. (Getting around by private vehicle is not permitted at Grand Canyon West; there is a large parking area where you can leave your car and pick up the shuttle.)

It's a good idea to book your general admission tickets and add-ons before you travel out to this remote sight. If you're coming from

Las Vegas (as many Grand Canyon West visitors do), you can easily find an all-inclusive tour that includes admission. Expect to spend a long day out here, and the drive back to anywhere (Peach Springs or Las Vegas) takes at least two hours. Because of its remoteness and rather high cost, consider beforehand whether it is worth it to you. While the views of the Grand Canyon are indeed spectacular along the western rim, they are vastly less dramatic than those from the South and North Rims—Grand Canyon West sits at around 4,000 feet (1,219 m) above sea level, so the views of the canyon are much shallower and more uniform than those in the park.

GRAND CANYON SKYWALK

The Skywalk (928/769-2636 or 888/868-9378, www.grandcanyonwest.com, $20 plus $39 admission fee to Grand Canyon West) is as much an art installation as it is a tourist attraction. A horseshoe-shaped glass and steel platform jutting out 70 feet (21 m) from the canyon rim, it appears futuristic surrounded by the rugged, remote western canyon. It's something to see for sure, but is it worth the long drive and the high price tag? Not really. If you have time for an off-the-beaten-path portion of your canyon trip, it's better to go to the North Rim and stand out on Bright Angel Point—you'll get a somewhat similar impression, and it's cheaper. There is something of the thrill ride to the Skywalk, however. Some people can't handle it: They walk out a few steps, look down through the glass at the canyon 4,000 feet (1,219 m) below, and head for (seemingly) more solid ground. It's all perfectly safe, but it doesn't feel that way if you are subject to vertigo. Another drawback of this site is that you are not allowed to take your camera out on the Skywalk. If you want a record of this adventure, you have to buy a "professional" photo taken by somebody else. You have to store all of your possessions, including your camera, in a locker

before stepping out on the glass, with covers on your shoes.

HUALAPAI RANCH

At **Hualapai Ranch** (928/769-2636 or 888/868-9378, www.grandcanyonwest.com), you can take a zipline ride, go horseback riding, and stay overnight in a rustic cabin.

DIAMOND CREEK ROAD

You can drive to the river's edge yourself along the 19-mile (31-km) **Diamond Creek Road** through a dry, scrubby landscape scattered with cacti. The road provides the only easy access to the river's edge between Lees Ferry, not far from the North Rim, and Pearce Ferry, near Lake Mead. You need a permit to drive the road; obtain one at the Hualapai Lodge in Peach Springs (the road is just across Route 66 from the lodge). A tribal police officer may check it at some point along the road.

At the end of the road, where Diamond Creek marries the Colorado, there's a sandy beach by an enchanting, lush oasis, and, of course, there's that big river rolling by.

The route is best negotiated in a high-clearance SUV; you have to cross Diamond Creek six times as the dirt road winds down through Peach Springs Canyon, dropping some 3,400 feet (1,036 m) from its beginning at Peach Springs on Route 66. The creek is susceptible to flash floods during the summer and winter rainy seasons, so call ahead to check **road conditions** (928/769-2230).

RECREATION
River Rafting

Though the Skywalk may not be worth the high price of admission and the long drive to reach it, the Hualapai offer one adventure that is worth the steep price tag: the canyon's only **one-day river rafting experience,** offered by **Hualapai River Runners** (928/769-2636 or 888/868-9378, www.grandcanyonwest.com, May-Oct., $450 pp). It generally takes up to a year of planning and several days of roughing it to ride the river and the rapids through the inner gorge, making a Colorado River

---

1: The Skywalk at Grand Canyon West **2:** Hualapai Ranch

Keepers of the Wild Nature Park

Though tawny cougars are known to occasionally haunt these windy high-desert plains, and some stretches of Historic Route 66 could perhaps stand in for a sweeping African savanna, one doesn't expect to encounter a shaggy-maned lion here, or for that matter a flitting lemur or a thoughtful baboon—except perhaps at **Keepers of the Wild Nature Park** (13441 E. Route 66, mile marker 87, www.keepersofthewild.org, 9am-5pm Wed.-Mon., all-day pass $20 adults, $12 children under 12), about 16 miles (26 km) east of Peach Springs on Historic Route 66. A hospital, retirement home, and haven for abused, neglected, and abandoned exotic animals, the park has tigers, a bear, a wolf, a whole village full of squealing, playful monkeys, and much more.

The animals live in large, fenced-in habitats, with big boulders and pools and mostly native trees and shrubs. The paths are easy, but there isn't a lot of shade, so bring a hat. The whole park is wheelchair-accessible, and there's a gift shop with snacks and drinks. Picnicking is encouraged, so feel free to bring a basket. The last tickets are sold at 4pm. For $10 more per person, a guide will take you on a driven "safari" tour of the park that lasts about 1.5 hours (10am, 1pm, and 3:30pm). This is an ideal stop for families with kids. Most of the animals here have cute names and sad life stories, so you run the risk of falling in love.

adventure something that the average tourist isn't likely to try. Not so in Grand Canyon West. For about $450 per person, Hualapai river guides will pick you up in a van early in the morning at the Hualapai Lodge in Peach Springs and drive you to the Colorado via the rough Diamond Creek Road, where you'll float downstream in a motorboat over roiling white-water rapids and smooth and tranquil stretches. You'll stop for lunch on a beach and take a short hike through a watery side canyon to beautiful Travertine Falls. At the end of the trip, a helicopter picks you out of the canyon and drops you on the rim near the Skywalk. It's expensive, yes, but if you want to ride the river without a lot of preplanning and camping, this is the way to do it. Along the way the Hualapai guides tell stories about this end of the Grand Canyon, sprinkled with tribal history and lore.

FOOD
Peach Springs

The Hualapai Lodge's restaurant, **Diamond Creek** (900 Route 66, 928/769-2230 or 928/769-2636, www.grandcanyonwest.com, 6am-9pm daily, $10-15), serves American and Native American dishes. The Hualapai taco (similar to the Navajo taco, with beans and meat piled high on a fluffy slab of fry bread)

and the Hualapai stew (with luscious sirloin tips and vegetables swimming in a delicious, hearty broth) are both recommended. The restaurant also offers a heaping plate of delicious spaghetti—great if you're carbo-loading for a big hike to Havasupai. The menu also includes a few vegetarian choices, good chili, and pizza.

The **Caverns Grille** (Historic Route 66, mile marker 115, 928/422-3223, www.gccaverns.com, noon-8pm daily), in the Grand Canyon Caverns complex, serves American grill-style burgers, sandwiches, salads, and more for lunch and dinner along with a selection of beer and wine. Deep inside the cave (about 200 ft/61 m, or 21 stories, down), the **Caverns Grotto** serves lunch and dinner combined with a tour of the cave (call 928/422-3233 for reservations, lunch served noon-4:45pm daily, dinner 5pm-9pm daily, $49.94-69.95 pp, includes tour).

Grand Canyon West

The dining scene at Grand Canyon West is not great, but there are three eateries with great views of the canyon. There's a restaurant and a café at Eagle Point and a café at Guano Point. To get a meal at one of the two viewpoints, you must add on a $19 meal ticket to your general admission price, which gives you the choice of a burger, veggie burger, or a chicken sandwich. As an alternative, consider eating at the excellent restaurant at the Hualapai Lodge in Peach Springs. Bringing outside food and beverages to Grand Canyon West is not permitted.

Seligman

The **Roadkill Café** (502 W. Route 66, 928/422-3554, 7am-9pm daily, $8-24) is more than just a funny name; it's a popular place for buffalo burgers, steaks, sandwiches, and other typical Old West-themed bar-and-grill eats. Have a few drinks in the **OK Saloon** and a look around at the cluttered interior.

The majestic, if stuffed, mountain lion that watches over diners at **Westside Lilo's Café** (22855 W. Old Hwy. 66, 928/422-5456, www.westsidelilos.com, 6am-9pm daily, $8-23) was shot not far from the restaurant by a member of the owners' family. It's just one of the backcountry touches that add to the ambience at this popular diner-style eatery (complete with counter service), which serves good burgers, excellent homemade potato salad, and other standard American fare. Lilo's is famous for its carrot cake, which is moist and flavorful.

ACCOMMODATIONS
Peach Springs

The **Hualapai Lodge** (900 Route 66, 928/769-2230 or 928/769-2636, www.grandcanyonwest.com, $150-170) in Peach Springs has a small heated saltwater pool, an exercise room, gift shop, 57 comfortable, newish rooms with soft beds, cable, free Wi-Fi, and train tracks right out the back door. This is a good place to stay the night before hiking into Havasupai, as it's only about 7 miles (11.3 km) west of the turnoff to Hualapai Hill and the trailhead.

Located on the 800-acre Route 66 property of Grand Canyon Caverns about 13 miles (20.9 km) east of Peach Springs, the **Caverns Inn** (Historic Route 66, mile marker 115, 928/422-3223, www.gccaverns.com, $117) is a basically updated old motor hotel with 48 units, all ground floor. The rooms are clean

and comfortable, and the complex has a pool open in summer, a laundromat, three restaurants, and hiking trails. The inn is just 66 miles (106 km) from the Havasupai Trailhead. The cave and the restaurants are about one mile from the motel area.

Grand Canyon West

Hualapai Ranch (928/769-2636 or 888/868-9378, www.grandcanyonwest.com) offers rustic cabins ($125-159, up to 6 people) with private bathrooms, refrigerators, and microwaves.

Seligman

There are several small, locally owned motels in Seligman, a tiny Historic Route 66 town about 37 miles (60 km) east of Peach Springs and about 90 miles (145 km) east of the Havasupai Trailhead. The accommodations here are nothing special, though they are typically quite affordable.

The **Supai Motel** (134 W. Chino St., 928/422-4153, www.supaimotelseligman.com, $69-82) has clean and comfortable rooms at a fair price. The **Historic Route 66 Motel** (22750 W. Route 66, 928/422-3204, www.route66seligmanarizona.com, $69-82) offers free Wi-Fi and refrigerators in clean, comfortable rooms. The **Canyon Lodge** (114 E. Chino St., 928/422-3255, www.route66canyonlodge.com, $70-100) has free Wi-Fi in its themed rooms (which means posters on the walls of James Dean, Marilyn Monroe, John Wayne, and other pop-culture icons), along with refrigerators and microwaves. It also serves a free continental breakfast.

CAMPING

Grand Canyon Caverns RV Park (Historic Route 66, mile marker 115, 928/422-3223, www.gccaverns.com, $40-50), about 13 miles (20.9 km) east of Peach Springs on the 800-acre property of Grand Canyon Caverns, has 48 sites with full hookups as well as tent sites. The tree-lined and private park has bathrooms and showers, a swimming pool open in summer, hiking trails, and many other activities.

TRANSPORTATION AND SERVICES
Driving and Parking

The best way to get to **Grand Canyon West** from the **South Rim** is to take I-40 to the Ash Fork exit and then drive west on Route 66. Starting at Ash Fork and heading west to Peach Springs, the **longest remaining portion of Route 66** moves through **Seligman,** a small roadside town that's caught in the heyday of the Mother Road. The route through Seligman, which stands up to a stop and a walk around if you have the time, is popular with nostalgic motorcyclists, and there are a few eateries and tourist-style stores in town. Once you reach **Peach Springs** (about 140 mi/225 km from the South Rim, about a 2.5-hour drive), continue west on Route 66 for 29 miles (47 km), turn right on Antares Road and drive 32 miles (52 km), turn right onto Pearce Ferry Road and drive 3 miles (4.8 km), and then turn right on Diamond Bar Road and drive 21 miles (34 km). Diamond Bar Road ends at the only entrance to Grand Canyon West. The drive from Peach Springs to Grand Canyon West is 85 miles (137 km) and takes about 2 hours. The total drive from the South Rim to Grand Canyon West is about 225 miles (360 km) and takes about 4.5 hours.

Hualapai Reservation's Skywalk is only 125 miles (201 km) from **Las Vegas** (about a 2.5-hour drive), so it makes sense to include this remote side trip if you're headed to the South Rim from Vegas anyway. To reach Grand Canyon West from Las Vegas, take U.S. 93 out of the city, heading south for about 65 miles (105 km) to mile marker 42, where you'll see the Dolan Springs/Meadview City/Pearce Ferry exit. Turn north onto Pearce Ferry Road. About 30 miles (48 km) in, turn east on Diamond Bar Road. Then it's about 20 miles (32 km) to Grand Canyon West.

Once you arrive at Grand Canyon West, you must park your vehicle and ride the free **hop-on/hop-off shuttle** between the viewpoints. There is a large parking area where you can leave your car and pick up the shuttle.

Services

All of the services in the Grand Canyon West area are located in Peach Springs.

Navajo Nation and the Hopi Mesas

Though it has been visited by tourists regularly for more than a century, the 27,000-square-mile Navajo Nation, within which stand the three separate Hopi Mesas, still feels like the American outback. This is one of the most isolated, undeveloped regions in the country, and one with a rare and haunting beauty all its own.

SIGHTS
Little Colorado River Gorge Navajo Tribal Park

The Little Colorado River drops some 2,000 feet (610 m) through the arid, scrubby land, cutting through gray rock on the way to its marriage with the big river and creating the **Little Colorado Gorge.** Stop here near mile marker 286 on AZ 64, near the road's junction with U.S. 89, and get a barrier-free glimpse at this lesser but still jaw-dropping chasm created by an important Arizona waterway that begins high in the White Mountains. The small park has two viewpoints, interpretive signs, and a ramada shaped like a Navajo hogan. There are also booths here selling Navajo arts and crafts and a lot of touristy souvenirs, as well as hiking trails and picnic tables.

Historic Cameron Trading Post and Lodge

Established in 1916, **Historic Cameron**

Trading Post and Lodge (800/338-7385, www.camerontradingpost.com) is a busy travel center in the western section of the Navajo Nation, about 30 miles (48 km) east of Grand Canyon National Park's Desert View section, at the junction of AZ 64 and U.S. 89. The stone and log complex has served the region as a trading post, hotel, restaurant, art gallery, and general oasis of civilization— it's hard not to stop here if you're traveling through Navajoland north of Flagstaff. The restaurant here is one of the best in the region, with delicious Navajo, Mexican, and American dishes served in a dining room with a stone fireplace and Navajo rugs on the walls. The lodge, which has been expanded and remodeled over the years, has kept its enchanting sandstone garden from the 1930s, a relaxing spot with terraced planting beds built with local sandstone rocks, shady trees, and fragrant flowers. Not far from the lodge, an old 1911 swayback suspension bridge still hovers over the Little Colorado Gorge.

Painted Desert and Dinosaur Tracks

Tuba City, a small settlement with a few chain hotels, is the capital of the western Navajo Nation. It's about 60 miles (97 km) east from the Grand Canyon National Park's South Rim via AZ 64, U.S. 89, and U.S. 160 East, and about 80 miles (129 km) north of Flagstaff via U.S. 89 and U.S. 160 East. Approaching the community from the west, you'll drive through a wondrous stretch of **Painted Desert,** red, dusty orange, and gray mounds rising above the ruins of washes, like the humped, craggy backs of buried dinosaurs, with not a shrub in sight.

About 5 miles (8 km) west of Tuba City on U.S. 160, look for a sign that says **Dinosaur Tracks.** Turn north onto the dirt road and expect to be greeted by one of several Navajo guides who hang around the area, especially during the busy summer season. You can follow one of the friendly guides onto a great red sandstone slab, where eons ago raptor dinosaurs and other ancient monsters populated

this land, back when it was swampy and fertile. Their birdlike tracks were sealed forever in the stone, and the guides, many of whom learned details about the tracks from Northern Arizona University archaeologists working in the area, will spray water on the dozens of claw prints to bring them out of the red rock while explaining exactly what you're seeing. Expect to tip $15-20 for the tour. Off to the northeast look for the lush green hillsides of **Moenave,** where several Navajo families live off the natural springs for which this area is known. This is also where Mormon farmers settled in the 1870s, and it was for generations prior to that a Hopi farming area.

★ The Hopi Mesas

When you visit Hopi, you step out of normal time into a kind of sacred time in which the Hisatsinom still speak to their modern-day descendants, the "People of Peace," and the lessons and stories of the ancients still guide and rule life in the 21st century, the dawning of which has mostly been ignored around Hopi. Go to Hopi if you want to have a quiet, spiritual experience touring crumbling villages occupied for centuries, interacting with the friendly and creative people whose direct and well-remembered ancestors built and lived in most of the spectacular Pueblo ruins around Indian Country, and searching for artistic treasures built on patterns and narratives laid down before time began.

The Hopi do not allow any photography, sketching, or recording in the villages, and they don't like it when you enter their villages without first asking a village leader or at least someone at a crafts store or gallery. Talk to the folks at the **Hopi Cultural Center** on Second Mesa or the **Moenkopi Legacy Inn & Suites** in Moenkopi if you have any questions about the rules. Be respectful, and remember, as it is with the Navajos, the Hopi people are living their lives, not participating in an anthropological experiment. Don't bring any drugs or alcohol onto the reservation, and don't take any pottery shards off of it.

Many Hopi live on three remote mesas on

Navajo Nation and the Hopi Mesas

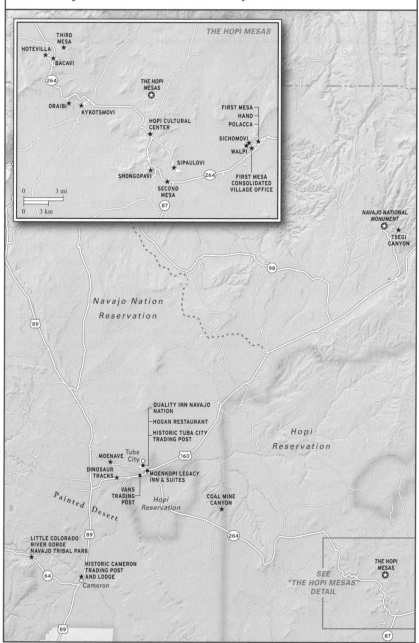

THE HOPI MESAS

THIRD MESA
HOTEVILLA ★
★ BACAVI

264

ORAIBI ★
★ KYKOTSMOVI

THE HOPI MESAS ✪

FIRST MESA
HANO
POLACCA

HOPI CULTURAL CENTER ★

SICHOMOVI
WALPI ★

SIPAULOVI ★

SHONGOPAVI ★

SECOND MESA ★

264

FIRST MESA CONSOLIDATED VILLAGE OFFICE

0 —— 3 mi
0 —— 3 km

87

NAVAJO NATIONAL MONUMENT ✪
TSEGI CANYON

98

Navajo Nation Reservation

89

QUALITY INN NAVAJO NATION
HOGAN RESTAURANT
HISTORIC TUBA CITY TRADING POST

Hopi Reservation

MOENAVE ★ Tuba City

DINOSAUR TRACKS

160

MOENKOPI LEGACY INN & SUITES

VANS TRADING POST

Hopi Reservation

COAL MINE CANYON ★

Painted Desert

264

LITTLE COLORADO RIVER GORGE NAVAJO TRIBAL PARK

89

64

HISTORIC CAMERON TRADING POST AND LODGE ★
Cameron

SEE "THE HOPI MESAS" DETAIL

THE HOPI MESAS ✪

87

89

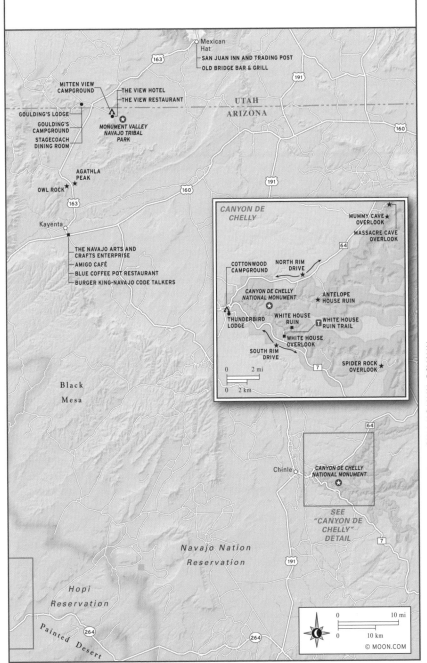

the southern tip of **Black Mesa,** a separate reservation carved out of the southwest portion of the Navajo Nation. There are 10 villages on the mesas, which are numbered east to west.

You can drive yourself up and over the mesas and enter many of the villages, but this is not an ideal, or even a very interesting way to visit Hopi. Without a bit of historical and cultural context, many of the mesa villages simply look like rundown rural outposts. But with a **guide,** a whole ancient, hidden world that exists beneath the rather hardscrabble surface opens up, and the mesas become sacred, mysterious ground.

TOURS

It's essential to call ahead to book a tour. The Hopi religious calendar is rather full, and often one village or another will close to outsiders for days at a time. Weather on the remote mesas can also cancel tours. The best place to book a tour is through the **Moenkopi Legacy Inn & Suites** (junction U.S. 160 and AZ 264, Tuba City, 928/283-4500, www.experiencehopi.com) or the **Hopi Cultural Center** (928/734-2401, www. hopiculturalcenter.com, 8am-5pm daily) on Second Mesa. The Moenkopi Legacy Inn's website has a comprehensive list of approved guides and their prices.

Left-Handed Hunter Tour Company (Second Mesa, 928/734-2567, $120-195 pp for 4-8 hours) offers exceedingly informative and memorable tours of the Taawaki Petroglyph Site, Moenkopi, Old Oraibi, Hotevilla, Bacavi, Kykotsmovi, Sipaulovi, and Musangnuvi, as well as visits with local artists. The Moenkopi Legacy Inn offers a highlight-filled **Experience Hopi Tour** (www.experiencehopi.com/tours, $145 pp), which includes a comprehensive exploration of the land, people, history, and art of the Hopi, plus lunch at the Hopi Cultural Center. A guide picks you up at the hotel in the morning and brings you back in the late afternoon.

MOENKOPI

The **Moenkopi Legacy Inn & Suites** (junction U.S. 160 and AZ 264, Tuba City, 928/283-4500, www.experiencehopi.com, $152), in the Upper Village of Moenkopi near Tuba City, has become the gateway to visiting Hopi. The all-Hopi staff at this gorgeous hotel and visitors center can help you book a guide to take you on an unforgettable tour of the Hopi Mesas.

Using Moenkopi as the gateway, it makes sense to start any tour of Hopi from the west and head east along AZ 264, which will take you to each of the mesas. From Moenkopi, Third Mesa is 45 miles (72 km), Second Mesa is 62 miles (100 km), and First Mesa is 70 miles (113 km).

About 15 miles (24 km) from Moenkopi along AZ 264, look for mile marker 336 and a dirt road that leads to **Coal Mine Canyon,** a spectacular gorge with magnificently eroded, multicolored hoodoos that's worth a few hundred snapshots from a sitting area near the rim.

THIRD MESA

The first of the mesa villages along AZ 264, and the first you reach on the road from Moenkopi, are **Hotevilla, Bacavi,** and **Kykotsmovi.** All are a mix of mostly ramshackle homes next to ancient, stacked-rock half-ruins hundreds of years old. The best place to stop on Third Mesa is **Oraibi,** also called Old Oraibi. Twenty-four families still live in the village, which sits at the edge of the mesa and looks out over the hazy flatland sea below. There's no electricity and no running water. "Our elders want no webbing above us and nothing buried in the ground," a Hopi woman who had been born and raised in the village explained. Some villagers have installed solar panels on the roofs of their small homes—each one built next to or on top of the ruin of an older one—to bring a little modern

---

1: aerial view of the Hopi Mesas **2:** Tsegi Canyon in Navajo National Monument **3:** ruins of Betatakin in Navajo National Monument **4:** Monument Valley Navajo Tribal Park

comfort. There are several kivas in the village that look exactly like those seen in the Hisatsinom ruins, with their rough ladders sticking out of their trapdoor entrances, except these are still in use. A walk around this village, in which people have made lives since at least AD 1100, is a strangely humbling experience. You may come away from it wondering why most of us think we need so much stuff to live that elusive good life.

SECOND MESA

The **Hopi Cultural Center** (928/734-2401, www.hopiculturalcenter.com, 8am-5pm daily) on Second Mesa has a small **museum** ($3) featuring blown-up photographs of Hopi taken in the 19th and early 20th centuries and displays on Hopi culture as well as many artifacts from around the mesas. It provides one of the few stops along the road through Hopi that can be enjoyed without a guide. The museum is an essential stop for anyone interested in Hopi culture. The center also has a restaurant serving traditional Hopi dishes and other food, as well as a small hotel. There are several interesting shops in the cultural center complex, including an excellent silversmith. The village of **Shongopavi** on Second Mesa is believed to have been the first Hopi village, and the village of **Sipaulovi** offers walking tours and other information about visiting Hopi.

FIRST MESA

Polacca, just below First Mesa, is one of the younger villages on Hopi, founded in 1890. There are many Hopi and Tewa potters living in Polacca. If you're interested in buying direct from the artists, keep a lookout for handmade signs outside of homes.

Next you'll come to **Hano,** founded in 1680 after the Pueblo Revolt by Tewas from New Mexico. The Hopi said the fleeing Tewas could stay in exchange for their vigilance in keeping enemies and attackers off the mesa trails. Hano is the home of the famous Tewa potter **Nampeyo;** in the early 1900s, Fred Harvey convinced Nampeyo to move to the Grand Canyon to demonstrate pottery making for tourists, creating a kind of living diorama at the famous Mary Colter-designed Hopi House. The area is still a center of pottery making, and artists directly related to Nampeyo—who is credited, even as a Tewa, with beginning a renaissance in Hopi pottery and thus creating a major modern art form and economy—still reside and work here, selling pottery out of their homes.

Just above Hano is **Sichomovi,** founded in 1750 by citizens of Walpi. This village has running water and electricity, unlike Walpi, a traditional village at the very edge of the mesa founded in the 1600s when villagers moved up the mesa from their village below to escape the predations of their neighbors.

WALPI GUIDED WALKING TOUR

If you have time for just one tour, make it of **Walpi,** a traditional Hopi village where the old ways live on. You will meet several Hopi artists on the tour of Walpi, sitting on the steps in front of their rock-carved homes, carving kachina dolls from cottonwood root. The people here are remarkably friendly—everybody says hello and smiles, welcoming visitors and inviting you into their homes to show you their art. If you are at all interested in Hopi art, this is the place to buy it. Not only will the price be significantly less than at a museum store or trading post, but you'll also get to meet the artist—and maybe even watch the final stages of creation. Take cash with you. Your Hopi tour guide will take you on a slow walk around the clifftop village, a time warp on the edge of the world. You'll learn all about the traditions and history, both temporal and spiritual, of this ancient place. It's a fascinating and memorable experience. The tour takes about an hour, but you can stay around after and talk to the artists and others.

You should book a tour a day in advance if you can, and don't be surprised if the village is closed due to weather or for religious reasons. Tours run through **First Mesa Consolidated Village Office** (928/737-2670, 8am-4:30pm daily summer, 9am-3pm daily winter, last tour at 2pm daily winter, $20 adults, $10 children under 18), about 71 miles (114 km) from Moenkopi in Polacca at the base of First Mesa, where you must stop and check in before heading up to Walpi. Take AZ 264 west to mile marker 390.8, turn north at the stop sign, and go 0.25 mile (0.4 km) to the office, which is next to the post office.

★ Navajo National Monument

Though it's within the Navajo Reservation, beautiful **Tsegi Canyon,** an eroded pink-rock landscape carpeted with gray-green pinyon pine and juniper forests, was once home to the Hisatsinom, ancestors of the Hopi. These Ancestral Puebloans (sometimes referred to by the Navajo name Anasazi) are credited with building the three cliffside villages in the canyon—some of the best-preserved and most awe-inspiring ruins in the Southwest. The Hopi, Navajo, Zuni, and Paiute cultures still consider this a sacred place, so only a few short hikes to promontories above the canyon are open to the general public. If you want to explore the area more deeply, you can sign up to take guided hikes to two of the ruins with a park ranger.

Only the ruins of the village called **Betatakin** by the Navajo and Talastima by the Hopi are visible from the canyon rim, tucked in a south-facing natural rock alcove that kept the village cool in the summer and warm in the winter; just below the village is a white-and-green aspen forest. Deeper in is **Keet Seel,** an older and larger village than Betatakin and one of the largest cliff dwellings in the Southwest. It's called Kawestima by the Hopi. **Inscription House,** or Tsu'ovi, is also perched in the canyon, but it has been closed to the public since the late 1960s.

Archaeologists believe that the Kayenta culture (one of three Ancestral Puebloan subgroups, along with Chaco and Mesa Verde) lived in the canyon as early as AD 950, with major building projects getting under way around AD 1250. But by AD 1300, for reasons only guessed at, all the villages had been abandoned.

The monument is about 50 miles (81 km)

northeast of Tuba City and 30 miles (48 km) southwest of Kayenta. Approaching from either way on U.S. 160, take AZ 564 for 9 miles (14.5 km) to the park entrance. Unlike most parks and monuments off the reservation, admission here is free. The **visitors center** (928/672-2700, www.nps.gov/nava, 9am-5pm daily, free) has a gift shop that sells books, T-shirts, hats, and small water bottles, as well as an interesting museum featuring items used in everyday life by the Puebloans and found in their left-behind villages.

★ Monument Valley Navajo Tribal Park

The **scenic drive** north 22 miles (35 km) from **Kayenta** along **U.S. 163** to **Monument Valley Navajo Tribal Park** ($20 per car with up to 4 people) is almost as dramatic as the destination itself. About a third of the way along the paved route you'll see the aptly named **Owl Rock** to the west and the hulking, jagged **Agathla Peak** to the east (also known as El Capitan), which tribal lore says marks the center of the world.

If there were any question that this is one of the most celebrated and enticing landscapes in the world, listen to the conversations around you as you visit Monument Valley—and you must visit Monument Valley, if only to prove that all the images you've seen are real. It sounds like "It's a Small World" out on this arid, dusty valley. Japanese, Chinese, Italian, German, British, and various Eastern European visitors gather at every lookout, looking for something distinctly Western, or American, in the iconic, jutting red rocks.

It was the director John Ford who brought this strange, remote place to the world and made it a stand-in for the West's dueling freedom and danger, most memorably in *The Searchers.* Now, to drive around the park is to enter a thousand car commercials, magazine layouts, road films, and Westerns, a landscape that's comfortably, beautifully familiar even if you're seeing it for the first time.

The Navajo have thankfully not overdeveloped this sacred place—some would argue it's underdeveloped for its potential—so the only way to see the park without a Navajo guide is to drive the 17-mile (27-km) unpaved **Valley Drive,** with pullouts for scenic views of the rock spires and lonely buttes. Upon entering the park you'll get a map of the drive with the name of each "Monument"—names like Wetherill Mesa, John Ford's Point, and The Thumb. If you can, it's worth arriving about an hour or so before sundown to see sunset over the valley—you'll wonder how you got here, and you'll stay until the lights go out. Be warned, though, that with the constant stream of cars driving the dry, dirt road, the air tends to get dusty.

You're allowed to take photographs here, but only of the natural wonders. Remember to ask permission before taking pictures of any Navajos or their private property.

VISITORS CENTER

The park's **visitors center** (435/727-5874 or 435/727-5870, 6am-8pm daily Apr.-Sept., 8am-5pm daily Oct.-Mar.), perched on a promontory overlooking the valley and the dirt road that snakes through it and around the eroded-sandstone sculptures, is an obvious place to start your visit. There's a small museum with displays on Navajo culture and history, as well as the history of Hollywood's use of this iconic landscape, and a wall or two showing contemporary Navajo art. Staff here can set you up with a guide if you want to go deeper into the valley and learn about the tribe's religious, cultural, and economic ties to it. There's a small patio outside the visitors center, which is right next to The View Hotel, restaurant, and trading post/gift shop, where you can sit and contemplate the natural art before you.

THE VALLEY DRIVE

The best way to see the valley and its monuments up close and on your own time is to head out into the hazy red lands via the 17-mile (27-km), self-guided **Valley Drive** (6am-8pm daily Apr.-Sept., 8am-5pm daily Oct.-Mar., $20 per car with up to 4 people).

The route, which is all dirt and a bit rough in some spots, has 11 pullouts for longer views of some of the more famous mesas, buttes, and spires. At many of these numbered stops, which otherwise have no services, you'll find Navajo families selling jewelry and souvenirs. Plan to spend at least two hours exploring the valley. If dust bothers you, so too will the Valley Drive, but try not to let that stop you: This is one of the most scenic, inspirational, and absolutely essential drives in the Southwest. Take water and food along, and check your tires before you head out. The roughest part of the drive is at the start, going down a steep hill into the valley, but the rest is easy and flat. Don't follow too close behind other cars; you'll be buried in red dust if you do. The tribe does not allow motorcycles or RVs on the Valley Drive.

The road into the valley starts just past the visitors center parking lot and has two lanes until Camel Butte, where it becomes a one-way loop around **Rain God Mesa.** The first stop, just as you enter the valley, provides a classic, much-photographed view of the "mittens," **West Mitten Butte** and **East Mitten Butte,** named because of the spires that rise from the side of each butte to form what looks like a hand in a mitten. Just a short scoot up the road is **Merrick Butte,** named, according to Richard Klinck in his classic history of the valley, *Land of Room Enough and Time Enough,* for James Merrick, a soldier turned prospector who was killed near the butte for trespassing on a Navajo silver mine. The huge mesa opposite Merrick Butte is called **Mitchell Mesa,** for it is said that at its base died Ernest Mitchell, Merrick's partner in trespass and violent death.

The second stop on the drive, **Elephant Butte,** is supposed to look like the titular pachyderm. The third and fourth numbered stops, **The Three Sisters** and **John Ford's Point,** are two of the best. The sisters are side-by-side spires on the edge of Mitchell Mesa, and the point is named for the famous director who revealed this valley to the world through his Westerns. The fifth stop is **Camel Butte,** named for the stone-frozen ungulate that to many it resembles. Just a bit up the road from the fifth stop, a ramshackle hut and corral provides **horseback tours of the backcountry** (30-minute to 6-hour tours, $45-165, credit cards accepted). You can also stop here and take pictures of the horses, but make sure to ask first, and be prepared to pay $5.

The sixth numbered stop on the drive provides a view of the formation called **The Hub,** which looks somewhat like the center of a wagon wheel, and of huge **Rain God Mesa,** marking the center of the valley. Here the road turns to loop around Rain God Mesa, with pullouts near **Thunderbird Mesa** (No. 7) and the edge of **Spearhead Mesa** (No. 8), from which you can see red sand dunes and, far off in the valley beyond the road, the impossibly delicate spire called the **Totem Pole,** which rises next to a gathering of thicker spires the Navajo call **Yei Bi Chei** ("dancers emerging from a Hogan"). The ninth stop is at the far tip of Spearhead Mesa, where there's a short, easy trail out to **Artist Point Overlook.** The view here is spectacular, and it's easy to see how the promontory got its name. Continuing on around the other side of Rain God Mesa, you'll see **Cly Butte,** at the base of which is buried "Old Cly," a beloved Navajo medicine man who died in 1934. Take a short side road from here up to the 10th stop, the **North Window Overlook,** which provides a breathtaking view of the valley's northern section. Return back to the loop, which ends at Camel Butte, behind which rises a spire called **The Thumb** (No. 11). Then it's back to the visitors center along the two-lane route from Camel Butte. You'll pass the same monuments on the way back, obviously, and feel free to stop at them again.

★ Canyon de Chelly National Monument

The most visually impressive wind- and water-worn canyon in Arizona save for the one they call Grand, **Canyon de Chelly**

(pronounced "de Shay"; the name is a Spanish approximation of the Navajo word for canyon, *tsegi*) is a labyrinth of eroded sandstone mesas, buttes, and spires washed in pink and red and varnished with black and purple. The canyon's fertile bottomlands and safe, hidden alcoves, seemingly designed beforehand to host stone cliff dwellings, have drawn people here for some 4,000 years. The greatest among the Southwest's ancients, the Ancestral Puebloans, built several hanging villages against the red-rock cliffs, the remains of which are still slowly crumbling in their shady alcoves.

The most beautiful, essential, intact, and wonderfully preserved ruin in the canyon is the amazing **White House Ruin,** which hangs above the canyon's sandy bottom and can be reached only via a 2.5-mile (4-km) out-and-back hike, and is the only ruin that you can view unaccompanied by a Navajo guide.

About 40 Navajo families call the canyon and its rimlands home. You'll pass some of their homesites and hogans as you drive the two scenic roads along the rim. Free-roaming horses like to munch on the grasses and weeds that grow along the side of the road; they will generally ignore you until you get out of your car for a photo, when they will promptly turn and trot away. The federal monument comprises about 84,000 acres of the canyon; however, as with the other federal parks on the reservation, the Navajos' interests trump all others here. Nearly all of the canyon is off-limits without a hired Navajo guide. Located near **Chinle,** a small Navajo Nation town about 200 miles (320 km) east of Grand Canyon National Park's South Rim, the **visitors center** (928/674-5500, www.nps. gov/cach, 8am-5pm daily, free) is a good place to start your visit. Here you can find out about guided tours (a ranger will give you a long list if you ask), learn about the history and science of the canyon, and browse a small bookstore stocked well with volumes on the Southwest and the Colorado Plateau. A map of the park's scenic drives is available here for free.

SCENIC DRIVES

Two paved scenic rimside drives offer the most comprehensive look at Canyon de Chelly without hiring a guide. The visitors center has a free map of the easy drives, and both can be done in a regular car. The 37-mile (60-km) round-trip **South Rim Drive** will take you to the **Spider Rock Overlook,** where you can see the eponymous 800-foot (244-m) red-rock spire, a must-see of any visit to the canyon. The south drive has seven overlooks, while the 34-mile (55-km) round-trip **North Rim Drive** has three: **Antelope House Ruin, Mummy Cave Overlook,** and **Massacre Cave Overlook,** each with a view of ruins. Many of the lookouts are at the end of a short but relatively strenuous hike, and most have no barriers whatsoever between you and the edge.

TOURS

You need a Navajo guide with you to travel deep into the canyon, and there are many available for hire throughout the year. Expect to pay about $50-60 per hour for 1-3 people for a private Jeep tour along the canyon bottom to some of the out-of-the-way ruins, caves, and rock-art sites.

Canyon de Chelly (Unimoq) Tours (Chinle, 928/349-1391 or 928/349-1600, http://canyondechellytours.com, $75 pp) offers a three-hour group tour in a big four-by-four (you ride with about 10 other passengers in the open bed). The tour will take you from Antelope House Ruin to White House Ruin.

Antelope House Tours (Chinle, 928/674-5231, www.canyondechelly.net) offers three-hour Jeep tours of all the ruins ($157 for three people) and three-hour hiking tours ($99 for three people) with guides versed in the lore and culture of the Navajo and the other peoples that lived in this spectacular place before them. It's a good idea to call ahead for reservations.

1: Elephant Butte in Monument Valley **2:** Canyon de Chelly National Monument

HIKING AND BACKPACKING

Below are the only hikes on the Navajo Nation open to the public without a Navajo guide. **Backcountry hiking and camping** trips on Navajo land require a **permit** from the tribe (https://navajonationparks.org/permits, $12 pp per day). Of the hikes below, only Keet Seel requires a permit.

Navajo National Monument

Just outside the visitors center at **Navajo National Monument** (www.nps.gov/nava) there are three short hiking trails that allow for optimum viewing of the canyon. The 1-mile (1.6-km) round-trip **Sandal Trail** is paved and easy (though a bit steep) and leads to an overlook perfect for viewing the village of Betatakin/Talastima sleeping in its alcove. It's steep going back up, and the hike should not be treated lightly just because it's short. Take water, especially in the summer. The 0.8-mile (1.3-km) round-trip **Aspen Forest Overlook** (easy but steep) descends about 300 feet (91 m) to provide a good look at the forest below the village, but you can't see the ruins. The **Canyon View Trail** (easy) leads 0.6 mile (1 km) round-trip to a nice view of the ruins near the Canyon View Campground. Allow about 30 minutes to an hour for each hike.

If viewing **Betatakin** from the ridgetop isn't enough for you, you can sign up to take a hike into the canyon to explore the ruins up close. The hike to Betatakin is 5 miles (8 km) round-trip and takes 3-5 hours to complete. A ranger guides you 700 feet (213 m) down into the canyon and then on to the ruins. It is a mildly strenuous hike, but the outing is memorable for its scenery, not its difficulty. Two hikes are available daily in the summer (May-Sept.), leaving from the visitors center at 8:15am and 10am. During the rest of the year, one hike leaves from the center daily at 10am. It's required that you sign up beforehand with the rangers at the visitors center if you want to take the hike.

The trek to **Keet Seel** (which roughly translates to "shattered house") is a bit more

involved. One of the best-preserved ruins in the Southwest, Keet Seel was "discovered," for the Anglo world anyway, by the famous Southwestern ruin-hunter Richard Wetherill while he was chasing a runaway burro.

Reaching the ruin involves a 17-mile (27-km) round-trip hike (which ranges from moderate to strenuous) through the canyon bottomlands along a meandering stream—with several small waterfalls—that you have to cross dozens of times. You will get your feet wet early and often on this hike; there's no way to avoid it. Many hikers take along a sturdy pair of hiking sandals and change into them after descending 1,000 feet (305 m) into the canyon along a rock-hewn trail. When you arrive at the primitive campground within sight of the ruin, a volunteer ranger who lives in a hogan-shaped log cabin nearby will take you on an hour-long tour of the ruin, which you reach by climbing a steep ladder into a cliffside rock alcove. He explains all about the people who once lived in this hidden canyon, and usually shows off a few astounding items found at the site from the everyday lives of the stone village's builders and residents. This is as close as you're likely to get to the ancients.

If you are some kind of world-champion hiker, you could go in and out in the same day, but a stay overnight at the campground, with the ruins dark and mute just across the wash, is a memorable experience. (There is no water available at the campground, nor are fires allowed, but there is a compost toilet.) You have to attend a short orientation meeting either the morning of your hike at 8am or the afternoon prior at 4pm. It's best to arrive the day before so you can get an early start. The best place to stay is at one of the chains in Kayenta, about a half-hour drive from the monument. It's a good idea to purchase and pack all your backpacking supplies before arriving on the reservation, as there aren't any good places to do so nearby.

Reservations and a backcountry permit are required for Keet Seel and are limited to 20 people per day. Call ahead for best results (928/672-2700). The hike is offered daily in the summer, May-September, but after September 15 it's offered every second weekend of the month only.

Monument Valley Navajo Tribal Park

The only hiking you can do in **Monument Valley** without a Navajo guide is along **Wildcat Trail,** a 3.2-mile (5.1 km) loop trail around **West Mitten Butte.** It's an easy, quiet walk along a red-dirt path among gray-green scrub and sagebrush, with the spires and buttes looming close and lizards whipping over red rocks. The trail starts 0.4 mile (0.6 km) north of the visitors center. It's easy enough for kids, but there's no shade, and it can get windy out there. Take water with you, and plan on being out for two hours or more.

★ Canyon de Chelly National Monument

The short but steep **White House Ruin Trail** (2.5 mi/4 km round-trip), a skinny trail hewn out of petrified pink sand dunes leading down to the **White House Ruin,** is the only route to the sandy, shady bottomlands of **Canyon de Chelly** (www.nps.gov/cach) that's open to the public without a Navajo guide, and it is one of the highlights of a visit to Indian Country. The trail offers a rare chance to see Ancestral Puebloan ruins up close and on your own. Once on the canyon bottom, you pass a traditional Navajo hogan and farm, and the canyon walls, streaked with purple, black, and orange, rise hundreds of feet above you. Hawks and ravens circle overhead as black and brown dots high in the bright blue sky. Cave-like hideouts built by natural forces in sandstone alcoves call for you to rest and sit back in their cool shade. Cottonwoods, willows, and peach trees grow in the bottomlands, while pinyon pine, juniper, scrub oak, cholla, and prickly pear cling to the sides of the precipitous trail, a dusty green set against the reddish pink of the de Chelly sandstone. Although you can

---

1: Spider Rock in Canyon de Chelly **2:** arriving in the Canyon de Chelly bottomlands

The Hopi Arts Trail

The Hopi are world renowned for their pottery, baskets, overlay jewelry, and kachina dolls. There are dozens of artists on the Hopi Reservation making and selling collectible, museum-quality crafts for much, much less than you are likely to pay in a museum store or trading post. Look for homemade signs advertising crafts for sale at homes in most villages, and take lots of cash with you.

In recent years many Hopi artists have banded together to form the **Hopi Arts Trail,** a marketing campaign that has made it easier than ever to meet and buy art from Hopi artists living on and below the mesas. A free pamphlet guide to the trail is available online at www.hopiartstrail.com or at the Moenkopi Legacy Inn. The guide features eight galleries spread out around Hopi in 12 villages along AZ 264 and lists the name, phone number, and specialty of 18 different Hopi artists. An artist will typically invite you into his or her home, where you can view the work and learn about the process.

Another great way to meet artists on Hopi is by taking the **Walpi Guided Walking Tour** on First Mesa.

also take two scenic drives to see all the canyon's wonders, there is no substitute for hiking in. Pick up the trailhead at the **White House Overlook,** the fourth signed stop along the South Rim Drive, about 6 miles (9.7 km) from the visitors center.

The hike is easy going down and moderate going back up, as it is pretty steep in a few places. Allow half a day for the round-trip hike and exploring the bottomlands.

If you're on the hunt for Navajo arts, take some cash with you on the hike; there are often artists sitting beneath the shady trees near the White House Ruin, offering their creations for sale.

EVENTS AND SHOPPING
Events
TUBA CITY

The **To'Nanees'Dizi Diné Fair** (aka the Western Navajo Fair, 928/283-3305, http://westernnavajonationfair.net), held once a year in mid-October, is the social event of the season in this corner of the reservation. It's not easy to secure reservations over the three-day fair, which brings hundreds of Navajo families to Tuba City from around the reservation for a rodeo, parade, traditional food and ceremonies, live bands, cutest baby and Miss Western Navajo pageants, and sporting events. It's a fun and illuminating time to be in Tuba City.

Shopping
TUBA CITY

The **Historic Tuba City Trading Post** (10 N. Main St. and Moenave Rd., 928/283-5441, 8am-5pm daily) in downtown Tuba City has been selling native crafts and a vast array of staples since the 1870s. It's still open, and though it has changed a lot over the decades, it offers a great assortment of handmade jewelry, rugs, and other popular Indian Country souvenirs and collectibles. **Van's Trading Post** (928/283-5343, 8am-8pm daily) along U.S. 160 is like a lesser Walmart, half grocery store and half other merchandise like clothing and furniture. There's a coin laundry next door, and a pawn shop is also operated on-site.

KAYENTA

The **Navajo Arts and Crafts Enterprise** has a retail store at Kayenta (928/697-8611, www.gonavajo.com, 9am-7pm Mon.-Sat., noon-6pm Sun.), at the junction of U.S. 160 and U.S. 163. Operated by Navajos, the company sells all kinds of local handmade arts and crafts, curios, rugs, silver jewelry, concha belts, bolo ties, pottery, and more.

FOOD
Cameron

With its professionally prepared, native-inspired cuisine and historical Indian

Country decor, the ★ **Historic Cameron Trading Post** (800/338-7385, www.camerontradingpost.com, 6am-9:30pm daily summer, 7am-9pm daily winter, $7-16), about 30 miles (48 km) east of Grand Canyon National Park on U.S. 89, has one of the best restaurants in the region, serving American and Navajo food including excellent beef stew, heaping Navajo tacos, chili, and burgers. The trading post also has a small grocery store that has packaged sandwiches, chips, and sodas.

Tuba City

In Tuba City, the **Hogan Restaurant** (Main St. and Moenave St., 928/283-5260, 6am-10pm daily, $10-20) is a diner-style place that serves decent food for breakfast, lunch, and dinner daily, including everything from burgers and fries to Navajo tacos and mutton stew as well as a few Mexican favorites.

Hopi

The **Hopi Cultural Center** (AZ 264, 928/734-2404, www.hopiculturalcenter.com, 6am-9pm daily, $5-12) on Second Mesa serves American diner- and grill-style favorites along with must-try traditional Hopi dishes such as Hopi hot beef, Hopi tacos, blue corn mush, and lamb stew.

Kayenta

One of the best restaurants on Navajoland, the ★ **Blue Coffee Pot Restaurant** (0.25 mi/0.4 km east of U.S. 160 and U.S. 163 junction, 928/697-3396, Mon.-Fri., $4-12) in Kayenta, about 25 miles (40 km) south of Monument Valley, serves outstanding home-style Navajo, American, and Mexican food in a hogan-shaped building just off U.S. 160. The Navajo taco here is simply terrific, as are the beef ribs. The staff is friendly, if a bit harried in this busy place. The ★ **Amigo Café** (U.S. 163, 928/697-8448, 10:30am-9pm Mon.-Fri., 8am-9pm Sat., $10-15), just north of the junction, serves fantastic Mexican, Navajo, and American food and is popular with the locals. The **Burger King** (928/697-3534) on U.S. 160 (near the Hampton Inn) has the usual, with

the added feature of a **Navajo Code Talkers** exhibit, which you can view as you chow down on your french fries.

Monument Valley

The View Restaurant (435/727-3468, www.monumentvalleyview.com, 7am-2pm and 5pm-8pm daily, $10-25) in Monument Valley inside the park has decent Navajo, Mexican, and American food for breakfast, lunch, and dinner. In between meals there are only packaged sandwiches, fruit, and snacks available.

At the junction of U.S. 163 and the park entrance road, there's a small shopping center where you can get snacks and fry bread, and there are a few gift shops selling local crafts and curios.

Mexican Hat, Utah

A couple steps from the San Juan Inn in Mexican Hat, Utah, the **Old Bridge Bar & Grill** (2256 U.S. 163, 435/683-2322, 7am-9pm daily, $5-20) serves a big, filling breakfast, tasty Mexican food, Navajo tacos, burgers, and all the other grill-style mainstays, plus a few vegetarian options. It also has a full bar and pool.

ACCOMMODATIONS
Cameron

The ★ **Historic Cameron Trading Post and Lodge** (800/338-7385, www.camerontradingpost.com, $79-199), at the junction of AZ 64 and U.S. 89, is a charming and affordable place to stay and makes a perfect base for a visit to the Grand Canyon, Indian Country, Lake Powell, and the Arizona Strip. It has a good restaurant, and there's also an art gallery, a visitors center, a huge trading post/gift shop, and an RV park ($35 full hookups, no bathroom or showers). The rooms are decorated with a Southwestern Native American style and are very clean and comfortable, some with views of the Little Colorado River and the old 1911 suspension bridge that spans the stream just outside the lodge.

Tuba City

The nicest hotel in Tuba City is the **Quality Inn Navajo Nation** (10 N. Main St. and Moenave Rd., 928/283-5260, www.choicehotels.com, $130-150), right next to the Historic Tuba City Trading Post. The two-story hotel has clean rooms decorated in a soft Southwestern style, free Wi-Fi, and free continental breakfast.

Moenkopi

The **Moenkopi Legacy Inn & Suites** (junction U.S. 160 and AZ 264, Tuba City, 928/283-4500, www.experiencehopi.com, $152) in the Upper Village of Moenkopi near Tuba City, set a new standard for accommodations on Hopi when it opened in 2010. It has luxury rooms with big, comfortable beds, tastefully decorated with photographs of Hopi and featuring a patio door that opens to a heated, saltwater pool and spa. There is a small eating area where a continental breakfast is served in the morning, or there's a café at the gas station across the street (also operated by the Hopi) that serves diner-style fare and some Hopi dishes. Each room has free wireless and a flat-screen TV, and there are some excellent examples of Hopi arts throughout the beautiful lobby. This is the best hotel in Indian Country for the price.

Kayenta

Because it is so close to Monument Valley, there are several nice chain hotels in Kayenta, most of them along U.S. 160 as you enter town. The **Hampton Inn** (U.S. 160, 928/697-3170, $215-220) is very comfortable and offers wireless Internet, a pool, a gift shop, a restaurant, and free continental breakfast. The **Wetherill Inn** (U.S. 163, 1000 Main St., 928/697-3231, www.wetherill-inn.com, $149) has comfortable rooms, an indoor pool, wireless Internet, a gift shop, and free breakfast.

Monument Valley

When the Navajo Nation developed **The View Hotel** (435/727-5555, www.monumentvalleyview.com, $249 and up), the only in-park, noncamping accommodations available at Monument Valley, they probably could have thrown up a few trailers and a kiddy pool and charged $100 per night. The location alone is the attraction; everything else just gets in the way. But they didn't do that, thankfully. The View is instead a complement to the landscape, a low and tucked-away line of rooms near the Mitten Buttes, with patios facing east over the valley where the sun comes alive in the morning. The color of the hotel fairly merges with that of the buttes, monuments, and vast red dunes, making it appear inevitable. The rooms are comfortable and decorated in a generic Southwestern style. It's the view that you're paying for, obviously, and you will pay a lot, if you can get a reservation. There are no cheap rooms, especially during the spring and summer high season. The hotel also rents out cabins with their own amazing views near the Wildcat Trail. These are a good option for families and groups ($199 for a cabin that sleeps four).

Just outside the park, the **Goulding's Lodge** (1000 Goulding Trading Post Rd., 866/313-9769, www.gouldings.com, $175-250) compound features a hotel with luxury amenities, a campground, a museum, and a trading post selling Navajo crafts. It keeps the name of the first trader to settle in the valley, Harry Goulding, who opened a trading post here in 1928, exchanging staples for Navajo jewelry and rugs. The story goes that in the late 1930s Goulding himself went to Hollywood to convince Ford to come to Monument Valley to film *Stagecoach*. Goulding's Lodge has 62 rooms and eight family-friendly, multiroom suites with kitchenettes. There's an indoor heated swimming pool and exercise room, wireless Internet, and satellite TV. The Stagecoach Dining Room ($13.99-16.99) serves American and Navajo food (such as lamb stew, Navajo tacos, and fry bread) for breakfast, lunch, and dinner.

Mexican Hat, Utah

The very small town of Mexican Hat, Utah, is just 27 miles (43 km) north of Monument

Valley along U.S. 163, about 40 minutes from the tribal park. As such, Mexican Hat, named for a precariously balanced rock near town that looks like a sombrero, is an excellent place to base your visit. The few accommodations in Mexican Hat are generally less expensive than the chain hotels in Kayenta and are much less expensive than The View Hotel in Monument Valley. Moreover, a few restaurants here serve alcohol, which is prohibited on the reservation.

The ★ **San Juan Inn and Trading Post** (U.S. 163 and the San Juan River, 800/447-2022, www.sanjuaninn.net, $130-145) is right on the banks of the beautiful San Juan River and next to a picturesque bridge. Offering basic rooms with air-conditioning, TV, and free but spotty Wi-Fi, the San Juan Inn is the best place to stay near Monument Valley for the money. It's in a quiet and relaxing setting, with red cliffs hovering above the bushy green riverbank and the river rolling by—plus there are always a few other explorers around here to talk to. The inn also rents well-appointed yurts, which are located on a different property nearby ($110).

Canyon de Chelly National Monument

Near the visitors center on Canyon de Chelly National Monument, ★ **Thunderbird Lodge** (3.5 mi/5.6 km east of U.S. 191 on Indian Rte. 7, 928/671-5841, http://thunderbirdlodge.com, $90-120) is the only hotel within the monument and feels faraway and rural with its grassy and shady grounds. The basic rooms come with free Wi-Fi, refrigerators, and TVs, and they are clean and comfortable. There's a decent cafeteria-style restaurant here, and a trading post-gift shop where you can book tours of the canyon.

CAMPING
Cameron

Just 30 miles (48 km) from Grand Canyon National Park's Desert View entrance, **Cameron Trading Post RV Park** (466 Hwy. 89, 800/538-7385, www.camerontradingpost.

com, $35) has basic sites with full hookups across U.S. 89 from the Cameron Trading Post, the lodge, and the restaurant. The sites are available first-come, first-served. The park has no cell service or Wi-Fi, though you can get on Wi-Fi at the trading post, reached by a tunnel beneath the highway. There are no bathrooms or showers.

Navajo National Monument

Navajo National Monument (928/672-2700, www.nps.gov/nava) has two campgrounds, both of them free and first-come, first-served. The **Sunset View Campground** is open year-round and has 31 sites for tents and RVs up to 28 feet, with potable water but no hookups or dump stations. The **Canyon View Campground** is open April 1-November 1 and has 14 primitive tent sites with a composting toilet, charcoal grills, and picnic tables.

Canyon de Chelly National Monument

At **Canyon de Chelly National Monument** (www.nps.gov/cach) is **Cottonwood Campground,** a free, first-come, first-served campground. It's open year-round, with running water and flush toilets in the summer only. For more information, contact the Navajo Parks and Recreation Department (928/674-2106).

Monument Valley

In Monument Valley, **The View Campground** (435/727-5802, www.monumentvalleyview.com, $20 tent sites, $40 RV sites) is open year-round. There are separate RV and tent sites. Each site has a table, grill, ramada, and trash can, and there are restrooms and coin-operated showers. No hookups are available, but a dump station is open during the summer. Check in at the visitors center to get a campsite. The well-equipped **Goulding's Campground** (435/359-0047, www.gouldings.com) offers tent sites for $19 per night and RV sites with full hookups for $48 per night. There's also a convenience store, a gas station, a coin laundry, a car wash, and an indoor pool at the campground.

TRANSPORTATION AND SERVICES

Driving

It's relatively easy to navigate Indian Country, as long as you have a steady vehicle and a good map. Remember that the distances between stations, much as it was in the old days of the territory, are generally long, so take advantage of off-road respite when it presents itself.

To reach the Navajo and Hopi Reservations from Flagstaff, take U.S. 89 north to **Cameron** (53 mi/85 km from Flagstaff, 1 hour), at the entrance to the Navajo Nation. To get to Cameron from Grand Canyon National Park's Desert View section, take AZ 64 east to the junction with U.S. 89 (30 mi/48 km, 1 hour). Past Cameron, turn east on U.S. 160, which will take you through **Tuba City** (26 mi/42 km from Cameron, 30 minutes) and **Kayenta** (75 mi/121 km from Tuba City, 1.25 hours), past the **Navajo National Monument** (63 mi/101 km from Tuba City, 1 hour). From Kayenta, head north on U.S. 163 to reach **Monument Valley Navajo Tribal Park** (22 mi/35 km, 30 minutes), or head east from Kayenta on U.S. 160 and then take U.S. 191 south to reach Chinle and **Canyon de Chelly National Monument** (71 mi/114 km, 1.25 hours).

Hopi land can be reached via the gateway village of **Moenkopi**, at the junction of U.S. 160 and AZ 264, about 2 miles (3.2 km) southeast of Tuba City.

The best map of this area is the American Automobile Association's (AAA) Indian Country Guide Map.

Services

Contact the **Navajo Tourism Department** (P.O. Box 663, Window Rock, AZ 86515, 928/810-8501, www.discovernavajo.com) for advice and information about traveling in this region.

Glen Canyon National Recreation Area

Sprawling over the Arizona-Utah border and some 1.25 million acres, **Glen Canyon National Recreation Area** (928/608-6200, www.nps.gov/glca, $30 per car for a seven-day pass, $25 motorcycles, $15 bikes) is a popular boating, fishing, and hiking area centered on **Lake Powell**, the continent's second-largest artificial lake. Created by the damming of the Colorado River and the submersion of the river-sculpted Glen Canyon, the lake is 186 miles (300 km) long and has more than a thousand miles (1,610 km) of meandering desert shoreline. Its waters run through a red-rock maze of narrow side canyons, like canals around an ornate sandstone city, now abandoned. During the spring and summer months the lake is crowded with sometimes rowdy Jet Skiers, water-skiers, and houseboat residents, but you could also visit the area and never get wet—the canyon-country scenery is enough to draw and keep even the most water-averse visitors. The whole area resembles one vast, salmon-pink sand dune frozen and petrified at once—it is a desolate, lonely place sometimes, beautiful and sacred but also a reminder of how humans can change a seemingly unalterable landscape at their will.

Probably the most popular activity on Lake Powell is houseboating. The floating mansions chug around the buttes and spires, while their residents shoot water cannons at each other and stop at night for parties on the beaches around the lake.

As it is on the nearby Navajo Reservation, some places around Lake Powell are an hour off Arizona time during daylight saving time.

The closest town to the lake is **Page**, which is about 3 miles (4.8 km) from Glen Canyon Dam.

Glen Canyon National Recreation Area

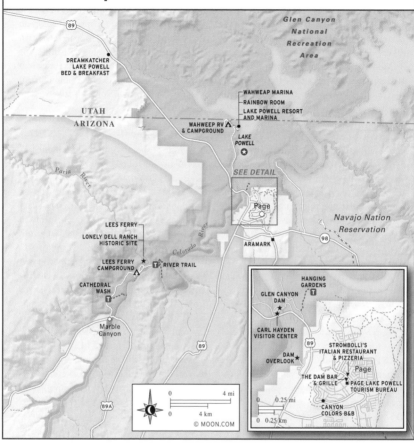

SIGHTS
Glen Canyon Dam

Looking out at **Glen Canyon Dam** through large picture windows in Glen Canyon's **Carl Hayden Visitor Center** (U.S. 89 on west side of dam, 928/648-6404 or 928/608-6072, www.nps.gov/glca, 8am-5pm daily, free tours offered), it's difficult not to be impressed. The great concrete slab shimmed into the narrow Navajo-sandstone channel allows for the storage of some 27 million acre-feet of water (an acre-foot of water is roughly the amount that a family of four uses in a year); it's a brash

reclamation feat if there ever was one. But it is also difficult to see Lake Powell, the reservoir and playground created by the dam, and not feel that something was lost in the flooding of once-spectacular Glen Canyon and the irrevocable alteration of the Colorado River's ecosystem.

The writer and desert-country anarchist Edward Abbey, whose famous 1975 trickster-novel *The Monkey Wrench Gang* envisions the destruction of Glen Canyon Dam by a group of ecowarriors, described the long-lost canyon, waiting silent about 300 feet (91 m) below

Lake Powell's glassy surface, as a "once lovely wonderland of grottoes, alcoves, Indian ruins, natural stone arches, cottonwood groves, springs and seeps and hanging gardens of ivy, columbine, and maidenhair fern—and many other rare things."

Along with sinking this natural wonderland, the dam severely altered the character of the Colorado River downstream. A sediment-laden river—a characteristic of the mighty flow that allowed it to carve those famous canyons—the Colorado River once ran warm and muddy, filled with native fish and lined by beaches, sandbars, and groves of cottonwood and willow. Now that the flow stops at the dam, the once sediment-heavy river runs cool and clear coming out the other side, which has encouraged invasive plant and fish species to thrive to the detriment of the native flora and fauna. Beaches that are eroded don't come back so easily because of the lack of sediment in the river flow, and a controlled flow has replaced the natural flood cycle of the river, leading to the disappearance of an entire ecosystem.

Many people, including some who once supported the dam's construction, now believe that too much was lost for what was gained. The dam is surely an awesome sight, and it will either draw your admiration for the brave and tough laborers who built it from 1957 to 1964 or your disgust for the loss of a once-wild river that it changed forever. More likely, you'll feel a little bit of both, and you will agree with Abbey, who conceded that "though much has been lost, much remains."

Since the 1990s the river below the dam has been purposely flooded several times with timed releases of flows from the reservoir. An army of scientists then moves into the canyon along the river to determine the flood's effects on the ecosystem. While these experiments have been helpful, many scientists believe they happen too infrequently to make much of a difference in combating the dam's negative influence downriver.

DAM OVERLOOK

A short but mildly strenuous walk to the Dam Overlook is worth the effort to see the front of the massive dam and the Colorado River going its merry way beyond it. Catch the trailhead off U.S. 89, about 1.5 miles (2.4 km) south of the Carl Hayden Visitor Center on Scenic View Road. It's a 940-foot (287-m) walk, one-way, down some relatively steep steps.

★ Lake Powell

If you make the drive to these remote corners of the Colorado Plateau, crossing Indian lands and canyonlands just to see the landscape, and fail to get out on the water, you are indeed missing something. Stark and beautiful, Lake Powell offers the opportunity to kayak or Jet-Ski through a drowned labyrinth of strangely sculpted canyons.

Many otherwise landbound folks who visit Lake Powell have their own boats, including a large contingent of locals and near-locals from the surrounding region. Others become lake-top locals for a week every year, conspiring with friends to lounge in luxury under the relentless sun, blushed in a more or less permanent buzz. You can rent a houseboat at **Wahweap Marina** (100 Lakeshore Dr., Page, 888/896-3829, www.lakepowell.com/houseboats), which also rents kayaks, Jet Skis, and powerboats.

Between April and October, the marina offers several **boat tours** of the lake, including dinner and breakfast cruises and day trips to Rainbow Bridge and elsewhere. The red rocks grow warm and flash their deep hidden colors during sunrise and sunset, and a boat tour is a great way to experience this. There are nighttime tours of the lake for a view of the city of stars that emerges from the huge, clear sky. Depending on length and destination, boat tours from Wahweap run $41-125. There's a booking desk inside the Lake Powell Resort at Wahweap Marina.

1: Glen Canyon Dam **2:** Lake Powell

Rainbow Bridge National Monument

Rainbow Bridge, the world's largest arched-rock span and one of the true wonders of the natural world, is a sacred site to the Navajo, who call it *Nonnezoshi* (rainbow turned to stone). An improbable arch of reddish-orange sandstone 290 feet (88 m) high, the "bridge" is one of the most popular sites within the recreation area, even with the difficulty in getting there and the admonitions against walking under it in deference to Navajo beliefs. While you can gear up for a multiday backpack trip across the hot, rugged land to reach the wonder on foot, most visitors take a 50-mile (81-km), all-day boat tour from Wahweap Marina or take their own boat to the well-signed port of call. **Aramark** (800/528-6154, www.lakepowell.com, $122) is in charge of tours. The trip includes an easy 2-mile (3.2-km) round-trip hike from the dock to the arch.

TOP EXPERIENCE

Lees Ferry

A boat launch and fishing spot with a campground, **Lees Ferry** (www.nps.gov/glca) is the only spot in hundreds of miles of canyonland where you can drive down to the **Colorado River.** It's reached via a paved access road from U.S. 89A—look for the Lees Ferry sign about 5 miles (8 km) west of Navajo Bridge.

Lees Ferry is named for a man who occupied the area briefly in the early 1870s, Mormon outlaw John D. Lee, one of the leaders of the infamous Mountain Meadows Massacre in Utah. Lee was exiled to this lonely spot after he and others attacked and murdered more than 100 westbound Arkansas emigrants moving through Utah Territory during a period when relations between the Utah Mormons and the U.S. government were strained, to say the least. One of Lee's wives, Emma Lee, ended up running the ferry more than Lee ever did; he soon lit out and lived as a kind of fugitive until he was finally, in 1877, recalled home and sentenced to death. The proclamation was carried out by firing squad on the same ground as the massacre. To the end and in a published memoir, Lee insisted that he was a scapegoat, and many believe Brigham Young ordered the massacre.

For long before and after Lee lent his name to the crossing, this 2-mile (3.2-km) stretch near the mouth of the Paria River was one of the few places to cross the river in southern Utah and northern Arizona, and it remained so until the bridging of the Colorado at Marble Canyon in 1929. Today the area is the starting block for thousands of brave river-trippers who venture into the Grand Canyon on the Colorado River every year. It's also a popular fishing spot, though the trout here have been introduced and were not native to the warm, muddy flow before the dam at Glen Canyon changed the Colorado's character.

RECREATION
Hiking and Backpacking

The stone landscapes of Glen Canyon National Recreation Area seem like an alien world. Hiking here is similar to being in the inner canyon—it's difficult to keep an eye on the trail for all the strange variegated strata and looming formations. The sun here is unforgiving, and there is no shade save under the odd jutting rock ledge. Hikes near **Lees Ferry** will lead you to the sandy banks of the typically inaccessible **Colorado River,** sculptor of Grand Canyon.

For an easy introduction to this unique world of rock and water, take a hike to **Hanging Garden,** an unlikely oasis out on the hard land where greenery hangs from the seeping rocks, providing a cool place to kick back and study the landscape. It's a 1-mile (1.6-km), one-way trek on a slickrock trail that's easy and okay for kids. The trailhead is 0.5 mile (0.8 km) from Glen Canyon Bridge on U.S. 89, on the east side of the bridge, across from the Carl Hayden Visitor Center. Just look for the sign.

CATHEDRAL WASH
Distance: 3 miles (4.8 km) round-trip

Duration: 1-2 hours
Elevation gain: 300 feet (91 m)
Effort: Moderate
Trail conditions: Dirt, rocky, slickrock, sand
Trailhead: Along Lees Ferry Road

Named for **Cathedral Rock,** a dramatic redrock formation jutting out of the earth just to the south, **Cathedral Wash** is an excellent short and relatively easy introduction to canyonland hiking, ending with an amazing encounter with the Colorado River as it flows on to Grand Canyon. For eons water falling off the Vermilion Cliffs toward the river cut this deep and narrow channel down to the Kaibab limestone and the darker Toroweap formation. The red, gray, and white walls lean in and overhang in parts as you negotiate the stone ledges through the narrow canyon, intensifying the thrilling strangeness of this popular hike. To reach the trailhead, drive 1.3 miles (2.1 km) from the junction of U.S. 89A and Lees Ferry Road; park at the trailhead, found on the left (the second pullout from the highway).

LONELY DELL

Distance: 1 mile (1.6 km) round-trip
Duration: 1 hour
Elevation gain: None
Effort: Easy
Trail conditions: Dirt, rocky, sand
Trailhead: Lees Ferry near the Paria River bridge

Park near the bridge over the Paria River and walk up the gravel road to the **Lonely Dell Ranch Historic Site** for a self-guided tour of the remains of a far-flung homestead. The Lee family and other ferry runners over the years operated this small ranch and orchard near the crossing. A log cabin, a stone-built ranch house, and a cemetery remain, and the orchard is still bearing fruit, which you are allowed to sample in season.

RIVER TRAIL

Distance: 1.2 miles (1.9 km) round-trip
Duration: 1 hour
Elevation gain: None
Effort: Easy

Trail conditions: Dirt, rocky, sand
Trailhead: Lees Ferry boat launch parking area

Pick up this easy hike along the Colorado River at the Lees Ferry boat launch parking area. A relatively flat route of gravel and river sand, the trail follows the river around Lees Ferry Historic Site, where you'll see the remains of past mining operations and ferry boat ventures. If you're lucky you may also see some rafters heading out on a trip into Grand Canyon, or at least preparing for one. Sit down on the sandy beach and relax to the sounds of the river rushing by.

Take the 2-mile (3.2-km) one-way **Spencer Trail** spur off the River Trail up some 1,500 feet (457 m) on a series of strenuous switchbacks for a condor's-eye view of the incredible landscape. Figure on adding another 2-3 hours for this difficult detour.

PARIA CANYON

Distance: 45 miles (72 km) one-way
Duration: Multiple days
Elevation gain: 1,300 feet (396 m)
Effort: Strenuous
Trail conditions: Dirt, slickrock, sand, some water
Trailheads: Lees Ferry, White House, Buckskin Gulch, and Wire Pass

The Paria River cuts through the northeast portion of the 294,000-acre Vermilion Cliffs National Monument, creating **Paria Canyon,** a gorgeous slickrock box canyon with pools and falling water—it's one of the most popular canyonland backpacking areas. You must obtain a **permit** from the Bureau of Land Management (435/688-3200, www.blm.gov) to hike in the canyon ($6 pp per day for day hikes, $5 pp per day for overnight hikes). Applying online is easy, but permits go fast during the spring, summer, and early fall. There are four trailheads from which to enter this remote and gorgeous canyon: Lees Ferry, White House, Buckskin Gulch, and Wire Pass. For more information, talk to the staff at the BLM Kanab Field Office (669 S. Hwy 89A, Kanab, UT, 435/664-1200, www.blm. gov/office/kanab-field-office, 8am-4:30pm Mon.-Fri.).

★ Boating

Most of the **houseboats** available for rent here sleep up to 12 people and have all the comforts of home. On average, expect to pay about $150-200 per person per day for a houseboat, which you can rent from three days up to seven days. The least expensive are about $1,800-2,500 for three days, while the luxury models are about $10,000 for five days. You can rent a boat at **Wahweap Marina** (100 Lakeshore Dr., Page, 888/896-3829, www.lakepowell.com/houseboats), and it's essential to plan far ahead (about six months in advance) and make a reservation.

The **boat rental facility** (8am-6pm daily) at Wahweap, which is just a short drive from the Lake Powell Resort along Lakeshore Drive, also rents **Jet Skis** ($180 for two hours, $375 all day, plus $500 deposit) and **powerboats** ($600 all day, plus $500 deposit). While these vehicles are pricey and a bit obnoxious, exploring the canyons and alcoves of Lake Powell on a speedy boat or Jet Ski seems otherwise ideal. There's no easier, or faster, way to see the whole lake and to explore its mysterious corners and beaches.

A more peaceful and contemplative activity, which also has the virtue of being great exercise, is **kayaking** on Lake Powell. It's even better with a loved one; the double sit-on-top kayak here is perfect for couples, especially if one of the pair is not inclined to do much paddling ($60 all day, plus $100 deposit). Make sure to take some water and food along with you. You can buy groceries in Page, and a store near the rental office sells a small selection of snacks and drinks (it also has bathrooms). Two or three hours is more than enough time to paddle across the lake to one of the white beaches spreading out from sheer white rock faces nearby, have a picnic, climb into the shallow caves in the rock face, and paddle back again. Don't forget the sunscreen.

Fishing

You'll need a valid Arizona fishing license from the **Arizona Game & Fish Department** (602/942-3000, www.azgfd. com, $55 nonresidents, $37 residents) to fish year-round in the Colorado River, Glen Canyon National Recreation Area, and Lake Powell.

In Lake Powell you'll find smallmouth, largemouth, and striped bass, as well as walleye, channel catfish, crappie, and bluegill. Just downriver at Lees Ferry, you'll find trout of all variety—about 20,000 wild trout per mile. Lees Ferry is managed as a trophy trout fishery and offers some of the best fishing on the lower Colorado.

For guides, gear, and any other information about the area, try **Lees Ferry Anglers** (928/355-2261 or 800/962-9755, https://leesferry.com, 6am-9pm daily), located at the Cliff Dwellers Lodge. The guides at **Marble Canyon Outfitters** (800/533-7339, www.leesferryflyfishing.com) and **Kayak the Colorado** (928/856-0012, www.kayakthecolorado.com) will also take you out fishing or kayaking on the Colorado River beyond the dam, including trips to Horseshoe Bend.

ACCOMMODATIONS AND FOOD

Wahweap Marina and Lake Powell Resort

The largest marina in the recreation area and the center of Arizona-side visits to Lake Powell, the **Wahweap Marina** (928/645-2433, www.lakepowell.com) offers lodging, food, boat and other watercraft rentals, camping, RV parking, tours, and shopping all within one area. Aramark is the main concessionaire at the marina, running the ★ **Lake Powell Resort and Marina** (100 Lakeshore Dr., 928/645-2433, $154-250), where you can rent the equipment to do just about anything on the lake. The hotel has two heated pools, a sauna, a hot tub, and a workout room. The resort is elegant but casual, with everybody walking around in flip-flops and swimsuits, and overlooks the marina and lake. The rooms are

How Green and Sustainable is GCNRA?

Operating the **Lake Powell Resort and Marina,** Aramark is **Glen Canyon National Recreation Area'**s main concessionaire. The company has an active sustainability program that includes water-efficient xeriscape landscaping, low-flow shower heads, and an opt-out linen option for guests. The resort also contributes to the Clean the World initiative, which recycles unused hotel soaps and shampoo and sends them to communities in need. The resort is also certified by the Clean Marine Program for its recycling and pollution-control efforts. Aramark uses recycled, locally sourced, and energy-efficient building materials, and more and more of the houseboats on Lake Powell come equipped with solar power. All these strategies contribute to making Lake Powell a more sustainable destination, but there's no getting away from the fact that the lake sits in the middle of a hot and arid desert.

comfortable, stylish, and dark and cool for those overheated summer days when you've had enough of the sun.

The marina's **Rainbow Room** (100 Lakeshore Dr., 928/645-2433, 6am-2pm and 5pm-10pm daily in season, 7am-1:30pm and 5pm-9pm daily winter, $10-32) at the Lake Powell Resort has lakeview tables and serves delicious fish, steak, pork chops, and pasta for dinner and a buffet at lunch. The hotel also has a stylish, relaxing bar, the **Driftwood Lounge,** inside with good drinks and tasty tapas. The marina has a sandy beach with chairs and cabanas, and it offers guided fishing tours and waterskiing instruction, among myriad other activities.

Page

As the gateway to Lake Powell, Page has all the usual chain hotels and several chain restaurants. Most of Page's services are found along Lake Powell Boulevard, the main drag through town.

Canyon Colors B&B (225 S. Navajo Dr., 928/645-5979, www.canyoncolorsbandb. com, $99-159, two-night minimum) rents two bright and homey rooms and has an outdoor barbecue area and a pool. The **Dreamkatcher Lake Powell Bed & Breakfast** (66 S. American Way, Big Water, Utah, 435/675-5828, www.dreamkatcherslakepowell.com, $99-215), about 20 minutes from Page on the Utah side of the recreation area, offers three pleasant rooms, a library with views of the

lake, and a hot tub with a spectacular view of the canyonlands.

The Dam Bar & Grille (644 N. Navajo, 928/645-2161, www.damplaza.com, 11am-11pm daily, $13-34) is the small resort town's entertainment complex, featuring a surf-and-turf restaurant. ★ **Strombolli's Italian Restaurant & Pizzeria** (711 N. Navajo Dr., 928/645-2605, https://strombollisrestaurant. com, 11am-10pm daily, $10-20) offers toothsome Italian entrées like baked ravioli with meat sauce, New York-style pizza, burgers, steaks, salads, and a decent wine list.

CAMPING

Wahweap RV & Campground (Lakeshore Dr., 888/896-3829, www.lakepowell.com, $62) has 36 tent-only sites and 139 sites with full hookups. There are 30- and 50-amp sites with water and septic year-round for rigs up to 45 feet (and there's a few spaces for big rigs up to 70 feet). The campground has a coin-operated laundry and showers, a camp store nearby, and free Wi-Fi. Each site has a picnic table, a fire ring, and a grill, but they are all lacking in shade, which makes staying here in the summer a bit uncomfortable, for tent campers especially. It's not recommended in summer, but it's nice in spring and early fall—and even in summer there's the cool balm of the lake and the swimming beach close by.

The **Lees Ferry Campground** ($20 per night) has 51 sites with grills, tables, and shade structures on a rise above the Colorado River.

The sites have access to bathrooms and potable water. For more information, call Glen Canyon National Recreation Area (928/608-6200). To reach the campground, drive about 4.5 miles (7.2 km) from the junction of U.S. 89A and Lees Ferry Road and turn left, following signs to the campground.

TRANSPORTATION AND SERVICES
Driving and Parking

The best and really the only practical, free-wheeling way to travel to and explore the Lake Powell region is by car. From **Flagstaff,** take U.S. 89 north across the western edge of the Navajo Reservation to Page; the drive is about 130 miles (209 km) and takes 2.25 hours.

A trip north to Lake Powell can easily be folded into a visit to the Grand Canyon's **South Rim.** Take AZ 64 east through the Desert View gate (the park's East Entrance) to Cameron, about 30 miles (48 km), then head north on U.S. 89 for about 80 miles (129 km) to Page. The total distance from the Desert View gate to Page is 110 miles (177 km) and takes about 2.5 hours. The **North Rim** is just as spectacular in its way but without the crowds. The North Rim is 154 miles (248 km) from Lake Powell along U.S. 89A. It will likely take you just as long as the drive from the South Rim; figure on 2.5 hours without stops.

If you're visiting the North Rim along with **Zion National Park** and **Bryce Canyon National Park,** consider a side trip to Lake Powell, especially if you're staying in **Kanab, Utah,** a central base camp for visiting all of the Arizona Strip and southern Utah. Kanab is 74 miles (119 km) from Lake Powell along U.S. 89, just to the north of the Arizona border. The drive across the vast sagebrush plain takes about 1.5 hours.

From **Kayenta** and **Monument Valley** on the Navajo Reservation, east of Lake Powell, take U.S. 160 west to AZ 98 for about 100 miles (161 km), a two-hour drive.

Services

The **Page Lake Powell Tourism Bureau** (647-A Elm St., 928/660-3405, www.visitpagelakepowell.com) has all kinds of information on Page, Glen Canyon, and the rest of the region, and the staff there can help you book tours. The bureau runs the **Visitor Information Center** (10am-4pm Mon.-Fri., 10am-2pm Sat.), located inside the Powell Museum (6 N. Lake Powell Blvd.).

The Arizona Strip and Kaibab Plateau

If there is any wild loneliness left in the United States, it is holed up on the Arizona Strip. This five-million-acre wilderness of crumbling red-rock walls, fallen boulders, and long sagebrush sweeps, humpbacked by the evergreen Kaibab Plateau, has only been accessible by highway from within Arizona since 1929 and the opening of the old Navajo Bridge across the Colorado River. Before that, only Paiutes and Latter-day Saints made a go of it here on any serious scale. The region is still inhabited primarily by ranchers, polygamists, hermits, river guides, and residents of the Kaibab Paiute Indian Reservation.

Think of the "strip" as exactly that: a narrow band of Arizona territory hemmed on the north by Utah's southern border, the south by the Grand Canyon, the east by the Colorado River, and the west by Nevada's eastern border. Within that band are several semi-desert grassland valleys; the long red-rock southern escarpment of the Paria Plateau, a vast tableland protected as the Vermilion Cliffs National Monument; and a green and meadowy forest, smothered by deep snow in winter.

After Fredonia, U.S. 89A begins to rise into a pinyon-juniper woodland that quickly becomes a ponderosa pine forest as the highway climbs the massive upsweep in the land known

The Arizona Strip and Kaibab Plateau

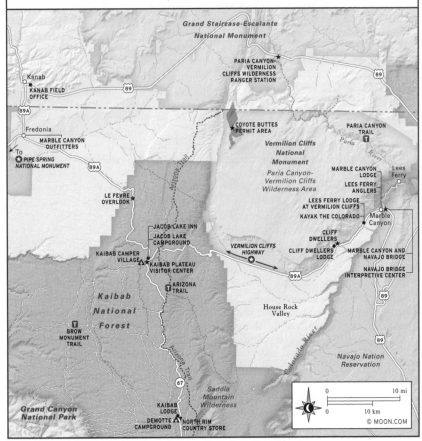

Grand Staircase-Escalante National Monument

Kanab

KANAB FIELD OFFICE

Fredonia

MARBLE CANYON OUTFITTERS

To PIPE SPRING NATIONAL MONUMENT

LE FEVRE OVERLOOK

JACOB LAKE INN

JACOB LAKE CAMPGROUND

KAIBAB CAMPER VILLAGE

KAIBAB PLATEAU VISITOR CENTER

ARIZONA TRAIL

Kaibab National Forest

BROW MONUMENT TRAIL

Grand Canyon National Park

KAIBAB LODGE

DEMOTTE CAMPGROUND

NORTH RIM COUNTRY STORE

Saddle Mountain Wilderness

PARIA CANYON-VERMILION CLIFFS WILDERNESS RANGER STATION

COYOTE BUTTES PERMIT AREA

Vermilion Cliffs National Monument

Paria Canyon-Vermilion Cliffs Wilderness Area

VERMILION CLIFFS HIGHWAY

PARIA CANYON TRAIL

Paria River

MARBLE CANYON LODGE

Lees Ferry

LEES FERRY ANGLERS

LEES FERRY LODGE AT VERMILION CLIFFS

KAYAK THE COLORADO

Marble Canyon

CLIFF DWELLERS

CLIFF DWELLERS LODGE

MARBLE CANYON AND NAVAJO BRIDGE

NAVAJO BRIDGE INTERPRETIVE CENTER

House Rock Valley

Navajo Nation Reservation

Colorado River

0 10 mi
0 10 km

© MOON.COM

as the Kaibab Plateau. This island-like highland, surrounded by arid valleys and giving way on its southern edge to Grand Canyon, measures about 60 miles (97 km) from north to south and roughly 45 miles (72 km) east to west, ranging in height—and so climate and flora—from 3,000 to 9,200 feet (914-2,804 m). In the plateau's highest ranges along AZ 67 from Jacob Lake to the North Rim, dark evergreen forests mixed with white and yellow aspens hedge the wide, green meadows. One of the state's best forest landscapes, the Kaibab has long been logged and hunted; there are old logging and Jeep trails crisscrossing the

tableland, which make backcountry exploring relatively easy, though only with four-wheel drive and not in the winter. From December to mid-May you'll find AZ 67 to the North Rim closed, but U.S. 89A usually stays open year-round, even when the plateau is covered in a thick blanket of snow.

SCENIC DRIVES
★ Vermilion Cliffs Highway
Don't think of this scenic journey in terms of political boundaries, for it clips two other states. Rather, it is a journey over a landscape, through a region with a history that cannot

be understood without seeing the formidable barriers thrown up by nature.

This is classic road-trip territory, and if you're already in the state with a rental car or your own vehicle, consider taking time to at least drive the **Vermilion Cliffs Highway,** a paved two-lane route that runs, more or less, from Marble Canyon to St. George, Utah, using U.S. 89A, AZ 389, and UT 59 in Utah. Along the way you'll pass through the entire strip, crossing the Colorado River and ascending and coming back down the Kaibab Plateau. This can be done in one long day from either the east or the west, but if you want to stop and really see the landscape, take at least two days. If you're heading east to west, the Cameron Trading Post and Lodge on U.S. 89, near the Little Colorado River and the eastern entrance to Grand Canyon National Park's South Rim, makes a good stopping destination. If you're heading west to east, you might want to stay the night in Fredonia or in Kanab, Utah; St. George, Utah; or even Mesquite, Nevada, near the Virgin River Gorge.

The most logical way to see the strip is to fold it into an excursion from the South Rim to the North Rim. Leave the South Rim early in the morning, cross the eastern strip, spend the night and the next day at the North Rim, and then keep heading west down the Kaibab Plateau to Pipe Spring National Monument and on to St. George. From there it's easy to go on and explore western Arizona and the lower Colorado.

If you plan on doing more than road-tripping, such as hiking the empty spaces of the Vermilion Cliffs, it's best to plan ahead and to have at least a high and tough SUV, if not a four-wheel-drive vehicle.

SIGHTS
Marble Canyon and Navajo Bridge

A few miles before U.S. 89A runs into U.S. 89 south toward Navajoland and the Grand Canyon, two bridges span **Marble Canyon,** where the Colorado River digs deep again after surfacing at Lees Ferry. This is the exit

from or the entrance to the heart of the strip, depending on which way you're headed. The original Navajo Bridge was opened in 1929, the first bridge to cross this part of the Colorado, putting Lees Ferry out of business for good. By 1995, a new bridge had opened, as the original was not up to the increased traffic along U.S. 89A. The original bridge is now kept open for sightseers, and you can walk over it and look down at the river flowing through magnificent Marble Canyon, here at the very start of the Grand Canyon. The **Navajo Bridge Interpretive Center** (U.S. 89A on west side of Navajo Bridge, 928/355-2319, www.nps.gov/glca, 9am-5pm daily Apr.-Oct.) has a book shop and displays about the bridge, and there are usually several booths selling Native American arts and crafts.

Vermilion Cliffs National Monument

Most Arizona Strip visitors see only the southern escarpment of the Paria Plateau as they cut through the valley along U.S. 89A. That edge's high, crumbling sandstone cliffs give this national monument of swirling slickrock and narrow, high-walled river canyons its name. The cliffs are best viewed from an established viewpoint about 30 miles (48 km) west of Navajo Bridge as the highway begins to climb out of the House Rock Valley.

There are no services or visitors centers on this remote monument, and much of it is within the **Paria Canyon-Vermilion Cliffs Wilderness Area** and so can't be accessed by car. The area is best explored from the north, along U.S. 89 in Utah between Kanab, Utah, and Page, Arizona. From Page, head west on U.S. 89 for about 30 miles (48 km) to reach the BLM's **Paria Canyon-Vermilion Cliffs Wilderness Ranger Station,** where you can get advice on visiting the area; it serves as a kind of visitors center and crossroads for backpackers and day hikers. This is really the kind of place you have to plan ahead for; most of the best areas require a permit, and those are given out on a lottery system for some of the most popular attractions.

You can also access the monument from the south on the compacted-dirt House Rock/Coyote Valley Road (BLM Road 1065), off the south side of U.S. 89A at House Rock, which leads to the **Coyote Buttes Permit Area.** Coyote Buttes has a north and south section—the north is best gained via U.S. 89 in Utah. This is a world-famous trekking area where there are several trails that lead through a strange rock world of twisted, undulating, multicolored sandstone formations, often appearing as if rough red, yellow, and pink water has been held up and petrified. Along these trails you'll see all the sandstone arches, alcoves, spires, domes, amphitheaters, and buttes that make the canyonlands so exotic and enticing. A limited number of people are allowed in each day, even for day hiking, so make sure to get a permit (www.blm.gov, $5) before traveling.

For more information on the monument, talk to the folks at the BLM's **Arizona Strip Field Office** (345 E. Riverside Dr., St. George, UT, 435/688-3200) or the **Kanab Field Office** (435/644-4600).

Cliff Dwellers and House Rock Valley

U.S. 89A continues on through the red-dirt and sagebrush **House Rock Valley** at the base of the Kaibab Plateau, overlooked by the Vermilion Cliffs. In the tiny settlement of **Cliff Dwellers,** you'll see a little sandstone-brick structure tucked beneath a fallen boulder. Like some kind of canyon-country Hobbit house, the red-rock slabs and sculpted boulder blend with the cliffs, and the chipped light blue trim paint matches the empty sky. This **little rock house,** nearly melding into the vermilion scenery, is one of the most enchanting structures in all of Arizona. There's usually a Navajo or two selling jewelry here, and you can walk around and duck in and out of the strange rock hovels, as long as you remember this is private property. The house and other small shelters were built by Blanche and Bill Russell, the area's original homesteaders. Operating a trading post out of the little rock house, the Russells also catered to Mormon travelers moving through the valley on their way to the St. George temple.

Kaibab Plateau Visitor Center

The rangers at the **Kaibab Plateau Visitor Center** (928/643-7298, www.fs.usda.gov, 8am-5pm daily mid-May-mid-Oct.), about 44 miles (71 km) from the North Rim, can give you advice on hiking and exploring the plateau, and there's a good selection of books for sale and a few displays on the area's flora and fauna.

Le Fevre Overlook

Stop at this observation point along U.S. 89A on the Kaibab Plateau, on the east side of the highway about 8 miles (12.9 km) north of Jacob Lake, and climb the short stairway to a sweeping view of the Vermilion Cliffs and the Arizona Strip.

★ Pipe Spring National Monument

A shady, watered spot on an otherwise dry and windy bunchgrass plain, **Pipe Spring National Monument** (928/643-7105, www.nps.gov/pisp, 8am-5pm daily June-Aug., 8:30am-4:30pm daily Sept.-May, $7) is the Arizona Strip's best historic site. A museum and visitors center fronts a well-preserved fortified ranch house and a few historic outbuildings, a compound built in the 1860s and 1870s by Mormon pioneers who raised cattle for meat and cheese here, much of it taken west weekly to feed workers building a temple in St. George.

The monument is located within the borders of the **Kaibab Paiute Indian Reservation,** and the nation operates the visitors center jointly with the National Park Service.

The excellent museum inside the visitors center has several displays telling the history

1: Vermilion Cliffs Highway **2:** Navajo Bridge over the Colorado River **3:** window in the wall of a home in the tiny settlement of Cliff Dwellers **4:** Pipe Spring National Monument

of both Native American and Mormon settlement on the strip, with artifacts of both cultures. For an in-depth introduction to the history and politics of the strip, this museum can't be beat. After looking over the displays, bookstore, and gift shop, you can head out to the fort for a personal tour by a volunteer (about every half hour in the busy season). The guide takes you through each room in the fortified home, called **Windsor Castle,** furnished with period furniture and still displaying rifle notches in the walls. The tour also takes you into the factorylike rooms where cheese and other provisions were made and stored, recalling the hardscrabble life on the 19th-century strip. The fort had the first telegraph in Arizona, part of which is still here. There is also a trail that goes about half a mile (0.8 km) up a rise behind the fort, where there's an expansive view of the vast plain stretching out toward lonely Mount Trumbull to the south. It is a beautiful, isolating view, quiet except for the wind and the crunch of your feet on the rocky red ground. The rangers at Pipe Spring are also excellent sources for tips on touring the area.

Pipe Spring National Monument is 32 miles (52 km) west of Le Fevre Overlook via U.S. 89A and AZ 389, about a 30-minute drive.

RECREATION
Hiking and Biking

Many of the trails (and backcountry dirt roads) on the Kaibab Plateau are open to both hikers and mountain bikers. Trails within Grand Canyon National Park and designated federal wilderness areas are closed to bikes. The best times to hike and bike on the plateau are late spring, summer, and early fall. The main road leading from U.S. 89A to the North Rim, AZ 67, is closed from December 1 to May 15. From July through September, morning excursions are best, as afternoon thunderstorms often roll in during these months, bringing high winds, lightning, and occasionally violent downpours. For more information about trails in this area, check the **Kaibab National Forest** website (www.

fs.usda.gov/kaibab) and talk to the rangers at the **Kaibab Plateau Visitor Center** (U.S. 89A and AZ 67, 928/643-7298, 8am-5pm daily mid-May-mid-Oct.).

You will need a high-profile vehicle or even a four-wheel drive to reach some of the backpacking trails in this area.

ARIZONA TRAIL
Distance: 50.5 miles (81 km) one-way
Duration: A few hours to multiple days
Elevation gain: Varies based on length of hike
Effort: Easy to moderate
Trail conditions: Dirt, rocky, some sand
Trailhead: Four developed trailheads: U.S. 89A Trailhead, Forest Road 205 Trailhead, East Rim Trailhead, Boundary Trailhead

Open to both hikers and mountain bikers, the Kaibab Plateau sections of the **Arizona Trail** run north across the plateau and into Grand Canyon National Park, offering views of Marble Canyon, the Arizona Strip, and the Navajo Reservation as it winds through the region's pinyon-juniper, ponderosa pine, and mixed-conifer forests. The oldest section of the 800-plus-mile (1,290-km) border-to-border trail (www.aztrail.org), the Kaibab Plateau sections are marked with brown fiberglass posts with Kaibab Plateau decals.

There are four trailheads. To reach the **U.S. 89A Trailhead,** drive 2 miles (3.2 km) east of the Kaibab Plateau Visitor Center on U.S. 89A; the trailhead is at the junction of U.S. 89A and Forest Road 205. To reach the **Forest Road 205 Trailhead,** drive 9 miles (14.5 km) south of the Kaibab Plateau Visitor Center on AZ 67; turn left on Forest Road 205, then go 0.3 mile (0.5 km) to the trailhead. To reach the **East Rim Trailhead,** drive 27.5 miles (44 km) south of the Kaibab Plateau Visitor Center on AZ 67; turn left on Forest Road 611 and go 4.4 miles (7.1 km) to trailhead. For the **Boundary Trailhead,** drive 27.5 miles (44 km) south of the visitors center and turn left on Forest Road 611, then drive 1.4 miles (2.3 km) and turn right on Forest Road 610. It's then another 6 miles (9.7 km) to the trailhead. It's best to have an SUV or truck to get to this trailhead.

EAST RIM TRAIL (FOREST TRAIL 7)

Distance: 3 miles (4.8 km) round-trip
Duration: 2-3 hours
Elevation gain: 1,000 feet (305 m)
Effort: Strenuous
Trail conditions: Dirt, rocky, some sand
Trailhead: East Rim Viewpoint

The **East Rim Trail** is in the **Saddle Mountain Wilderness** and so is open to hikers only. The steep trail descends North Canyon through mixed conifers and oaks. Turn around and head back the same way when you reach the two forks of the **North Canyon Trail** (Forest Trail 4); this trail joins other trails and is often used as a link to multiday trips through the wilderness area. It's a short but strenuous day hike that provides a decent introduction to the steep trails of the canyonlands.

From the Kaibab Plateau Visitor Center, take AZ 67 for 27.5 miles (44 km) south and turn left at Forest Road 611, just past the DeMotte Campground entrance. Another 4 miles (6.4 km) on is the East Rim Viewpoint; the trail starts at the wilderness boundary. It's best to have an SUV or truck to get to this trailhead.

BROW MONUMENT TRAIL

Distance: 2 miles (3.2 km) one-way
Duration: 1-2 hours
Elevation gain: Negligible
Effort: Easy
Trail conditions: Dirt, rocky, some sand
Trailhead: Forest Road 252

Take this short and easy hike through the pinyon-juniper and ponderosa pine forest to one of the rare survey markers left from the explorer John Wesley Powell's survey expedition of 1872. There are U.S. Forest Service interpretive signs about the history of the area along the trail, explaining the purpose and methods of the early geological surveys of the Arizona Strip.

From the Kaibab Plateau Visitor Center, take AZ 67 for 27.5 miles (44 km) south and turn right at Forest Road 22, just past the DeMotte Campground entrance. Drive 16 miles (26 km) north to Forest Road 477, then drive 0.25 mile (0.4 km) west to Forest Road 252. The trailhead is about 2 miles (3.2 km) farther. It's best to have an SUV or truck to get to this trailhead.

RAINBOW RIM TRAIL

Distance: 22.5 miles (36.2 km) one-way
Duration: 2-3 days
Elevation gain: 800 feet (244 m)
Effort: Moderate
Trail conditions: Dirt, rocky, some sand
Trailhead: Parissawampitts Viewpoint or Timp Viewpoint

The 22.5-mile (36.2-km) one-way **Rainbow Rim Trail** is a fun and challenging single-track through forests and meadows and along the north rim of Grand Canyon. The trail reaches five different overlooks. To start at **Parissawampitts Viewpoint,** take AZ 67 south from its junction with U.S. 89A for 26.5 miles (43 km), turn right on Forest Road 22 and drive 10.5 miles (17 km), turn left on Forest Road 206 and drive 3.5 miles (5.6 km), and turn right on Forest Road 214 and drive 8 miles (12.9 km) to Parissawampitts Viewpoint. To start from **Timp Viewpoint** at the other end, take Forest Road 206 for 1.5 miles (2.4 km) to Forest Road 271, turn right and then drive 8 miles (12.9 km) to the trailhead. The drive to the trailheads from the Kaibab Plateau Visitor Center may take up to 1.5-2 hours one-way. It's best to have an SUV or truck to get to these trailheads.

FOOD

The **Marble Canyon Lodge** (U.S. 89A near Marble Canyon, 800/726-1789, www.marblecanyoncompany.com, $10-20) has an excellent restaurant serving tasty fry bread and other Southwestern staples.

The restaurant at **Cliff Dwellers Lodge** (U.S. 89A near Marble Canyon, 928/355-2261 or 800/962-9755, https://leesferry.com, $10-30) serves good breakfasts, lunches, and dinners, with everything from fajitas and ribs to falafel and halibut. It also serves liquor, beer, and wine.

Jacob Lake Inn (junction U.S. 89A and AZ 67, 928/643-7232, www.jacoblake.com) has a restaurant that offers excellent homemade bread and soups and hearty, delicious scratch creations, with a few vegetarian options, including a delicious garden burger. The diner-style **counter** here serves breakfast 6:30am-11am daily ($3-10) and lunch 11am-close daily ($5-15), and there's also a **dining room** for a more formal dinner service 5:30pm-9pm daily ($10-25).

The **Kaibab Lodge** (AZ 67, mile marker 605, 928/638-2389) has a cozy restaurant that serves hearty and delicious food for breakfast ($6-12) and dinner ($11-30) daily during the high season (mid-May-mid-Oct.) and is closed in the winter (mid-Oct.-mid-May). The menu includes burgers, ribs, and steaks. The restaurant offers gluten-free options, and for vegetarians there's a garden burger and a few pasta dishes.

The **North Rim Country Store** (AZ 67, mile marker 605, 18 mi/29 km north of the rim, 928/638-2383, www.northrimcountrystore.com, 7am-7pm daily mid-May-late Oct.) has a small selection of premade packaged sandwiches, cheese, fruit, a few vegetables, sodas, and a selection of beer and wine.

ACCOMMODATIONS

The small **Cliff Dwellers Lodge** (U.S. 89A near Marble Canyon, 928/355-2261 or 800/962-9755, https://leesferry.com, $90) is nearly drowned by the scenery around it, tucked beneath the base of the red cliffs. This lodge offers charming, rustic-but-comfortable rooms with satellite television.

The **Lees Ferry Lodge at Vermilion Cliffs** (U.S. 89A near Marble Canyon, 928/355-2231 or 800/451-2231, www.vermilioncliffs.com, $65) has romantic little rooms in a retro-West, rock-built structure that blends into the tremendous background wonderfully. This lodge has undergone major renovations in recent years.

The trading post first established by Lorenzo Hubbell at **Marble Canyon Lodge**

(U.S. 89A near Marble Canyon, 800/726-1789, www.marblecanyoncompany.com, $82-185) has been open for business since 1920, serving wanderers under the ever-blue sky—which is the only thing bigger out here than the wide-open landscape. This is a friendly and comfortable place to stop. Some rooms have kitchenettes, and the trading post here has a superior selection of books about the region. The lodge also operates a gas station and convenience store just up the road.

The main lodging in the northern portion of the Kaibab Plateau is the **Jacob Lake Inn** (junction U.S. 89A and AZ 67, 928/643-7232, www.jacoblake.com, $128-165 rooms, $96-144 cabins, about 45 miles (72 km) from the North Rim. It features rustic cabins greatly in need of an update, basic motel-style rooms with outside entrances, and a fairly nice hotel-style building with inside hallways, televisions, and Wi-Fi. There's also a bakery, gift shop, small general store, and gas station here.

Kaibab Lodge (AZ 67, mile marker 605, 928/638-2389, mid-May-mid-Oct., $100-185), about 18 miles (29 km) from the North Rim, has cabins and motel-style rooms, generally rustic but comfortable. There are no TVs, Wi-Fi, or cell phone service. The Hiker's Special is one of the best deals on the plateau: $100 per night for a small, basic room with a double bed and a bathroom.

CAMPING

DeMotte Campground (Forest Road 616, 877/444-6777, www.recreation.gov, mid-May-mid-Oct., $22) has 38 nonelectric campsites for tents, trailers, and small motorhomes, with tables and fire grills, drinking water stations, and vault toilets. There are no hookups. The campground is about 18 miles (29 km) north of the North Rim along AZ 67.

Jacob Lake Campground (Jacob Lake, U.S. 89A and AZ 67, www.recreation.gov, mid-May-mid-Oct., $18) is a Kaibab National Forest-administered campground with 51

1: Lees Ferry Lodge at Vermilion Cliffs **2:** Marble Canyon Lodge

nonelectric campsites, ADA-accessible vault toilets, and drinking water, close to hiking, biking, and equestrian trails. There are no hookups. The campground is about 44 miles (71 km) from the North Rim.

Also in Jacob Lake, about 45 miles (72 km) north of the rim, **Kaibab Camper Village** (928/643-7804, www.kaibabcampervillage.com, mid-May-mid-Oct., $20-45) has pull-through and back-in spots for rigs up to 40 feet with full hookups, and tent sites with tables and fire pits. The complex has chemical toilets, coin-op laundry and showers, and a store. Head south on AZ 67 from the U.S. 89A junction; after 0.25 mile (0.4 km), turn right on Forest Road 461, then drive 1 mile (1.6 km) to reach the campground.

The **Kaibab National Forest** (www.fs.usda.gov/kaibab) allows free dispersed camping across the Kaibab Plateau for up to 14 days per month.

TRANSPORTATION AND SERVICES

Driving

U.S. 89A runs east-west through the Arizona Strip and is usually open year-round. The main road leading from U.S. 89A to the North Rim, AZ 67, is closed from December 1 to May 15. Sitting at the junction of U.S. 89A and AZ 67, about 45 miles (72 km) north of the rim, is Jacob Lake, a small settlement without a lake

of any kind, which serves as the gateway to the Kaibab Plateau.

The many Forest Service roads around the Kaibab Plateau are mostly dirt or gravel and should be taken case by case; some should be avoided unless you have a high-profile vehicle. In July, August, and September, expect daily late-afternoon thunderstorms that can quickly wash out a road or inspire a flash flood. To reach some of the backpacking trails here, you will need a high-profile vehicle or even a four-wheel drive.

Gas Stations and Repairs

The **North Rim Country Store** (AZ 67, mile marker 605, 928/638-2383, 7am-7pm daily mid-May-late Oct.) fixes tires and sells a small selection of car supplies. For repairs involving batteries, belts, hoses, and other auto emergencies, you'll have to make it 45 miles (72 km) north of the rim to the service station at **Jacob Lake** (928/643-7232).

Services

The Kaibab Plateau and Grand Canyon National Park's North Rim have no emergency medical resources save for rangers. The closest hospital is in Kanab, Utah, 37 miles (60 km) from the Kaibab Plateau Visitor Center (junction U.S. 89A and AZ 67), about a 45-minute drive. The closest emergency room is in Page, Arizona, 80 miles (129 km) from the visitors center, about a 1.5-hour drive.

Gateways to the Grand Canyon

The four main gateway towns near Grand Canyon each serve a different kind of trip.

Flagstaff, the largest city near the canyon and the capital of the Colorado Plateau, has the most diverse restaurants and accommodations in the region, including many chain hotels as well as independent hotels, inns, and hostels. Most river trips will convene at a prearranged hotel in Flagstaff before moving on to launch at Lees Ferry.

Williams, about 40 minutes west of Flagstaff, is the most direct gateway town, being only an hour's drive along AZ 64 from the South Rim. Though much smaller than Flagstaff, Williams is a popular

Highlights

Look for ★ to find recommended sights, activities, dining, and lodging.

★ Stroll **Flagstaff**'s charming **historic downtown,** popping in and out of shops, galleries, bars, and restaurants and soaking up the Route 66 and railroad-town atmosphere (page 236).

★ Hike up **Mount Humphrey Trail** to the rocky peak of Arizona's tallest mountain, with one of the greatest views in the Southwest (page 247).

★ Join the long history of Grand Canyon tourists who have spent the day shopping, eating, and drinking along the quaint main drag in **historic downtown Williams,** the last place on earth to give up Route 66 for I-40 (page 259).

★ Watch the Colorado River wind around a lone sandstone butte, **Horseshoe Bend,** from the edge of a high sheer cliff (page 265).

★ View the swirling and surreal beauty of the sublime slot canyon at **Antelope Canyon Navajo Tribal Park** (page 265).

Gateways to the Grand Canyon

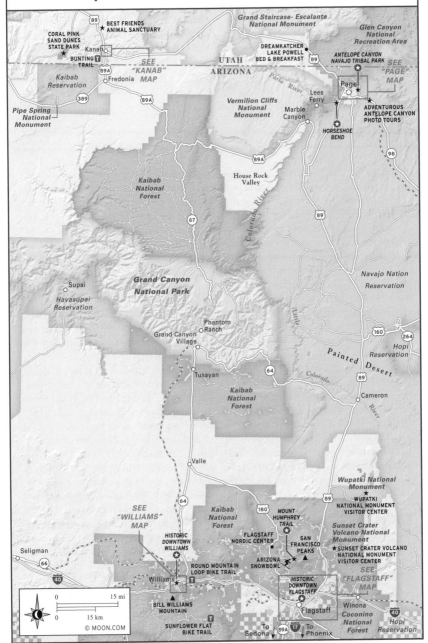

CORAL PINK SAND DUNES STATE PARK
BEST FRIENDS ANIMAL SANCTUARY
Kanab
BUNTING TRAIL
89
Kaibab Reservation
Fredonia
89A
Pipe Spring National Monument
389
89A
UTAH
ARIZONA
SEE "KANAB" MAP

Grand Staircase-Escalante National Monument
DREAMKATCHER LAKE POWELL BED & BREAKFAST
89
Paria River

Glen Canyon National Recreation Area
ANTELOPE CANYON NAVAJO TRIBAL PARK
Page
SEE "PAGE" MAP
ADVENTUROUS ANTELOPE CANYON PHOTO TOURS
98
Lees Ferry
Marble Canyon
HORSESHOE BEND

Vermilion Cliffs National Monument

House Rock Valley
89A

Kaibab National Forest
67
Colorado River

Grand Canyon National Park

Supai
Havasupai Reservation

Navajo Nation Reservation

Phantom Ranch
Grand Canyon Village
Tusayan
64
Colorado
Little Colorado River

160 264
Hopi Reservation

Painted Desert

Kaibab National Forest

Cameron
89

Valle

64

SEE "WILLIAMS" MAP

Kaibab National Forest

HISTORIC DOWNTOWN WILLIAMS
ROUND MOUNTAIN LOOP BIKE TRAIL

180
MOUNT HUMPHREY TRAIL
FLAGSTAFF NORDIC CENTER
SAN FRANCISCO PEAKS
ARIZONA SNOWBOWL

Wupatki National Monument
WUPATKI NATIONAL MONUMENT VISITOR CENTER

Sunset Crater Volcano National Monument
SUNSET CRATER VOLCANO NATIONAL MONUMENT VISITOR CENTER

SEE "FLAGSTAFF" MAP

Seligman
66
40
Williams

HISTORIC DOWNTOWN FLAGSTAFF
Flagstaff
Winona
Coconino National Forest
40
Hopi Reservation

0 15 mi
0 15 km
© MOON.COM

BILL WILLIAMS MOUNTAIN
SUNFLOWER FLAT BIKE TRAIL

To Sedona
89A 17
To Phoenix

tourist area with many excellent hotels, motels, and restaurants, and it is the best place to base your visit if you plan to ride the Grand Canyon Railway into and out of the park.

Page, about 2.5 hours from both the South and North Rims, is a good base for those visiting both rims plus Lake Powell and Glen Canyon National Recreation Area. While surrounded by stark sandstone beauty, Page has little to recommend itself other than its easy chain hotels and restaurants.

About an hour's drive west from Page is **Kanab, Utah,** a pleasant small town with many hotels, inns, and restaurants, a great choice if you're wrapping a trip to Zion and Bryce Canyon National Parks in with your visit to Grand Canyon, or if you're just visiting the North Rim and the Kaibab Plateau.

Flagstaff

Flagstaff is a highland forest town on the southern cliff of the Colorado Plateau with a population of about 74,000, by turns a charming sylvan college town with a historic core and a sprawling, volcanic-rock-strewn hub for interstate semitrucks and graffiti-covered train cars. Its fortunes have been linked to those of Grand Canyon since the 1880s. In the early days of Grand Canyon tourism, before the Santa Fe Railroad came to the South Rim, travelers had to catch a stagecoach out of Flagstaff and endure an expensive ($15 per person), cramped, dusty, and jarring eight-hour ride. Tourist traffic shifted somewhat to Williams after the Santa Fe finished the South Rim spur in 1901, but through it all Flagstaff has remained the main port for Grand Canyon visitors and has grown over the years into a place that deserves attention in its own right, with a major Colorado Plateau museum, three national monuments featuring fascinating Native American ruins, and a charming, historic downtown with unique restaurants, shops, and galleries.

SIGHTS
★ Historic Downtown Flagstaff

Flagstaff has managed to hold on to many of the historic downtown redbrick buildings and quaint storefronts that served the needs of the railway and its passengers, housed and kept Route 66's argonauts, and marked the social and commercial heart of the town for generations. Its many restaurants, shops, and bars make it an ideal spot for tourists. On the National Register of Historic Places since the 1980s, many of the buildings in the downtown area date from the late 19th and early 20th centuries, including the Babbitt Brothers Building, which was constructed in 1888, and the Coconino County Courthouse, built in 1894. Just across Route 66 from the downtown area is the old Santa Fe Depot, built in the Tudor Revival style in 1926.

Downtown is a pleasant place to be any time of year, and the traveler will find myriad places to eat, drink, and hunt for all manner of artistic and handmade treasures. Take a half day or so and walk along Humphreys Street, Beaver Street, Leroux Street, San Francisco Street, and Route 66 (also called Santa Fe) across from the train depot, ducking in and out of shops, galleries, watering holes, and eateries. **Heritage Square** (Aspen Ave. between Leroux and San Francisco Sts., 928/853-4292, www.heritagesquaretrust.org) hosts live music, outdoor movies, and arts and crafts fairs on weekends during the warmer months.

Southside Historic District
After exploring downtown, walk south of

Previous: Antelope Canyon Navajo Tribal Park; Horseshoe Bend; Hotel Monte Vista in downtown Flagstaff.

the tracks, where there are more shops, restaurants, and bars in the Southside Historic District, which is a bit shaggier than downtown and offers a look at Flagstaff's left-of-center scene. It's just south of downtown and bordered by Route 66 and the Santa Fe Railroad, the Rio de Flag, and Northern Arizona University (NAU). The neighborhood was added to the National Register of Historic Places in 2010. Check out the ruins of the **Historic Basque Handball Court** (east side of San Francisco St.), built in 1926 by tourist-homeowner Jesus Garcia, who emigrated from Spain to Flagstaff in 1912. The building has been wonderfully restored and is now an excellent restaurant and bakery. The ruins of the 40-foot-high (12-m) sandstone court remain. It's said to be the last such court standing in Arizona and one of only a few in the nation. Route 66 enthusiasts will want to seek out the imaginative mural on a wall along West Phoenix Avenue. The nearby Flagstaff Visitor Center offers a free walking guide to other historic Route 66 sites around downtown and the Southside.

Riordan Mansion State Historic Park

Riordan Mansion State Historic Park (off Milton Rd. at 409 W. Riordan Rd., 928/779-4395, https://azstateparks.com, 9:30am-5pm daily, $10 adults, $5 children 7-13) is a rock-and-log mansion sprawling amid a stand of pines in the middle of Flagstaff's commercial section and abutting the NAU campus. Its origin is a great American success story that would have been perfectly depicted in Technicolor. Two brothers, Michael and Timothy Riordan, make it big on the western frontier, denuding the Arizona northland of its harvestable lumber. The boys are rich, powerful, and run in Flagstaff's founding circles, helping to build a lasting American community out of a rough, arid wilderness. The close brothers marry close sisters, Caroline and Elizabeth Metz, and the two fledgling families get on so well that they decide to build a

40-room, 13,000-square-foot (1,208-m) Arts and Crafts-style masterpiece and live in it together. They hire El Tovar designer Charles Whittlesey to design two mansions in one, each shooting off in separate directions and linked by a pool hall and communal space. They decorate their majestic home with Stickley furniture, stained glass, and enough elegant details to draw crowds of visitors for the next 100 years. And everybody lives happily ever after.

The park offers **tours** (on the hour 10am-4pm, reservations recommended) of the Arts and Crafts treasure, one of the best examples of the distinctive architecture that left a stylish stamp on the Southwest in the late 19th and early 20th centuries. Only a small portion of the structure is included in the tour, but it's full of original furniture and displays about the family and life in Flagstaff's formative years.

Lowell Observatory

The hilltop campus of **Lowell Observatory** (1400 W. Mars Hill Rd., 928/774-3358, www.lowell.edu, 10am-10pm Mon.-Sat., 10am-5pm Sun., $17 adults, $12 on Sun., $10 children 5-17, $6 on Sun.), just west of downtown, occupied by tall, straight pines and a few small, white-domed structures with round concrete bases, has had a good deal of influence over the science of astronomy since its founders began searching the clear rural skies over Flagstaff in 1894. The historic viewpoint has had something to do with contemporary ideas about the beginnings of the universe as well.

It was here between 1912 and 1914 that Vesto Slipher discovered that the universe's galaxies are moving away from Earth, a phenomenon measured by changes in the light spectrum called redshifts. This in turn helped Edwin Hubble and others confirm that the universe is expanding, thus providing the first observable evidence for the Big Bang. Another historic distinction came a few years later in 1930, when 24-year-old Clyde Tombaugh looked out from atop Mars Hill and discovered Pluto.

Flagstaff

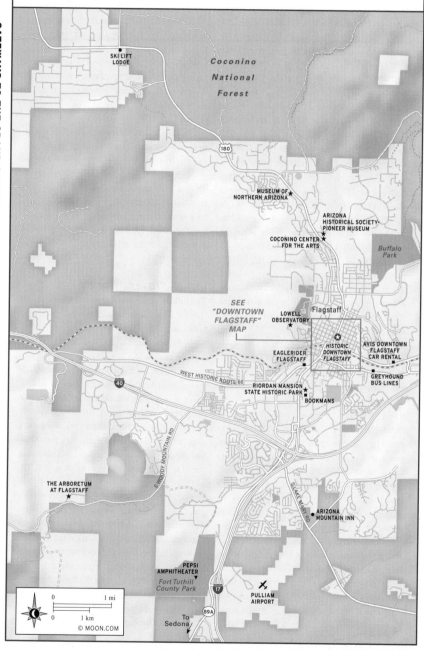

Coconino National Forest

180

SKI LIFT LODGE

MUSEUM OF NORTHERN ARIZONA ★

ARIZONA HISTORICAL SOCIETY–PIONEER MUSEUM ★

COCONINO CENTER FOR THE ARTS ★

Buffalo Park

SEE "DOWNTOWN FLAGSTAFF" MAP

LOWELL OBSERVATORY ★

Flagstaff

EAGLERIDER FLAGSTAFF

HISTORIC DOWNTOWN FLAGSTAFF

AVIS DOWNTOWN FLAGSTAFF CAR RENTAL

GREYHOUND BUS LINES

40

WEST HISTORIC ROUTE 66

RIORDAN MANSION STATE HISTORIC PARK

BOOKMANS

S MILTON RD

S WOODY MOUNTAIN RD

S LAKE MARY RD

THE ARBORETUM AT FLAGSTAFF

ARIZONA MOUNTAIN INN

PEPSI AMPHITHEATER

Fort Tuthill County Park

17

PULLIAM AIRPORT

89A

To Sedona

0   1 mi

0   1 km

© MOON.COM

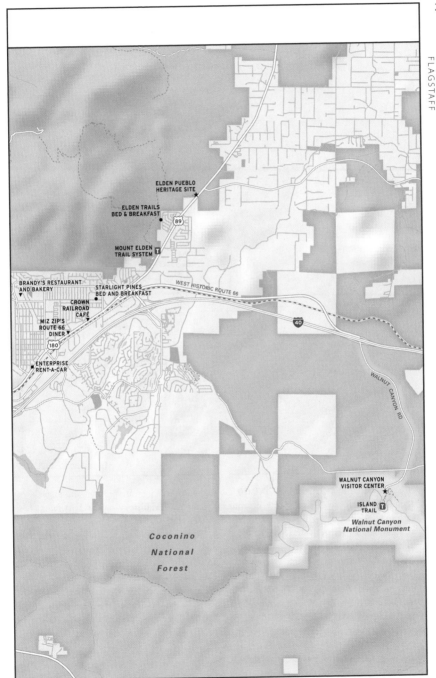

Downtown Flagstaff

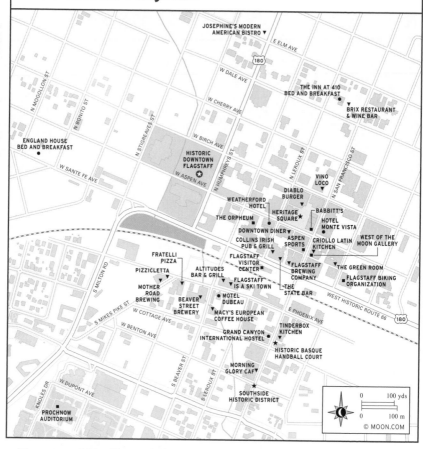

JOSEPHINE'S MODERN
AMERICAN BISTRO ▼
E ELM AVE
180
W DALE AVE

W CHERRY AVE
THE INN AT 410
BED AND BREAKFAST
▼
BRIX RESTAURANT
& WINE BAR

W BIRCH AVE
N MOGOLLON ST
N BONITO ST
N STIGREAVES ST
N HUMPHREYS ST
N LEROUX ST
N SAN FRANCISCO ST

ENGLAND HOUSE
BED AND BREAKFAST

W SANTE FE AVE

HISTORIC
DOWNTOWN
FLAGSTAFF
W ASPEN AVE

VINO
LOCO
▼

DIABLO
BURGER
▼
WEATHERFORD
HOTEL
HERITAGE
THE ORPHEUM   SQUARE ★   BABBITT'S
HOTEL
MONTE VISTA
DOWNTOWN DINER ▼
COLLINS IRISH   ASPEN   CRIOLLO LATIN   WEST OF THE
PUB & GRILL   SPORTS   KITCHEN   MOON GALLERY

FLAGSTAFF
FRATELLI   VISITOR
PIZZA   CENTER ■   ▼FLAGSTAFF   ▼THE GREEN ROOM
PIZZICLETTA   ALTITUDES   BREWING
BAR & GRILL ▼   COMPANY   ■ FLAGSTAFF BIKING
MOTHER   ▼ FLAGSTAFF   ORGANIZATION
ROAD   IS A SKI TOWN   THE
BREWING   BEAVER ▼   ● MOTEL   STATE BAR
STREET   DUBEAU   WEST HISTORIC ROUTE 66   180
S MILTON RD   BREWERY   MACY'S EUROPEAN
COFFEE HOUSE   E PHOENIX AVE
S MIKES PIKE ST   W COTTAGE AVE
W BENTON AVE   TINDERBOX
GRAND CANYON   KITCHEN
INTERNATIONAL HOSTEL ●

HISTORIC BASQUE
HANDBALL COURT
S BEAVER ST
S LEROUX ST

MORNING
GLORY CAF ▼

KNOLES DR
W DUPONT AVE   SOUTHSIDE
HISTORIC DISTRICT

PROCHNOW
AUDITORIUM

0   100 yds
0   100 m
© MOON.COM

Museum of Northern Arizona

A couple of well-educated and adventurous easterners, Mary and Harold Colton, an artist and a zoologist, respectively, who first came to northern Arizona on their honeymoon, founded the **Museum of Northern Arizona** (3101 N. Fort Valley Rd., U.S. 180, 3 mi/4.8 km north of downtown, 928/774-5213, www.musnaz.org, 10am-5pm Mon.-Sat., noon-5pm Sun., $12 adults, $8 children 10-17) in 1928 to preserve and encourage the indigenous arts and crafts of the Colorado Plateau. Since then this essential museum has become the cultural and scientific center of the Four Corners

region, collecting, interpreting, and displaying the natural history, art, and artifacts of timeless landscapes and human cultures.

The museum's main building is itself a dark-wood and river-rock work of art, set among the pines along the shallow Rio de Flag, with Arts and Crafts-era touches such as the handmade tile borders by Hopi potter Sadie Adams around the main entrance. Inside there are comprehensive exhibits on the Four Corners region's ancient and

1: Flagstaff's historic downtown 2: Riordan Mansion State Historic Park 3: Wupatki National Monument 4: Lowell Observatory

current biomes and its buried and blowing strata, plus one of the better introductions to Ancestral Puebloan and Puebloan cultures you'll find, with displays from the Basket Makers up to the Hopi and Navajo of today. Volunteer docents stroll about eager to discuss and supplement any of the exhibits. The collection of Pueblo Indian pottery, jewelry, kachina, and basketry is the museum's high point, but the galleries showing contemporary Hopi and Pueblo art, including oil paintings, watercolors, and sculpture, tend to open one's eyes to the vibrancy of the region's current cultural moment. Those who appreciate design should stroll into the lounge to see the Arts and Crafts flourishes in this cozy living-room setting. There's also a beautiful and relatively easy **nature trail** on the museum's forested grounds. Maps to the 0.5-mile (0.8-km) trail are available at the front desk.

Arizona Historical Society-Pioneer Museum

Stop at the **Arizona Historical Society-Pioneer Museum** (2340 N. Fort Valley Rd., 928/774-6772, www.arizonahistoricalsociety. org, 10am-5pm Mon.-Sat., 10am-4pm Sun., $6 adults, $3 children 7-17), near the Museum of Northern Arizona, to see how the early Anglo settlers lived in Flagstaff and northern Arizona. It's rather fascinating, after just learning about the ancient plateau lifeways of the Hopi and other tribes, to see how a completely different culture adapted to the same relatively harsh conditions. The building is something to see in itself: It's the old Coconino County Hospital for the Indigent, built in 1908. The museum has several displays on, among other things, frontier farming, education, transportation, and medicine, including a bedroom kept exactly as a hardworking nurse would have left it a century ago. There's also a retired steam train and various old farming implements parked on the beautiful forested grounds, where the museum puts on a host of events throughout the spring and summer.

Coconino Center for the Arts

Not a few artists and artisans lurk among the tall pines in Flagstaff, and many more sit atop the Hopi Mesas nearby, carving kachinas out of cottonwood root, while others walk the wide, empty roads of Navajoland and then re-create the landscape. Throughout the year the local arts group Flagstaff Cultural Partners gathers them together for a series of art exhibitions and concerts at the **Coconino Center for the Arts** (2300 N. Fort Valley Rd., 928/779-2300, http://flagartscouncil. org, 11am-5pm Tues.-Sat., donation recommended), a sleek, modern gallery that looks somewhat futuristic among the trees and contrasts with the historical architecture of the nearby Museum of Northern Arizona and the Pioneer Museum. Check the website for an up-to-date calendar of events at this, the "cultural hub of Flagstaff."

The Arboretum at Flagstaff

A 200-acre botanical garden and research station spotlighting the flora (and, if you're lucky, the fauna) typical of the Colorado Plateau, **The Arboretum at Flagstaff** (4001 S. Woody Mountain Rd., 928/774-1442, www.thearb.org, 9am-4pm Wed.-Mon. Apr. 15-Oct. 31, $10 adults, $5 children 3-17) offers 50-minute guided walking tours daily at 11am and 1pm and shows off birds of prey at noon and 2pm (Thurs.-Sat.). The forested property on the volcanic lands southwest of downtown Flagstaff has easy, winding trails, tall, shaggy trees, a pond, a tree-ring maze, and much more. A few hours here and you'll be able to recognize and appreciate the unique plants and animals that flourish in this high and dry plateau country. The arboretum is about 4 miles (6.4 km) south of Route 66 on Woody Mountain Road, only the first mile of which is paved. The rest is OK for all vehicles.

Elden Pueblo Heritage Site

The **Elden Pueblo Heritage Site** (Townsend-Winona Rd., off U.S. 89, 928/527-3452, free), a Sinagua ruin in the shadow of 9,280-foot (2,829-m) Elden Mountain, on

Who Were the Sinagua... and Where Did They Go?

The Sinagua people left their architecture and masonry all over north-central Arizona: the red-rock apartment buildings rising from the cinder plains below the San Francisco Peaks, the sandstone-cliff hideouts of Walnut Canyon, the limestone castles in the lush, easy-living Verde Valley, and the brick-stone rooms leaning against Sedona's red walls.

We don't really know what they called themselves, but according to tradition more than anything else, we call them the Sinagua, Spanish for "without water"—which alludes to the name used by early Spanish explorers for this region of pine-covered highlands still stuck somehow in aridity: *Sierra Sin Agua* (mountains without water).

Their cultural development followed a pattern similar to that of the Ancestral Puebloans in the Four Corners region. They first lived in pit houses bolstered by wooden beams and made a living from small-scale dryland farming, hunting, and gathering pinyon nuts and other land-given seasonal delicacies. They made strong and stylish baskets and pottery (though they didn't decorate theirs in the manner of the Ancestral Puebloans and others); they were weavers, craftspeople, and traders.

Around AD 700 a branch of the Sinagua migrated below the Mogollon Rim to the Verde Valley and began living the good life next to fish-filled rivers and streams that flowed year-round; these migrants are now called the Southern Sinagua, and the ones who stayed behind are called the Northern Sinagua. When, around AD 1064, the volcano that is now Sunset Crater, northeast of Flagstaff, erupted, there were Sinagua villages well within reach of its spewing ash and lava, though archaeologists have found evidence that nearby pit houses had been disassembled and moved just before the eruption, leading to the assumption that they probably knew the big one was coming.

The eruption would not be the end of the Sinagua—quite the contrary. Though the reasons are debated—it could have been that crops grew to surplus because a post-eruption cinder mulch made the land more fertile, or it could be that the years following the big blow were wetter than normal, or it could be a bit of both—after the eruption Sinagua culture began to become more complex, and soon it would go through a boom time. From roughly 1130 to 1400 or so, Sinagua culture flourished as the Sinagua lands became an important stop in a trade network that included Mexico to the south, the Four Corners to the north, and beyond. At pueblo-style ruins dating from this era, archaeologists have found shells, copper bells, and macaw bones, all from Mexico. Sinagua architecture became more Puebloan, and villages often had Mexican-style ball courts and kivas similar to those of the Ancestral Puebloans. It is from this era that the famous ruins protected throughout this region date.

Then it all ended. Owing to drought, disease, war, civil strife, a combination of these, or some other strange tragedy we may never learn about, by the early 1400s the Sinagua culture was on the run. By 1425, even the seemingly lucky farmers of the Verde Valley had abandoned their castles. The survivors and stragglers mixed with other tribes, their kind never to be seen again. Lucky for us they were such good builders.

To learn more about the Sinagua, check out the easy-to-read booklet *Sinagua*, written by Rose Houk, part of the Western National Park Association's series Prehistoric Cultures of the Southwest. This and many other booklets in the series are available at Wupatki and other Sinagua sights near Flagstaff and in the Verde Valley. There are also displays on the Northern and Southern Sinagua at all of the ruins near Flagstaff and in the Verde Valley. The information above comes from various museum displays and Houk's excellent booklet.

Flagstaff's eastern edge, was once a bustling trading center related to the more dramatic Wupatki and Walnut Canyon settlements to the north and east. These easily accessible volcanic-rock ruins were first studied in 1926 by the great Southwestern archaeologist and ethnologist Jesse Walter Fewkes, who also supervised digs at Casa Grande in southern Arizona and Mesa Verde in southern Colorado. The settlement in its heyday (about 1100-1275) had 60-70 rooms and hosted a fairly well-connected population: Archaeologists have found macaw skeletons and other evidence of trade with the far south. The site is still being studied and excavated today, often with the help of students and volunteers. Tall ponderosa pines guard the ruin along the 250-yard (229-m) dirt path (ADA accessible) that circles the site. This is a perfect first stop on a daylong tour of the Sinagua ruins around Flagstaff. There's a sign for the parking lot on Townsend-Winona Road, 1 mile (1.6 km) north of the Flagstaff Mall on the west side of U.S. 89.

Sunset Crater Volcano and Wupatki National Monuments

Sunset Crater Volcano isn't really a volcano at all anymore but a nearly perfectly conical pile of cinder and ash that built up around the former volcano's main vent. Sunset Crater erupted, probably several different times, between 1049 and 1100. The eruptions transformed this particularly arid portion of the not exactly lush Colorado Plateau, and now huge cinder barrens, as surprising as an alien world the first time you see them, stretch out along the loop road leading through these popular national monuments. You can't climb the crater cone anymore—years of scarring by the crowds saw to that—but you can walk across the main lava field at the crater's base, a cinder field with scattered dwarfed, crooked pines and bursts of rough-rock-adapted flowers and shrubs, all the while craning up at the 1,000-foot-high (305-m), 2,550-foot-wide (777-m) cone.

Along with turning its immediate environs

into a scorched but beautiful wasteland, the volcano's eruptions may have inadvertently helped the Sinagua culture thrive for a brief time in this formidable environment, the subject and object of Sunset Crater's sister monument, Wupatki. The series of eruptions spewed about a ton of ashfall over 88 square miles (228 sq km), and closer to the source the ash created a kind of rich mulch that, combined with a few years of above-average rainfall, may have stimulated a spike in population growth and cultural influence. Archaeological findings in the area suggest that the five pueblos in the shadow of the crater, especially the large Wupatki, were at the center of a trading crossroads and the most important population center for 50 miles (81 km) or more, with about 2,000 people living within a day's walk from the sprawling red-rock apartment building by 1190. Times seem to have been good for about 150 years here, and then, owing to a variety of factors, everybody left. The Hopi and other Pueblo people consider Wupatki a sacred place, one more in a series of former homes their ancestors kept during their long migrations to Black Mesa. Today you can walk among the red and pink ruins, standing on jutting patios, looking out over the dry land, wondering what that waterless life was like, and marveling at the adaptive, architectural, and artistic genius of those who came before.

VISITING THE MONUMENTS

The monuments sit side by side on an arid sweep covered with clump-grass, humps of volcanic remains, pine stands, and, if you're lucky, blankets of yellow wildflowers, about 12 miles (19.3 km) north of Flagstaff along U.S. 89. Turn onto the Sunset Crater-Wupatki Loop Road, which will lead you across the cinder barrens, through the forest, out onto the red-dirt plains and the ruins, and then back to U.S. 89. One ticket is good for both monuments.

Heading north from Flagstaff, you'll get to the **Sunset Crater Volcano National Monument Visitor Center** (6082 Sunset

Crater Rd., 928/526-0502, www.nps.gov/sucr, 9am-5pm daily, $25 per vehicle for 7-day pass to both monuments) first, about 2 miles (3.2 km) from the junction. Take a few minutes to look over the small museum and gift shop; there are several displays about volcanoes and the history of the region. Pick up the guidebook ($1, or free if you recycle it) to the 1-mile (1.6-km) loop **Lava Flow Trail** out onto the **Bonito Lava Flow** and head up the road a bit to the trailhead. This is an easy walk among the cinder barrens, a strange landscape with a kind of ruined beauty about it—only squat pines will grow, but there are surprising flushes of life throughout, small niches in which color can find a foothold. The trail skirts the base of the great crater cone and takes about an hour or so.

Another 16 miles (26 km) on the loop road and you're at the **Wupatki National Monument Visitor Center** (25137 N. Wupatki Loop Rd., 928/679-2365, www.nps.gov/wupa, 9am-5pm daily, $25 for both monuments), a total of 21 miles (34 km) from the junction, near the last of the five pueblos, the titular Wupatki. The other pueblos before Wupatki are reached by two separate short trails, each with its own parking lot along the loop road. At Wupatki, you can purchase a guidebook ($1, or free if you recycle it) to the 0.5-mile (0.8-km) **Wupatki Pueblo Trail,** which leads around the village complex and back to the visitors center. If you don't have time to see all five pueblos, head straight to Wupatki, the biggest and best of them all.

Walnut Canyon National Monument

Not far from Wupatki, another group of Sinagua people farmed the forested rim and built stacked limestone-and-clay apartments into the cliffsides of Walnut Canyon, a 20-mile-long (32-km), 400-foot-deep (122-m) gathering of nearly every North American life zone in one relatively small wonderland. Near the rim, a huge island of rock juts out of the canyon innards,

around which residents constructed their cells, most of them facing south and east to gather warmth. Depending on how much sunlight any one side of the island received, the Sinagua could count on several seasons of food gathering, from cactus fruit to pinyon nuts and wild grapes. A creek snakes through the canyon's green bottomlands, encouraging cottonwoods and willows. The Sinagua lived in this high, dry Eden for about 125 years, leaving finally for good around 1250. This is an enchanting, mysterious place that should not be missed.

VISITING THE MONUMENT

Take I-40 east from Flagstaff for 7.5 miles (12.1 km) to Exit 204. Then it's 3 miles (4.8 km) south to the canyon rim and the **Walnut Canyon Visitor Center** (928/526-3367, www.nps.gov/waca, 9am-5pm daily, $15 pp for 7-day pass), where there are a few displays, a small gift shop, and a spectacular window-view of the canyon. An hour or more on the **Island Trail,** a 1-mile (1.6-km) loop past 25 cliff dwellings (close enough to examine in detail) and into several different biomes high above the riparian bottomlands, is essential to a visit here, but it's not entirely easy; you must climb down (and back up) 240 rock-hewn steps to get to the island, descending 185 feet (56 m). Once you're on the island, though, it's an easy, mostly flat walk, and one you won't soon forget. There's also a short trail up on the rim with some great views.

RECREATION
Hiking

Flagstaff sits below the towering **San Francisco Peaks,** surrounded by a six-million-year-old, 1,800-mile (2,900-km) volcanic field, and everywhere you walk you hear the crunch of cinders beneath your boots. The last eruption was back in 1085, now celebrated at Sunset Crater National Monument, so there's not much to worry about—though the USGS's Volcano Hazards Program lists the threat here as "moderate."

Launching a Rafting Tour from Flagstaff

Just two hours south of Lees Ferry (the launching point for most river trips through Grand Canyon) and 2.5 hours north of Phoenix's Sky Harbor Airport, Flagstaff is home to six National Park Service-approved river-rafting concessionaires and the natural place to base your once-in-a-lifetime Colorado River adventure.

A river trip with any of the outfitters listed below will likely begin with a night at a Flagstaff chain hotel, where you'll attend a lengthy and required orientation, before a sleepy ride in a van or shuttle bus to Lees Ferry early the next morning. If you are running just the upper canyon, you'll probably hike out from the river to the South Rim, in which case a return to Flagstaff to rest and recuperate is a good option. Most trips include round-trip transportation to and from Flagstaff. If you are coming from Phoenix, you can rent a car there and drive to Flagstaff or take a shuttle from the airport. As with any river trip, you must secure a reservation with these companies up to a year in advance.

- **Canyoneers** (7195 N. U.S. Hwy. 89, 928/526-0924 or 800/525-0924, https://canyoneers.com), the oldest concessionaire on the river, goes all the way back to the 1930s and Nevills Expeditions, the first to take passengers through Grand Canyon. Still going strong, the company offers motor trips of 4 to 8 days and oar trips of 6 to 14 days.

- **Arizona Raft Adventures** (4050 E. Huntington Dr., 928/526-8246 or 800/786-7238, https://azraft.com) is a third-generation family operation whose guides have an average of 14 years of experience on the great river. ARA offers full-river trips with oars, paddles, or motors (or a combination), as well as upper- and lower-river trips.

- **Canyon Explorations/Expeditions** (675 W. Clay Ave., 928/774-4559 or 800/654-0723, www.canyonexplorations.com) is a family-owned operation offering oar and paddle trips of the upper, lower, and entire river. They also offer 8- and 10-day motor trips of the entire river.

- **Grand Canyon Whitewater** (100 N. Humphreys St., Ste. 202, 928/779-2979 or 800/343-3121, www.grandcanyonwhitewater.com) takes out 6-, 8-, and 10-day oar trips and motorized trips of varying lengths, including an 8-day full canyon adventure.

- Started by Colorado River rafting pioneer Bus Hatch, **Hatch River Expeditions** (5348 E. Burris Ln., 928/526-4700 or 800/856-8966, www.hatchriverexpeditions.com) offers 4- and 7-day motorized trips and 6-, 7-, and 12-day oar trips.

- **Outdoors Unlimited** (6900 Townsend Winona Rd., 800/637-7238, www.outdoorsunlimited.com) takes out 13- and 15-day oar trips of the entire river, as well as 5- to 14-day all-paddle river trips.

The Spanish conquistadores called them the Sierra Sinagua, the "mountains without water." Franciscans later affixed the high forested peaks with the less daunting name of their patron saint of Assisi. Sacred to the region's Native Americans, who call the mountains by many names, most northern Arizonans call them simply "the peaks." You can see their snowcapped heights from the scrubby deserts below Prescott all the way to the North Rim, a sharp fixed point ever by your side as you move around the region.

Now named for mostly forgotten white men who once beat towns out of the wilderness—Humphrey, Agassiz, Fremont, Abineau—the peaks are covered with excellent highland hiking trails and ski runs.

Most of the hiking and recreation areas around Flagstaff are in the **Coconino National Forest** (1824 S. Thompson St., 928/527-3600, www.fs.usda.gov/coconino, 8am-4pm Mon.-Fri.), whose website has a comprehensive list of trails, biking trails, and campgrounds.

ASPEN LOOP TRAIL

A short, moderately difficult introduction to the world of the San Francisco Peaks, the **Aspen Loop Trail** runs 2.5 miles (4 km) along the western slope of Mount Humphrey, the tallest of the peaks. The trail moves up about 300 feet (91 m) west from Mount Humphrey Trailhead through lush green meadows lined with aspens, spruce, and high-elevation bristlecone pines. The views are incredible, stretching far and wide over the northland landscape all the way to Grand Canyon. From downtown Flagstaff, take U.S. 180 north for 8 miles (12.9 km), then turn right on Snowbowl Road (Forest Road 516) and drive 7 miles (11.3 km) to reach the trailhead.

★ MOUNT HUMPHREY TRAIL

The **Mount Humphrey Trail** (Snowbowl Rd./Forest Road 516) is a tough hike that leads to the highest reaches of Humphrey Peak at 12,633 feet (3,851 m)—the very top of Arizona and near to the sacred realms wherein the Hopi kachina dwell and watch. The 10-mile (16.1-km) round-trip is very strenuous but beautiful and rewarding. The trail moves through a shady aspen forest and up above the tree line to a windy and rocky alpine stretch where only ancient bristlecones grow. The view from the wind-battered peak is unspeakably thrilling. Plan on the hike taking 5-6 hours, and be careful of altitude sickness if you're a habituated lowlander. The trailhead is signed 7.4 miles (11.9 km) up Snowbowl Road.

INNER BASIN TRAIL

The moderate, 3.9-mile (6.3-km) one-way **Inner Basin Trail** leads from Lockett Meadow along forested trails into the caldera, the old volcano's hidden soul, which is covered in spring with wildflowers and green-and-white aspens. Take U.S. 89 northeast from Flagstaff for 12.5 miles (20.1 km) and turn left onto Forest Road 552, across from Sunset Crater. Take Forest Road 552 about 1 mile (1.6 km) to Lockett Meadow and the trailhead.

KACHINA TRAIL

The **Kachina Trail** (Snowbowl Rd./Forest Road 516), which begins at the first parking lot on the right 7 miles (11.3 km) up Snowbowl Road, is one of the most popular trails in the peaks. It's a moderate 10-mile (16.1-km) round-trip hike across the south face of the peaks at 9,500 feet (2,896 m), through thick stands of conifers and aspens with sweeping views at every corner, and across an ancient lava flow. This is a particularly beautiful route in the fall, with fiery yellows and reds everywhere.

Mountain Biking

Mountain biking is very popular in Flagstaff, and many of its trails are up-and-down exciting and technical to the point of mental and physical exhaustion. Enthusiasts will want to head straightaway to the series of moderate-to-difficult interconnected trails of the **Mount Elden Trail System,** northeast of town along U.S. 89. There are enough loops and mountainside single-tracks in this area to keep you busy for a while.

The **Flagstaff Biking Organization** (http://flagstaffbiking.org) offers information on northland biking events and issues. The experts at **Absolute Bikes** (202 E. Route 66, 928/779-5969, www.absolutebikes.net, 9am-7pm Mon.-Fri., 9am-6pm Sat., 10am-4pm Sun. Apr.-Dec., 10am-6pm Mon.-Sat., 10am-4pm Sun. Jan.-Mar.) have info on some of the best local trails on their website. They also have a store in the nearby slickrock paradise of Sedona, and they rent out mountain bikes in both areas.

Arizona Snowbowl

On the slopes of the San Francisco Peaks, **Arizona Snowbowl** (Snowbowl Rd. off U.S. 180, 928/779-1951, www.arizonasnowbowl. com, all-day lift tickets $75) offers skiers and snowboarders over 2,300 feet (701 m) of vertical drop and 32 scenic trails that cover 777 acres. In wet years the first snow usually falls in December, but in recent, drought-ridden years the snow has stayed away until late in

the season. The resort prevailed in a dispute with Native Americans over artificial snow and now makes powder from reclaimed water when Mother Nature won't play along. The Hopi and other regional tribes consider the mountains sacred.

In the summer, the ski lift becomes the **Scenic Chairlift** (10am-4pm Fri.-Mon., $19 adults and children over 12, $15 children 6-12), lifting passengers slowly up to 11,500 feet (3,505 m), where you need a jacket in July and the hazy flatland stretches out for eternity.

Flagstaff Nordic Center

A complex of trails and sledding hills, the **Flagstaff Nordic Center** (U.S. 180, mile marker 232, 928/220-0550, www.flagstaffnordiccenter.com) is a popular place for cross-country skiing, sledding, snowshoeing, and all manner of snow play as long as there's snow on the Coconino National Forest at the base of the peaks. Equipment rentals, lessons, and races are available.

There's even more to do here in the summer. The high-meadow trails offer excellent hiking and biking during the cool mountain days, and if you just can't stand to leave, camp in a yurt or rustic cabin ($50-60) for an unforgettable night in the starlit forest, with the majestic San Francisco Peaks watching over your slumber.

ENTERTAINMENT AND EVENTS
Nightlife
BARS, BREWPUBS, AND LOUNGES

Most of Flagstaff's favorite nightspots can be found in and around the historic downtown, the Southside Historic District, and on the edges of the Northern Arizona University campus. The nightlife here is naturally full of college students, but you'll find plenty of older locals and tourists in the mix.

The **Monte Vista Cocktail Lounge** (100

N. San Francisco St., 928/779-6971, www.hotelmontevista.com, 1pm-2am daily) is a genial and historic place to sip cocktails or cry into your beer, with live music on the weekends, DJs, and pool. It's in what feels like the low-ceilinged basement of the Monte Vista Hotel, built way back in 1927. On entering this little old-school joint down the steps from the hotel lobby, you can smell fourscore years of spilled beer and general revelry imprinted deeply into the walls and floor. They say there are even a few ghosts still hanging around, unwilling to go home. Also off the Monte Vista's lobby is the more modern-minded **Rendezvous Coffee House and Martini Bar** (100 N. San Francisco St., 928/779-6971, www.hotelmontevista.com, 6:30am-2am daily), a coffeehouse-cum-cocktail lounge with an impressive selection of spirits and creative cocktail creations. The coffee here is superior, but don't be surprised if you start drinking early after looking at all those bottles as you sip your brew. The sleek, elegant interior and big windows that look out on bustling downtown Flagstaff encourage lounging and a "let's have another" attitude.

The **State Bar** (10 E. Route 66, 928/266-1282, 3pm-midnight Mon.-Thurs., noon-2am Fri.-Sat., noon-midnight Sun.) proves that the locavore movement is alive and well in Arizona, serving a surprisingly wide selection of beer and wine made right here in the Grand Canyon State.

Charley's Pub (23 N. Leroux St., 928/779-1919, www.weatherfordhotel.com, 8am-10pm daily) and **The Gopher Hole Pub** (5pm-close daily), both in the historic Weatherford Hotel downtown, are historic and fun places to have a beer or cocktail, hang out for happy hour, and watch live rock and blues bands.

Flagstaff Brewing Company (16 E. Route 66, 928/773-1442, www.flagbrew.com, 11am-2am daily), along Route 66 in downtown, offers expertly crafted microbrews in a pub-style setting where locals and tourists meet and mix. Try the dark-as-midnight Sasquatch Stout and sit on the patio, letting the strong beer and high-country air adjust

1: Inner Basin Trail **2:** Kachina Trail **3:** Arizona Snowbowl

your outlook on the laid-back mountain town. **Mother Road Brewing** (7 S. Mikes Pike, 928/774-9139, www.motherroadbeer.com, 2pm-9pm Mon.-Thurs., noon-10pm Fri.-Sat., noon-9pm Sun.), just across the train tracks in the Southside, has a casual tasting room, a patio with a fire pit, and a rotating menu of creative small-batch beers. Order a pizza from Pizzicletta next door or bring your own food if you prefer. Mother Road also has a tap room at its 20-barrel brewhouse at 1300 Butler Avenue.

Beaver Street Brewery (11 S. Beaver St., 928/779-0079, www.beaverstreetbrewery.com, 11am-11pm Sun.-Thurs., 11am-midnight Fri.-Sat.), on the historic Southside, serves award-winning microbrews and fantastically delicious pizzas in a bar-and-grill setting. IPA lovers should not miss the HopShot IPA served here. Connected on the inside and owned by Beaver Street Brewery, a fun atmosphere prevails at **Brews & Cues** (11am-1am Sun.-Wed., 11am-2am Thurs.-Sat.), where a few games of eight ball provide the perfect complement to the tasty ales.

The Green Room (15 N. Agassiz St., 928/226-8669, http://flagstaffgreenroom.com, 5pm-2am Mon.-Thurs., 3pm-2am Fri.-Sun.) has a super-fun happy hour, a big dance floor, and a party vibe nearly every night. On the weekends this dance club and live music venue brings in local and touring bands and has karaoke.

Flagstaff is a ski town, and the Southside's **Altitudes Bar & Grill** (2 S. Beaver St., 928/214-8218, www.altitudesbarandgrill.com, 11am-10pm daily) celebrates that fact with its snow-sports decor and "Skishots," a convivial way to get hammered quickly. A friendly bartender, perhaps with a full cold-weather beard and a wool cap, serves three or four shots of your favorite spirit affixed to an old ski. You and your drinking buddies must cooperate to sink them, a task that becomes increasingly tricky as the night progresses. Altitudes also offers a good selection of local beers and live music and serves a sufficiently tasty American grill-style menu until 10pm.

Collins Irish Pub & Grill (2 N. Leroux St., 928/214-7363, www.collinsirishpub.com, 11am-2am daily) downtown is a decent place to watch the game and sock back a few pints of Guinness. The emphasis here is on sports, and the menu of pub food is a strange amalgam (Irish nachos?). But if you forget that it's supposed to be an Irish pub, it turns instantly into a regular old American joint with a friendly crowd and all sorts of fun distractions.

Vino Loco (22 E. Birch Ave., 928/226-1764, www.vinolocoflag.com, noon-close daily) is a charming little bar and shop downtown that features wines made by Arizona's many small vineyards, including those in the Verde Valley just an hour or so south of Flagstaff. There's live music here Thursdays and Fridays.

LIVE MUSIC

Flagstaff's a pretty laid-back town, and it has its share of mountain men, bohemians, and creative types. Northern Arizona University's more than 20,000 students, many from abroad, help give the old frontier town a dash of do-it-yourself cosmopolitanism. It's not surprising, then, that the area attracts headlining acts and smaller indie favorites to its bars and theaters at a steady clip. If you're a fan of alternative pop, alt-country, classic country, bluegrass, classic rock, and just plain rock and roll, it's a good idea to check the websites of the following venues before making your travel plans. Odds are some funky act you love or have barely heard of will be playing during your visit.

The Orpheum (15 W. Aspen St., 928/556-1580, www.orpheumpresents.com), a retro-cool theater and bar that was Flagstaff's first movie house, hosts practitioners of modern music from Ozomatli to Modest Mouse and shows classic, neoclassic, and first-run movies on special nights each month. True to Flagstaff's crunchy reputation, the venue hosts a party every year on Jerry Garcia's birthday. The **Pepsi Amphitheater** (2446 Fort Tuthill Loop, 928/774-0899, www.pinemountainamphitheater.com), out in the pines at Fort Tuthill Park, is the region's best outdoor venue and attracts great bands from all over, many of the bluegrass and country persuasion. **Prochnow Auditorium** (Knoles Dr., North Campus, Northern Arizona University, 928/523-5638 or 888/520-7214) at NAU books national and international acts into an intimate setting.

Festivals and Events

Flagstaff hosts a variety of cultural events, mostly during its cool springs and warm summers.

During Flagstaff's year-round **First Friday Artwalk** (6pm-9pm), downtown comes alive with local art, crafts, music, and food. Students and townies mix it up and celebrate the vibrancy of the northland's culture at this fun monthly street festival. A walking guide to participating galleries is available on the **Flagstaff Art Council's website** (http://flagartscouncil.org). In the summer, it joins forces with **Downtown Friday Nights/First Friday,** a monthly street festival on the first Friday of every month May-October with live bands, artwalks, food, and crowds of northlanders seeking fun and diversions. The party is centered at Heritage Square.

In May, world-renowned authors come to town for lectures, signings, readings, and panel discussions at the **Northern Arizona Book Festival** (928/380-8682, www.nazbookfest.org).

The **Museum of Northern Arizona Heritage Program** (928/774-5213, www.musnaz.org) puts on several important and well-attended cultural festivals each year, featuring Native American arts and crafts markets, food, history displays, and entertainment: the **Zuni Festival of Arts and Culture** in late May; the **Hopi Festival of Arts and Culture** in early July; the **Navajo Festival of Arts and Culture** in early August; and, in late October, **Celebración de la Gente,** marking Día de los Muertos (Day of the Dead). The second week in September, just before it starts to get cold in the north country, Flagstaff ushers in **Route 66 Days** (www.flagstaffroute66days.com), celebrated with a parade, a classic car show, and all

manner of special activities along the downtown portion of the Mother Road. In October the **Flagstaff Mountain Film Festival** (www.flagstaffmountainfilms.org) screens the year's best independent films with an environmental, outdoor-adventure, and social-justice bent at The Orpheum.

If you find yourself in the northland on New Year's Eve, head over to the historic downtown **Weatherford Hotel** (23 N. Leroux St.) for the popular local party known as the **Pine Cone Drop.** Among rocking bands and general revelry, the hotel lowers a 6-foot-tall (1.8-m), lit-up pinecone from its roof, as if this little railroad town in Arizona were Times Square. Thousands attend to meet the new year with cheer and watch the fireworks that attend the pinecone's fall. They do it twice: once at 10pm to coincide with the party on the East Coast and again at midnight.

SHOPPING

The best place to shop for distinctive gifts, souvenirs, decorations, clothes, and outdoor gear is Flagstaff's historic downtown. You'll find Native American arts and crafts, Western wear, New Age items, art galleries specializing in handmade objects, antiques stores, and more.

Outfitters

Babbitt's (12 E. Aspen Ave., 928/774-4775, www.babbittsbackcountry.com, 9am-8pm Mon.-Sat., 10am-6pm Sun.) sells top-notch outdoor gear from a famous old building with a famous old northland name. The store's 1880s-era, local sandstone building once housed the state's largest general store, built by a pioneer family of traders. The knowledgeable staff here can help you plan a northland backcountry adventure and will recommend the best gear for the conditions; they also have an excellent map and book section. Another locally owned outfitter downtown, **Aspen Sports** (15 N. San Francisco St., 928/779-1935, http://aspensportsflagstaff.com, 9am-7pm Mon.-Fri., 8am-7pm Sat., 10am-5pm Sun.), sells the best in outdoor, hiking, skiing,

Side Trip to Sedona

Sedona's rare beauty is the result of geologic circumstance—the slow work of wind, rain, trickling water, and the predictable restless rocking of the Colorado Plateau. The little resort town sits at the base of the plateau, and its red-rock monuments rise dramatically alone into the light blue sky. High concentrations of iron oxide, or rust, in the sediment layers stain the rock statues many shades of red as a finishing flourish. The result is one of the most beautiful and sought-after landscapes on earth.

Only an hour or so along incredibly scenic AZ 89A, Sedona can be easily enjoyed in an unhurried day trip from Flagstaff. The waters of **Oak Creek** are so inviting that you may want to stop along the side of the road and put your feet in. It's illegal to park along most stretches of the road, but there are a few pullouts and several lodges and stores along the way where you can stop. The best and easiest place to get in the creek is at **Slide Rock State Park** (6871 N. Hwy. 89A, 928/282-3034, https://azstateparks.com, 8am-6pm daily summer, 9am-6pm daily winter, $10 per vehicle, $20 summer), where you can try out the 80-foot (24-m) natural red-rock slide, walk around the short nature trails, picnic, or just soak in the creek and lounge around on the warm rocks. There will likely be crowds in the summer, including many families with children. It's best to stop at Slide Rock on your way back up through Oak Creek Canyon along AZ 89A to Flagstaff, as you're going to get wet and likely smell like a creek after you jump in the inviting water.

After a slow drive through beautiful **Oak Creek Canyon,** find a place to park in **Uptown Sedona** (along AZ 89A north of its junction with AZ 179, the town's main intersection) and check out the shops and scenery. (Don't worry if you didn't get enough of Oak Creek Canyon—you'll be driving back through it at the end of the day.) If you're in a shopping and people-watching mood, don't miss a stop at **Tlaquepaque Arts and Crafts Village** (336 Hwy. 179, 928/282-4838, www.tlaq.com), an enchanting collection of Mexican-style courtyards with all kinds of unique shops, south of Uptown on AZ 179. Head farther south toward I-17 on AZ 179, also called the **Red Rock Scenic Byway,** with otherworldly scenery along both sides of the road. Take a stroll on one of the trails around **Bell Rock** (about 8 mi/12.9 km south of Uptown), and then stop at the towering **Chapel of the Holy Cross** (780 Chapel Rd., www.chapeloftheholycross.com, 9am-5pm Mon.-Sat., 10am-5pm Sun., free), which appears to be emerging full born from a red-rock

---

snowboarding, and trekking gear and has an experienced staff of experts, all of whom would likely rather be skiing the peaks or hurling themselves into a canyon somewhere nearby. In this wilderness, those are the folks you want on your side.

Books

Bookmans (1520 S. Riordan Ranch Rd., 928/774-0005, www.bookmans.com, 9am-10pm daily), Arizona's original used-media supercenter, is the best bookstore in northern Arizona bar none, with a huge selection of used books, CDs, vinyl records, DVDs, and musical instruments.

Galleries

Stop by the **West of the Moon Gallery** (14 N. San Francisco St., 928/774-0465, www.westofthemoongallery.com, 10am-5pm daily) in Flagstaff's downtown to see the best work of contemporary painters, artists, and artisans from around the region, including both classic and experimental work from Navajo artists. This is one of several places in Arizona to see and purchase the luminous, swirling, mysterious paintings of Shonto Begay, one of the best Native American artists working today.

FOOD

Flagstaff has a fairly sophisticated restaurant scene, with places serving cuisines from all over the world as well as creative and inspired American fare. The downtown and Southside areas have the best local eateries,

one of the trails around Sedona's Bell Rock

cradle. Next take a drive up to **Airport Mesa** (on Airport Rd., off AZ 89A) for a glorious look at the buttes all spread out before you. Have lunch in Uptown before heading back into Oak Creek Canyon for some fun in the water.

GETTING THERE

From Flagstaff, follow Milton Road south out of town and get onto I-17 South. In 2 miles (3.2 km), take Exit 337 for AZ 89A South toward Sedona/Oak Creek Canyon. You'll be on AZ 89A for 25 steep and winding miles (40 km) through Oak Creek Canyon, a cool green landscape. The highway will lead you directly into Uptown and then West Sedona.

including many dedicated to sustainability and using locally and regionally sourced ingredients.

Mexican and Latin American

★ **Criollo Latin Kitchen** (16 N. San Francisco St., 928/774-0541, http://criollolatinkitchen.com, 11am-10pm Mon.-Fri., 9am-10pm Sat.-Sun., $10-30), in Flagstaff's historic downtown, creates an eclectic, ever-changing menu of gourmet, Latin-inspired dishes for brunch, lunch, and dinner from sustainable ingredients grown regionally on small farms and ranches. The sleek and refined interior, with eye-catching paintings and small tables that look out on downtown through a glass front, creates an urbane atmosphere that complements the

creative food and somewhat belies the rural mountain setting.

American and Southwestern

For the very best burgers in the northland, head to **Diablo Burger** (20 N. Leroux St. #112, 928/774-3274, www.diabloburger.com, 11am-9pm Sun.-Wed., 11am-10pm Thurs.-Sat., $10-13), which serves a small but stellar menu of beef raised locally on the plains around Flagstaff. All the finely crafted creations, such as the "Cheech" (guacamole, jalapeños, and spicy cheese), or the "Vitamin B" (bleu cheese with bacon and a beet), come on Diablo's branded English muffin-style buns alongside a mess of Belgian fries. It also has a terrific veggie burger.

Brandy's Restaurant and Bakery

(1500 E. Cedar Ave. #40, 928/779-2187, www. brandysrestaurant.com, 6:30am-3pm daily, $6-10) often wins the "Best Breakfast" honors from readers of the local newspaper, and those readers know what they're talking about. The homemade breads and bagels make everything else taste better. Try the Eggs Brandy, two poached eggs on a homemade bagel smothered in hollandaise sauce. For lunch there are crave-worthy sandwiches (Brandy's Reubens are some of the best in the business), burgers, and salads. Brandy's also serves beer, wine, and mimosas.

Josephine's Modern American Bistro (503 N. Humphreys St., 928/779-3400, www. josephinesrestaurant.com, 11:30am-2pm and 5pm-9pm Mon.-Fri., 10am-2pm and 5pm-9pm Sat., 9am-2pm Sun., $10-30) offers a creative fusion of tastes for lunch and dinner, such as the roasted pepper and hummus grilled-cheese sandwich and the chile relleno with sun-dried cranberry guacamole, from a cozy historic home near downtown. This is one of the best places in town for brunch.

Charly's Pub and Grill (23 N. Leroux St., 928/779-1919, www.weatherfordhotel. com, 8am-10pm daily, $11-26), inside the Weatherford Hotel, serves Navajo tacos, enchiladas, burritos, and a host of other regional favorites for breakfast, lunch, and dinner. The Navajo taco, a regional delicacy featuring fry bread smothered in chili and beans, might be the best off the reservation. Try it for breakfast topped with a couple of fried eggs. Charly's also has more conventional but appetizing bar-and-grill food such as hot, high-piled sandwiches, juicy burgers, steaks, and prime rib.

★ **Brix Restaurant & Wine Bar** (413 N. San Francisco St., 928/213-1021, http:// brixflagstaff.com, 5pm-close Tues.-Sun., $18-36) operates out of a historic building a few blocks north of downtown and serves creative and memorable food using local and sustainable ingredients. The menu here changes often based on what's new at Arizona's small farms, ranches, and dairies. The New American cuisine that results is typically spectacular. It also

has fine selections of wine, a slew of creative cocktails, and desserts that should not be missed.

The **Tinderbox Kitchen** (34 S. San Francisco St., 928/226-8400, www. tinderboxkitchen.com, 5pm-10pm daily, $18-26), in the Southside District, serves a revolving menu of gourmet takes on familiar American favorites and has an elegant lounge (4pm-close daily) where you can wait for your table with a martini. The chef uses seasonal ingredients, and there's always something new and exciting here—like venison served with blue cheese grits, bacon creamed corn, or jalapeño mac-and-cheese. It's one of those places where the chef is limited only by ingredients and imagination, and the chef here is lacking in neither.

Diners

For a big breakfast of eggs, bacon, and potatoes, or an omelet stuffed with cheese, a hot cup of coffee, and friendly service, head over to the **Downtown Diner** (7 E. Aspen Ave., 928/774-3492, 6am-6pm daily, $5-15), right across from Heritage Square. This clean little greasy spoon also has good burgers, shakes, and hot dogs. There's similar fare at local favorite **Miz Zip's Route 66 Diner** (2924 E. Route 66, 928/526-0104, 6am-9:30pm Mon.-Sat., 7am-2pm Sun., $5-15) on Flagstaff's east side. Open since the 1950s, it still serves the same diner classics of the golden age, such as hot open-faced sandwiches smothered in rich gravy, juicy burgers, and filling breakfasts. Miz Zip's only takes cash.

The **Crown Railroad Café** (3300 E. Route 66, 928/522-9237, http:// thecrownrailroadcafes.com, 6am-9pm daily, $8-12) celebrates the golden era of the railroad. Sit among model trains, iron road memorabilia, and Navajo blankets while enjoying the huge, three-egg "Route 66" omelet, expertly prepared huevos rancheros, and a fresh homemade biscuit.

Pizza

Named Flagstaff's favorite pizza since 2002,

Fratelli Pizza (119 W. Phoenix Ave., 928/774-9200, www.fratellipizza.net, 10:30am-9pm daily, $10-20) swears by its "stone deck oven" and eschews the "conveyer belt" mentality of the chains. The results are sublime. Try the popular Flagstaff, with basil pesto, sun-dried tomatoes, and artichoke hearts. You can also build your own pie from among dozens of fresh toppings or stop in for a huge slice ($3). Fratelli also serves salads, antipasti, and calzones and offers a decent selection of beer and wine. There's also a location on 4th Street (2120 N. 4th St., 928/714-9700, 10:30am-9pm daily).

The wonderful **Pizzicletta** (203 W. Phoenix Ave., 928/774-3242, www.pizzicletta.com, 5pm-close Tues.-Sun., $11-15), in the Southside neighborhood, offers soppressata rather than pepperoni and prosciutto di Parma rather than ham. Among the carefully chosen, rather spare list of toppings are almonds and charred kale. But it's the dough that makes the pizza here so good. Pizzicletta also serves fantastic bread, beer, wine, and house-made gelato.

Vegetarian

The **Morning Glory Café** (115 S. San Francisco St., 928/774-3705, http://morningglorycafeflagstaff.com, 10am-2:30pm Tues.-Fri., 9am-2:30pm Sat.-Sun., $8-11) serves natural, tasty vegetarian eats from a cozy little spot on San Francisco Street. Try the hemp burger for lunch, and don't miss the blue corn pancakes for breakfast. With local art on the walls, free wireless internet, and friendly service, this is an ideal place to get to know the laid-back Flagstaff vibe. There are a lot of vegan and gluten-free options here. The café doesn't take credit cards, so bring some cash.

Macy's European Coffee House (14 S. Beaver St., 928/774-2243, www.macyscoffee.net, 6am-8pm daily, $5-10), south of the tracks, is the best place to get coffee and a quick vegetarian bite to eat, or just hang out and watch the locals file in and out.

ACCOMMODATIONS

Being an interstate town close to several world-renowned sights, Flagstaff has all the chain hotels. A good value and a unique experience can be had at one of the historic downtown hotels. Along Route 66 as you enter town from the east, there are a large number of chain and locally owned small hotels and motels, including several old-school motor inns, and a few places that are likely inexpensive for a reason. East Flagstaff, while it lacks the charm of the downtown area, is an acceptable place to stay if you're just passing through. If you're a budget traveler and don't mind students, hippies, and folks from other lands, try the hostels in Flagstaff's Southside Historic District.

Under $50

The **Grand Canyon International Hostel** (19 S. San Francisco St., 888/442-2696, www.grandcanyonhostel.com, $26-78) is a clean and friendly place to stay on the cheap, located in an old 1930s building in the Southside neighborhood, in which you're likely to meet some lasting friends, many of them foreign tourists tramping around the Colorado Plateau. The hostel offers bunk-style sleeping arrangements and private rooms, mostly shared bathrooms, a self-serve kitchen, Wi-Fi, a free breakfast, and a chance to join in on tours of the region. It's a rustic but cozy and welcoming hippie-home-style place to stay. The same folks operate the **Motel DuBeau** (19 W. Phoenix St., 800/398-7112, www.modubeau.com, $26-75), a clean and charming hostel-inn with a small dorm and eight private rooms. It offers a free breakfast, Wi-Fi, and a friendly atmosphere in an old motor hotel built in 1929. Make sure to spend some time at the on-site **Nomad's Global Lounge** (4:30pm-10pm Mon.-Thurs., 4pm-11pm Fri.-Sat., 4pm-9pm Sun.), kicking back a few cold ones with your new friends.

$100-250

The **Weatherford Hotel** (23 N. Leroux

St., 928/779-1919, www.weatherfordhotel. com, $80-190) is one of two historic hotels downtown. It's basic but romantic, like stepping back in time when you head off to bed. There are no TVs or phones in most of the rooms, the cheapest of which share a bathroom. While the whole place is a little creaky, the location and the history make this a fun place to rest. With live music at the hotel's two pubs and the odd wedding or private party in the historic ballroom, the Weatherford can sometimes get a bit noisy. It's not for those looking for the tranquility of the surrounding pine forest.

The ★ **Hotel Monte Vista** (100 N. San Francisco St., 928/779-6971 or 800/545-3068, www.hotelmontevista.com, $85-175 Apr. 15-Nov. 5, $70-140 Nov. 6-Apr. 14), the other historic downtown hotel, is a retro-swanky, redbrick high-rise built in 1927, which once served high-class and famous travelers heading west on the Santa Fe Railroad. These days it offers comfortable and convenient rooms with historic charm, cable TV, and private bathrooms, as well as hostel-style rooms with a shared bathroom. There's a cocktail lounge and sleek coffee bar off the lobby. As with many of the grand old railroad hotels, there are lots of tales to be heard about the Hollywood greats who stayed here and the restless ghosts who stayed behind. Parking is not easy downtown, so if you have a big rig consider staying somewhere else.

The Inn at 410 Bed and Breakfast (410 N. Leroux St., 928/774-0088 or 800/774-2008, www.inn410.com, $195-325) has eight artfully decorated rooms in a classic old home on a quiet, tree-lined street just off downtown. This is a wonderful little place, with so much detail and stylishness. Breakfasts are interesting and filling, often with a Southwestern tinge, and tea is served every afternoon. You certainly can't go wrong here. Booking far in advance, especially for a weekend stay, is a must.

The stately **England House Bed and Breakfast** (614 W. Santa Fe Ave., 928/214-7350 or 877/214-7350, www. englandhousebandb.com, $149-219) is located in a quiet residential neighborhood near downtown at the base of Mars Hill, where sits the famous Lowell Observatory. This beautiful old Victorian has been sumptuously restored, and its rooms are booked most weekends. If you're just passing through, the innkeepers are happy to show you around, after which you will probably make a reservation for some far future date. They pay as much attention to their breakfasts here as they do to details of the decor. This is one of the best little inns in the region.

The hosts at ★ **Elden Trails Bed & Breakfast** (6073 Snowflake Dr., 928/266-0203, www.eldentrailsbedandbreakfast.com, $149-169 d, $40 per night each additional adult) are committed to living a sustainable-as-possible lifestyle, including growing a lot of their own food in a large garden and greenhouse full of native plants and organic crops. Both ecotourists and foodies will feel at home in this comfortable and inspiring B&B at the base of Mount Elden, about 5 miles (8 km) east of downtown Flagstaff. It's a small place, just one detached studio suite that sleeps four adults. A healthy, organic (and if you prefer, vegan) breakfast is served in the studio's sunny nook, and your new home-away-from-home sits amid tall pines and hiking trails. Make reservations far in advance.

Forest Inns

The **Ski Lift Lodge** (6355 N. Hwy. 180, 928/774-0729 or 800/472-3599, www. arizonasnowbowl.com, $109-179) has simple, rustic cabins and rooms with cozy fireplaces and a good restaurant. Best of all, it's in the forest beneath the San Francisco Peaks, about 7 miles (11.3 km) northwest of downtown, right near the road up the peaks to the Snowbowl. It's dark out there, and you can see all the stars in the galaxy on many nights. This lodge is a good bet if you're skiing or engaging in other snow-related activities. Make reservations in advance for ski season, as there are few other places to stay in the immediate area. The drive from Flagstaff proper is about 10-20 minutes, longer in inclement weather. Prices are considerably lower on weekdays.

The **Starlight Pines Bed and Breakfast** (3380 E. Lockett Rd., 928/527-1912 or 800/752-1912, www.starlightpinesbb.com, $169-179) is located about 3 miles (4.8 km) northeast of town in the forest at the foot of Mount Elden, offering four rooms stuffed with antiques and style in a Victorian-era home. There's a porch swing, deep tubs perfect for bubble baths, and fresh-cut flowers in every room—but no TVs. They'll even bring your breakfast to your room. This is a perfect place for couples looking for a romantic mountain getaway.

For a touch of wilderness adventure with all the comforts, try the **Arizona Mountain Inn** (4200 Lake Mary Rd., 928/774-8959, www.arizonamountaininn.com), offering 17 rustic but comfortable family-perfect cabins ($135-600) in the pines not far from town as well as four B&B-style rooms ($120-160). Dogs are welcome in most rooms and cabins.

INFORMATION

The **Flagstaff Visitor Center** (1 E. Route 66, 928/774-9541 or 800/379-0065, www. flagstaffarizona.org, 8am-5pm Mon.-Sat., 9am-4pm Sun.), located in the old train depot in the center of town, has all kinds of information on Flagstaff and the surrounding area.

TRANSPORTATION
Air

Flagstaff's small **Pulliam Airport** (FLG, 928/556-1234, www.flagstaff.az.gov), located about 5 miles (8 km) south of downtown, offers five flights daily to and from Sky Harbor in Phoenix through **American Airlines** (800/443-7300, www.aa.com). It's a roughly 50-minute flight, as opposed to a 2.5-hour drive from Phoenix, and generally costs about $400. This is not your best option, though, as you must rent a car to explore the northland properly. If you are coming from Phoenix, it's best to rent a car there and make the scenic drive north.

Car

The best and, really, the only easy way to properly see Flagstaff and the surrounding country is by car. From **Phoenix,** take I-17 north for about 2.5 hours (144 mi/232 km), and you're in another world. The scenic route to Flagstaff from I-17 starts at AZ 260 in the Verde Valley, about 1.5 hours (about 100 mi/161 km) north of Phoenix near Cottonwood. Get off the interstate at Exit 287, heading west toward Cottonwood. About 12 miles (19.3 km) on, take AZ 89A north through Sedona and Oak Creek Canyon and all the way to the mountains and the pines. It's only about 50 miles (81 km) from Cottonwood to Flagstaff, but it takes at least an hour and probably more to drive the scenic route through the verdant riverside valley and past the otherworldly red rocks of Sedona. You can also pick up AZ 89A at the Village of Oak Creek, which is 39 miles (63 km) from Flagstaff, and take it straight north through Sedona and Oak Creek Canyon. This route is spectacular, as it includes about 8 miles (12.9 km) of travel on AZ 179 past some of the Sedona area's most famous eroded rock attractions. Get off the interstate at Exit 298 (AZ 179) and pick up AZ 89A about 8 miles (12.9 km) north at Sedona. From there, Sedona and Flagstaff are separated by about 30 slow miles (48 km) of winding two-lane road with amazing views.

Once in "Flag," as the locals sometimes call this mountain town, you're ideally situated to visit a long list of unique attractions. Chief among these is Grand Canyon National Park's **South Rim,** a mere 80 scenic miles (129 km) away. Take U.S. 180 north from downtown, driving through the pine forest in the shadow of the towering San Francisco Peaks. Pick up AZ 64 at the tiny, windswept roadside stop known as Valle, about 50 miles (81 km) from Flagstaff. From there it's a straight shot across a barren plain to the South Rim gate. The whole trip takes about 1.5 hours, making Flagstaff a logical place to base your Grand Canyon visit if you don't want to stay in the park.

A trip to the **North Rim** from Flagstaff takes quite a bit longer. Take U.S. 89 north across the volcanic cinderlands, through the western edge of the vast Navajo Reservation, and into the lonely landscape near the Utah border known as the Arizona Strip. After about two hours (123 mi/198 km), pick up U.S. 89A going west at Bitter Springs. Cross the Colorado River at Marble Canyon and skirt the edge of Vermilion Cliffs National Monument toward the Kaibab Plateau, climbing to the forested highlands and Jacob Lake, the center of plateau life. The 50-mile (81-km) drive from Bitter Springs to Jacob Lake usually takes an hour or more. When you pass the hotel and restaurant at Jacob Lake, you have another 45 miles (72 km) to go on AZ 67, a drive that takes an hour or more through a mountain forest of evergreens and aspen, with patches blackened by fire. The whole gorgeous, unforgettable, 208-mile (340-km) drive will take you at least four hours and probably longer. It's not a great idea for a day trip from Flagstaff unless you want to spend all day in the car. It's a better idea to take two days and stay overnight in the park or at Jacob Lake.

The sights closest to town are **Sunset Crater** and **Wupatki,** 14 miles (22.5 km) and 30 miles (48 km) north on U.S. 89, respectively, and **Walnut Canyon,** a quick 10.5-mile (16.9-km) drive east on I-40. These places attract visitors from around the world and are easy to find. You can't miss them if you follow the signs along the highway and the interstate. The **Navajo Nation**'s reservation begins about 50 miles (81 km) north of Flagstaff on U.S. 89, and **Lake Powell** spreads across the hard land 136 miles (219 km) to the north on the same route.

The 467-mile (750-km) drive from **Los Angeles** to Flagstaff typically takes about seven hours, most of it along I-40. If you're starting from **Las Vegas,** take U.S. 93 past Hoover Dam and over the Colorado River to I-40. The 252-mile (405-km) drive takes about four hours.

CAR RENTAL

Most of the major car-rental companies have a presence at Flagstaff's small **Pulliam Airport** (928/556-1234, www.flagstaff.az.gov), about 5 miles (8 km) south of downtown. **Avis Downtown Flagstaff Car Rental** (175 W. Aspen Ave., 928/714-0713, www.avis.com, 7am-6pm Mon.-Fri., 8am-4pm Sat., 9am-1pm Sun.) is located right in the middle of all the action at the corner of Aspen Avenue and Humphreys Street. **Budget** (800/527-7000, www.budget.com) operates out of the same facility with the same hours and phone number. **Enterprise Rent-A-Car** (213 E. Route 66, 928/526-1377, www.enterprise.com, 8am-6pm Mon.-Fri., 9am-noon Sat.) is located on the eastern edges of town along I-40.

If you're looking for a mythic Southwestern experience, stop by **EagleRider Flagstaff** (800 W. Route 66, 928/637-6575, www.route66rider.com, 8am-6pm daily, $109-145 per day) and rent a Harley-Davidson.

Long-Distance Bus

Flagstaff's **Greyhound Bus Lines** (800 E. Butler Ave., 928/774-4573, www.greyhound.com) station is located along the industrial wasteland that is East Butler Avenue. The company offers bus service to Flagstaff from most points on the map.

Shuttle

Groome Transportation aka Arizona Shuttle (928/350-8466, https://groometransportation.com/arizona) offers several daily trips between Flagstaff's Amtrak station and Phoenix's Sky Harbor International Airport ($48 pp one-way). The company also offers rides from Flagstaff to the Grand Canyon three times daily (Mar.-Oct., $60 round-trip for adults) as well as from Flagstaff to Sedona, the Verde Valley, and Williams ($35-43 one-way).

Train

The **Amtrak** *Southwest Chief* **route** (800/872-7245, www.amtrak.com), which mirrors the old Santa Fe Railroad's *Super Chief* route of the grand Fred Harvey days, stops twice daily (one eastbound, one westbound) at Flagstaff's classic **downtown depot** (1 E. Route 66), the former Santa Fe headquarters and also the town's visitors center. The route crosses the country from Chicago to L.A., dipping into the Southwest through northern New Mexico and northern Arizona.

Public Transportation

Flagstaff's city bus, the **Mountain Line** (928/779-6624, www.mountainline.az.gov, $1.25 per ride, $2.50 for day pass), runs 6am-10pm weekdays and 7am-8pm weekends to stops all over town.

Bike

Flagstaff is a relatively bicycle-friendly city, with a well-established and active bike culture. You'll likely see a lot of people riding mountain bikes around town, even in the winter. It's pretty easy to get around most of the town on a bike, following a network of multiuse paths laid out in the **Flagstaff Urban Trails and Bikeways Map,** available for free at the **Flagstaff Visitor Center** downtown. You can pedal from downtown to the east side of town while avoiding the always busy traffic along Route 66 using the popular **Route 66 Trail.** The 4.4-mile (7.1-km) paved trail runs along the south side of Route 66 east from downtown and is popular with bike commuters. The ambitious 42-mile (68-km) **Flagstaff Loop Trail** is about half finished. The trail will someday circle the town and feed smaller, spoke-like paths to various points in town.

Williams

This small, historic town along I-40 (what used to be Route 66), surrounded by the Kaibab National Forest, is the closest interstate town to AZ 64 and thus has branded itself "The Gateway to the Grand Canyon." It has been around since 1874 and was the last Route 66 town to be bypassed by the interstate (not until 1984). As a result, and because of a resurgence over the last few decades owing to the rebirth of the Grand Canyon Railway, Williams, with about 3,000 full-time residents, has a good bit of small-town charm—the entire downtown area is on the National Register of Historic Places. It's worth a stop and an hour or two of strolling around, and there are a few good restaurants. It's only about an hour's drive to the South Rim from Williams, so many consider it a convenient base for exploring the region, though the drive is not as scenic as either AZ 64 from Cameron or U.S. 180 from Flagstaff. This is the place to stay if you plan to take the **Grand Canyon Railway** to the rim, which is a highly recommended way of reaching the South Rim. It's fun, it cuts down on traffic and emissions

within the park, and you'll get exercise walking along the rim or renting a bike and cruising the park with the wind in your face.

SIGHTS
★ Historic Downtown Williams

On a walk through the **Williams Historic Business District** you'll see how a typical pioneer Southwestern mountain town might have looked from territorial days until the railroad died and the interstate came. Williams wasn't bypassed by I-40 until the 1980s, so many of its old buildings still stand and have been put to use as cafés, boutiques, B&Bs, and gift shops. Walk around and look at the old buildings; shop for Native American and Old West knickknacks, pioneer-era memorabilia, and Route 66 souvenirs you don't need; and maybe stop for a beer, cocktail, or a cup of coffee at an old-school, small-town saloon or a dressed-up café. The district is bounded on the north by Railroad Avenue, on the south by Grant Avenue, and on the east and west by 1st and 4th Streets, respectively. About 250 acres, the district has 44 buildings

Williams

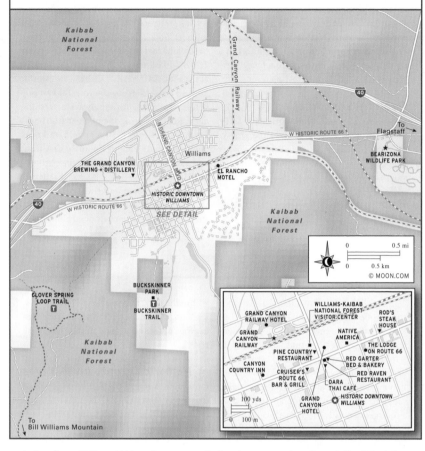

dating from 1875 to 1949 and an array of Route 66-era business signs and midcentury commercial architecture worth a few snapshots. Historic Route 66 is variously termed Bill Williams Avenue, Grand Canyon Avenue, and Railroad Avenue, and it splits into parallel one-way streets through the historic downtown before meeting up to the west and east.

Bearizona

Don't be surprised if a big brown bear, gone lazy from living the easy life in beautiful pine-covered **Bearizona Wildlife Park** (1500 E. Route 66, I-40 Exit 165, 928/635-2289, www.

bearizona.com, 8am-5pm daily, $25 adults, $23 seniors, $15 children 4-12), decides to lounge on his back in front of your car; it's best to drive around the old beast, one of the many rescued animals that call this family-friendly drive-through wildlife park home. Along the 3-mile (4.8-km) drive through the forested park, which the park insists be done with windows up, you'll see many brown and black bears wrestling and lounging in the meadows, as well as wolves, bison, bighorn sheep, and other classic western animals. A walk-through section at the end of the drive called **Fort Bearizona** features adorable baby animals frolicking with innocence and wonder, along with a few regal birds of prey that would probably like to eat all those fuzzy little morsels.

Kids absolutely love this place, and it makes for an easy side trip on the way to the Grand Canyon: It's located just outside of Williams near the junction of I-40 and AZ 64, right on the route to the South Rim. Allow about two hours to visit this fun park; many of the animals here have a bit of personality, and you might get hooked if you stay too long. Bearizona is busiest in the summer, but the park is open year-round. The hours may vary according to season and weather.

Grand Canyon Railway

The **Grand Canyon Railway** (800/843-8724, www.thetrain.com) runs daily out of the original depot built by the Santa Fe Railroad back in 1908, which also housed the Fray Marcos Hotel, one of the first Harvey Houses in Arizona. The building is the oldest poured-concrete structure in Arizona. Though the original hotel inside the depot has been turned into a gift shop and offices, across the tracks is the sprawling Grand Canyon Railway Hotel, built in 1995 to resemble the Fray Marcos; it has some of the most luxurious

accommodations in the region, including a "pet resort" and an indoor pool and spa.

A fun, history-soaked, and environmentally conscious way to visit the canyon, the Grand Canyon Railway runs between the station in Williams and the South Rim depot in Grand Canyon Village. The train has several different ticket levels ($67-226 adults, $32-153 children 2-15), including bar cars and luxury packages, and the rides feature strolling musicians, bandits, and other Old West tropes. Moving across the open highland landscape, the trip takes about 2.5 hours in each direction. From mid-June to mid-July, there are two morning departures from Williams and two afternoon departures from the South Rim; the rest of the year there is a single morning departure from Williams and a single afternoon departure from the South Rim.

RECREATION
Hiking

The best trails near Williams are in the **Kaibab National Forest** (www.fs.usda.gov/main/kaibab) around **Bill Williams Mountain,** the 9,259-foot (2,822-m) volcanic peak named after the famous Arizona mountain man Old Bill Williams. The mountain is about 3.5 miles (5.6 km) south of Williams,

Route 66 runs through downtown Williams.

but it can be accessed from **Buckskinner Park** at the end of 6th Street on the south end of town.

An easy 2-mile (3.2-km) loop through the lower forested reaches of the mountain begins at the **Buckskinner Trail** in the park and hooks up with the **Clover Spring Loop Trail** and **Bill Williams Mountain Trail** before looping back.

If you're looking for something a bit more epic, take the **Bill Williams Mountain Trail** to the top, a moderately steep 8.5-mile (13.7-km) round-trip through the beautiful pine and aspen forests, ending with amazing views of the territory from on high. Take Railroad Avenue west of downtown for a mile (1.6 km) and turn left at the sign for the **Williams Ranger District** (742 S. Clover, 928/635-5600, www.fs.usda.gov/kaibab, 8am-4:30pm Mon.-Fri.), then follow the signs to the trailhead. You can also drive to the top of the mountain via Forest Road 111.

Mountain Biking

There are several excellent mountain bike rides in the forest around Williams, many of them using old fire and logging roads. To reach many of the backcountry mountain biking areas here, you'll need at least a high-clearance rig.

The 10-mile (16.1-km) **Round Mountain Loop Bike Trail** is a fun series of undulating, disused dirt roads through the ponderosa pine forest. Take 4th Street/Perkinsville Road 8.5 miles (13.7 km) from Williams to Forest Road 110 (White Horse Rd.), then turn left and go 10 miles (16.1 km) to Forest Road 105.

In the same general area, the 16-mile (26-km) **Sunflower Flat Bike Trail** is a bit more strenuous and includes a couple of killer climbs. The route follows Sunflower Flat Road, aka Forest Road 14, through a clear-cut area—flat, open, and denuded for generations—then turns left on Forest Road 747 and left again on Forest Road 110, where it passes a beautiful meadow with spectacular views of the peaks. Combine the loop with the **Perkins Tank Loop** (Forest Road 747) for a longer ride. Take 4th Street/Perkinsville Road 8.5 miles (13.7 km) from Williams to Forest Road 110, then turn left and drive 2.5 miles (4 km) to Forest Road 147.

For more bike trails in the area, check with the **Kaibab National Forest** (www.fs.usda.gov/main/kaibab).

ENTERTAINMENT AND EVENTS

In June, classic car enthusiasts gather in Williams for the **Historic Route 66 Car Show,** which includes a retro evening of cruising a 2-mile (3.2-km) loop around town showing off refurbished masterpieces.

Northland kids wait all year for the Grand Canyon Railway's celebration of author Chris Van Allsburg's classic holiday story *The Polar Express.* The always sold-out **Polar Express and Mountain Village Holiday** (800/848-3511, www.thetrain.com, 5:30pm and 7:30pm daily mid-Nov.-early Jan., $45-58 adults, $33-45 children 2-15) features a one-hour nighttime pajama-party train ride, complete with cookies and hot cocoa, to a lit-up Christmastown that kids ooh and ahh at from their train seats. Riders dressed up like characters in the book read the story as kids follow along in their own copies. Then Santa boards the train and gives each kid some individual attention and a free jingle bell like the one in the famous book. On the return trip, everybody sings Christmas carols, while the younger tykes generally fall asleep. This annual event is *very* popular with kids and their families from all over northern Arizona, and tickets generally sell out early (even as early as August).

SHOPPING

There's a gathering of boutiques and gift shops in Williams's quaint, historic downtown area, between Railroad, Grant, 1st, and 4th Streets.

Don't miss **Native America** (117 E. Route 66, 928/635-4600, 8am-9pm daily summer, 8am-6pm daily winter), a Native American-owned shop with Hopi and Navajo arts and crafts and some fun and interesting Old West kitsch sculptures holding up the front porch.

FOOD

A northland institution with some of the best steaks in the region, ★ **Rod's Steak House** (301 E. Route 66, 928/635-2671, www.rodssteakhouse.com, 11am-9:30pm Mon.-Sat., $12-25) has been operating at the same site since 1946. The food is excellent, the staff is friendly and professional, and the menus are shaped like steers.

The **Pine Country Restaurant** (107 N. Grand Canyon Blvd., 928/635-9718, http://pinecountryrestaurant.com, 6:30am-9:30pm daily, $8-19) is a family-style place that serves good diner-style food and homemade pies. Check out the beautiful paintings of the Grand Canyon on the walls.

Cruiser's Route 66 Bar & Grill (233 W. Route 66, 928/635-2445, www.cruisers66.com, 11am-9pm daily, $7-18) offers a diverse menu, with superior barbecue ribs, burgers, fajitas, pulled-pork sandwiches, and homemade chili. It has a full bar and offers live music most nights. During the summer evenings the patio is lively and fun.

For something a bit more upscale and romantic, try the **Red Raven Restaurant** (135 W. Route 66, 928/635-4980, www.redravenrestaurant.com, 11:30am-2pm and 5pm-close daily, $11-25), a charming little place along Route 66 with big windows looking out on the bustling sidewalk and the tourists strolling by. It serves delicious and inventive dishes: steak wraps, Guinness stew, tasty lamb, sweet potato fries, and Southwest egg rolls, to name just a few. The restaurant also has a deep beer list with selections mainly from Arizona and Colorado, and a good wine selection heavy on Italy and California. Make a reservation for dinner.

The vegetarian's best bet this side of downtown Flagstaff is the **Dara Thai Café** (145 W. Route 66, 928/635-2201, 11am-2pm and 5pm-9pm Mon.-Sat., $7-15), an agreeable little spot in the Grand Canyon Hotel. The café serves a variety of fresh and flavorful Thai favorites and offers quite a few meat-free dishes.

Brewing and serving craft beers in a cavernous building near the railroad tracks, **The Grand Canyon Brewing + Distillery** (301 N. 7th St., 800/513-2072, www.grandcanyonbrewery.com, 2pm-close daily, $9-22) is a favorite with locals and tourists alike. It gets pretty busy here at times, especially around quitting time. Along with several excellent craft beers, it serves pub-style food and pizzas that do not disappoint.

ACCOMMODATIONS

Williams has some of the most affordable independent accommodations in the Grand Canyon region, as well as several chain hotels.

It's difficult to find a better deal than the clean and basic **El Rancho Motel** (617 E. Route 66, 928/635-2552 or 800/228-2370, www.elranchomotelwilliams.us, $80-125), an independently owned, retro motel on Route 66 with few frills save comfort, friendliness, and a heated pool open in season.

The **Canyon Country Inn** (442 W. Route 66, 928/635-2349, www.thecanyoncountryinn.com, $89-115) is an enchanting little place right in the heart of Williams's charming historic district. Its country-Victorian decor is not for everyone, but it's a comfortable and friendly place to stay while exploring the canyon country.

The **Grand Canyon Railway Hotel** (235 N. Grand Canyon Blvd., 928/635-4010, www.thetrain.com, $169-189) stands now where Williams's old Harvey House once stood. It has a heated indoor pool, two restaurants, a lounge, a hot tub, a workout room, and a huge gift shop. The hotel serves riders on the Grand Canyon Railway and offers the highest-end accommodations in Williams.

The original **Grand Canyon Hotel** (145 W. Route 66, 928/635-1419, www.thegrandcanyonhotel.com, $79-195) opened in 1891, even before the railroad arrived and made Grand Canyon tourism something not just the rich could do. New owners refurbished and reopened the charming old redbrick hotel in Williams's historic downtown in 2005, and now it's an affordable, friendly place to stay with a lot of character and a bit of an international flavor. Spartan single-bed rooms go for $79 a night with a shared bathroom, and individually named and eclectically decorated double rooms with private baths are $93-105 a night—some of the most distinctive and affordable accommodations in the region. There are no televisions in the rooms. Several larger rooms with private baths and other amenities go for $150-195. There are also hostel rooms for $33-38.

The **Red Garter Bed & Bakery** (137 W. Railroad Ave., 928/635-1484, www.redgarter. com, $175-199) makes much of its original and longtime use as a brothel (which, like many similar places throughout Arizona's rural regions, didn't finally close until the 1940s), where the town's lonely, uncouth miners, lumberjacks, railway workers, and cowboys met with unlucky women, ever euphemized as "soiled doves," in rooms called "cribs." The 1897 frontier-Victorian stone building, with its wide, arching entranceway, has been beautifully restored with a lot of authentic charm, without skimping on the comforts—like big brass beds for the nighttime and delightful, homemade baked goods, juice, and coffee in the morning. Famously, this place is haunted by some poor unquiet, regretful soul, so you might want to bring your night-light along.

★ **The Lodge on Route 66** (200 E. Route 66, 877/563-4366, http://thelodgeonroute66. com, $99-189) has stylish rooms with sleep-inducing pillow-top mattresses; it also has a few civilized two-room suites with kitchenettes, dining areas, and fireplaces—perfect for a family that's not necessarily on a budget. The motor court-style grounds, right along the Mother Road, feature a romantic cabana with comfortable seats and an outdoor fireplace. No pets.

INFORMATION

Stop at the **Williams-Kaibab National Forest Visitor Center** (200 W. Railway Ave., 928/635-1418 or 800/863-0546, 8am-6:30pm daily spring-summer, 8am-5pm daily fall-winter) for information about Williams, the Grand Canyon, and camping and hiking in the Kaibab National Forest.

TRANSPORTATION
Car

Williams is 33 miles (53 km) west of Flagstaff via I-40, a 40-minute drive, and about 160 miles (260 km) north of Phoenix via I-17, a 2.75-hour drive. The drive from Williams to Grand Canyon National Park's South Entrance on AZ 64 is about 60 miles (97 km) and takes roughly an hour.

Shuttle

Groome Transportation aka Arizona Shuttle (928/350-8466, https:// groometransportation.com/arizona) offers trips from Flagstaff to Sedona, the Verde Valley, and Williams ($35-43 one-way).

Train

The **Grand Canyon Railway** (800/843-8724, www.thetrain.com) runs daily between the Williams station and the South Rim depot in Grand Canyon Village, with several different ticket levels ($67-226 adults, $32-153 children 2-15).

Page

The town would not exist without the lake, and the lake would not exist without the dam: Such is the symbiotic chain of existence here in the slickrock lands around sunken Glen Canyon, where water lovers come to play among the red and pink sandstone labyrinths.

Page is a small, tidy town with a higher-than-normal number of churches for its size; they are all lined up along one long block at the beginning of the main drag. The population here was once composed primarily of dam builders and their families, for the town was founded in 1957 as a government-run camp for Glen Canyon Dam workers, built on land formerly owned by the Navajo but traded for a slice of property in Utah. These days Page has sizable Latter-day Saint and Navajo communities, and the population swells with boaters, water-skiers, swimmers, and houseboat loungers visiting **Lake Powell** and **Glen Canyon National Recreation Area** in the spring and summer. The business life of Page is now dedicated to that influx, and to the town's relative proximity to Grand Canyon's South and North Rims, so there are plenty of chain hotels and restaurants here.

SIGHTS
★ Horseshoe Bend

As you drive into Page from the south along U.S. 89, look for mile marker 545 (about 4 mi/6.4 km south of town), where you can walk 0.75 mile (1.2 km) one-way to a viewpoint above the famous, much-photographed **Horseshoe Bend,** where the Colorado River curves like a horseshoe around a lonely pink butte far below. You'll likely know you're there by the crowds. In recent years this barrier-free roadside lookout has become very popular. It's of course incredibly beautiful—the green river meanders in a tight curve around red rock—but it's also thrilling because there's nothing between you and the river far, far below. If you're hoping to get a good photograph here,

make sure to bring a wide-angle lens. Take water, a hat, and sunscreen with you; though short, the hike moves over sand and up and down a few inclines.

There is a large dirt parking lot at the trailhead, which also has some bathrooms that are quite dirty. The parking lot is dusty and busy, and there are a lot of tour buses and motorhomes, so use caution.

John Wesley Powell Museum

Just off Page's main drag is the **John Wesley Powell Museum** (6 N. Lake Powell Blvd., 928/645-9496 or 888/597-6873, www.powellmuseum.org, 9am-5pm daily, free, donation welcomed), named, as is the nearby reservoir, for the one-armed Civil War veteran, scientist, writer, and explorer who led the first two scientific river expeditions through the Grand Canyon. The center has an excellent bookstore, and the friendly staff can help you book boat and air tours, but the museum itself takes a little more effort to enjoy. There is a lot of fascinating information on Powell and the river runners who followed in his path, but most of the displays are made up of long articles that you have to stand there and read. Children will likely be impatient, though there's a small interactive display on the natural science of the area. Inside the museum is Page's **Visitor Information Center** (www.visitpagelakepowell.com).

★ Antelope Canyon Navajo Tribal Park

A color-swirled, water-worn slot in a mesa on Navajoland, **Antelope Canyon Navajo Tribal Park** (928/698-2808, 8am-5pm daily Apr.-Oct., shorter hours Nov.-Mar., $8 admission, required guided tours extra) is a few miles southeast of Page off AZ 98. This popular crevice of twisting and twirling slickrock requires a Navajo guide, but it's easy to find one. You pile into a big four-wheel drive

Page

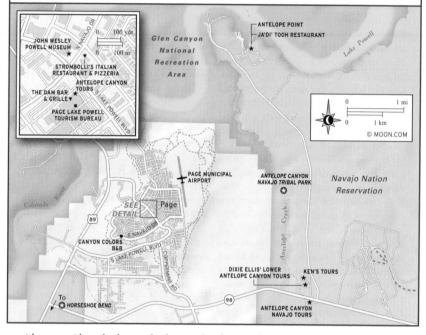

with your guide and others and ride several bumpy miles down a sandy wash to the slit in the rocks rising up out of the ground—the entrance to a wonderland. The guide then takes you through the short slot canyon, out the other side, and then back again. It's an easy walk along a sandy bottomland, with the canyon walls rising 130 feet (40 m) and impossibly narrow in some stretches. It's a strange, fantastic, and very memorable stroll, and one that is highly recommended despite the relatively high cost of a tour. The tours are staggered, so you are never crammed in there with too many other people. The earlier you go the better; the light and the colors are said to be at their best between 10am and noon, but it's really only important for serious photographers to go at these ideal times of the day.

The slot canyon's unique undulations and warm reds and pinks, especially in the summer with the sun high in the sky and shining in laser-like shafts through small gashes high above, make it one of the most photographed in the canyonlands, if not the world. It is a very popular attraction, and you'll find no shortage of guides in Page. Still, it's a good idea to make a reservation. Park admission is generally wrapped into what you pay the guide. You can also go to the park yourself and hire a guide there.

Antelope Canyon Navajo Tours (928/698-3384, http://navajotours.com, tours 8:45am-4pm daily, $60 adults, $30 children) start about 3 miles (4.8 km) southeast of Page off AZ 98 at Antelope Canyon Navajo Tribal Park. Knowledgeable Navajo guides drive you through the desert landscape in a big four-wheeler for a 1.5-hour general tour.

Antelope Canyon Tours (22 S. Lake Powell Blvd., 928/645-9102, www.antelopecanyon.com, $60 adults, $50 ages 8-22, $42 children under 8) offers two different tours every day, year-round, departing from Page. The 1.5-hour general tour leaves at

7am, 8am, 9:30am, 11:30pm, 1:30pm, 3:30pm, and 4:30pm.

One of the better photography tours of Antelope Canyon is offered by **Adventurous Antelope Canyon Photo Tours** (AZ 98, mile marker 302, 928/380-1874, www.navajoantelopecanyon.com, $158-297), and they will also take you out to a few other, though lesser, slot canyons that aren't as well known and heavily visited as Antelope Canyon. This company is recommended for serious amateur and professional photographers.

Lower Antelope Canyon

Across AZ 98 from the tribal park, a few tour operators offer hike-in access to **Lower Antelope Canyon,** a similarly beautiful and mysterious slot canyon. Tours ($40, $20 children 8-12, plus $8 Navajo permit fee) run about every 20 minutes and last 1.25 hours. The 1.1-mile (1.8-km) round-trip hike is easy and OK for kids. **Dixie Ellis' Lower Antelope Canyon Tours** (928/640-1761, http://antelopelowercanyon.com) has tours 10am-4:10pm daily. **Ken's Tours** (928/606-2168, www.lowerantelope.com) operates in the same area and has tours 8:20am-4pm daily.

Antelope Point Marina

The Navajo Nation's **Antelope Point** (537 Marina Pkwy., Navajo Rte. N22b, 928/645-5900, www.antelopepointlakepowell.com, $25) has a tasteful sandstone welcome center (8am-4pm daily) and offers a variety of services as well as access to Lake Powell in a starkly beautiful setting. The **Ja'di' Tooh Restaurant** (11am-8pm daily in summer, $14-28) serves decent American food (burgers, sandwiches, steaks, salads) and looks out over the stark, red land and the glowing blue lake. A hotel is planned for the future. You can rent houseboats and other watercraft or get flicked across the water at the wakeboarding park, and there are slips to park your boat and a store to purchase supplies.

The marina is about 9 miles (14.5 km) outside Page on Navajo land. Take AZ 98 east to Navajo Route 222. It's not far from Antelope Canyon Navajo Tribal Park.

ENTERTAINMENT AND EVENTS

Every year on the first weekend in November, about 50 hot-air balloonists bring their colorful crafts to Page for the **Page Balloon Regatta** (928/645-2741, www.pagechamber.com, early Nov.). The highlight of the event is

Antelope Canyon Navajo Tribal Park

the Balloon Glow, when the balloonists light up their balloons on the ground, creating dozens of glowing orbs. There's also a street festival and other events that attend this busy weekend near Lake Powell.

FOOD

Millions of tourists drive through Page every season to see Lake Powell and the canyonlands, and as a result the area has all the usual chain hotels and several chain restaurants—more than is usual for a small town in the middle of nowhere. You'll find most of Page's services along Lake Powell Boulevard, the main drag through town.

The Dam Bar & Grille (644 N. Navajo, 928/645-2161, www.damplaza.com, 11am-11pm daily, $13-34) is the small resort town's entertainment complex, featuring a surf-and-turf restaurant with well-made baby back ribs, steaks, prime rib, sandwiches, and salads.

For dinner or lunch try ★ **Strombolli's Italian Restaurant & Pizzeria** (711 N. Navajo Dr., 928/645-2605, https://strombollisrestaurant.com, 11am-10pm daily, $10-20) for toothsome Italian entrées like baked ravioli with meat sauce, calzones, New York-style pizza, chicken parmigiana, stuffed eggplant parmigiana, burgers, steaks, salads, and a decent wine list.

ACCOMMODATIONS

Canyon Colors B&B (225 S. Navajo Dr., 928/645-5979, www.canyoncolorsbandb.com, $99-159, two-night minimum) rents two bright and homey rooms in Page and has an outdoor barbecue area and a pool, friendly hosts, and big, delectable breakfasts. The **Dreamkatcher Lake Powell Bed & Breakfast** (66 S. American Way, Big Water, Utah, 435/675-5828, www.dreamkatcherslakepowell.com, $99-215) is

about 20 minutes from Page on the Utah side of the recreation area. There are three pleasant rooms with private baths, a library with views of Lake Powell, and a hot tub with a spectacular view of the canyonlands.

INFORMATION

The **Page Lake Powell Tourism Bureau** (647-A Elm St., 928/660-3405, www.visitpagelakepowell.com) has all kinds of information on Page, Glen Canyon, and the rest of the region, and the staff there can help you book tours. The bureau runs the **Visitor Information Center** (10am-4pm Mon.-Fri., 10am-2pm Sat.), located inside the Powell Museum (6 N. Lake Powell Blvd.).

TRANSPORTATION

Page is 129 miles (208 km) north of Flagstaff via U.S. 89, a 2.25-hour drive. It's a good base for those visiting both the North Rim and South Rim as well as Lake Powell and Glen Canyon National Recreation Area. (Page is about 3 miles/4.8 km from the Glen Canyon Dam.)

There are two routes to the **North Rim** from Page: For the **Arizona route,** take U.S. 89 south to Bitter Springs, head west on U.S. 89A to Jacob Lake, and then south on AZ 67 to the rim; the drive is 123 miles (198 km) and takes about 2.5 hours. For the **Utah route,** take U.S. 89 to Kanab, Utah, and then head south on U.S. 89A and AZ 67 to the rim; the drive is 153 miles (246 km) and takes closer to three hours.

To get to the **South Rim,** head south on U.S. 89 and turn west onto AZ 64. Grand Canyon National Park's East Entrance station is about 30 miles (48 km) from the junction. The drive from Page to the East Entrance is 110 miles (177 km) and takes about 2.5 hours. From the East Entrance to Grand Canyon Village is another 25 miles (40 km).

Kanab, Utah

About 7 miles (11.3 km) north of the Arizona border along U.S. 89A in Utah, Kanab is the pleasant, relatively bustling capital of the Arizona Strip. Here you'll find varied accommodations, including several chain hotels and restaurants. It's a tiny, rural burg, far from the real world. Isolated out here on the western end of the Colorado Plateau, Kanab is home to only about 4,000 year-round residents. It is nonetheless well set up for travelers and tourists. Kanab makes an ideal base for visiting Grand Canyon National Park's North Rim, which is just 80 miles (129 km) or about 1.5 hours away; Zion National Park, 40 miles (64 km) to the northwest; Bryce Canyon National Park, 77 miles (124 km) to the northeast; and Lake Powell, 70 miles (113 km) to the east.

SIGHTS

Little Hollywood Museum

For nearly 100 years Kanab's often clear, blue skies and classic plateau landscapes have brought movie and television producers to the area to such an extent that it sometimes calls itself Little Hollywood. Since the 1920s, more than 100 movies and television shows have been filmed in and around Kanab—including portions of such classics as *Brighty of the Grand Canyon, Planet of the Apes,* and *The Outlaw Josey Wales.* This fact is celebrated at the **Little Hollywood Museum** (297 W. Center St., 435/644-5337, www.littlehollywoodmuseum.org, 9am-6pm daily, free) in central Kanab. The museum has some interesting displays and memorabilia and is worth a stop for Western film buffs. The complex also has a restaurant and a gift shop, and during the high season is a stop for tour buses.

Grand Staircase-Escalante National Monument Visitor Center

One of several regional visitors centers for the vast and lonely Grand Staircase-Escalante National Monument, the **Kanab Visitor Center** (745 E. U.S. Hwy. 89, 435/644-1300, www.blm.gov, 8am-4:30pm daily mid-Mar.-mid-Nov., 8am-4:30pm Mon.-Fri. mid-Nov.-mid-Mar.) has information and advice on visiting the monument's remote stretches, where geologists, paleontologists, and archaeologists search the red rocks for clues. A trip out here requires a lot of planning and backcountry expertise. The visitors center also has a helpful topographical model and a geologic cross section of the region. Rangers here watch over a daily walk-in lottery for permits to visit the Vermilion Cliffs' popular Wave and Coyote Buttes areas, and they offer various programs throughout the high season.

The one-million-acre Grand Staircase-Escalante National Monument has three units, and the Escalante Canyon section is by far the most popular for hikers with its rare and shady riparian areas, strange sandstone formations, and cool waterfalls. Escalante is about a two-hour drive from Kanab one-way.

Best Friends Animal Sanctuary

The largest no-kill animal shelter in the country, **Best Friends Animal Sanctuary** (5001 Angel Canyon Rd., 435/644-2001, http://bestfriends.org, 8am-5pm daily, free) keeps some 1,600 homeless dogs, cats, pigs, burros, horses, sheep, goats, mules, and more, on a beautiful red-rock canyon property about 5 miles (8 km) north of Kanab. Call ahead to book a free tour of the property and a chance to interact with the animals. Tours leave daily at 8:30am, 10am, 1pm, and 2:30pm.

Coral Pink Sand Dunes State Park

About 22 miles (35 km) west of Kanab, the 10,000- to 15,000-year-old **Coral Pink Sand Dunes** (435/648-2800, $10 per car) shift endlessly with the wind, the sandy remains of the

The Mystery of Everett Ruess

Everett Ruess (pronounced Roos) disappeared in 1934 into the canyonland wilderness around Escalante, Utah. He was 20 years old and a seasoned desert rat. Friends, strangers, and newspaper reporters searched long hours and many miles looking for the talkative, eccentric young artist. But nobody ever saw him again.

At the astonishing age of 16, Ruess embarked on a series of epic solo journeys across the Colorado Plateau. He employed companionable mules to carry his camping gear and ventured into the uninhabited sandstone wilds for weeks at a time, searching for beauty and Puebloan ruins to inspire his watercolors, linocuts, sketches, photographs, and poetry.

Reuss came to the great Southwest during the worst days of the Great Depression. He never had much money and was often destitute, doing odd jobs and befriending tourists for his meals. He received a steady stream of books and art supplies from his parents back home in Hollywood, packages that he regularly picked up at some of America's most isolated outposts of proto-civilization. Obsessed with art and literature, he read Thomas Mann's *Magic Mountain* while working as a cowboy on Arizona's Mogollon Rim, and recited T. S. Eliot's "The Love Song of J. Alfred Prufrock" to the stones and stars in Canyon de Chelly.

Ruess was talkative and easy company, and he managed to know several of the era's great artists, including the painter Maynard Dixon and photographers Dorothea Lang, Ansel Adams, and Edward Weston. He briefly lived in San Francisco and tried to make it as an artist, but the canyons kept calling his name.

We know about Ruess and his romantic travels because he wrote eloquent letters to family and friends and kept a detailed and compelling diary. *Desert Magazine* published a few of his letters in 1939, about five years after he disappeared. Hundreds of readers called for more, so the next year the magazine published a book-length collection: *On Desert Trails with Everett Ruess*, edited by Hugh Lacy. When R. L. Rusho's edition of the letters, *A Vagabond for Beauty*, appeared in 1983, and later the *Wilderness Journals of Everett Ruess*, the artist's cult grew mightily, and his story became a favorite mystery and legend of the canyonlands.

The early search parties found his two burros grazing in an isolated canyon, but his gear and body have never been recovered. Strangely, he carved the word NEMO in at least two places, in a cave and near a ruin around the area where he was last seen. His father later wrote that Ruess was probably referring to Captain Nemo from *20,000 Leagues Under the Sea*, by Jules Verne. While most experts believe he died as a result of an accident or foul play and that his body sank forever beneath the roiling waters of the Colorado River, the carvings and Reuss's own words have fueled speculation over the years that he disappeared by choice. If he had planned to run away and live out his life as a desert hermit, this magical canyon country would have been the ideal setting for such a spiritual quest.

Just before he walked off into desert and the unknown, Ruess wrote what would be his last letter to his brother Waldo.

"As to when I shall revisit civilization, it will not be soon, I think," he wrote. "I have not tired of the wilderness; rather I enjoy its beauty and the vagrant life I lead more keenly all the time. I prefer the saddle to the streetcar, and the star-sprinkled sky to the roof."

area's eroded Navajo sandstone cliffs trapped here at 6,000 feet (1,829 m) above sea level. The dunes are popular with ATV riders and sandboarders, but's it also fun just to climb them. There aren't any developed trails, for obvious reasons. There are two campgrounds here, one with hookups and one without ($20-30 per night). Take U.S. 89 north 7.5 miles (12.1 km), turn left onto Hancock Rd for 9.4 miles (15.1 km), and then left at Coral Pink Sand Dunes Road.

RECREATION
Hiking

There are several easy to moderate hiking and equestrian trails in the red-and-green

Kanab

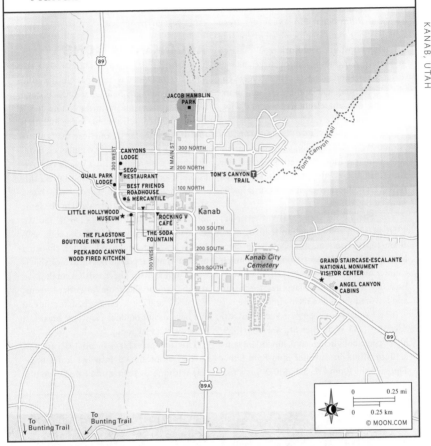

wildlands around Kanab. For a comprehensive list, try Trailskanab.com.

The 2.5-mile (4-km) round-trip **Bunting Trail** climbs 860 feet (262 m) to a panel of petroglyphs and amazing views of the region, growing steeper as you reach the top. The trailhead is 3.5 miles (5.6 km) from downtown Kanab—head east on U.S. 89 and south on U.S. 89A, turn right at Kanab Creek and drive through the Ranchos subdivision, then turn right on Stanfield.

The popular **Tom's Canyon Trail** is a beautiful 3-mile (4.8-km) round-trip hike over easy and flat terrain to a box canyon and a weeping spring at a picnic area. The trailhead is just 1 mile (1.6 km) from downtown—head north on Main Street, turn right on 300 North, enter the La Estancia subdivision, then turn right at the waterwheel and park on the street.

Mountain Biking

Two fun single-tracks loop through **Jacob Hamblin Park** (566 N. 100 E., 435/6442534) in Kanab. Short (1.5 mi/2.4 km) but pleasingly technical, the Raven and Roadrunner Trails were built by the local bike club, and riders from beginners to experts will want to do multiple figure eights here.

FOOD

The **Rocking V Café** (97 W. Center St., 435/644-8001, www.rockingvcafe.com, 11:30am-10pm daily, $15-48) serves fresh and delicious food, and there's an interesting art gallery upstairs. The Rocking V makes a good burger, including a Boca burger, as well as tasty chicken and pasta dishes, veggie enchiladas, creamy mac-and-cheese, and more. It also has a decent selection of beer and wine, including microbrews.

The more upscale **Sego Restaurant** (190 N. 300 W., 435/644-5680, www.segokanab.com, 5pm-9pm Mon.-Sat.) serves regional new American dishes with a dose of international flavor, using local, regional, and sustainably sourced ingredients.

The Soda Fountain (176 W. Center St., 435/644-3401, www.kanabuniteddrug.com, 10am-10pm Mon.-Sat. Apr.-Oct., 11am-8pm Mon.-Sat. Nov.-Mar., $4-10) is an old lunch counter inside the local United Drug, a throwback spot featuring diner favorites, ice cream, and flavored sodas in a retro atmosphere.

The **Peekaboo Canyon Wood Fired Kitchen** (233 W. Center St., 435/689-1959, http://peekabookitchen.com, lunch 11:30am-2:30pm Mon.-Fri., dinner 5pm-8pm Sun.-Thurs., 5pm-10pm Fri.-Sat., $10-20) is a fun and casual spot attached to the Flagstone Boutique Inn & Suites, with excellent pizza and a full range of Impossible Burgers and other vegetarian options.

ACCOMMODATIONS

The **Quail Park Lodge** (125 N. 300 W., 435/215-1447, www.quailparklodge.com, $109-129), along U.S. 89 as it rolls through Kanab, is clean and affordable and has a freshly painted, retro motor lodge look to it that draws in the fan of American road culture and popular architecture. A small pool, tasteful motel-style rooms with TVs and free Wi-Fi, and a location that can't be beat make this one of the best places to stay on the Arizona Strip. Right next door and owned by the same folks, the **Canyons Lodge** (236 N. 300 W., 435/644-3069, www.canyonslodge.com, $89-179) is less nostalgic than its sister, choosing instead a nattier, posh-wilderness look that is warm and stylish. There's also a small pool, and the comfortable rooms offer flat-screens, free Wi-Fi, and crisp, relaxing beds for the end of a hard day of outdoor play. Free breakfast comes with every room.

The nation's largest no-kill animal haven has branched into the hotel business with the **Best Friends Roadhouse &**

Coral Pink Sand Dunes State Park

Mercantile (30 N. 300 W., 435/644-3400, www.bestfriendsroadhouse.org, $129-249), a stylish and comfortable central Kanab inn that welcomes your pets. Best Friends Animal Sanctuary (5001 Angel Canyon Rd., 435/644-2001, http://bestfriends.org) also rents the **Angel Canyon Cottages** (up to 6 guests and 3 pets, $130-150 Mar.-Nov., $95 Dec.-Feb.) and the smaller **Angel Canyon Cabins** (1-2 people and 2 pets, $85-105 Mar.-Nov., $60 Dec.-Feb.) on its gorgeous property outside Kanab, where it also operates a small **RV park** (full hookups, $30-50 Mar. 15-Oct. 31, closed in winter).

The Flagstone Boutique Inn & Suites (233 W. Center St., 844/322-8824, www.theflagstoneinn.com, $139-149) in central Kanab is a wonderfully restored old travel lodge from the 1940s, now with 32 comfortable and stylish bungalows featuring kitchens, flat-screens, and full-sized tubs.

TRANSPORTATION

Kanab is 74 miles (119 km) west of Page via U.S. 89, a 1.25-hour drive. Grand Canyon National Park's North Rim is about 80 miles (129 km) south of Kanab via U.S. 89A and AZ 67; the drive takes about 1.5 hours.

Background

The Landscape

GEOGRAPHY

When dinosaurs roamed the earth, this dry land was a swampy and wet place. Over the eons, different portions of Arizona, the U.S. state through which all of Grand Canyon spreads, were covered by shallow seas that flowed in, flourished, and then dried up and retreated. Eventually the landscape you see took shape—mountains rose, volcanoes burst and created new land, and plates slid apart and crashed into each other, creating upland plateaus and digging deep canyons with the erosional help of rivers, wind, and aridity.

The plateau country dominates the northern reaches of Arizona, covering about two-fifths of the state. The **Coconino Plateau** creates the **South Rim** of Grand Canyon, the **Kaibab Plateau** creates the **North Rim,** and several other intermontane plateaus of various sizes stand to the east and west. Together, the plateaus form the **Colorado Plateau Province** (often simply called the **Colorado Plateau**), centered on the Four Corners region, where the states of Arizona, Utah, New Mexico, and Colorado meet. The Colorado Plateau's 200-mile (320-km) southern edge, the **Mogollon Rim** of central Arizona, borders ponderosa pine forests and scrubby, rocky, cactus-strewn midlands around 5,000-6,000 feet (1,524-1,829 m) above sea level. Off the plateaus, lower down in the **basin and range** territory, the hot and bushy Sonoran Desert takes over.

A land of towering red sandstone cliffs, vast slickrock plains, large evergreen forests, streamside oases, unforgiving deserts, and deep jagged canyons, the Colorado Plateau and the Four Corners region have more national parks and national monuments than any other place in the United States outside of Washington, D.C. And the greatest one of them all is **Grand Canyon National Park,** in which can be found most of the varied biomes that exist throughout the Four Corners.

The bottom of Grand Canyon is a low, hot **desert** similar to the Salt River Valley around Phoenix, while the North Rim, with sections above 8,700 feet (2,652 m), has spruce-fir and ponderosa pine **forests,** and the South Rim is covered in pinyon-juniper woodland and ponderosa pines. The highest **mountains** in the plateau country reach nearly 13,000 feet (3,962 m), and their peaks are dominated by tundra and bare, cold boulders. The lowest areas in the region are along the **Colorado River,** which cuts through the province as it falls headlong from high in the Rocky Mountains in Colorado through Grand Canyon and then on to the lowland deserts of western Arizona. Other wondrous niches of greenery and bursting life pop up throughout the region where **springs** trickle out of the rock cliffs, creating paradisal spots inside the canyon as well as perennial creeks that marry the Colorado River from the south and north. Most of the humans who have made a go of life in this otherwise hard and arid land have done so along these scattered creeks and springs.

GEOLOGY

Grand Canyon was formed by the great cosmic need of all water to return to the sea from whence it came. Water falls—that's its sole mission in life—and huge torrents of water carrying loads of dry, rocky sediment fall hard and fast, cutting deep into the rocks of an uplifted plateau. As the cuts get deeper, the land then gives way and falls apart, forming canyons deep and wide.

The plateau country began to form in its current shape around 600 million years ago, when the continent was relatively flat and layer after layer of limestone, sandstone, siltstone, and shale were deposited by tropical seas moving in and then receding, leaving behind dunes and stream deposits and eroding the older layers for some 300 million years. Then the dune deposits hardened and petrified, creating the strange, swirling sandstone you see all over the plateau region. Volcanic eruptions around the plateau added to the great piling of sediment, while rivers and lakes and inland seas flushed in and then dried up or receded. But the plateau itself, while it was eroded and cut and sculpted and formed, remained relatively stable in contrast to the other lands around it, which changed mightily. About 70 million years ago the land all around the Southwest began to rise, pushing the plateau from about sea level to more than 10,000 feet (3,048 m) above it. Great mountains were thrust up out of the ground all around the

---

region, and the earth stretched with underground tension to create the basin and range province to the west and south of the plateau. About 20 million years ago, the basin and range province broke into the land of deep valleys and long mountain ranges that it is today. The Colorado Plateau eventually rose nearly a mile (1.6 km) higher than the basin and range region. The Colorado River fell through the plateau and cut deep into the rock, carving Grand Canyon—a process that started less than 6 million years ago.

Today, Grand Canyon's high rock walls represent an open book of **geologic strata,** with each descending rock layer revealing the environmental conditions of its formation. It is not a complete book, however; there are missing layers called **unconformities,** eroded away to nothing over time by wind and water. The layers that do remain grow older as you descend into the canyon's hot desert depths. The caprock on the rims, the **Kaibab Formation,** is about 270 million years old. Head down the Bright Angel Trail from the South Rim and watch deep time take shape; below the Kaibab Formation, the strata slip by, streaked red, pink, and black, minerals bleeding one into another—the **Toroweap Formation** (273 million years), the **Coconino Sandstone** (275 million years), the **Hermit Formation** (280 million years), the **Supai Group** (285-315 million years), the **Redwall Limestone** (340 million years), the **Temple Butte Formation** (385 million years), the **Muav Limestone** (505 million years), the **Bright Angel Shale** (515 million years), the **Tapeats Sandstone** (525 million years), and the **Grand Canyon Supergroup,** a series of sedimentary strata between 650-1,250 million years. The oldest rocks in Grand Canyon, 1.7-1.8 billion-year-old layers of ancient schist, gneiss, and granite called the **Vishnu basement rocks,** form the dark walls of the inner gorge, about 3,000 feet (914 m) below the rim.

CLIMATE

Weather conditions in and around Grand Canyon National Park vary by season and elevation.

The **South Rim,** around 7,000 feet (2,134 m), has a generally mild four-season climate, which keeps that section of the park open and busy year-round. In summer, average high temperatures range in the 70s F (21-26°C) and 80s F (27-32°C). Winter, from around December to early March, is cold, sometimes wet and sometimes snowy. Spring and fall are cool, with high temperatures in the 50s F (10-15°C) and 60s F (16-21°C).

Snow and bitter cold close down the park's **North Rim,** which is significantly higher in elevation than the South Rim, from December until mid-May. High temperatures in the summer range from the mid-60s F (18°C) to the high 70s F (24-26°C). Spring and fall see highs in the 40s F (4-9°C) and 50s F (10-15°C).

A desert climate prevails **inside Grand Canyon,** where it's generally about 20 degrees warmer than on the rims. It's hot in the summer, mild ranging toward idyllic in spring and fall, and cold at night and brisk during the day in the winter months.

The Grand Canyon region has two relatively predictable (though sometimes entirely absent) **wet seasons.** Slow pour-downs come from time to time in **winter,** along with snowstorms of various weight and staying power. In **summer,** the so-called monsoon season brings the entire Southwest back to life after the May-June heat hibernation. Starting in July and lasting until September, warm air from the south rises and cools over the plateau, forming epic **thunderstorms** that both bless and plague the rims and inner canyon. Rolling in dark and blustery in the late afternoon, threatening with lightning flashes and booming thunder, these relatively frequent storms sometimes last only a few minutes, which can be enough time to fill all the dry washes and send everything caught in them, hikers included, careening through the canyons.

ENVIRONMENTAL ISSUES

The primary environmental issues facing Grand Canyon are the same as those facing the entire Southwest: **climate change** and **megadrought.** The region is generally getting hotter and drier, and has been for at least the last 30 to 40 years. Tree-ring data reveals that ancient droughts in the region have lasted even longer and caused widespread disruption of human cultures. Unfortunately for the most recent human cultures to call the Southwest home, the builders of the desert megacities like Phoenix, Las Vegas, and Los Angeles made a pact to divide the waters of the **Colorado River** during what they did not know at the time was a historically wet year, essentially sealing a deficit into the agreement forevermore.

The level of mining activity and other resource extraction in the canyonlands tends to rise and fall with the nation's politics, but over the long-term industrial uses like this have been on a precipitous downturn, and much of the land throughout the Colorado Plateau Province benefits from federal protection as national parks, national monuments, national forests, and federal wilderness areas.

Perhaps the greatest environmental disaster to hit Grand Canyon was the construction of **Glen Canyon Dam** upriver in 1963. The dam completely changed the river through Grand Canyon, turning the very name of the once-mighty Colorado into a standing joke. Where once the river flowed a muddy red (Colorado means "colored red" in Spanish) through the canyon, warm and filled with rocks and other carving materials, after the dam closed it turned green and cold, changing the entire nature of the river corridor, from what kinds of fish could live in the water to what kinds of plants grew on its banks. While calls over the years to bring the dam down have so far gone unanswered, extensive research and periodic planned floods have given scientists new insights into why it should eventually be dismantled.

Plants and Animals

There must be some rule from long ago that says you can't discuss Grand Canyon's plant and animal communities without first mentioning old C. Hart Merriam. Head of the first large U.S. Biological Survey of the canyon country in 1889, Merriam hiked the inner canyon and lived for a time on the San Francisco Peaks near Flagstaff, where he observed that different "life zones" appeared relative to the elevation, and that to hike from the bottom of Grand Canyon to the top of Humphrey Peak at over 12,000 feet (3,658 m) above sea level was, in terms of the flora and fauna you'd encounter, something like walking from Mexico to Canada in about 50 miles (81 km). While essentially true, biologists today tend to use the term "communities" rather than life zones. Merriam's categories are too broad for this varied land of niches and microclimates, where zones bleed into each other based on slope aspect, relative air temperature, and other mysterious factors—allowing, for example, highland species like Douglas fir to grow several miles down the Bright Angel Trail, thanks to a cool, north-facing alcove, and desert plants to thrive on the 7,000-foot (2,134-km) South Rim with the help of warm air rising out of the depths.

You can download a comprehensive **checklist of plant and animal species** known to exist in Grand Canyon National Park at www.nps.gov/grca/learn/nature/plants.htm.

PLANTS

Let's take a hike through Grand Canyon, starting at the South Rim, venturing down into the canyon, and then climbing back up to the North Rim.

The **South Rim** rises to around 7,000 feet (2,134 km) above sea level and is covered with **ponderosa pine forest** and **pinyon-juniper woodland.** Adapted to aridity and fire, the tall and skinny ponderosa pine is northern Arizona's representative species and has a complex, symbiotic relationship with other plants and animals in the region. A healthy ponderosa pine forest is open and parklike, not choked with brush, and wildfire plays a major role in keeping it that way. Gambel's oak and other dry-forest denizens typically appear throughout the ponderosa community as well. Close to the rim, you'll encounter the so-called pygmy forest of twisted pinyon pines, junipers, cliffrose, silvery sagebrush, and little leaf mountain mahogany, all similarly drought-adapted plants. This community thrives across the Colorado Plateau, and these species figure largely in the traditions and larders of the region's Native American tribes.

Now we head into the **inner canyon.** Descending to the Tonto Platform about 3,900 feet (1,189 m) below the South Rim, but still towering 1,200 feet (366 m) above the Colorado River, we find ourselves in another world—the **desert scrub** community. Mostly bushes and cacti with deep roots in loose sand, look for creosote, brittlebush, blackbrush, catclaw, mesquite, saltbush, wolfberry, Mormon tea, turpentine broom, and sagebrush among the scrub, along with prickly pear and claret cup cactus, teddy bear and buckhorn cholla, yucca, and century plants. The desert scrub is particularly beautiful in the spring after heavy winter snowstorms, when all the brush, cacti, and dormant hidden wildflowers bloom in a riot of yellow, red, purple, pink, and orange.

A bit farther down the Bright Angel Trail there's another plant community to discover: the **riparian** community. At the spring-fed desert oasis of Indian Garden, groundwater spilling out of the rock walls creates a small green paradise of hanging gardens, mosses, monkeyflowers, maidenhair ferns, columbines, lobelia, poison ivy, and other water-loving plants that could not exist in the canyon outside of this safe and wet haven. The spring then becomes a perennial creek, which inspires a beautiful riparian area as it falls and flows through its well-worn channel toward the river, creating rare greenbelts of cottonwoods (many of them planted by humans over the years), willows, and other streamside plants that act like a magnet to all of the canyon's living things. Such spring-fed and riparian oases pop up throughout the canyon—Vasey's Paradise, Elves Chasm, Bright Angel Creek, Havasu Creek, to name just a few—and have allowed small human communities to thrive in this otherwise hard and arid land for thousands of years.

Mesquite, coyote willow, catclaw, arrowweed, and the invasive tamarisk or saltcedar dominate the river corridor, while fragrant night-blooming flowers such as the sacred datura and tufted evening primrose thrive along the banks. We cross the Colorado at Bright Angel Canyon and continue toward the North Rim on the North Kaibab Trail, hiking along Bright Angel Creek, one of those life-giving canyon riparian zones.

As we rise finally to the **North Rim,** we enter the highland **mixed-conifer forest** of the Kaibab Plateau, which ranges in elevation from around 6,000 to 9,200 feet (1,829-2,804 m); the area within the park is on the higher end. This enchanted upland of boreal forests and green mountain meadows is still generally arid, but its high elevation, winter snow, and summer rainstorms have made an evergreen home for Engelmann spruce; alpine, white, and Douglas fir; quaking aspen; and ponderosa pine, along with seasonal wildflowers such as lupine, yarrow, and aster.

ANIMALS

Across the five distinct but ranging Grand Canyon plant communities (ponderosa pine forest, pinyon-juniper woodland, desert scrub, riparian, and mixed-conifer forest), predator and prey carry on the amoral game of survival. Some animals here are generalists willing to ignore borders and boundaries, while other niche-bound natives exist here, precariously, and nowhere else in the world.

On the **South Rim** it's usually not difficult to spot **Abert's squirrels, mule deer,** and **elk,** and on the **North Rim** look for **deer, Kaibab squirrels,** and **wild turkeys.** You will likely never see the **mountain lions** that are watching it all from some hidden place on either rim and inside the canyon.

The skies over Grand Canyon are the province of magnificent birds of prey, and one of the great pleasures of viewing the canyon from the rims is watching the **California condors, peregrine falcons,** and **red-tailed hawks** soaring overhead. About 40 bird species live in the canyon country year-round; among the most common are **ravens,** which are found throughout Grand Canyon, especially on the rims. The area is also a seasonal home to some 300 species of winged visitors, including water- and shorebirds such as **avocets, grebes, mallards, stilts,** and **great blue herons** along the river corridor. (Download a comprehensive **checklist of Grand Canyon birds** at www.nps.gov/grca/learn/nature/bird-checklists.htm.)

Inside the canyon, around the river and the perennial creeks, you might see a **ringtailed cat,** a **spotted skunk,** and the ubiquitous **mule deer,** as well as rarer species such as the outspoken **canyon tree frog** and the **red-spotted toad.** The skies inside Grand Canyon at dusk are ruled by more than 20 different species of **bats,** and as morning warms the high rock cliffs, the **bighorn sheep** come out to greet you, unafraid and seemingly even willing to pose for photographs.

Reptiles are found throughout Grand Canyon, from the rims to the river. These include numerous species of lizards, such as the **short-horned lizard, collared lizard,** and **yellow-backed spiny lizard.** Among the many snake species that live here are six rattlesnake species, including the pinkish **Grand Canyon rattlesnake,** which is found nowhere else in the world.

Human History

Humans have lived in and around Grand Canyon for at least 12,000 years. The earliest were **Paleoindian hunter-gatherers** who left behind animal effigies called split-twig figurines, dating from around 3000 BCE and made of coyote willow. Some 200 have been found in a dozen caves around Grand Canyon, twisted into the shapes of bighorn sheep and deer and believed to have been left behind as part of a sympathetic-magic hunting ritual. Similar figurines were left throughout the Southwest for some 1,700 years, between 2900 and 1250 BCE.

Around AD 700 the **Cohonina,** Hopi for "the people who live to the west," began farming and hunting on the canyon's western rim and in its depths. The Little Ice Age seems to have pushed the Cohonina out of the plateau region by about AD 1200, leaving the area to the **Ancestral Puebloans** that had begun to move in around AD 800. These communities, ancestors of the Hopi tribe who still live on three remote mesas east of the canyon, built settlements along the river and on the rims, farming corn, beans, squash, and cotton in the Unkar Delta and the Colorado River's side canyons by AD 1100. The ruins of these early canyon settlers can still be seen today on both rims and inside the canyon.

In September of AD 1540, a few Hopi guides took Spanish explorer **Garcia Lopez Cardenas** and his men to the South Rim of Grand Canyon. According to canyon historians, the party first viewed the canyon somewhere between Moran Point and Desert View. Three of these Spanish adventurers, all of whom had come north from Mexico with the Coronado Expedition on an eventually disappointing search for fabled riches, attempted to descend into the canyon, but none could make it. Cardenas and other explorers after him for centuries declared the gorge worthless and an impassable barrier to the region's settlement and exploitation. And so the canyon country was largely left alone while the Spanish transformed the native cultures throughout the Southwest, introducing the horse, the sheep, and new technologies that significantly altered the tribes' ancient lifeways.

While other Spanish explorers, mountain men, and wanderers came through the region from time to time, it wasn't until the mid-19th century that explorations and surveys of the canyon country commenced in earnest. The **Ives Expedition of 1857-1858** entered the western Grand Canyon with F. W. Von Egloffstein and H. B. Mollhausen, the first artists to sketch the canyon. The famous one-armed Civil War veteran **John Wesley Powell** explored the Colorado River through Grand Canyon on two expeditions in 1869-1872, and the **1871 Wheeler Expedition** took along **Timothy O'Sullivan,** who became the first man to photograph Grand Canyon. In 1875, the geologist **Clarence Edward Dutton** explored Grand Canyon and named what he saw after Shiva, Zoroaster, and other figures that reflected his deep interest in Eastern religions.

The Native Americans living in the Grand Canyon region during this era of exploration typically did not fare well after contact. In an area so lacking in basic resources, confrontations over springs, arable land, hunting rights, and mining claims were inevitable, and these confrontations often turned deadly, sowing hatred and distrust in each new generation, feeding a cycle of violence. Eventually the federal government confined many of the tribes to reservations that included only a fraction of their ancestral lands, with some members attempting to live according to the old ways but many more being forced into assimilation and exploited by the invading culture.

By the late 19th century South Rim miners and pioneers such as **John Hance, Ralph Cameron,** and **William "Buckey" O'Neill** were discovering that outfitting and guiding tourists was a lot less difficult and much more profitable than the hard-rock mining speculations that had brought them to the rim.

O'Neill came to Arizona in 1879 at the age of 19 and was a miner, journalist, judge, mayor of nearby Prescott, and presidential candidate. But perhaps his greatest contribution to northern Arizona was selling his canyon mining claims and in doing so helping to bring the **Santa Fe Railroad** to the rim in 1901, allowing the general middle-class public access to the great wonder for the first time.

Cameron was also an early canyon miner and entrepreneur—and eventually a U.S. senator who helped Arizona win statehood. He developed the Grandview and Bright Angel Trails and, after the railroad came to the rim, constructed a two-room hotel where Bright Angel Lodge now stands from the remains of his obsolete stagecoach station. He later fought for decades to control the Bright Angel Trail and Indian Garden with a $1 per-person toll and a string of questionable mining claims. Cameron eventually lost the fight and the National Park Service took over the trail in 1928.

The **El Tovar** hotel opened in 1905 with "electric lights powered by a steam generator" and high-class service provided by the famous **Fred Harvey Company.** By the late 1800s Harvey had an exclusive contract with the Santa Fe Railroad to manage all the eateries and Harvey Houses west of Missouri. The company had high standards and supplied each location with fresh, locally grown food and impeccable, stylish service. While Harvey died of cancer at the age of 65 in 1901, not living to see Grand Canyon come under his company's great influence, the South Rim hotel was the culmination of all the Harvey company stood for.

After decades of debate, advocacy, and increasing levels of protection, President

Woodrow Wilson signed the bill creating **Grand Canyon National Park** in 1919. The Harvey Company and the Santa Fe Railroad remained and hired Southwestern architect **Mary Jane Colter** to design and build many of the enchanting and unique buildings that still stand today and are seen by millions of visitors every year.

People and Culture

Many of Arizona's Native American nations have an ancient cultural and spiritual attachment to the Grand Canyon and the rimlands beyond it. To the Hopi, Navajo, Kaibab Paiute, and others, the canyon is much more than a beautiful, heart-stopping view. It is the place where their stories begin, where their seeds first sprouted—their ultimate homeland and their sacred space in the world.

HOPI

The **Hopi** people have deep ties to Grand Canyon, believing that their distant ancestors ascended into this world through a Sipapu, or navel, located inside the canyon near the confluence of the Colorado River and Little Colorado River. Though they have changed and adapted somewhat over time, in the way of all human cultures, the Hopi are known for their retention and protection of the ancient lessons of the people that came before.

A visit to the **Hopi Mesas** some 70 miles (113 km) east of Grand Canyon National Park is in part a trip back in time. Some of the oldest villages near the mesa edges are said to be around 1,000 years old, and you can still see small plots of drought-adapted crops growing along the roads, and ancient ladders sticking out of underground ceremonial kivas. And for all those centuries the Hopi have seen the canyon as a sacred place, and have found within it the raw materials for their ritual and artistic endeavors.

The Hopi encountered Spanish conquistadores in the 16th century. The Spanish brought priests with them into the region, and later missionaries made the journey into this vast area, intent on converting the native peoples to Spanish Catholicism. Their methods were often cruel and destructive, and most Pueblo people, including the Hopi, largely resisted conversion and fought to save their ancient cultures. These conflicts culminated in the great Pueblo Revolt of 1680, a coordinated, surprise attack throughout the region that beat the Spanish back south for generations. One Hopi village, Awatovi, allowed the Spanish to return and reestablish a mission. In 1700, the other Hopi villages, intent on preserving their traditional culture, attacked Awatovi with overwhelming force and burned it to the ground, ensuring that missionaries did not return to the mesas for some 200 years.

Throughout the late 19th and 20th centuries the Hopi drew many ethnologists, artists, photographers, and writers to canyon country, attracted by the tribe's seemingly peaceful and creative modes of life so far away from the increasingly demoralizing patterns of industrialization and modernity. Romantic scenes from the Hopi Mesas figure in a large number of the professional paintings and photographs made in the canyonlands during this period. Eventually the tribe banned photography and even sketching on the mesas, though they still allowed respectful tourists and visitors to watch some of their unique and colorful ritual dances.

In recent years the Hopi have been encouraging more tourists to visit the mesas, though you still can't take photographs or make a sketch there. Through the Moenkopi Legacy Inn at the off-mesa Hopi settlement of **Moenkopi,** near Tuba City, the tribe now offers a wide range of guided tours of the mesas, and encourages tourists to drive the **Hopi Arts Trail,** a collection of shops and galleries across all three mesas where you can buy one-of-a-kind works of art—kachina dolls, jewelry, pottery, textiles, and more—straight from the artists themselves.

NAVAJO

The **Navajo** people, also known as the **Diné** (the name the Navajo give to themselves, meaning "The People"), are the largest and most populous Native American nation. They migrated from Canada to the Colorado Plateau about a century before the Spanish arrived from the south, and lived a semino-madic life of hunting, gathering, and raiding that sometimes had them at odds with their neighbors, who were sedentary, pueblo-dwelling farmers.

After contact with the Spanish and the Pueblos, the Diné also became pastoralists and farmers, one of many occasions when these resilient people borrowed from another culture to expand their own. As the anthropologist Edward T. Hall explains: "In their natural state all people are highly adaptable, but the Navajos seem to be the most adaptable people on earth—not simply in adapting to new technologies . . . but in their ability to live with, even absorb into their society, people who are different."

The Navajo Nation's modern story is largely one of survival in the face of government antagonism and neglect. In 1863, Col. Kit Carson was sent in to exert government control over the Navajo, loosing a brutal campaign to round up what remained of the tribe and forcibly march them some 300 miles (485 km) toward isolation and death at Fort Sumner, New Mexico Territory. This event, called the **Long Walk,** remains an indelible scar on the collective heart of the Diné, a before-and-after dividing line in the Navajo Nation's modern history. About 8,000 Navajo were interned at Fort Sumner. Four years later, when the tribe returned to Navajoland, some 5,000 remained.

After years of extreme privation, the Diné eventually returned to their adaptive ways, becoming very successful pastoralists, weavers, and artists. They were aided by the Anglo traders who found worldwide markets for high-quality Navajo crafts and brought modern goods to the remote reservation. The Diné have thrived and grown and now number 298,000 (about 180,000 of whom live on the reservation).

KAIBAB PAIUTE

A tribe with strong ties to Grand Canyon's North Rim, the **Kaibab Paiute** are part of the larger Southern Paiute Nation that once hunted and gathered over traditional lands north and west of the Colorado River from Utah through Nevada and all the way to California.

Arriving in the canyonlands from the north around AD 1250-1300, the Kaibab Paiute for centuries ranged across the Kaibab Plateau, the Arizona Strip, and southern Utah, living around the region's few perennial water sources such as Pipe Spring. In the 1860s, Latter-day Saints from Utah moved into the area and diverted all the springs, severely disrupting the Paiute way of life and displacing them from their land. By the late 1800s and early 1900s, the Southern Paiute were largely confined to reservations, with the Kaibab Paiute Indian Reservation (with only about 240 members today) on the Arizona Strip, and others established in southern Utah and to the east near Navajoland.

The **Pipe Spring National Monument** is located within the borders of the Kaibab Paiute Indian Reservation, and the nation operates the visitors center jointly with the National Park Service. An excellent museum inside the visitors center explores the history of the Kaibab Paiute and the Mormon settlers.

HAVASUPAI

The **Havasupai** people have been living in Grand Canyon for at least 800 years, tending small irrigated fields of corn, melons, beans, and squash and small orchards of peach, apple, and apricot trees. For centuries the Havasupai farmed in **Havasu Canyon** and other spring-fed areas of Grand Canyon—**Indian Garden** along the Bright Angel Trail

The Emergence of the Zuni People

Though they live far from Grand Canyon in the western badlands of **New Mexico,** the **Zuni** people believe that their ancestors emerged into this world inside Grand Canyon at a place called *Chimik'yama'kya dey'a,* and tribe members still make pilgrimages there. Today this sacred spot along Bright Angel Creek is called **Ribbon Falls,** and it's a popular detour off the North Kaibab Trail to the Colorado River.

From this place of emergence, the Zuni's ancestors migrated eastward, following Bright Angel Creek down to the Colorado River, then the great river east through the canyon to its confluence with the Little Colorado River, whose headwaters are located at Zuni Pueblo.

and **Santa Maria Spring** along the Hermit Trail—in the summer and then hunted and gathered on the rim during the winter. These ancient patterns were disrupted by the settling of northern Arizona in the late 19th century.

Like the other Pai bands in and around Grand Canyon, the Havasupai were confined in 1882 to an inadequately small reservation, theirs being the only one actually inside the canyon itself. After years of advocacy the reservation was expanded in 1975, and the tribe members were allowed to move seasonally to the rims to hunt and gather as they had done for centuries. Later, the modern world overtook the Havasupai as it has almost every other Indigenous culture, and today the tribe's fortunes are tied to global tourism. Every year some 25,000 visitors from around the world—just a small fraction of the numbers that really wanted to go but could not secure a reservation fast enough—hike, ride a horse, or descend in a helicopter to **Supai,** the tribe's inner-canyon hometown and the gateway to Havasu Canyon's famous blue-green **waterfalls.**

HUALAPAI

Closely related to the Havasupai, the **Hualapai** ("people of the tall pines") came to the canyonlands around AD 1200-1300, but before the 1860s the tribe itself did not exist. It was the federal government's idea to group together 13 autonomous bands of Yuman-speaking Pai Indians living on the high, dry plains in Grand Canyon's western reaches.

The U.S. Army nearly wiped out the bands during the land wars of the 1860s, and the internment of the survivors almost finished the job. But the bands persisted, and in 1883 the government established the million-acre Hualapai Reservation, with its capital at **Peach Springs.** Then the government spent the next 100 years or so trying to take the reservation away from them for the benefit of white ranchers, the railroad, and the National Park Service.

These days the Hualapai Nation, though still impoverished, have successfully launched a worldwide brand—**Grand Canyon West.** The tribe partnered with Las Vegas entrepreneur David Jin in the early 2000s and built **The Skywalk,** a 70-foot-long (21-m) glass walkway hanging from the Grand Canyon's western rim, transforming the once empty and lonely corner of Grand Canyon into a thriving tourist enterprise focused on tours from Las Vegas.

Essentials

Getting There

Though neither is too close to the mainstream of American life, northern Arizona and the Colorado Plateau have long been popular destinations for explorers, scientists, settlers, artists, and tourists. This is the great Southwest, the iconic landscape of so many cowboy films and road-trip movies, of all those tall tales and all that legendary history which often turns out to be true—you need your own ride and an easygoing spirit to really do this right. Out here there are often long and empty distances between towns and stations, and help could be a long time coming

Coronavirus and Grand Canyon

At the time of writing in fall 2020, the coronavirus pandemic had significantly impacted the United States, including Grand Canyon and other areas covered in this guide. Most, if not all, destinations required that face masks be worn in enclosed spaces, but the situation was constantly evolving.

Now more than ever, Moon encourages its readers to be courteous and ethical in their travel. We ask travelers to be respectful to residents and mindful of the evolving situation in their chosen destination when planning their trip.

BEFORE YOU GO

- Check local websites (listed below) for updated **local restrictions** and the **overall health status** of destinations in this area.

- If you plan to fly, check with your airline as well as the **Centers for Disease Control and Prevention** (www.cdc.gov) for updated **recommendations** and **requirements.**

- Check the website of any museums and other venues you wish to patronize to confirm that they're open, if their hours have been adjusted, and to learn about any specific visitation requirements, such as **mandatory reservations** or **limited occupancy.**

- Pack **hand sanitizer,** a **thermometer,** and plenty of **face masks.** Consider packing **snacks, bottled water,** or even a **cooler** to limit the number of stops along your route.

- **Assess the risk** of entering crowded spaces, joining tours, and taking public transit.

- Expect **general disruptions.** Some park entrances and roads may be closed. Events may be postponed or cancelled. Some tours and venues may require reservations, enforce limits on the number of guests, be operating during different hours than the ones listed, or be closed entirely.

RESOURCES

- **National Park Service:** Grand Canyon National Park (www.nps.gov/grca), Glen Canyon National Recreation Area (www.nps.gov/glca)

- **U.S. Forest Service:** Southwestern Region (www.fs.usda.gov/r3)

- **State of Arizona:** Arizona Department of Health Services (www.azdhs.gov)

- **Native American Nations:** Havasupai (http://theofficialhavasupaitribe.com), Hopi (www.hopi-nsn.gov), Hualapai (http://hualapai-nsn.gov), Kaibab Paiute (www.kaibabpaiute-nsn.gov), Navajo (www.navajo-nsn.gov)

the farther you stray from the Grand Canyon National Park's South Rim section.

Many travelers fly into Sky Harbor International Airport in Phoenix and then rent a car for the 225-mile (360-km) drive north to the South Rim and environs, which takes about four hours. Many other canyon tourists drive or take bus tours to the South Rim from Las Vegas, Nevada (280 mi/450 km, 5-hour drive), and from Los Angeles, California (494 mi/795 km, 7.5-hour drive).

SUGGESTED ROUTES

Most Grand Canyon National Park visitors reach the **South Rim** from either **Flagstaff** or **Williams** and enter the park through

Previous: biking into Grand Canyon National Park on the Tusayan Greenway.

the **South Entrance.** It's the park's busiest entrance by far; during the summer there's likely to be a long line at the South Entrance, especially on weekends and holidays. (A smart way to skip these lines is to leave your car at the IMAX theater in Tusayan, purchase a pass there, and then hop on the free shuttle bus into the park.) From the South Entrance you're just minutes away from prime parking spots, the Grand Canyon Visitor Center, and Grand Canyon Village.

Reached by taking U.S. 89 north from **Flagstaff** to Cameron and then heading west on AZ 64, the **East Entrance** receives much less traffic. The eastern route enters the park at the **Desert View** section, about an hour's scenic drive from Grand Canyon Village and the main visitor center.

South Entrance (South Rim)
FROM WILLIAMS
Just off I-40, **Williams** bills itself as the gateway to Grand Canyon. It has carried this distinction since the early 1900s, when the Santa Fe Railroad built a spur and a Harvey House here, opening a new era in Grand Canyon tourism. It's still a great place to base your canyon visit, and it's worth a short stop to stroll around the historic downtown. If you're not stopping, avoid driving through the town by taking Exit 165 off I-40 to AZ 64. Once you're on AZ 64, just keep going straight and in about an hour (60 mi/97 km) you'll be saying hello to a friendly ranger at the park's **South Entrance.** AZ 64 traverses a bunchgrass flatland after leaving the piney forests around Williams—a dry and open landscape with a string of wildcat mobile homes. It's not exactly scenic, especially compared with what's to come. Near Tusayan (a small settlement of hotels and restaurants just outside the park gates), a pinyon-juniper woodland ranging into tall, thin ponderosa pines passes by outside the window. Watch out in this area for elk and other wildlife.

FROM FLAGSTAFF
From downtown **Flagstaff** take North Humphreys Street to U.S. 180 and turn left at the junction (follow signs to Grand Canyon National Park). The road skirts the base of the San Francisco Peaks and moves across the open cinder lands, popping with yellow wildflowers in the spring, and through a beautiful highland pine forest peppered with those beloved stands of northern Arizona aspens. About 50 miles (81 km) on, U.S. 180 meets AZ 64 at **Valle,** a small settlement with a travel center-style gas station. Turn right onto AZ 64 for about 30 miles (48 km) to the park gates, passing through Tusayan along the way. The entire drive from Flagstaff to the park gate is about 80 miles (129 km) and typically takes about 1.5 hours.

East Entrance (South Rim)
FROM FLAGSTAFF
To reach the **East Entrance** from **Flagstaff,** take U.S. 89 north for an hour (46 mi/74 km) to **Cameron,** on the Navajo Reservation. At Cameron head west on AZ 64 for about another hour (30 mi/48 km) to Grand Canyon National Park's **East Entrance,** near the park's Desert View section. It's another hour or so on AZ 64/Desert View Drive to Grand Canyon Visitor Center and Grand Canyon Village.

FROM PAGE
To reach the South Rim from **Glen Canyon National Recreation Area** and **Page,** take U.S. 89 south to **Cameron,** then head west on AZ 64 to the East Entrance. The drive from Page to the East Entrance is 110 miles (177 km) and takes about 2.5 hours.

North Rim Entrance
While few visitors to Grand Canyon National Park make the long trip to the remote and magical North Rim, those who do are rewarded with the Kaibab Plateau's uncommon high-country grandeur and evergreen beauty. The northside park has only one

entrance, one small booth among the Douglas fir and ponderosa pine near the end of AZ 67, a 45-mile (72-km) two-lane highway that ends where Grand Canyon begins. AZ 67 is the only road into and out of the park's North Rim section, and heavy snows close it every year from December 1 to May 15, limiting visitation here to a few short but intensely lived seasons.

FROM THE SOUTH RIM

The 215-mile (345-km) drive to the North Rim from Grand Canyon National Park's **South Rim** leaves the park through the East Entrance at Desert View and cuts through the far western edge of the **Navajo Reservation** on U.S. 89 from Cameron to Bitter Springs, a haunting territory of crumbling sandstone ridges and wide, dry flatlands. The highway splits near the Colorado River: U.S. 89 continues north to **Glen Canyon National Recreation Area, Lake Powell,** and Utah, while U.S. 89A crosses the river at **Marble Canyon** over Navajo Bridge, and then skirts the towering Vermilion Cliffs heading west across the wild Arizona Strip. Climbing high onto the forested Kaibab Plateau, U.S. 89A continues on to Fredonia, and then meets back with U.S. 89 at Kanab, Utah, not far from Zion National Park. For the North Rim-bound, U.S. 89A ends on the plateau at Jacob Lake, not a town so much as a motel, restaurant, gas station, and campground scattered through the forest at the AZ 67 junction. The North Rim falls away about 45 miles (72 km) south of here at the end of AZ 67, just beyond the back deck of Grand Canyon Lodge. The entire drive typically takes about 4.5 hours.

FROM FLAGSTAFF

The journey from **Flagstaff** to the North Rim is nearly the same as that from the park's South Rim, except that you pick up U.S. 89 on Flagstaff's east side rather than at Cameron, about an hour (53 mi/85 km) north of Flagstaff. Expect the 210-mile (340-km) drive to take about 4-4.5 hours.

FROM PAGE

There are two routes to the North Rim from **Page:** For the **Arizona route,** take U.S. 89 south to Bitter Springs, head west on U.S. 89A to Jacob Lake, and then south on AZ 67 to the rim; the drive is 123 miles (198 km) and takes about 2.5 hours. For the **Utah route,** take U.S. 89 to Kanab, Utah, and then head south on U.S. 89A and AZ 67 to the rim; the drive is 153 miles (246 km) and takes closer to 3 hours.

FROM KANAB

The North Rim is about 80 miles (129 km) south of **Kanab** via U.S. 89A and AZ 67; the drive takes about 1.5 hours.

FROM PHOENIX

Phoenix rises all glass and asphalt from an unbearably hot Sonoran Desert dry-river valley about 225 miles (360 km) south of Grand Canyon. Simmering across this sprawling metroland called the Valley of the Sun, Phoenix and its sister cities—Scottsdale, Tempe, Mesa, Glendale, etc.—have both obvious and hidden pleasures, but for many Grand Canyon tourists it is a large airport, a maze of freeways, and a hectic start to a four-hour drive in a rental car. Fortunately Phoenix lends itself equally to lingering for a few days, especially in the spring or fall, or to getting out of town and into the piney northland as quickly as possible. To do the latter, just get on I-10 West at Sky Harbor and then take I-17 North out of the city, into the desert, and on to the canyonlands.

Car

Car travel is the ideal way to visit northern Arizona and the canyonlands, a landscape created for the road trip if there ever was one. Most of the roads to, from, and around Grand Canyon National Park's South and North Rims can be traversed and negotiated in a regular sedan or compact rental car. An SUV is preferable if you're planning to do a lot of backcountry driving to remote trailheads. If you have an electric car, there are recharge stations at Grand Canyon National Park's

South Rim and on the Hopi Reservation at Moenkopi, near Tuba City.

There are two routes from Phoenix to Grand Canyon National Park's South Rim, one that goes through Williams and one that goes through Flagstaff. The **Flagstaff route** is recommended for its vastly superior scenery, offering a chance to see the towering San Francisco Peaks, Arizona's highest range, and to drive through Flagstaff, a fun, interesting town with excellent museums and national monuments dedicated to the natural and human history of the Colorado Plateau. Take I-17 out of Phoenix, across the desert, down through the Verde Valley, and up into the high country for 144 miles (232 km), a drive of about 2.5 hours. After reaching Flagstaff, take U.S. 180 across the volcanolands at the base of the San Francisco Peaks to AZ 64 at Valle, and then turn north for the final stretch to the park's South Entrance. The total trip from Phoenix is about 225 miles (360 km) long and takes about four hours. About 10 miles (16.1 km) longer and less scenic, the **Williams route** takes I-17 from the valley to I-40 West to AZ 64. It's 60 miles (97 km), about a one-hour drive, from Williams to Grand Canyon—a total trip of 235 miles (380 km) from Phoenix to the South Rim.

The drive north on I-17 from the Valley of the Sun to Grand Canyon ascends from a saguaro-filled desert to the tall pines and aspens at the base of the San Francisco Peaks in a matter of a few hours—it's truly astounding how completely the landscape changes as you climb, a constant display of Arizona's great natural diversity. The interstate route, then, is scenic enough, but if you're up for a bit of a longer drive, take the off-interstate route through **Sedona** and **Oak Creek Canyon** to Flagstaff. About 1.5 hours (100 mi/161 km) north of the valley on I-17, take Oak Creek/Sedona Exit 298 to AZ 179. This scenic highway passes some of Sedona's most famous red rocks and has several pullouts and parking lots near hiking and biking trails. Pick up AZ 89A and move through uptown Sedona and into Oak Creek Canyon, twisting up through the lush riparian canyon onto the Colorado Plateau to Flagstaff. While the drive from Sedona to Flagstaff through Oak Creek Canyon is only about 30 miles (48 km), expect it to take about an hour, and that's only if you aren't tempted to stop along the green and shady way.

Air

If you're flying into Arizona from anywhere in the known world, you'll likely find yourself at **Phoenix Sky Harbor International Airport** (PHX, 3400 E. Sky Harbor Blvd., 602/273-3300, www.skyharbor.com). One of the Southwest's largest airports, Sky Harbor has two terminals served by many domestic and international airlines—United, American, Air Canada, British Airways, Delta, Frontier, Southwest, JetBlue, and more. The airport is just 3 miles (4.8 km) east of downtown Phoenix and easy to reach off the freeway. There's a free shuttle system, PHX Sky Train, that moves between the two terminals (3 and 4—there is no Terminal 2; it was closed due to its age in 2019). A recent remodel of the airport put new emphasis on opening locally owned shops and restaurants in the terminals, including a boutique featuring work by local artists and "express" locations of favorite valley restaurants and breweries.

Train

The **Amtrak** *Sunset Limited* (800/872-7245, www.amtrak.com), which runs along the southern route through the desert Southwest three times a week from New Orleans, stops in Maricopa, Arizona, a small town about 30 miles (48 km) east of Phoenix. Transportation options from Maricopa to Phoenix are tough to come by and expensive. The better Amtrak train to take is the northern route that stops at Flagstaff.

Bus and Shuttles

Phoenix's **Greyhound bus station** (2115 E. Buckeye Rd., 602/389-4200, www.greyhound.com) is located near Sky Harbor International Airport.

Valley of the Sun Essentials

Phoenix and the Valley of the Sun have a lot to offer the tourist, whether you're just passing through on your way from the airport to Grand Canyon National Park, or plan to stay in the desert for a few days on either end of your canyonland adventure. For dining, nightlife, and culture, check out downtown Phoenix (especially the artsy Roosevelt Row neighborhood). Tempe's fun vibe really comes out around Mill Avenue and Arizona State University, and Scottsdale has a world-famous upscale scene with resorts, fashionable nightclubs, and Southwestern art galleries. Beyond the urban areas, there are vast desert preserves with hiking and biking trails. If you're lucky enough to be in the valley in March, take in an MLB Spring Training game, or go see the Arizona Diamondbacks play one of their National League rivals from April to September.

If you only have time to take in one sight, make a stop at the Heard Museum (2301 N. Central Ave., 602/252-8848, www.heard.org, 9:30am-5pm Mon.-Sat., 11am-5pm Sun., $18 adults, $7.50 children 6-12) in downtown Phoenix before heading north to Grand Canyon National Park. The museum has 10 galleries featuring the art, artifacts, and historical narratives of each of the state's tribes. The large display on the Hopi is particularly comprehensive and includes the late U.S. Senator Barry Goldwater's collection of Hopi kachinas.

If you're willing to sacrifice just a bit more time, take a tour of legendary architect Frank Lloyd Wright's winter headquarters in north Scottsdale. Taliesin West (12621 Frank Lloyd Wright Blvd., 480/860-2700, recorded tour info 480/860-8810, www.franklloydwright.org, 9am-4pm daily). Familiar Wright motifs, like his ubiquitous compression-and-release entranceways, Asian-inspired touches, and native-rock-and-mortar aesthetic are on display at this truly unique and important attraction. There are several tours to choose from, including an in-depth, three-hour, behind-the-scenes look around ($75). The most popular tour is the 90-minute Insights Tour (8:45am-4pm daily, every half hour Nov.-Apr., every hour May-Oct., $36 adults, $17 children 12 and under), which includes a look at the beautiful Garden Room and the living quarters as well as all the sights included in the one-hour Panorama Tour (10:15am and 2:15pm daily, $28 adults, $10 children 12 and under).

Groome Transportation aka Arizona Shuttle (928/350-8466, https://groometransportation.com) offers several daily round-trip shuttles between Phoenix's Sky Harbor Airport and Flagstaff's Amtrak depot ($48 pp one-way). Groome also offers shuttles between Flagstaff and Grand Canyon National Park (Mar.-Oct., $60 round-trip for adults).

Tours

If you're looking for the assistance of an expert, you can hire Open Road Tours (602/997-6474, www.openroadtoursusa.com) to guide and shuttle you in comfort all over the state. Such tours are only recommended for those who enjoy groups. Grand Canyon National Park is well established and easy to negotiate—a tour guide is not necessary, and rangers are always on hand to answer questions and give free, informative tours.

Car Rental

It is easy to rent a car at Phoenix's Sky Harbor airport, but the exorbitant airport taxes and fees make doing so a bad idea; you'll get price shock that will ruin your trip in advance. That said, Sky Harbor provides a free rental car shuttle from the baggage claim at each terminal to the Rental Car Center (1805 E. Sky Harbor Circle S., 602/683-3741), just west of the airport. All the major rental companies are represented at the center, including Hertz (602/267-8822 or 800/654-3131, www.hertz.com) and Budget (800/527-7000, www.budget.com).

It's better to head outside the airport to rent a car. Try the locally owned Phoenix Car Rental (2934 E. McDowell Rd., 602/269-9310, and 3625 W. Indian School Rd., 602/269-9310, www.rentacarphoenix.com). The McDowell Road site is about 7 miles (11.3 km) from the airport. Take Sky Harbor Boulevard east to Priest, then get on the 202 Loop to Exit 1C or 32nd Street, then turn left on McDowell. You can also arrange for them to pick you up.

RV Rental

This is definitely RV country, and you'll be in good company if you decide to rent your own house-on-wheels. Expect to pay about $175-275 per day for large RVs and $150-200 for smaller rigs. Many of the RVers out on these roads rent from **Cruise America** (800/671-8042, www.cruiseamerica.com)—you'll see their trademark on about every third rig you pass. The **RV Rental Outlet** (2126 W. Main St., Mesa, 480/461-0023, 480/461-0025, or 888/461-0023, www.rvrentaloutlet.com) in Mesa has a wide range of RVs for rent, including campervan-style and other smaller, sleeker rigs. Expect to pay about $200-250 per day.

Equipment Rental

Lower Gear Outdoors (2155 E. University Dr., Ste. 112, Tempe, 480/348-8917, www. lowergear.com, 9am-6pm Mon.-Fri., 10am-4pm Sat., noon-4pm Sun.), a longtime valley outfitter, rents a huge range of outdoor camping and adventuring gear—tents, backpacks, sleeping bags, stoves, etc. You can order your gear online, with their help if you need it, and then they'll ship it to you before you travel or to an address in Arizona, including Grand Canyon National Park. You can also pick up your order at their Tempe shop on your way from the airport to the canyon.

Food and Accommodations

If you're staying a few days and nights in the Valley the Sun, there's certainly no shortage of things to do and places to eat and stay. The sprawling cityscape is alive with new restaurants and bars as well as local favorites that have served generations. To narrow down your options, check the dining and entertainment sections of the *Arizona Republic* and the *Phoenix New Times,* or try one the following local gems:

- **Pizzeria Bianco** (623 E. Adams St. at Heritage Square, 602/258-8300, www. pizzeriabianco.com, 11am-9pm Mon.-Thurs., 11am-10pm Fri.-Sat., $9-16)

- **Loving Hut** (3239 E. Indian School Rd., 602/264-3480, www.lovinghut.us, 11am-2:30pm and 5pm-9pm Tues.-Sat., 4pm-8pm Sun., $6-10)

- **Four Peaks Brewing Company** (1340 E. 8th St., Tempe, 480/303-9967, www. fourpeaks.com, 11am-2am Mon.-Sat., 10am-2am Sun., $10-15)

- **Windsor** (5223 N. Central Ave., 602/279-1111, http://windsoraz.com, 11am-11pm Mon.-Thurs., 11am-2am Fri., 9am-midnight Sat., 9am-10pm Sun., $12.50-20)

- **Maricopa Manor** (15 W. Pasadena Ave., 602/264-9200, www.maricopamanor.com, $239)

- **Arizona Biltmore** (2400 E. Missouri Ave., 602/955-6600, www.arizonabiltmore.com, $400-450)

- **Arizona Grand Resort** (8000 S. Arizona Grand Pkwy., 602/438-9000, www. arizonagrandresort.com, $229-300)

FROM LAS VEGAS
Car

The drive from **Las Vegas** to the South Rim (280 mi/450 km) is roughly five hours. Even if you get a late-morning start and make a few stops along the way, you're still likely to arrive at the park by dinnertime. Take U.S. 93 from Las Vegas to Kingman, then take I-40 to reach Williams or Flagstaff and head north to the park. The speed limit on most sections of I-40 in Arizona is 75 mph, so all that highland forest scenery flashes by unless you stop a few times to take it in. Most summer weekends you'll find the route crowded but manageable. At all times of the year you'll be surrounded by 18-wheelers barreling across the land. If you feel like stopping overnight, do so in Williams. It's just an hour or so from the park's South Entrance, has a bit of Route 66 charm, and offers several distinctive and memorable hotels and restaurants.

Air

McCarran International Airport (LAS, 5757 Wayne Newton Blvd., 702/261-5211, www.mccarran.com) is the primary airport for Las Vegas and the surrounding area. Served by most major airlines—including Delta, American Airlines, and United—the airport has three unconnected terminals and a tramway. Several helicopter and plane air-tour companies operate out of **North Las Vegas Airport** (2730 Airport Dr., North Las Vegas, http://vgt.aero).

Train

There is no **Amtrak** (www.amtrak.com) train stop in Las Vegas. You can take a shuttle from McCarran Airport to Kingman, Arizona, about 107 miles (172 km) east, catch the train there to the Flagstaff Amtrak depot, and then take another shuttle to the South Rim.

Bus and Shuttles

The **Las Vegas Greyhound** station (200 S. Main St., 702/384-9561 or 800/231-2222, www.greyhound.com) is always open. **SuperShuttle** (800/258-3826, www.supershuttle.com) and **Airline Shuttle Corp.** (702/444-1234, www.airlineshuttlecorp.com) pick up at the airport.

Tours

All of the Grand Canyon air tours originating in Las Vegas concentrate on the West Rim, far from the confines of Grand Canyon National Park. **Grand Canyon Helicopters** (855/326-9617, www.grandcanyonhelicopter.com) offers many tours of the canyon that start in Las Vegas, including one that lands in the western canyon for a champagne toast (3.5-4 hours, $519). **Papillon Helicopters** (888/635-7272, www.papillon.com), a popular South Rim tour company, also flies out of Vegas to the western

rim, as does **Grand Canyon Scenic Airlines** (928/638-2359, www.grandcanyonairlines.com), which gives flights from Las Vegas over the western canyon in its small and "ultra-quiet" De Havilland Twin Otter Vistaliner and Cessna Caravan planes.

Grayline (877/333-6556, https://graylinelasvegas.com) offers 12- and 14-hour motorcoach tours to the South Rim from Las Vegas ($180-240), as well as tours of the West Rim and Skywalk ($266 pp).

Car Rental

McCarran Rent-A-Center (7135 Gilespi St.) is open all day every day and is connected to the airport via shuttles that take renters back and forth to the lot about 3 miles (4.8 km) away. The center has 11 major car rental desks.

RV Rental

Las Vegas is one of only three places in the United States that you can rent a campervan, or mini RV, from **Jucy Rentals** (800/650-4180, www.jucyusa.com)—the others are L.A. and San Francisco. These sleek rigs are easier to drive than a motorhome but still have small kitchens, tables, beds, and other amenities. Expect to pay about $45-110 per day. For more traditional rolling mansions, check out **Cruise America** (800/671-8042, www.cruiseamerica.com) and plan on spending about $175-275 per day for large RVs and $150-200 for smaller ones.

Equipment Rental

The warehouse for **Basecamp Outdoor Gear Rental** (2595 Chandler Ave., 702/637-2456, www.basecampoutdoorgear.com, $50-300) is only about a mile (1.6 km) from McCarran Airport. Choose your gear online—including from several convenient all-in-one packages for backpacking and camping—and then pick it up before heading east across the desert to Grand Canyon and environs.

Food and Accommodations

Las Vegas has its guilt-ridden charms and

overheated mists of low-end fantasy, yes; compared to Grand Canyon, however, its attractions are ephemeral and soon forgotten, often willfully. Sometimes it's best to leave town directly from the airport. But staying a few days in Sin City is an option as well, and perhaps after its debaucheries the wonders of nature will seem all the more meaningful and lasting. If you just need to flop for the night before heading out, try one of the chains near the airport. Otherwise, don't miss the spectacle of the Strip if it's your first time in Vegas. Below are a few quick suggestions on places to eat and stay.

- **The Egg & I** (4533 W. Sahara Ave., Ste. 5, 702/364-9686, https://theeggworks.com, 6am-3pm daily, $10-20)

- **Bacchanal Buffet** at Caesar's Palace (3570 Las Vegas Blvd. S., 702/731-7928, www. caesars.com, 7:30am-10pm Mon.-Fri., 8am-10pm Sat.-Sun., $30-60)

- **Libertine Social** at Mandalay Bay (3950 Las Vegas Blvd. S., 702/632-7558, www. mandalaybay.com, 5pm-10:30pm daily, $35-55)

- **Stratosphere Casino, Hotel, and Tower** (2000 Las Vegas Blvd. S., 702/380-7777, www.stratospherehotel.com, $103-146)

- **The Palazzo** (3325 Las Vegas Blvd. S., 702/607-777 or 866/263-3001, www. palazzo.com, $239-349)

- **Paris Las Vegas** (3655 Las Vegas Blvd. S., 877/242-6753, www.caesars.com/paris-las-vegas.com, $149-276)

Getting Around

DRIVING

Driving to, around, and inside Grand Canyon National Park's busy **South Rim** section can be challenging, especially in the summer when the park is at its busiest. Some six million visitors come here every year to gawk at the gorge and take in the high-country sunshine, and most of them travel in cars. During the high season most of the parking lots near Grand Canyon Visitor Center and in Grand Canyon Village fill up by 10am. Arrive before 9am or after 4pm to secure the best parking spots.

Driving from sight to sight in your own vehicle is not the ideal way to visit the park. This strategy works better during the winter months when the **Hermit Road**, which leads to nine viewpoints on the western end of the park, is open to cars. From March to November, the 7-mile (11.3-km) one-way scenic road is open only to shuttle buses, bicycles, and pedestrians.

You will need your own car to travel to the park's **Desert View** section, about an hour's drive from Grand Canyon Village on

the park's eastern edge, as the shuttle buses only go as far as the Yaki Point and the South Kaibab Trailhead.

While driving in and around the park, keep a careful lookout for wildlife, especially along AZ 64 just outside the South Entrance. Inside the park, drive slowly and watch for pedestrians and bicycles.

SHUTTLES, BUSES, AND TOURS
Shuttles

Grand Canyon National Park's **South Rim** has a fleet of buses that run on natural gas. Operated by friendly and knowledgeable drivers, these shuttle buses crisscross the park all day and into the night, taking passengers to various viewpoints and sights for free. During the high season there may be long lines at the many shuttle stops throughout the park, but it is still the best strategy for getting around. The shuttle buses run every 10-30 minutes, beginning about an hour before sunrise and stopping about an hour after sunset.

You also have the option to leave your

vehicle outside the park's South Entrance in the small town of Tusayan. The shuttle's free **Tusayan Route (Purple)** runs from early spring to fall, allowing you to leave your car behind, skip the long entrance lines, and head straight for the main Grand Canyon Visitor Center without worrying about finding parking. The shuttle runs every 20 minutes and takes about 20 minutes from Tusayan to the visitors center inside the park. It stops at the IMAX Theater, the Best Western Grand Canyon Squire Inn, and the Grand Hotel, all of which have large parking lots. You must have your park entrance pass before you board the shuttle; you can buy one at various places in Tusayan. The best place to buy an entrance pass, park your car, and hop on the shuttle is at the **Grand Canyon Visitor Center and IMAX Theater** (unless you are staying at one of the hotels mentioned above). You can also buy an entrance pass at www. recreation.gov.

The **Trans-Canyon Shuttle** (928/638-2820, www.trans-canyonshuttle.com, $90 one-way, reservations required) makes a daily round-trip excursion between the North and South Rims, departing the North Rim at 7am and arriving at the South Rim at 11:30am. The shuttle then leaves the South Rim at 1:30pm and arrives back at the North Rim at 6pm. During the high season (spring and summer), the shuttle runs twice daily from the South Rim to the North Rim (8am-12:30pm and 1:30pm-6pm) and twice daily from the North Rim to the South Rim (7am-11:30am and 2pm-6:30pm).

Bus Tours

Throughout the year Xanterra, the company that runs most of the hotels and restaurants on the South Rim, offers various **motorcoach tours** (303/297-2757 or 888/297-2757, www. grandcanyonlodges.com) within the park. Options include sunrise and sunset tours and longer drives to the eastern Desert View area and the western reaches of the park at Hermit's Rest. Typically done in vans or large, comfortable buses, these tours are generally

fun and informative. The best tour offered is of the Desert View section of the park. It's the only section that's not accessible by free shuttle bus, and if you don't want to take your own vehicle to the eastern edges, it's the only way to get there.

Train Tours

Another way to make it to the South Rim without taking your car is to book passage on the **Grand Canyon Railway** (800/843-8724, www.thetrain.com). Starting from the small town of Williams, about 60 miles (97 km) from the South Rim, the train chugs across the high-country plains and through the pine forests near the rim at a fairly slow pace, allowing passengers to enjoy the scenery. After arriving at Grand Canyon Village's historic train depot, you have several hours to explore the park before boarding the train for the return trip. The train has several different cars and offers more luxurious seating at higher prices, including in a car with a full bar and one with a glass-roof observation area.

Mule Tours

Park concessionaire Xanterra's **Canyon Vistas Mule Ride** (303/297-2757 or 888/297-2757, www.grandcanyonlodges.com) along the South Rim goes year-round and includes one hour of orientation and a two-hour ride. Xanterra also offers overnight mule trips below the rim to Phantom Ranch.

On the North Rim, **Grand Canyon Trail Rides** (435/679-8665, www.canyonrides.com) offers three daily options during the high season: a one-hour trail ride through the forest and along the rim; a three-hour trail ride along the rim to Uncle Jim's Point; and a three-hour trail ride down the North Kaibab Trail to Supai Tunnel.

Horseback Tours

Outside the park, **Apache Stables** (928/638-2891, www.apachestables.com) offers one- and two-hour trail rides, an evening ride with a campfire, and an evening wagon ride with a campfire.

RV

South Rim

The South Rim's in-park RV campground, **Trailer Village** (877/404-4611, www. visitgrandcanyon.com), is about a half mile (0.8 km) from Mather Campground and right near Market Plaza. Open year-round, it has full hookups and pull-throughs for vehicles up to 50 feet (15.2 m) long. Reservations are a must during the high seasons.

In Tusayan, about 1 mile (1.6 km) from the park entrance, **Grand Canyon Camper Village** (549 Camper Village Ln., Tusayan, 928/638-2887, www. grandcanyoncampervillage.com) is open year-round for trailers, motorhomes, and tents. It has coin-op showers, laundry, and limited Wi-Fi.

In Cameron, about 30 miles (48 km) from the park's eastern Desert View entrance, **Cameron Trading Post RV Park** (466 Hwy. 89, 800/338-7385, www.camerontradingpost. com), also open year-round, has basic sites with full hookups but no bathrooms or showers.

North Rim

The only campground on the North Rim with full hookups for RVs is **Kaibab Camper Village** (928/643-7804, www. kaibabcampervillage.com, mid-May-mid-Oct.), which has pull-through and back-in spots for rigs up to 40 feet (12.2 m), chemical toilets, coin-op laundry and showers, and a store. The campground is in Jacob Lake, about 45 miles (72 km) north of the rim.

BICYCLE

It's becoming easier and easier to ride your bike into and around Grand Canyon National Park's **South Rim** section. All of the roads and greenways (narrow paved trails meant for bikes and pedestrians) within the South Rim section are open to bicycles, including the 7-mile (11.3-km) one-way **Hermit Road,** one of the best places to ride in the park as it is closed to regular car traffic for much of

the year and includes many of the best viewpoints. Bikes are not allowed on most sections of the Rim Trail, which offers the best vantages from which to see the canyon. However, there is one 2.8-mile (4.5-km) section of the Rim Trail, the **Hermit Road Greenway Trail,** that is open to bikes.

All of the South Rim's hotels, stores, restaurants, and most of the viewpoints now have bike racks, so it's easy to stop and explore. Don't forget your lock.

Experienced and fit riders should consider leaving their car outside the park and riding in to the South Rim via the **Tusayan Greenway,** a 6.5-mile (10.5-km) one-way paved route through the forest. There's a large parking lot at the trailhead, about a mile (1.6 km) south of the main park entrance.

MOTORCYCLE

Northern Arizona is motorcycle country. You'll see packs of riders everywhere, many of them on easy-rider Harleys or big-rig touring bikes with all the bells and whistles. Keep your eyes open for wildlife, especially off the interstates on the two-lane state highways and backroads.

The **best times** to ride through the region are in **late spring, early fall,** and **early summer.** Before April the northland air is generally cold, bitterly so if cruising the blacktop at 75 mph (121 km/h). In May and June expect demoralizing heat everywhere, and from July through September you may have to pull over and seek shelter every afternoon around 2pm, when the thunderstorms roll in and drench the land.

You'll find support, gear, and repair shops in most of the towns in the region, but Flagstaff is your best bet if you need service near the park's South Rim section.

A few of the best, most scenic and inspiring places to ride in the canyonlands include:

- Flagstaff to Grand Canyon National Park along U.S. 180 and AZ 64

- Desert View Drive and Hermit Road on the South Rim

- U.S. 89A from Bitter Springs across the Colorado River to the Kaibab Plateau
- AZ 67 from Jacob Lake to the North Rim
- Point Imperial Road on the North Rim
- U.S. 89 between Glen Canyon National Recreation Area and Kanab and continuing north into southern Utah
- Historic Route 66 near the West Rim
- U.S. 160 across the Navajo Reservation

Recreation

A trip to Grand Canyon is almost necessarily an active one filled with fresh air and outdoor recreation. That's not to say that you can't enjoy the canyon without hiking or biking or at least strolling along the Rim Trail; it's worth it just to sit on a bench and stare at the great sandstone maze before you. But odds are that the high-country air, temperate weather, and inviting trails will have you up and ready to explore. It's best to go to the park prepared to do some hiking, or at least a bit more walking than you would typically do in regular life. While day hiking is by far the most popular activity at the canyon, bicycling around the park is becoming increasingly popular, and backpacking into the great gorge is still the reason Grand Canyon exists for a relatively small but growing and passionate subset of park visitors.

DAY HIKING

Day hiking at Grand Canyon National Park includes everything from strolls along the flat and paved Rim Trail to all-day rim-to-rim marches. For most hikers, sticking to one of the corridor trails and under 6 miles (9.7 km) or less round-trip will ensure a memorable but safe outing that's relatively easy to accomplish. Beginning hikers and families with young children should consider a short hike of just a mile (1.6 km) or two (3.2 km) round-trip with a specific destination.

On the **South Rim,** try the 1.4-mile (2.3-km) round-trip stroll along the **Rim Trail** between **Mather Point,** near the main visitors center and parking lot, and **Yavapai Geology Museum and Observation Station,** the best place in the park to learn

about the canyon's geology. To get a sense of what the canyon is like below the rim, try the 1.8-mile (2.9-km) round-trip hike on the **South Kaibab Trail** to **Ooh Aah Point.** Day hikers looking for a longer day should try the 3-mile (4.8-km) round-trip hike to **Mile-and-a-Half Resthouse** or the 6-mile (9.7-km) round-trip hike to **Three-Mile Resthouse** on the **Bright Angel Trail.**

On the **North Rim,** beginning hikers and families with small kids should try the 0.5-mile (0.8-km) round-trip walk on a paved trail to **Bright Angel Point,** as well as the **Transept Trail** (3 mi/4.8 km round-trip) through the forest between Grand Canyon Lodge and the campground. Relatively short but steep day hikes into the canyon via the **North Kaibab Trail** include the 1.5-mile (2.4-km) round-trip jog down to **Coconino Overlook** and the 4-mile (6.4-km) round-trip hike to **Supai Tunnel.**

Rules of the Trail

Hikers going up out of the canyon have the right-of-way; step aside and let them pass if you are heading down. Mule trains along the South Kaibab and North Kaibab Trails have the right-of-way whether they are headed up or down. Step aside and let the entire group pass before entering the trail again. Never go off the trails or take shortcuts, and don't harass wildlife or take away artifacts, rocks, or items of any kind, whether natural or man-made.

Perhaps the most important rule of the trail in Grand Canyon is to take seriously the warnings that the National Park Service is ever at pains to impart via signs at trailheads and all around the park. These are simple and stark: Don't hike unprepared and don't underestimate the canyon's steep, rocky trails and desert environment. Hikers who are legendary in more familiar, less challenging country and climes could be in for a shock once they get a few miles down. And, as the Park Service often points out, just because you are young, healthy, and in prime physical shape doesn't mean you can take preparation for granted. Grand Canyon is different. Many have died after failing to learn this lesson, or after willfully ignoring it. Much of the trouble that hikers get into, it seems, is rooted in the massive public delusion that summer is the best season to hike Grand Canyon. Summer is the worst time to be a hiker below the rim. If you hike down into the canyon in the summer, you'll want to be off the trail by about 10am-11am to avoid the deadly heat's domain, and wait until the relative cool of early evening before moving on again.

What to Wear

In all seasons, it's best to take a layered approach and to emphasize comfort over the long term. Winter hiking demands a lightweight but warm coat that stuffs small into your daypack, at least two more layers including a thermal base, and flexible, warm gloves. In summer, wear a long-sleeved shirt and, preferably, long hiking-style pants that ward off ultraviolet rays and dry quickly. Wear a hat that shades your face and a bandanna that protects your neck from the sun. Your hiking shoes should be well worn and comfortably your own before starting down the trail.

What to Take

A small backpack filled with water and salty, fatty snacks is the minimum you should carry on a day hike into Grand Canyon. And while you should never overload yourself, a few other lightweight items—such as a first-aid kit, headlamp, compass, and lighter—might come in handy in an emergency. If you're not sure how much water to take on your day hike, ask a ranger for advice. A lot of hikers

in Grand Canyon use hiking poles; these are great for keeping your balance and hefting yourself up the trail, but hikers with arthritis in their hands may find them too painful to use. In winter and early spring the trails into the canyon are often icy and muddy. In icy conditions, take crampons along.

BACKPACKING

Just a small percentage of Grand Canyon visitors spend a night or two below the rim, most of them at only a few developed campgrounds along the **corridor trails—Bright Angel, South Kaibab,** and **North Kaibab Trails.** A fraction of that small percentage dares to venture beyond the main trails into the far backcountry scattered with primitive campsites. That said, it's fairly easy to launch a backpacking expedition into the heart of the canyon and spend the night on the banks of Bright Angel Creek. A popular way to visit the inner canyon is to backpack from rim to rim, starting at the South Rim and ending at the North Rim (or the other way around), and camping for one, two, or even three nights along the way. Perhaps the most popular, time-honored Grand Canyon backpacking trip is a few nights at Bright Angel Campground near the Colorado River and Phantom Ranch, hiking in and out via the South Kaibab Trail, the Bright Angel Trail, or both.

Backcountry Permits

All overnight backpacking trips into Grand Canyon require a **backcountry permit** ($10 plus $8 pp per night), and they are not always easy to obtain. You must plan your trip carefully and follow the park's strict guidelines for applying, and there is no guarantee that you will be successful. Camping below the rim at any of the corridor campgrounds is limited to two consecutive nights from March 1 to November 14; between November 15 and February 28, you can stay up to four consecutive nights. You have a better chance of obtaining a permit for groups of less than seven people. In the more remote sites, you can stay up to seven consecutive nights in a particular backcountry use area.

WHEN TO APPLY

You can apply for a permit 10 days before the first of the month that is four months before your hike. So, for hikes starting in, say, January, get your permit request in between August 20 and September 1 by 5pm. It doesn't matter which day you turn it in; it just has to be there between the dates to receive "Earliest Consideration" status, to which the rangers give equal and random attention. Similarly, for hikes in September, apply between April 20 and May 1; for August, apply between March 20 and April 1, and so on (there's a handy schedule on the park's website). Expect to hear back within about three weeks.

HOW TO APPLY

Go to the **park's website** (www.nps.gov/ grca), print out a backcountry permit request form, fill it out, and then **fax** (928/638-2125) it first thing in the morning on the date in question—so, if you want to hike in October (one of the best months to be below the rim), you would fax your request May 20-June 1. On the first day of the month the fax number is usually busy throughout the day. On the permit request form you'll indicate at which campgrounds you plan to stay. The permit is your reservation. For more information on obtaining a backcountry permit, call the **Backcountry Information Center** (928/638-7875, 8am-noon and 1pm-5pm daily).

IN-PERSON AND LAST-MINUTE PERMITS

Rangers don't consider **in-person permit requests** until three months before the date of the hike—for example, if you want to hike in October, you can't apply for a permit in person until July 1, when most if not all of the permits for that month will have likely been issued. However, there is a way to obtain **last-minute permits** to hike into the canyon if you have the flexibility and money to stay in the park for a few days and hike on short notice. Last-minute permits are available only for corridor campgrounds—Indian Garden, Bright Angel, and Cottonwood— and are for one or two consecutive nights. To try for a last-minute permit, head over to the Backcountry Information Center between 8am and noon and 1pm and 5pm and request a wait-list number. This determines your place in line the following morning at 8am, and when your number is called you request the permit.

There are backcountry offices on both the South Rim and the North Rim:

- **South Rim Backcountry Information Center** (1 Backcountry Rd., Grand Canyon Village, 928/638-7875, 8am-noon and 1pm-5pm daily)

- **North Rim Backcountry Information Center** (North Rim Administration Bldg., 8am-noon and 1pm-5pm daily May 15-Oct. 15)

BIKING

Bikes are allowed on greenways and most roads throughout Grand Canyon National Park. However, bikes are not permitted below the rim or on hiking trails within the park, with the exception of the South Rim's **Hermit Road Greenway Trail** (a section of the Rim Trail— and about as close as you can get to the rim on a bike) and the North Rim's **Bridle Path.**

Bright Angel Bicycles and Café (10 S. Entrance Rd., 928/814-8704, www. bikegrandcanyon.com) rents comfortable, easy-to-ride bikes and safety equipment, and offers bike tours of the South Rim. Bright Angel Bicycles is located on the South Rim, right next to the Grand Canyon Visitor Center near the South Entrance and Mather Point.

Mountain Biking

Mountain bikes are not allowed on the trails inside the Grand Canyon, but just outside the park, near the South Entrance, there's a series of single-track trails and old mining and logging roads that have been organized into several easy to moderate loop trails called the **Tusayan Bike Trails.** Mountain bikes are also allowed on the **Arizona Trail** outside the park, trailheads for which are located on Forest Road 605 and at the historic Grandview Lookout Tower.

On the North Rim, try the rough road to **Point Sublime** as a mountain bike trail within the park boundaries, and outside the park try the **Rainbow Rim Trail,** a single-track through forests and meadows along the rim.

Road Biking

There are several roads in and around Grand Canyon National Park that make memorable and stunningly scenic road-bike rides. Very few of the roads outside the towns in this region have bike lanes, and the roads and highways leading into and around the park have little in the way of safe shoulders. The best bike rides around the canyon include **Desert View Drive** and **Hermit Road** on the South Rim and **AZ 67** from Jacob Lake to the North Rim.

FISHING

You must have a valid Arizona fishing license from the **Arizona Game & Fish Department** (602/942-3000, www.azgfd.com, $55 nonresidents, $37 residents) to fish in the Colorado River and Lake Powell, where you'll find trout, striped and largemouth bass, catfish, and other species. Outfitters near Lees Ferry and Lake Powell offer guided fishing trips throughout the year.

BIRDWATCHING

Some of the best birdwatching inside Grand Canyon National Park is from the South Rim, where you can see the majestic California condors, once on the brink of extinction, soaring through the turquoise skies. Birds of prey are really the stars of the canyon's bird-watching scene, with hawks, kestrels, eagles, and falcons stopping over every year during their migrations.

CLIMBING

There are rock climbing options that don't require an overnight permit in the Kaibab limestone along the South Rim. Inside the canyon, the most popular climb is Zoroaster Temple, but you will need an overnight permit to take it on.

Travel Tips

WHAT TO TAKE

Unless you like getting dressed up from time to time for no particular reason, there's no need to bring anything but outdoor- and adventure-style clothing with you to Grand Canyon National Park. Indeed, the only dress codes in the entire canyonlands, or really in the whole of the great American Southwest for that matter, are the ones requiring you to wear comfortable shoes and a shade-giving hat. If you're visiting during the early spring and fall, make sure to bring warm clothes that you can layer; it can get cold quickly. During the summer, you might find that you need a lightweight jacket, preferably waterproof, for the sometimes cool nights and afternoon thunderstorms. A small day pack for water and snacks, cameras, binoculars, and guidebooks is a must, and a few bandannas will always come in handy out here, whether to keep the sun off your neck or to wipe the red dirt off your forehead.

Don't forget to pack multiple reusable water bottles—or you can always wait and buy a souvenir bottle in one of the park's gift shops. Your water bottle will become your close friend as you carry it around the rims (and maybe even below), refilling it whenever it goes dry at one of several water stations serving cold and delicious spring water from deep within the canyon.

Budget Tips

Spending a lot of money at Grand Canyon National Park is really easy to do; but so is *not* spending a lot, as long as you plan well and are willing to do a little extra work.

- You can save a lot of money depending on **when you visit** the park. Everything is less expensive in **January and February.** If you plan it right, you could easily stay inside the park at Bright Angel Lodge or Maswik Lodge for just over $100 per night. It's cold at night, brisk during the day, and on many weekdays the park will be far from crowded.

- Reserve a spot at one of the **campgrounds** inside or outside the park to save money on accommodations during the spring, summer, and early fall **high seasons.** If you have the right vehicle and gear, you can even camp for free in parts of the Coconino and Kaibab National Forests.

- For relatively inexpensive but still charming and memorable accommodations, try the **vintage hotels and hostels** in downtown **Flagstaff.**

- To save on **food,** stock a cooler with groceries, drinks, and ice from a supermarket in Flagstaff and take it with you to the park, which has some of the grandest **picnic** sites in the world.

- If you plan on visiting any of the many other national parks and monuments around Grand Canyon and the Colorado Plateau, purchase an **America the Beautiful Pass,** with which, for just $80 per year, you can visit any federal park, monument, or forest as many times as you want.

TIME ZONES

While most of the country moves up an hour on the second Sunday of March, aka daylight saving time, Arizona, the 49th state, does not. And so it follows that when all the clocks drop back an hour on the first Sunday of November, nothing happens here. However, the Navajo and Hopi Nations do recognize daylight saving time, so there's an hour's difference between the time at Grand Canyon National Park and the time on the nearby reservations to the east.

INTERNATIONAL TRAVELERS

Grand Canyon National Park is well equipped for international tourists. Rangers on both rims offer guides and other literature in a variety of major languages and are used to working with international travelers. Arizona and the Southwest in general are very popular destinations for European, Japanese, and Chinese travelers especially, and in the summer, no matter where you're from, you could very well meet one of your compatriots on the South Rim or at Monument Valley.

The U.S. government's **Visa Waiver Program** allows tourists from many countries to visit without a visa for up to 90 days. To check if your country is on the list, go to https://travel.state.gov. Even with a waiver, you still need to bring your passport and present it at the port of entry.

ACCESS FOR TRAVELERS WITH DISABILITIES

The **National Park Service's Access Pass** (888/467-2757, www.nps.gov), a free lifetime pass, grants admission for the pass-holder and three adults to all national parks, national forests, and the like, as well as discounts on interpretive services, camping fees, fishing licenses, and more. Apply in person at any federally managed park or wilderness area; you must show medical documentation of blindness or permanent disability.

Grand Canyon has many **accessible**

viewpoints, and a large portion of the **Rim Trail**, the best vantage from which to see the canyon, is accessible to wheelchairs.

The park operates free shuttle bus service along the South Rim. All shuttle buses are wheelchair accessible (up to 30 in/76 cm wide and 48 in/122 cm long), with wheelchair ramps and low entrances and exits.

The National Park Service offers an *Accessibility Guide* for Grand Canyon National Park that outlines accessible facilities, services, and activities. It can be found at the park's visitors centers or downloaded from the park website (www.nps.gov/grca).

For advice and links to other helpful Internet resources, go to www.disabledtravelers.com, which is based in Arizona and is full of accessible travel information, though it's not specific to the state. For questions specific to Arizona, you may want to contact the state Department of Administration's **Office for Americans with Disabilities** (100 N. 15th Ave., Ste. 361, Phoenix, 602/542-6276 or 800/358-3617, TTY 602/542-6686).

TRAVELING WITH CHILDREN

Grand Canyon National Park is the perfect place for an active, outdoor vacation involving the whole family. Rangers are usually eager to explain and illuminate the sights for kids, and the National Park Service's **Junior Ranger** program is a fun and educational way to get your kids engaged with nature—it even includes a photo-ready swearing-in ceremony. Children under 16 are admitted free to federal parks, monuments, and recreation areas.

TRAVELING WITH PETS

Throughout the park dogs must be kept on a leash at all times, and they are not allowed in buildings, on shuttle buses, or below the rim. **Yavapai Lodge** on the South Rim is the only in-park hotel that allows dogs, but there are several hotels in Williams and Flagstaff that are dog-friendly. The **South Rim Kennel,** next to Maswik Lodge, takes dogs and cats with proof of vaccinations, including for overnight boarding; reservations are highly recommended.

HEALTH AND SAFETY
Extreme Temperatures

The least of what the Arizona sun can do to you is not to be taken lightly. A **sunburn,** which comes on quicker than you'd think, can lead to skin cancer, and that can lead to death. If you get a sunburn, there's little you can do, save try to make yourself more comfortable. Stay out of the sun, of course, and try to keep cool and hydrated. There are dozens of over-the-counter balms available, but simple aloe works as well as anything. A popular home remedy is to gently dab the burned areas with vinegar. **Heat exhaustion** and **heatstroke** can affect anyone during the hot summer months, particularly during a long, strenuous hike in the sun. Common symptoms include nausea, lightheadedness, headache, or muscle cramps. **Dehydration** and loss of electrolytes are the common causes of heat exhaustion. The risks are even higher in the desert regions. If you or anyone in your group develops any of these symptoms, get out of the sun immediately, stop all physical activity, and drink plenty of water. Heat exhaustion can be severe, and if untreated can lead to heatstroke, in which the body's core temperature reaches 105°F (40.5°C). Fainting, seizures, confusion, and rapid heartbeat and breathing can indicate the situation has moved beyond heat exhaustion.

Similar precautions hold true for **hypothermia,** which is caused by prolonged exposure to cold water or weather. This can happen on a canyon hike or backpacking trip without sufficient rain gear, or by staying too long in a cold body of water without a wetsuit. Symptoms include shivering, weak pulse, drowsiness, confusion, slurred speech, or stumbling. To treat hypothermia, immediately remove any wet clothing, cover the person with blankets, and feed him or her hot liquids.

Altitude Sickness

Grand Canyon's South Rim sits at about 7,000 feet (2,134 m), its North Rim at 8,000 feet (2,438 m) and above, and some of the surrounding mountains reach 10,000 feet (3,048 m) or higher. Some of the mountain towns in the canyonlands sit between 5,000 feet (1,524 m) and 8,000 feet (2,438 m) above sea level. Lowlanders in relatively good shape may get headaches, a little dizziness, and shortness of breath while walking around Flagstaff and Grand Canyon, but very few will experience serious altitude sickness—the result of not getting enough oxygen, and therefore not enough blood flow to the brain. Still, take it easy in the higher elevations if you begin to feel tired and out of breath, dizzy, or euphoric. If you have heart or lung problems, you need to be more aware in the higher elevations.

Dangerous Animals

In this region, **poisonous rattlesnakes** and **scorpions** are a threat. When hiking or climbing in desert areas, never put your hand onto a ledge or into a hole that you can't see. Both are perfect lairs for snakes and scorpions. While snakebites are rarely fatal anymore, they're no fun either. If you are bitten, immobilize the affected area and seek immediate medical attention.

A scorpion's sting isn't as painful as you'd expect (it's about like a bee sting), and the venom is insufficient to cause any real harm. Still, it's not what you'd call pleasant, and experienced desert campers know to shake out their boots every morning, as scorpions and spiders are attracted to warm, moist, dark places.

Tarantulas and **black widow spiders** are present across much of the Colorado Plateau. Believe it or not, a tarantula's bite does not poison humans; the enzymes secreted when they bite turn the insides of frogs, lizards, and insects to a soft mush, allowing the tarantula to suck the guts from its prey. Black widow spiders, on the other hand, have a toxic bite. Although the bite is usually painless, it delivers a potent neurotoxin, which quickly causes pain, nausea, and vomiting. It is important to seek immediate treatment for a black widow bite; although few people actually die from these bites, recovery is helped along considerably by antivenin.

In the extremely rare case that you come into contact with a mountain lion (also called a cougar), stay calm. Do not run, do not bend down, do not approach the big cat; try to give it space to leave, but also attempt to make yourself seem bigger and more intimidating—raise your arms slowly, open your jacket, speak loudly. Odds are it will leave eventually, but if it continues to come at you, start throwing stones and sticks in its direction—but don't crouch or turn your back to pick them up. If you encounter a mountain lion on a trail, tell a ranger as soon as possible.

ILLNESS AND DISEASE

West Nile virus from mosquitoes and **hantavirus** from rodents are the longshot threats to your health in this region, and both can be avoided by taking precautions. Use a DEET-based insect repellent to ward off mosquitoes and simply stay away from rodents. Hantavirus is an airborne infectious disease agent transmitted from rodents to humans when rodents shed hantavirus particles in their saliva, urine, and droppings and humans inhale the infected particles. It is easiest for a human to contract hantavirus in a contained environment, such as a cabin infested with mouse droppings, where the virus-infected particles are not thoroughly dispersed. Simply traveling to a place where the hantavirus is known to occur is not considered a risk factor. Camping, hiking, and other outdoor activities also pose low risk, especially if steps are taken to reduce rodent contact. The very first symptoms can occur anywhere between five days and three weeks after infection. They almost always include fever, fatigue, and aching muscles (usually in the back, shoulders, or thighs) and other flu-like conditions. Other early symptoms may include headaches, dizziness, chills, and abdominal discomfort (such as vomiting, nausea, or diarrhea). These are shortly followed by intense coughing and shortness of breath. If you have these symptoms, seek medical help immediately. Untreated infections of hantavirus are almost always fatal.

Resources

Suggested Reading

ECOLOGY AND NATURAL HISTORY

Houk, Rose. *An Introduction to Grand Canyon Ecology.* Grand Canyon, Arizona: Grand Canyon Association, 1996. This small but jam-packed guide to the whole Grand Canyon ecosystem is really all you need for a relatively deep understanding of all the different competing and cooperating biomes on the rims and within the canyon. Should be available in a more recent edition at the Grand Canyon Conservancy stores inside the park.

Summit, April R. *Contested Waters: An Environmental History of the Colorado River.* Boulder: University Press of Colorado, 2013. A deeply researched and well-argued history of the use and misuse of the Colorado River through history, written by a professor at Arizona State University.

Water, Frank. *The Colorado.* Athens, Ohio: Swallow Press, 1946. Though written long before the changes wrought by Glen Canyon Dam, this regional classic is still one of the best descriptions, histories, and contemplations on the land drained by the Colorado River.

HUMAN HISTORY
General Overview

Hughes, J. Donald. *In the House of Stone and Light: A Human History of the Grand Canyon.* Grand Canyon, Arizona: Grand Canyon Association, 1978. First written in the 1960s by history professor and Grand Canyon ranger J. Donald Hughes, this is still the best complete history of people at Grand Canyon. Should be available in a more recent edition at the Grand Canyon Conservancy stores inside the park.

Native American History and Archaeology

Hirst, Stephen. *I Am the Grand Canyon: The Story of the Havasupai People.* Grand Canyon, Arizona: Grand Canyon Association, 2006. The definitive history of the "People of Blue-Green Water" and their beautiful inner-canyon home.

James, Harry C. *Pages from Hopi History.* Tucson: University of Arizona Press, 1979. A fascinating history of the Hopi from prehistory to today, as told by elders of the tribe to an ethnologist in the 1960s and 1970s.

Lister, Robert H. and Florence C. *Those Who Came Before: Southwestern Archaeology in the National Parks System.* Tucson: University of Arizona Press, 1983. An excellent survey of and introduction to the archaeology of Grand Canyon, Zion, Bryce Canyon, and other federal parks.

Plog, Stephen. *Ancient Peoples of the American Southwest.* London: Thames & Hudson, 1997. A fine introduction to the main themes of Southwestern prehistory and archaeology.

Explorations and Expeditions

Dellenbaugh, Frederick S. *A Canyon Voyage: The Narrative of the Second Powell Expedition.* Tucson: University of Arizona Press, 1991. An artist on John Wesley Powell's second expedition, Dellenbaugh is a great writer and his account is more interesting than Powell's.

Hoig, Stan. *Came Men on Horses: The Conquistador Expeditions of Francisco Vazquez de Coronado and Don Juan de Onate.* Boulder: University Press of Colorado, 2013. A scholarly but highly readable account of the Entrada and the Spanish exploration of Grand Canyon.

Powell, John Wesley. *The Exploration of the Colorado River and Its Canyons.* New York: Dover Publications, 1964. The narrative of John Wesley Powell's first and second expeditions down the Colorado River, with a preamble that describes the canyonlands in great detail.

Warner, Ted J., ed. *The Dominguez-Escalante Journal.* Salt Lake City: University of Utah Press, 1995. An interesting and readable primary document of an early expedition across the hard lands around Grand Canyon.

Grand Canyon National Park

Armstrong, Patrick. *Fred Harvey, Creator of Western Hospitality.* Bellemont, Arizona: Canyonlands Publications, 2000. A fascinating, easy-to-read, and slim volume detailing Fred Harvey's great influence on Grand Canyon National Park.

Colter, Mary Elizabeth Jane. *Watchtower at Desert View: Manual for Drivers and Guides.* Grand Canyon, Arizona: Grand Canyon Association, 2015. Colter, the park's great architect, wrote this guide to her masterpiece, Desert View Watchtower, for the guides and bus drivers to make sure

they described her work as she saw it. It's a fascinating glimpse into a master artist's work. Available at the Grand Canyon Conservancy stores inside the park.

Stafford, Cindy. *In a Better Place: At Rest in Grand Canyon Cemetery.* Flagstaff: Vishnu Temple Press, 2015. This illustrated and annotated map of Grand Canyon Cemetery is a trove of early canyon history. Available at the Grand Canyon Conservancy stores inside the park.

ESSAYS AND LETTERS

Rusho, W. L. *Everett Ruess: A Vagabond for Beauty.* Salt Lake City: Peregrine Smith Books, 2007. The unforgettable account of artist Everett Ruess's journeys to the canyonlands in the 1930s, along with a collection of his beautiful letters describing the landscape.

Schullery, Paul, ed. *The Grand Canyon: Early Impressions.* Boulder: Pruitt Publishing, 1989. A collection of illuminating essays and impressions of Grand Canyon by Theodore Roosevelt, Zane Grey, John Muir, and others.

RECREATION

Belknap, Bill et al. *Belknap's Grand Canyon River Guide.* Evergreen, Colorado: Westwater Books, 2019. Waterproof and easy to pack, this essential map and guide to the river and environs is a must-purchase for anyone going on, or even planning on going on, a Colorado River trip.

National Geographic Society. *Trails Illustrated Topographic Map of Grand Canyon National Park North and South Rims.* Evergreen, Colorado: National Geographic Maps, 2009. The best map of the park and its trails, updated often, waterproof, and detailed. Available at the Grand Canyon Conservancy stores inside the park.

Thybony, Scott. *Official Guide to Hiking Grand Canyon: Day Hiking and Backpacking South and North Rims.* Grand Canyon, Arizona: Grand Canyon Association, 2005. The author of many useful pocket-guides to the park's trails, Scott Thybony brings them all together in this slim, easy-to-pack volume full of essential information, directions, and advice.

Internet Resources

GRAND CANYON

Grand Canyon National Park
www.nps.gov/grca
The Grand Canyon's official website has extensive information on the park; go here for information about backcountry permits.

Federal Campground Reservations
www.recreation.gov
Use this site to make reservations at all federal parks, monuments, and national forests.

Grand Canyon Conservancy
www.grandcanyon.org
The main Grand Canyon nonprofit, Grand Canyon Conservancy publishes the best books about the canyon and operates the Field Institute, which offers guided backpacking and hiking trips, classes, and tours.

Grand Canyon Hikers and Backpackers Association
www.gchba.org
Find trail-level information and advice for your great Grand Canyon expedition.

Grand Canyon History
www.grcahistory.org
Arizona State University's comprehensive collection of essays, documents, and images related to Grand Canyon's natural and human history.

BEYOND THE BOUNDARIES

Coconino National Forest
www.fs.usda.gov/coconino
Here you'll find detailed trail and campground information for the Coconino National Forest around Flagstaff and Grand Canyon.

Glen Canyon National Recreation Area
www.nps.gov/glca
Go here for information on camping and boating at Lake Powell and Lees Ferry.

Havasupai Nation
http://theofficialhavasupaitribe.com
The official website of the Havasupai Tribe.

Hopi Nation
www.experiencehopi.com
The official tourism site of the Hopi Reservation.

Hualapai Nation
www.grandcanyonwest.com
The official tourism site of the Hualapai Reservation.

Kaibab National Forest
www.fs.usda.gov/kaibab
Go here for trail and campground descriptions in the Kaibab National Forest.

Navajo Nation
www.navajonationparks.org
For information on permits and recreation opportunities on Navajoland.

GATEWAYS

Flagstaff
www.flagstaffarizona.org

This site has general information on visiting Flagstaff, the northland, and the Grand Canyon along with helpful listings.

Kanab, Utah
www.visitsouthernutah.com
This site offers information on Kanab and southern Utah, including recreation, accommodations, and dining.

Page
www.visitpagelakepowell.com
This site has visitor information for Page and Lake Powell, including places to stay.

Williams
www.experiencewilliams.com
For information on staying in this gateway city, including lists of accommodations and restaurants.

ARIZONA
Arizona Office of Tourism
www.visitarizona.com
The official site for the state's office of tourism has basic information on the state's regions and lists various possible itineraries.

Arizona Department of Transportation
www.azdot.gov
For information about the conditions of Arizona's roadways.

Index

List of Maps

Photo Credits

For when your friends want your recommendations.
Keep track of your favorite...

Restaurants and Meals

Neighborhoods and Regions

Cultural Experiences

In these books:

Coverage of gateway cities and towns

Suggested itineraries from one day to multiple weeks

Advice on where to stay (or camp) in and around the parks

MOON

GREAT SMOKY MOUNTAINS NATIONAL PARK

HIKING · CAMPING SCENIC DRIVES

JASON FRYE

MOON

JOSHUA TREE & PALM SPRINGS

JENNA BLOUGH

MOON

YELLOWSTONE & GRAND TETON

HIKE, CAMP, SEE WILDLIFE

BECKY LOMAX

MOON

YOSEMITE SEQUOIA & KINGS CANYON

ANN MARIE BROWN

MOON

ZION & BRYCE

Including Arches, Canyonlands, Capitol Reef, Grand Staircase-Escalante & Moab

W. C. McRAE & JUDY JEWELL

Get inspired for your next adventure

Follow @**moonguides** on Instagram or subscribe to our newsletter at **moon.com**

#TravelWithMoon

MAP SYMBOLS

▦▦▦	Expressway	○	City/Town	✈	Airport	⚲ Golf Course
▬▬	Primary Road	◉	State Capital	✕	Airfield	🅿 Parking Area
▬	Secondary Road	✺	National Capital	▲	Mountain	⬘ Archaeological Site
‐ ‐ ‐	Unpaved Road	◎	Highlight	✚	Unique Natural Feature	⬍ Church
‐ ‐ ‐	Trail	★	Point of Interest			
··········	Ferry	•	Accommodation	⚑	Waterfall	⬓ Gas Station
▬▬▬	Railroad	▼	Restaurant/Bar	⬆	Park	⬭ Glacier
▦▦	Pedestrian Walkway	■	Other Location	🆃🅷	Trailhead	⬚ Mangrove
▥▥▥	Stairs	Λ	Campground	⛷	Skiing Area	⬭ Reef
						⬭ Swamp

CONVERSION TABLES

°C = (°F - 32) / 1.8
°F = (°C x 1.8) + 32
1 inch = 2.54 centimeters (cm)
1 foot = 0.304 meters (m)
1 yard = 0.914 meters
1 mile = 1.6093 kilometers (km)
1 km = 0.6214 miles
1 fathom = 1.8288 m
1 chain = 20.1168 m
1 furlong = 201.168 m
1 acre = 0.4047 hectares
1 sq km = 100 hectares
1 sq mile = 2.59 square km
1 ounce = 28.35 grams
1 pound = 0.4536 kilograms
1 short ton = 0.90718 metric ton
1 short ton = 2,000 pounds
1 long ton = 1.016 metric tons
1 long ton = 2,240 pounds
1 metric ton = 1,000 kilograms
1 quart = 0.94635 liters
1 US gallon = 3.7854 liters
1 Imperial gallon = 4.5459 liters
1 nautical mile = 1.852 km

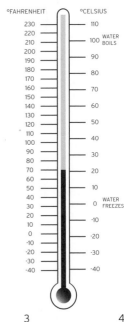

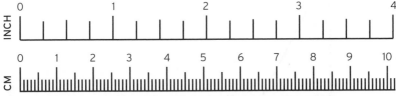

MOON GRAND CANYON

Avalon Travel
Hachette Book Group
1700 Fourth Street
Berkeley, CA 94710, USA
www.moon.com

Editor: Kathryn Ettinger
Acquiring Editor: Nikki Ioakimedes
Copy Editor: Ann Seifert
Graphics Coordinator: Darren Alessi
Production Coordinator: Darren Alessi
Cover Design: Faceout Studios, Charles Brock
Interior Design: Domini Dragoone
Moon Logo: Tim McGrath
Map Editor: Albert Angulo
Cartographer: John Culp
Indexer: Greg Jewett

ISBN-13: 978-1-64049-407-7

Printing History
1st Edition — 1999
8th Edition — April 2021
5 4 3 2 1

Text © 2021 by Tim Hull.
Maps © 2021 by Avalon Travel.

2198231984914

Front cover photo: the Colorado River meandering through the Marble Canyon section of Grand Canyon National Park © Inge Johnsson - www.robertharding.com
Back cover photo: aspen trees near Flagstaff © John Sirlin | Dreamstime.com

Printed in Malaysia for Imago